Illustrated
WordStar® 6.0

Russell A. Stultz & Dianne Stultz

Wordware Publishing, Inc.

Library of Congress Cataloging-in-Publication Data

Stultz, Russell A. (Russell Allen)
    Illustrated Wordstar 6.0 Russell A. Stultz and Dianne Stultz.
        p.   cm.
    Includes index.
    ISBN 1-55622-192-4
    1. WordStar (Computer program).   2. Word processing.
    I. Stultz, Dianne.   II. Title.
    Z52.2.W68S78   1990   90-46919
    652.5'536 — dc20

Copyright © 1991, Wordware Publishing, Inc.

All Rights Reserved

1506 Capital Avenue
Plano, Texas 75074

No part of this book may be reproduced in any form or by any means
without permission in writing from Wordware Publishing, Inc.

Printed in the United States of America

ISBN 1-55622-192-4
10 9 8 7 6 5 4 3 2 1
  9011

MicroPro, MicroPro International Corporation, WordStar, and TelMerge are registered trademarks, and Advanced Page Preview, MailList, and ProFinder are trademarks of MicroPro International Corporation.
Brown Bag Software is a registered trademark and PC-Outline is a trademark of Telemarketing Resources.
dBASE, dBASE III, dBASE III Plus are registered trademarks of Ashton-Tate.
Quattro is a registered trademark of Borland International, Inc.

All inquiries for volume purchases of this book should be addressed to Wordware Publishing, Inc., at the above address. Telephone inquiries may be made by calling:

(214) 423-0090

Contents

Module	Title	Page
1	About This Book	1
2	Program Overview	4
3	A Sample Session with WordStar	15
4	Abandon Document without Changes	21
5	Aligning Text (Auto-Align)	23
6	Block Hide/Display	26
7	Block Math	27
8	Block Selection	30
9	Calculator (Quick Math)	32
10	Centering Text on a Line or Page	35
11	Character Count	37
12	Columnar Editing	38
13	Copy Block to File (Write Block)	42
14	Copy Blocks of Text	44
15	Copy File	46
16	Copy File into Document (Read File)	48
17	Cursor Control	50
18	Cursor Movement, Quick	53
19	Custom Print Codes	56
20	Delete Blocks of Text	62
21	Delete Characters, Words, and Lines	64
22	Delete File	66
23	Disk Drive and Directory Selection	68
24	Dot Commands (Print and Format Control Codes)	70
25	Dot Leader	76
26	Drawing Lines and Boxes	78
27	Exit WordStar	80
28	File Directory Display	81
29	File Operations During Word Processing	83
30	Find and Find-Replace Again	85
31	Find Block Marker	87
32	Find Place Marker	89
33	Find-Replace	91
34	Find-Replace, Global	95
35	Find Specified Page, Character	98
36	Find Text String	100
37	Footnotes, Endnotes, Annotations, and Comments	103
38	Format Ruler	109
39	Help and Help Levels	113
40	Hyphenation	117

Contents (Cont.)

Module	Title	Page
41	Indent (Paragraph Tabs)	119
42	Indexing	121
43	Insert On/Off	125
44	Inset (Merging Graphics)	127
45	Justification Off/On	134
46	Line Numbering	136
47	Line Spacing	138
48	MailList	140
49	Margin Settings	148
50	Merge Print	153
51	Move Blocks of Text	163
52	Open a Document or Nondocument File	165
53	Page Breaks, Page Length	168
54	Page Preview	170
55	Paragraph Numbering	173
56	Paragraph Styles	176
57	PC-Outline	180
58	Print Alternate Pitch	188
59	Print Binding (Non-Break) Space	190
60	Print Color	191
61	Print Document	193
62	Print Extended Character Set (Special Symbols)	198
63	Print From Keyboard	201
64	Print Pause (Stop) Code	204
65	Print Phantom Space and Rubout (Special Characters)	206
66	Print Special Effects	208
67	Printer Select	213
68	ProFinder	215
69	Protect a File	226
70	Reformat (Realign) Text	228
71	Rename a File	230
72	Repeat a Keystroke Automatically	232
73	Run a Program	233
74	Save and Exit Document	235
75	Save and Exit WordStar	237
76	Save and Print Document	238
77	Save and Resume Edit	240
78	Scroll Screen	242
79	Scroll Screen, Quick	244
80	Shorthand (Macro Substitution)	246

Contents (Cont.)

Module	Title	Page
81	Sort Blocks of Text	251
82	Spelling Check	254
83	Status Line	258
84	Tab Settings (Decimal or Align)	260
85	Tab Settings (Typewriter)	263
86	Table of Contents Creation	266
87	TelMerge	269
88	Thesaurus	278
89	Undo, Unerase	280
90	Upper/Lower Case Conversion	282
91	Window (Working with Two Documents)	284
92	Word Wrap Off/On	287
93	WSCHANGE and PRCHANGE (Customizing WordStar)	289
Appendix A	Terms and Definitions	307
Appendix B	Converting Files from Other Word Processors	312
Appendix C	Word Processing Exercises	316
Index		331

Recommended Learning Sequence

Sequence	Title	Module	Page
1	About This Book	1	1
2	Program Overview	2	4
3	A Sample Session with WordStar	3	15
4	Open a Document or Nondocument File	52	165
5	Exit WordStar	27	80
6	Undo, Unerase	89	280
7	Help and Help Levels	39	113
8	Disk Drive and Directory Selection	23	68
9	File Directory Display	28	81
10	Copy File	15	46
11	Delete File	22	66
12	Rename a File	71	230
13	Save and Exit Document	74	235
14	Save and Resume Edit	77	240
15	Abandon Document without Changes	4	21
16	Save and Exit WordStar	75	237
17	Status Line	83	258
18	Protect a File	69	226
19	Cursor Control	17	50
20	Cursor Movement, Quick	18	53
21	Scroll Screen	78	242
22	Scroll Screen, Quick	79	244
23	Insert On/Off	43	125
24	Delete Characters, Words, and Lines	21	64
25	Block Selection	8	30
26	Block Hide/Display	6	26
27	Delete Blocks of Text	20	62
28	Move Blocks of Text	51	163
29	Copy Blocks of Text	14	44
30	Columnar Editing	12	38
31	Sort Blocks of Text	81	251
32	Copy Block to File (Write Block)	13	42
33	Copy File into Document (Read File)	16	48
34	Upper/Lower Case Conversion	90	282
35	Window Editing	91	284
36	Paragraph Numbering	55	173
37	Line Numbering	46	136
38	Drawing Lines and Boxes	26	78
39	File Operations During Word Processing	29	83
40	Margin Settings	49	148
41	Line Spacing	47	138

Recommended Learning Sequence (Cont.)

Sequence	Title	Module	Page
42	Indent (Paragraph Tabs)	41	119
43	Reformat (Realign) Text	70	228
44	Aligning Text (Auto-Align)	5	23
45	Save and Print Document	76	238
46	Repeat a Keystroke Automatically	72	232
47	Tab Settings (Typewriter)	85	263
48	Tab Settings (Decimal or Align)	84	260
49	Page Breaks, Page Length	53	168
50	Format Ruler	38	109
51	Word Wrap Off/On	92	287
52	Centering Text on a Line or Page	10	35
53	Justification Off/On	45	134
54	Hyphenation	40	117
55	Find Place Marker	32	89
56	Find Block Marker	31	87
57	Find Text String	36	100
58	Find-Replace	33	91
59	Find-Replace, Global	34	95
60	Find and Find-Replace Again	30	85
61	Find Specified Page, Character	35	98
62	Block Math	7	27
63	Calculator (Quick Math)	9	32
64	Dot Leader	25	76
65	Print Extended Character Set (Special Symbols)	62	198
66	Printer Select	67	213
67	Footnotes, Endnotes, Annotations, and Comments	37	103
68	Page Preview	54	107
69	Inset (Merging Graphics)	44	127
70	Print Document	61	193
71	Print Special Effects	66	208
72	Print Non-Break (or Binding) Space	59	190
73	Print Phantom Space and Rubout (Special Characters)	65	206
74	Print Pause (Stop) Code	64	204
75	Print Alternate Pitch	58	188
76	Print Color	60	191
77	Print From Keyboard	63	201
78	Paragraph Styles	56	176
79	Dot Commands (Print and Format Control Codes)	24	70
80	Custom Print Codes	19	56
81	Table of Contents Creation	86	266
82	Indexing	42	121

Recommended Learning Sequence (Cont.)

Sequence	Title	Module	Page
83	Run a Program	73	233
84	Shorthand (Macro Substitution)	80	246
85	Spelling Check	82	254
86	Character Count	11	37
87	Thesaurus	88	278
88	Merge Print	50	153
89	MailList	48	140
90	PC-Outline	57	180
91	ProFinder	68	215
92	TelMerge	87	269
93	WSCHANGE and PRCHANGE (Customizing WordStar)	93	289

Preface

ABOUT WORDSTAR 6.0

WordStar 6.0 now includes new printer drivers for printers such as the HP Laserjet III. This lets WordStar 6.0 users take full advantage of emerging printer technology and available type fonts. In addition, WordStar 6.0 also includes those features and utility programs introduced in Releases 5.0 and 5.5. Among these features are an on-line spell checker, a thesaurus with dictionary-style word definitions, a window function that lets you display and interact with two documents at the same time, an advanced page preview feature, footnotes and endnotes, multi-line headers and footers, and the ability to embed extended characters within documents. WordStar 6.0 also lets you embed graphics within text documents. The use of graphics and scalable fonts lets you produce documents that compare favorably with ones produced by desktop publishing software.

Other features include an outliner, a file manager, a list manager, and a telecommunications program. WordStar 6.0 also gives you the ability to import Lotus and Quattro spreadsheets and graphics directly, without an intermediate ASCII file conversion step. Star Exchange, which is supplied with WordStar 6.0, converts document files to and from such word processing programs as WordPerfect, MS Word, DisplayWrite, MultiMate, and earlier versions of WordStar.

With these many new features, WordStar still lets those familiar with the standard WordStar commands and key sequences use the old, time-tested commands they've used for many years. This is accomplished by two menu interfaces — a set of "pull-down" menus and the old familiar WordStar "classic" menus.

ABOUT ILLUSTRATED BOOKS

Illustrated books are found in many languages and countries. Books that were initially introduced in the English language have been adopted by computer book publishers around the world. Illustrated books are presently used in over thirteen languages around the world, and more are being added each year.

Wordware Publishing, Inc. thanks the readers, computer science and technology instructors, and dozens of publishers who are buying, using, translating, and promoting Illustrated books. We also appreciate the continued words of encouragement from our readers and friends. We shall continue to do our best to provide you with the newest titles and updates. And these books will contain information you can trust — programs that run and operating procedures that have been thoroughly tested.

As both writers *and* users of books in the Illustrated series, we look forward to many more.

Russ and Dianne Stultz

Module 1
ABOUT THIS BOOK

INTRODUCTION

This book describes MicroPro International's WordStar 6.0. WordStar has been around for several years and is used by more than five million people around the world.

The information in this book covers the many features offered by WordStar 6.0. It describes all text creation, editing, and printing operations. It also describes the use of merge print, spell check, thesaurus, shorthand (or *macro*), math, paragraph styles, and WordStar's MailList, TelMerge, PC-Outline, and ProFinder. Two new programs, Inset graphics and Star Exchange conversion, have been added.

The book is designed for a broad range of users. It is for beginning users who wish to learn the series of WordStar programs from scratch. It is for intermediate and advanced users as a quick reference that contains command examples that work. And finally, it is for the classroom instructor as an instructionally designed WordStar textbook.

The WordStar program is sophisticated and often appears overwhelming to inexperienced computer users. But it's not as bad as it looks. In fact, if you are a beginning user who is not afraid to experiment with WordStar functions, you will discover in a matter of minutes that WordStar is really quite easy to use. You may want to jump over to the sample session in Module 3 to see just how easy and powerful WordStar can be. You can do useful things by learning only a few commands. The more you use WordStar, the richer it becomes. After a week or so, you'll begin to feel like a veteran computer user. That's one reason why so many people like WordStar — it can be as simple or as powerful as you want to make it.

ORGANIZATION

To fit the broad range of users that this book addresses, the book is organized into small, easy-to-read *modules*.

This module describes the use of this book, its organization and contents, and some information about your computer and what you should know.

In Module 2 a brief overview of the programs covered in this book is provided. The WordStar menu network, which features both the pull-down menus and the classic WordStar menus familiar to many old WordStar users, is also described and illustrated.

Module 1

Module 3 is provided for the impatient user. It lets you dive into WordStar word processing in a single session. Easy-to-follow, step-by-step instructions tour you through WordStar, including a merge print operation.

A list of all the modules organized in a simple-to-complex order is located at the front of this book. Use this recommended learning sequence to chart your progress if you are learning or teaching WordStar.

Modules 4 through 93 provide descriptions, applications, and illustrations for each of the WordStar program functions. These modules describing WordStar word processing operations are arranged in alphabetical order for easy reference. Each module provides insight to WordStar's use in solving practical, everyday problems. Literally hundreds of useful examples, or *illustrations*, are presented in the Description, Applications, and Typical Operation sections of the modules.

These examples, particularly those using merge print, can be used as models to design word processing applications of your own. Having working examples that let you experiment with program commands takes the mystery out of what might otherwise be a technical obscurity. In addition to conducting "hands-on" experimentation, you will probably find yourself having a lot of fun, because WordStar is fun to use.

Appendix A contains terms and definitions used in word processing with WordStar. Some of these are functions that are not given their own module in the book.

Appendix B provides information on how to use Star Exchange, WordStar's utility for converting word-processed files to and from other word processing programs, such as WordPerfect, Microsoft Word, MultiMate, DisplayWrite, and prior versions of WordStar.

Appendix C is provided for both classroom and self-teaching situations. It contains WordStar word processing exercises. If you are a classroom instructor, you may wish to include these exercises in student assignments. If you are learning the WordStar series on your own, the exercises may be a good way to see what you've learned about an operation. If you can answer the questions, you are ready to move on to the next module in the learning sequence.

HARDWARE AND SOFTWARE REQUIREMENTS

WordStar programs operate with PC- and MS-DOS operating systems. You should have at least 384K of random access memory and two floppy disk drives or one floppy and one fixed disk drive. Because of the number of features supplied with WordStar, a fixed disk is recommended.

You should also have a printer connected to your microcomputer. WordStar supports a large variety of printers; therefore, your current printer is probably okay. However, it is important to install WordStar to operate with your printer and the unique set of control codes that it uses. Use either WINSTALL, which includes both installation and customization, or WSCHANGE to set up WordStar for your printer. You can also use PRCHANGE for printer setup, although this utility is called by the WSCHANGE utility when printer setup is selected.

Before running WordStar, you must have a CONFIG.SYS file on your system disk containing the line

    FILES = 20

This lets WordStar open multiple files during complex operations, such as spell checking.

WHAT YOU SHOULD KNOW

You should be familiar with your computer, its keyboard, and the rudimentary DOS commands. If you are not familiar with the rudimentary MS/PC-DOS commands used to format diskettes and to copy, rename, and delete files, obtain a copy of *Illustrated MS/PC-DOS* from Wordware Publishing, Inc.

Module 2
PROGRAM OVERVIEW

DESCRIPTION

WordStar is a popular word processor for a number of reasons. First, it produces ASCII text files, making it compatible with most popular database, spreadsheet, and communications programs. Indeed, its ability to read and write files directly into and out of text documents is a powerful feature that is often unavailable in other word processing programs.

WordStar's nondocument mode is popular among programmers who use WordStar as a programming editor to write source code for a host of programming languages, including BASIC, Pascal, C, and Assembler.

WordStar includes a number of powerful companion programs. WordStar's spelling checker finds typographical errors and misspelled words and suggests correctly spelled alternatives.

A built-in thesaurus lets you select a word and display a list of substitute words. You can choose an alternate word and replace the original one with a few strokes.

A merge print feature lets you merge a list of information into a base document, such as a form letter, phone directory, or series of mailing labels. Merge print lets you process mail lists and assemble "canned" text files, such as frequently used paragraphs, to create a new document.

A shorthand utility lets you save and recall frequently used key sequences at the touch of a few keys. The block math function lets you add columns and rows of numbers; a quick math feature provides a pop-up equation solver with a single key sequence.

Format control is extremely versatile. You can set margins, tabs, and indents; design and use footnotes; and then preview your pages before you print them.

WordStar features a list manager and a communications capability. The list manager, called MailList, lets you maintain lists, sort them, and prepare a variety of reports based on the lists. The communications feature, called TelMerge, lets you exchange documents with other computers.

WordStar's conversion program, Star Exchange, lets you convert documents to and from WordStar.

Program Overview

This book shows you how to use all of these features and how to perform many other time-saving operations.

RUNNING WORDSTAR

To run WordStar, you should put all WordStar program and overlay (.OVR) files on a hard disk within the same directory. The directory name \WS is recommended. Get in the habit of using a separate directory for your document files to avoid mixing data files with your program files.

Hard disk installation is made simple with WordStar's WSSETUP program, which leads you through each step of installation with on-screen instructions.

If you have a floppy disk system, copy the WordStar disks and run WINSTALL. Since program files are on one diskette and dictionary files on another, as they are distributed from MicroPro, you will have to tell WordStar where to "look" for these files using the WSCHANGE utility. Spelling checks will require a disk swap. Use a separate data diskette for your work, as the program and overlay files fill the program diskette.

Be sure that a CONFIG.SYS file with the line FILES = 20 is available on your DOS boot diskette or fixed disk root directory when you turn on your computer. You can create this file using the following steps.

1. Log the root directory of your boot disk.
2. Type **COPY CON: CONFIG.SYS** and press **Return**.
3. Type **FILES = 20** and press **Return**.
4. Press **Ctrl-Z** and **Return**.

The displayed results should look like this.

```
COPY CON: CONFIG.SYS
FILES = 20
^Z
```

The DOS message "1 File(s) copied" verifies that your typed text was copied from the screen (or *console* device) to disk.

Finally, you should include the line PATH=\WS in your AUTOEXEC.BAT file, which gives you access to WordStar from any subdirectory on your hard disk. If you already have a path command, you can add the \WS path to the end of the current line by preceding it with a semicolon. Use the following example as a model:

```
PATH=C:\;\DOS;\WS
```

Upon installation, be sure to tell WordStar where all files are located. If you install WordStar for a floppy disk system, you are prompted to swap diskettes during spelling checks. Review Module 93 and examine the WSCHANGE menus. These are used to customize WordStar for your system.

Once WordStar is installed, all that is necessary to start the WordStar word processing program is to type WS and press Return from the DOS prompt.

WORDSTAR MENUS

WordStar features two independent menu systems. You can adjust the menu systems to suit your individual needs. When first learning WordStar, you may want to maximize the display of on-screen menus and help information and operator prompts. Then, as you become more proficient, you may want to gradually suppress menus and corresponding help information. When you reach the "expert user" level, you may want to suppress all help information.

The first WordStar menu system features "pull-down" menus. These are accessed from the EDIT menu by pressing the Alt key in combination with the first letter of a menu category located on the menu bar (or line) at the top of the screen.

You can also display the old "classic" WordStar menus using WordStar's familiar key sequences known to WordStar users for more than a decade. Regardless of the menu system you select, you will find that they all work in concert to provide a powerful yet easy-to-use word processing environment. Examples from both menu systems are shown and described on the following pages of this module.

When you start WordStar, the OPENING menu is displayed. This menu is used to select editing, printing, file handling, or system commands. The following WordStar menus are included for your examination. Later, you may wish to turn back to these menus to review how to access certain WordStar operations. First, the WordStar pull-down menus are shown. Next, the WordStar classic menus are shown.

WORDSTAR PULL-DOWN MENUS The first screen you see when you start WordStar resembles the following illustration. This is WordStar's OPENING menu. Notice the menu bar at the top of the screen.

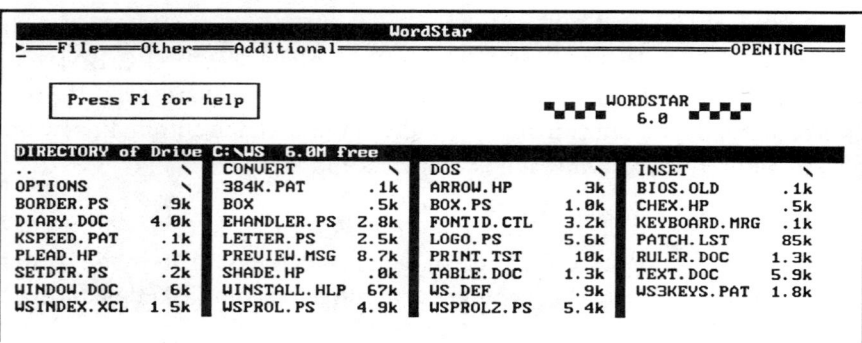

Program Overview

Pressing F, O, or A (File, Other, or Additional) displays one of the following pull-down menus in a window.

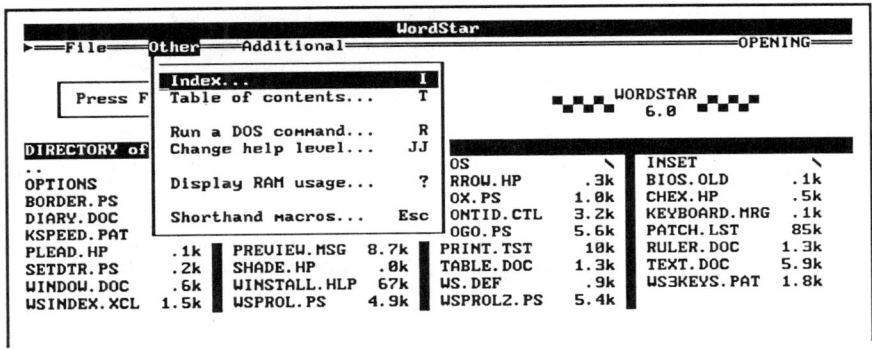

Notice that the File menu lets you create, edit, copy, rename, delete, and print files. It also lets you quit (exit) WordStar by typing X.

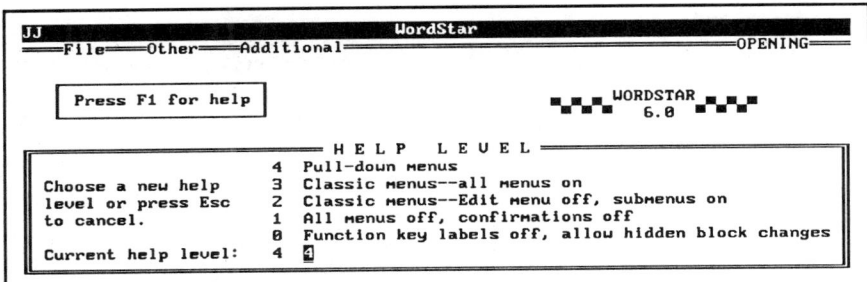

The Other menu is used to perform special functions, including indexing, preparing tables of contents, running DOS commands, setting the help level and menu system, using shorthand (or macro) commands, and checking your system's memory. Some Other pull-down menus are included for your review.

Other — Change help level (JJ)

Module 2

Other —Display Ram usage (?)

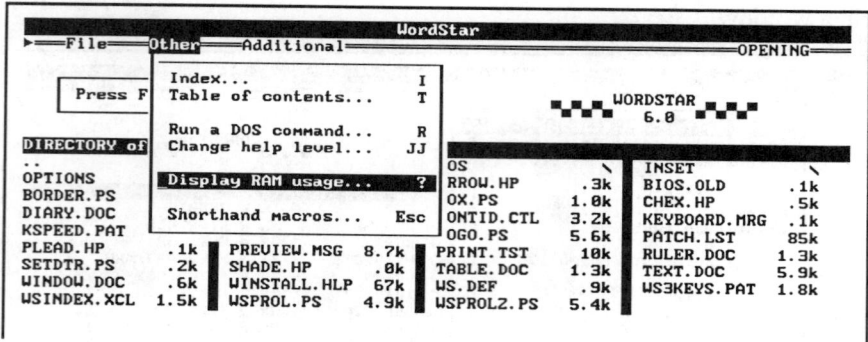

Other —Shorthand macros (Esc)

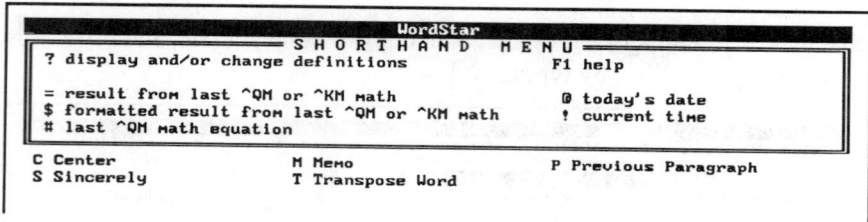

The Additional menu accesses WordStar's TelMerge and MailList utilities for telecommunications and mail list management.

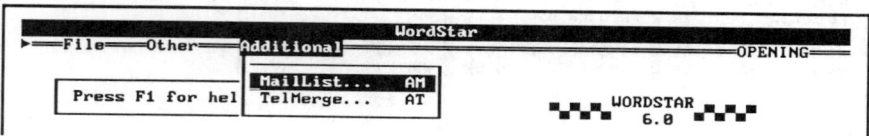

WordStar's editing screen also uses a pull-down menu system or the classic WordStar menus, depending on how you configure the help system. The EDIT menu bar is shown in the following illustration.

EDIT Menu Bar

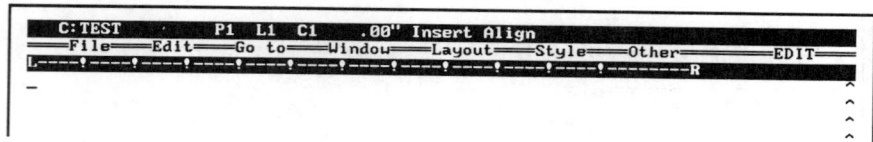

Program Overview

Pressing Alt-F pulls down the following menu.

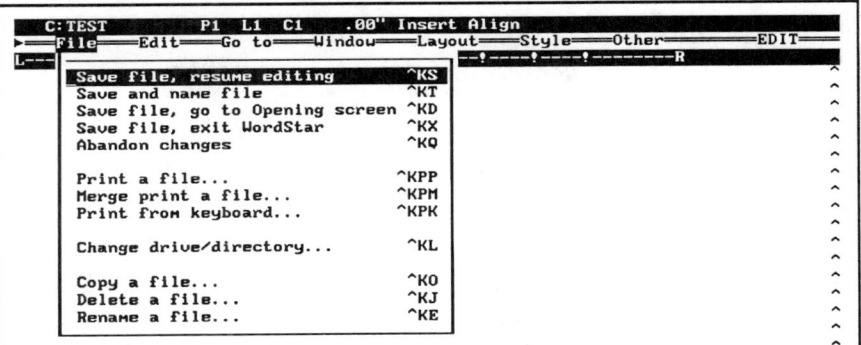

Pressing Alt-E pulls down the following menu.

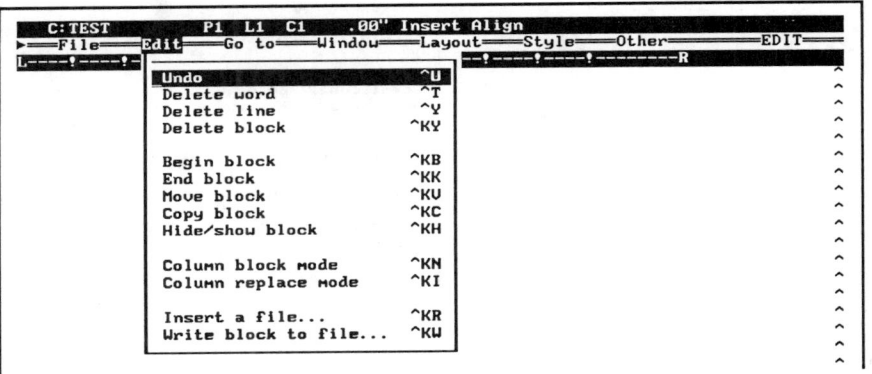

Pressing Alt-G pulls down the following menu.

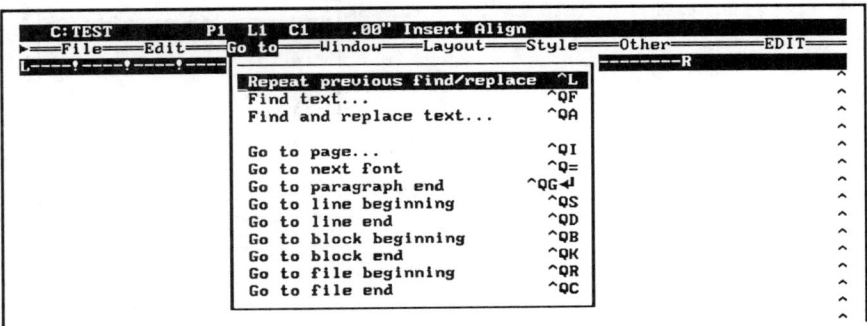

Module 2

Pressing Alt-W pulls down the following menu.

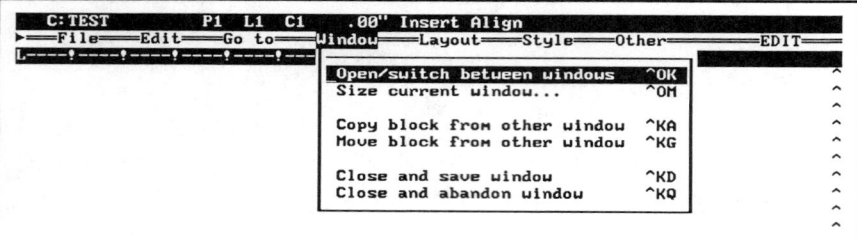

Pressing Alt-L pulls down the following menu.

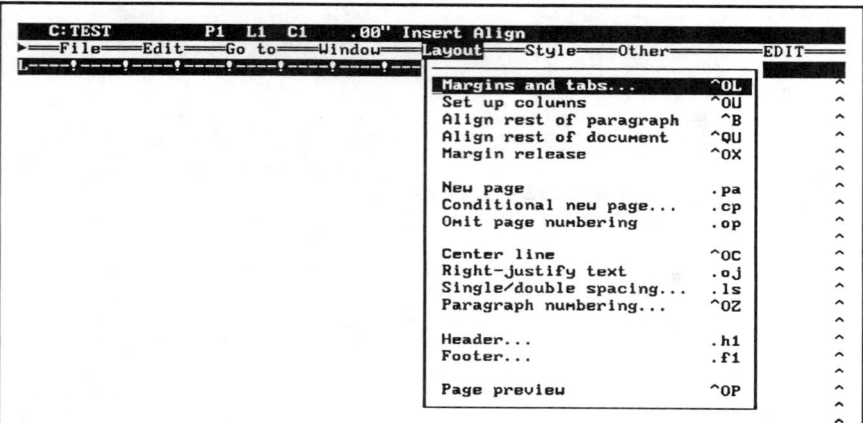

Pressing Alt-S pulls down the following menu.

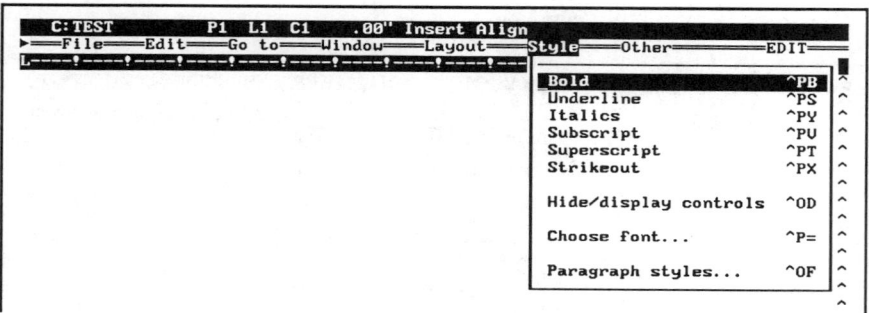

Pressing Alt-O pulls down the following menu.

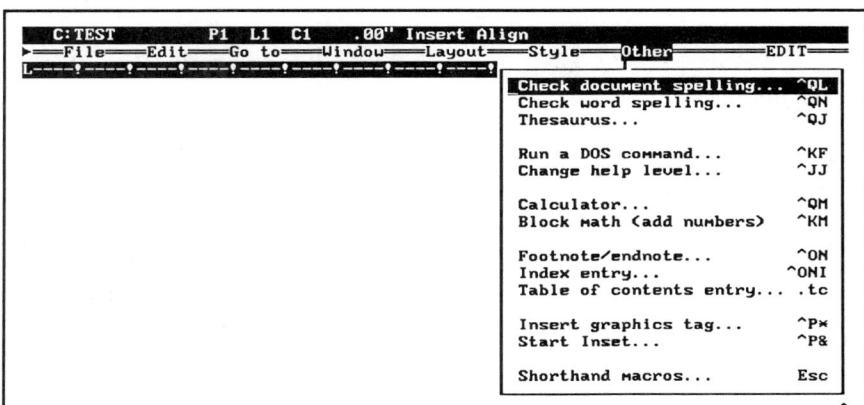

As mentioned earlier in the module, your dependence on the on-screen assistance diminishes as you memorize the commonly used commands. You can suppress the on-screen help as you become more experienced. It is changed temporarily by typing O at the OPENING menu or pressing Alt-O at the EDIT menu. Select the "Change help level..." line using the Down Arrow and press Return. Respond to the HELP LEVEL prompt by typing a number between 0 and 4 that corresponds to the desired help level. The default help level is set using the WSCHANGE utility furnished with WordStar.

WORDSTAR'S CLASSIC MENU NETWORK The WordStar classic menu network provides operator help information through context-sensitive operator menus, prompts, and on-screen help information. Figure 2-1 shows this menu structure and the key sequences used to access each of the menus within the network.

NOTE
The Ctrl-X notation is used throughout this book. It signifies that the Ctrl key is pressed and held while the indicated character key is typed. Both are released simultaneously. This is like typing a capital letter on a typewriter — you hold down the Shift key while typing a character key. The Ctrl key in the sequence is sometimes represented by the circumflex, or caret, symbol (^).

Module 2

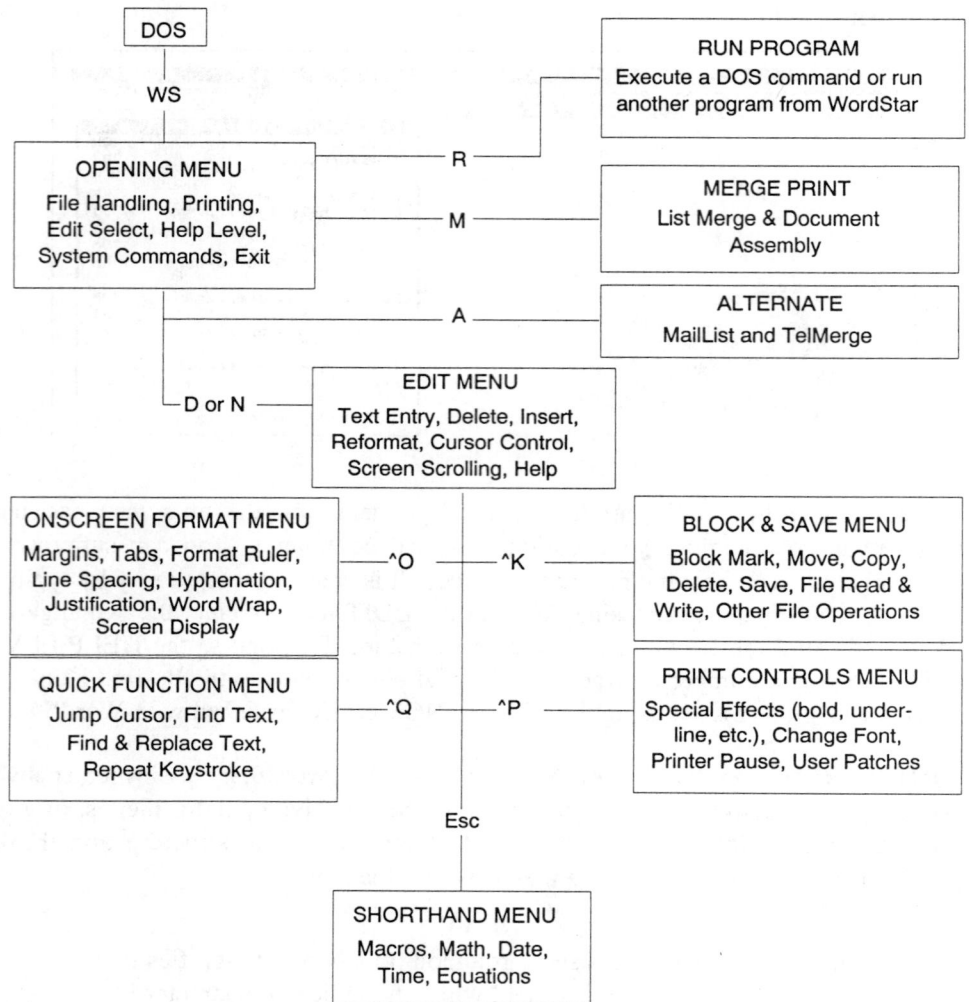

Figure 2-1. WordStar's Classic Menu Structure

The WordStar Classic menus are illustrated next. These menus give you the same capability as the pull-down menus. In fact, you may prefer the classic menus as they often access a function with fewer keystrokes. For example, to change help using the pull-down menu system, you must:

1. Type **Alt-O**.
2. Point to the "Change help level..." line.

Program Overview

3. Press **Return**.
4. Type the desired number.

To change help using the classic menu system, you must:

1. Press **Ctrl-JJ**.
2. Type the desired number.

OPENING MENU:

```
                        WordStar
              ═══════ O P E N I N G   M E N U ═══════
         D  open a document           L  change drive/directory
         S  speed write (new file)    C  protect/unprotect a file
         N  open a nondocument        E  rename a file
         P  print a file              O  copy a file
         M  merge print a file        Y  delete a file
         K  print from keyboard       F  turn directory off
         I  index a document         Esc shorthand
         T  table of contents         R  run a DOS command
         X  exit WordStar             A  additional
         J  help                      ?  memory usage
```

EDIT MENU:

```
    C:TEST         P1 L1 C1    .00" Insert Align
    ═══════════════════ E D I T   M E N U ═══════════════════
      CURSOR        SCROLL         DELETE       OTHER                MENUS
    ^E up         ^W up          ^G char     ^J help           ^O onscreen format
    ^X down       ^Z down        ^T word     ^I tab            ^K block & save
    ^S left       ^R screen up   ^Y line     ^U turn insert off ^P print controls
    ^D right      ^C screen     Del char     ^B align paragraph ^Q quick functions
    ^A word left     down        ^U undo     ^N split the line  Esc shorthand
    ^F word right                             ^L find/replace again
```

ONSCREEN FORMAT MENU:

```
   O  C:TEST         P1 L1 C1    .00" Insert Align
     ═══════════════ O N S C R E E N   F O R M A T   M E N U ═══════════════
        MARGINS & TABS          TYPING                    DISPLAY
     L  left    X release   W  turn word wrap off    D  turn print controls off
     R  right   U columns   J  turn justification on H  turn auto-hyphenation off
     T  turn ruler off      E  enter soft hyphen     P  page preview
     O  ruler to text       S  set line spacing      B  turn soft space dots on
     I  set/clear tabs      C  center line           K  open or switch window
     G  temporary indent    U  vertically center     M  size current window
     Z  paragraph number    A  turn auto-align off   N  notes
     F  paragraph styles    ]  right flush line      ?  memory usage
```

BLOCK & SAVE MENU:

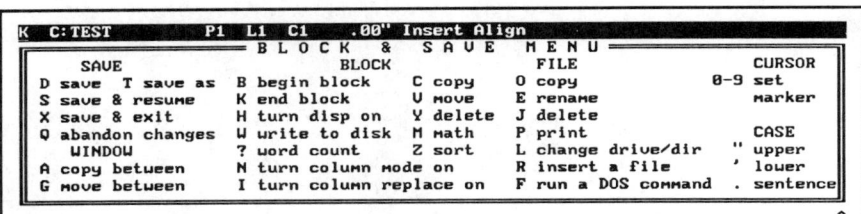

Module 2

PRINT CONTROLS MENU:

```
^P C:TEST       P1 L1 C1     .00" Insert Align
═══════════════ P R I N T   C O N T R O L S   M E N U ═══════════════
         BEGIN & END                                OTHER
   B bold         X strikeout       H overprint char   O binding space
   S underline    D double strike   ↵ overprint line   C print pause
   U subscript    Y italics         F phantom space    I 8-column tab
   T superscript  K indexing        G phantom rubout   . dot leader
                                    * graphics tag     0 extended chars
            STYLE                   & start Inset
   = select font   N normal font
   - select color  A alternate font       Q W E R ! custom    ? select printer
```

QUICK MENU:

```
^Q C:TEST       P1 L1 C1     .00" Insert Align
═══════════════ Q U I C K   M E N U ═══════════════
        CURSOR              FIND              OTHER              SPELL
   E upper left    P previous    F find text       U align rest doc   L check rest
   X lower right   U prev find   A find/replace    M math  Q repeat   N check word
   S begin line    B beg block   G char forward    J thesaurus        O enter word
   D end line      K end block   H char back           DELETE            SCROLL
   R beg file      0-9 marker    I page/line       Del line to left   W up, repeat
   C end file      ? char count  = next font       Y line to right    Z dn, repeat
                                  T to character
```

WORDSTAR CONTROL KEYS

Although the WordStar key sequences may at first seem convoluted, they are designed ergonomically, not logically. In fact, the typewriter keyboard is a cumbersome tool, designed to impede speed rather than to accelerate it.

This is a carryover from the early typing machines. Fast typing caused mechanical jams on these crude, gravity return typing machines. Therefore, it was necessary to design a keyboard that made typing as difficult as possible. Sometime later, an improved D'Vorak keyboard was invented. Too late for, alas, we continue to struggle to reach the frequently used keys, like E, I, and O, while our power fingers rest on the seldom used *home keys* like D, F, J, and K.

Module 3
A SAMPLE SESSION WITH WORDSTAR

GETTING READY

This module lets you experience WordStar and perform some merge print operations. Your DOS root directory should contain a CONFIG.SYS file with the line FILES = 20. You should also have the line PATH=\WS in your AUTOEXEC.BAT file on your root directory. This module assumes that your WordStar programs are on a fixed disk. Your program files should be in a \WS subdirectory. If you are using a two-floppy drive system, your program files should be on a disk in drive A and your working text (or data) files on a disk in drive B. (Look at Module 2 if you need more information about these installation requirements.)

SAMPLE SESSION

In this session you create a letter, then edit it for use with a merge print data file as a form letter. Next you prepare a data file for use with the form letter and use the merge print function to print the form letters. The procedures in this session use the pull-down menus.

NOTE

Control key sequences are shown Ctrl-#, where # is any character key. This indicates that the Ctrl key is pressed and held while the designated character key is typed. Both keys are released simultaneously. This is like typing a capital letter by pressing the Shift key and then typing the character.

If you are using a 101-key keyboard with Ctrl in the lower left-hand corner and Caps Lock to the left of A, you can use SWITCH.COM, supplied on the Advanced Customization disk, to convert Caps Lock to Ctrl. Type SWITCH and press Return from the DOS prompt to cause Caps Lock to operate as Ctrl.

Module 3

STARTING WORDSTAR AND PREPARING A LETTER Start WordStar and create a letter by performing the following steps.

1. Log to the WordStar program directory (C:\WS), type **WS**, and press **Return**. Notice that WordStar's OPENING menu is displayed.

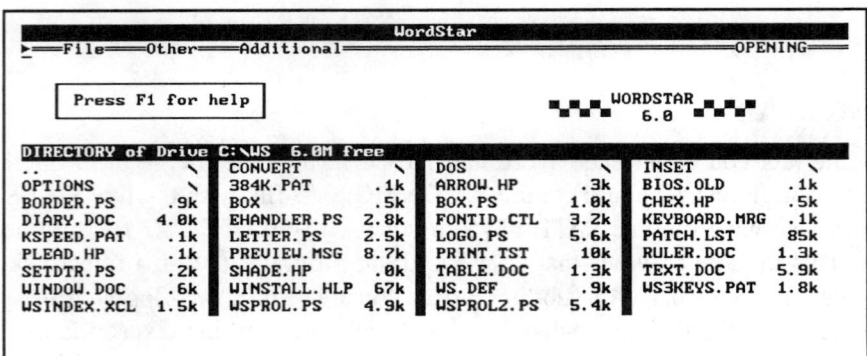

2. Type **F** and notice the pull-down File menu.

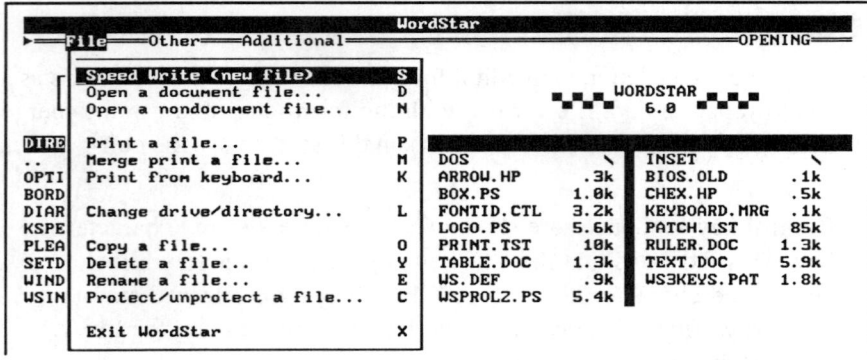

NOTE

In the following step, if you are using a floppy system, log to drive B. If you have a hard disk, make a \WS subdirectory named \DOC and log this subdirectory for document files.

3. Log the appropriate disk drive or subdirectory using step a if you have a floppy system or step b if you have a hard disk.

   a. Type **L** to "Change drive/directory...," then type **B** and press **Return** to log to drive B.

   b. Type **L** to "Change drive/directory...," then type **\WS\DOC** and press **Return** to log to the subdirectory \WS\DOC.

A Sample Session with WordStar

WordStar is now using the selected disk drive or subdirectory.

4. Type **FD** to open a document file. Then type the filename **CUSTOMER.LTR** and press **Return**.
5. Type **Y** in response to the "Can't find that file. Create a new one (Y/N)?" prompt. Notice that the EDIT menu is displayed.

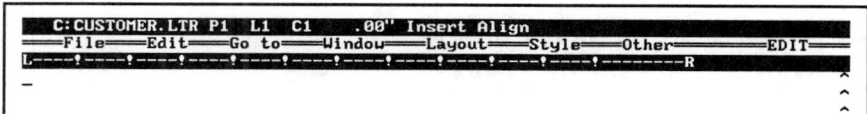

6. Use the ONSCREEN FORMAT menu to turn off hyphenation and justification as follows:
    a. Press **Ctrl-OH** to turn off hyphenation help.
    b. Press **Ctrl-OJ** to turn off justification.

    NOTE
    In following modules, hyphenation and justification are assumed to be off. The authors recommend that you set these off with WSCHANGE.

7. Type **.RM6.5"** and press **Return** to set the right margin to 6.5 inches. The period should be on line 1 column 1 (L1 C1) as shown on the status line at the top of the screen.

Notice the format ruler. It shows tab settings and the left and right margin settings.

8. Type the letter to Mr. Johnson, as shown in the following screen illustration.

TIP: When lines reach the right margin, let WordStar's automatic word wrap end the line automatically. End short lines by pressing Return, which places a < at the right side of the screen. Use the arrow keys for cursor control. If you prefer, you can press the Ctrl key in combination with the following letter keys for cursor control. This is the universal cursor control diamond used by such programs as dBASE, Sidekick, Multiplan, and many others.

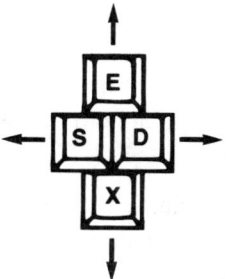

Figure 3-1   Cursor Control Diamond

17

Module 3

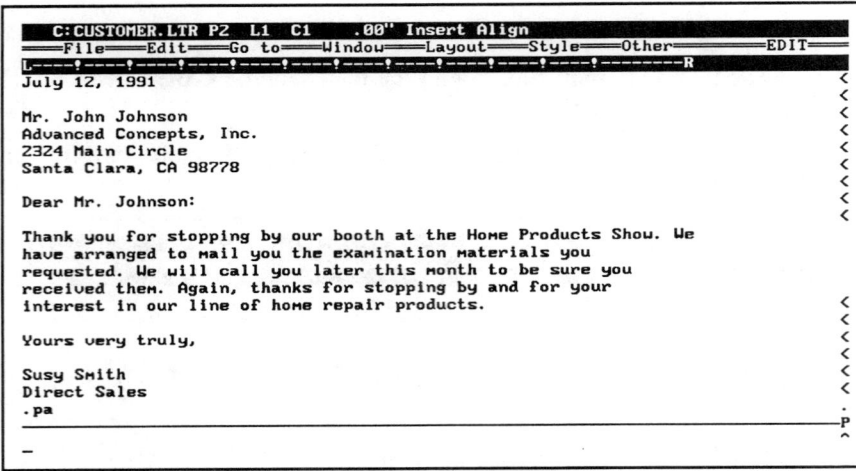

9. Press **Ctrl-KD** to save the letter. Check the file directory on the OPENING menu for the filename CUSTOMER.LTR.

PRINTING THE LETTER For proper printer operation, WordStar must have been installed for use with your printer. Most popular printers are included on the Printer selection menu within the WSCHANGE program, which calls the PRCHANGE utility supplied with WordStar. You can also install multiple printers using WSCHANGE. Once installed, you can select from a list of printers displayed at the bottom of the print prompt screen.

1. Check to see that your printer is ready for printing. Your printer must be properly connected to your computer, loaded with paper and ribbon, and turned on.
2. From the OPENING menu, type **FP** to print your letter. WordStar displays a PRINT menu. Notice that WordStar "remembers" the name of the last file you worked on. Press **Return** to accept the supplied filename CUSTOMER.LTR.
3. Press **F10** to accept the print default values if they are correct. Notice that your letter is printed.

MODIFYING THE LETTER FOR MERGE PRINT PRINTING In this section you edit your CUSTOMER.LTR for use with merge print. Special dot codes are embedded in the document that make use of a customer data file, which you create in the next section of this module. Note that the periods in the dot codes must be in column 1 (against the extreme left margin).

1. Type **FD**; notice that the last filename used is recalled. If it is the correct one, press **Return**. If the proper file is not recalled, you can type the filename and then press Return.

2. Press **Ctrl-O** and verify from the menu that hyphenation and justification are off. Press **Spacebar** to leave them as set.
3. Modify the letter as shown. Press **Del** (or Ctrl-G) to delete characters.

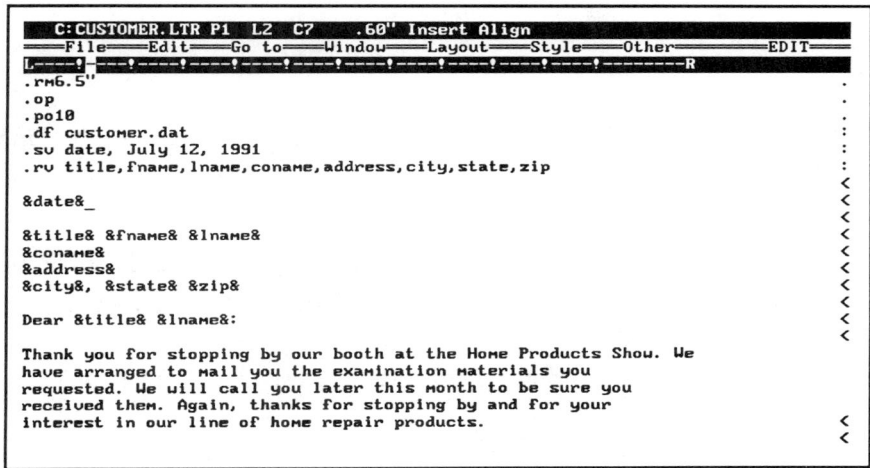

4. Save the document by pressing **Ctrl-KD**.

CREATING A MERGE PRINT DATA FILE Now that you have a form letter, you need a data file from which the form letter extracts variable information. In this section you use WordStar to prepare a data file containing sample customer data.

1. From the OPENING menu type **FN** (for *nondocument* file), type **CUSTOMER.DAT** and then press **Return**.
2. Type **Y** to answer the "Can't find that file. Create a new one (Y/N)?" prompt. Notice that the ruler line does not appear on the nondocument EDIT menu.

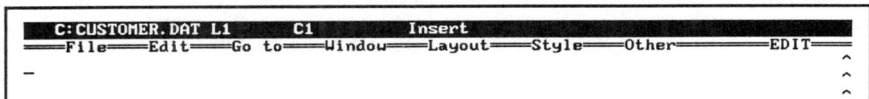

3. Type the following data file. Be sure you have a comma between each entry (*field*) on a line (*record*). End each line by pressing **Return**. Notice that the second record (Phyllis Berry) has a field with an internal comma. It is set off with quotes to keep merge print from treating the comma as a field separation character (called a *delimiter*).

Module 3

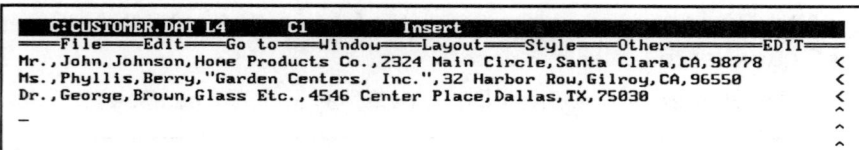

4. Save the data file by pressing **Ctrl-KD**.

PRINTING A MERGE PRINT DOCUMENT Now that you have a form letter and a corresponding data file, you are ready to print your form letters.

1. From the OPENING menu, type **FM** to merge print the document.
2. Respond to the prompt by typing **CUSTOMER.LTR** and pressing **Return**.
3. Check to see that your printer is ready. Then press **F10** to accept the merge print defaults.
4. Notice that three letters are printed. Each letter corresponds to a customer record in the CUSTOMER.DAT data file.

QUITTING WORDSTAR To exit WordStar:

1. Type **FX** from the OPENING menu. Note that the DOS prompt is displayed.
2. Turn to Module 52 to continue the recommended learning sequence.

Module 4
ABANDON DOCUMENT WITHOUT CHANGES

> Classic: ^KQ
> Pull-Down: Alt-F, select "Abandon Changes..."

DESCRIPTION

If you begin a document and decide either to quit or to start over, you can abandon your work without saving it by pressing Ctrl-KQ. The Q is the first letter of the word quit. Any Ctrl-K sequence controls block, save, and file operations.

If the displayed document is changed before it is abandoned without saving, WordStar displays the following message:

```
Changes have been made. Abandon anyway (Y/N)?
```

If you change your mind, type N and the cursor returns to its last position within the document. If you type Y, WordStar abandons the document without recording changes.

If you open a document and abandon it without making changes, WordStar briefly displays "Abandoning..." before returning to the OPENING menu:

APPLICATIONS

There are a number of reasons for using the abandon document operation. You may want simply to review a document and abandon it without changes. If you review a document and save it using Ctrl-KD instead of Ctrl-KQ, WordStar creates a duplicate file identified with a BAK extension.

If you are in the middle of modifying a document and decide that you want both the new and old versions, you can save the new version with Ctrl-KD and rename the .BAK (backup) file to make it usable.

If you accidentally delete portions of text from an existing document, it may be necessary to start over. Abandoning restores the original version of the document before it was changed.

There is still another common use of the abandon document operation. There are times when you make an error when typing the filename to open a document. Either the wrong document or a new document screen is displayed. For example, if you want to edit a

Module 4

document named LET and you type LTR, WordStar lets you know that you have opened a new document (if LTR doesn't already exist). To quit and start over, just press Ctrl-KQ. Once the OPENING menu is displayed, you're ready to try again by typing FD to open a document, typing the document name correctly, and pressing Return.

TYPICAL OPERATION

In this activity, you begin with the OPENING menu displayed, open a new document named TEST, then abandon it without saving.

1. At the OPENING menu, type **FD**, then type **TEST**, and press **Return**.
2. Type **Y** in response to "Can't find that file. Create a new one (Y/N)?"
3. Notice that a blank screen is displayed, ready for text entry.
4. Abandon the document by pressing **Ctrl-KQ**; the message "Abandoning..." is briefly displayed followed by the OPENING menu.
5. Turn to Module 75 to continue the learning sequence.

Module 5
ALIGNING TEXT (AUTO-ALIGN)

```
                    ^OA
```

DESCRIPTION

WordStar's auto-align feature is normally on. This feature aligns text as you type it. If you insert or delete a word in an existing paragraph, the text following the change realigns automatically. If you do not want this to happen, you can turn off auto-align by pressing Ctrl-OA. It is turned back on using the same key sequence.

When auto-align is off, you can align a paragraph within the margins or the indent level (set with Ctrl-OG) and the right margin by pressing Ctrl-B. If you change a document's margins, you can realign the entire document by placing the cursor at the beginning of the document and pressing Ctrl-QU.

When realigning a document, you may wish to protect certain passages from the effect of auto-align. This is done by placing the dot command .AW OFF on a line above the protected passage. To turn auto-alignment back on, enter the dot command .AW ON.

If you wish to change the margins of footnotes and endnotes (see Module 37), use Ctrl-ON and type U.

You should also check the hyphenation and justification settings before editing or realigning a document. This is done by pressing Ctrl-O and examining the ONSCREEN FORMAT menu. In particular, check the on/off status following the control characters J and H. If the settings are satisfactory, press the Spacebar. If not, type the letter J or H as required.

If you find the auto-align bothersome, you may wish to turn it off as a default value using WordStar's WSCHANGE utility.

APPLICATIONS

The auto-align function adjusts your document as it is edited. This eliminates the need to manually align edited passages with Ctrl-B. There are times, however, when auto-align should be suppressed. For example, if you are modifying centered or indented text, the auto-align feature shifts text back to the left margin. This requires you to readjust text to the center or indent level manually.

Module 5

Another problem encountered by auto-alignment activity is that your text entry is delayed during text readjustment. This is often annoying to fast typists. To prevent this action, you can turn off auto-align by pressing Ctrl-OA. When you are ready for auto-align to resume its effect, press Ctrl-OA again.

TYPICAL OPERATION

In this activity, you create a temporary document named TEMP. Then you turn auto-align off and on to determine its effect.

1. Open a new document named TEMP.
2. Press **Ctrl-O** and check the status of auto-align, hyphenation, and justification. If necessary, turn hyphenation and justification off; leave auto-align on. Press **Spacebar** to leave the settings unchanged if they are correct.
3. Type the following passage. After typing each step number and period, press **Ctrl-OG** to indent the following text. Press **Return** after the text in each step.

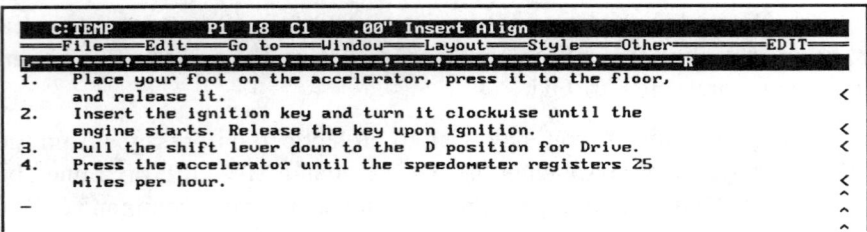

4. Move your cursor to the comma following the word "accelerator" in step 1. Press the **Spacebar** and type **pedal**. Notice that the second line of step 1 is auto-aligned to the left margin. (This is not desirable.)

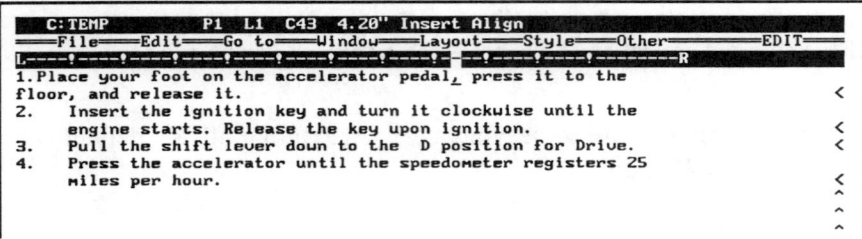

5. Move the cursor to the period at the end of step 4. Press **Ctrl-OA** to turn auto-align off.

Aligning Text (Auto-Align)

6. Type **, but no more**. Notice that the left indent is not realigned. (This is desired for this editing change.)

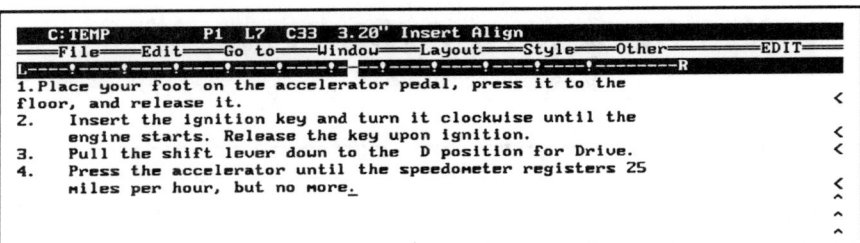

7. Continue to experiment with auto-align until you understand its operation.
8. Press **Ctrl-KQ** and type **Y** to abandon the document without saving.
9. Turn to Module 76 to continue the learning sequence.

Module 6
BLOCK HIDE/DISPLAY

> Classic: ^KH
> Pull-Down: Alt-E, select "Hide/show block"

DESCRIPTION

Marked blocks are normally highlighted in reverse video or half intensity. You can unmark (or hide) the block, which eliminates the highlighting. This is accomplished by pressing Ctrl-KH. Even though the block is hidden, WordStar "remembers" the block. If you decide to turn the highlighting back on, press Ctrl-KH again and the highlighting is reinstated.

APPLICATIONS

When a block is either moved or copied, block highlighting remains in effect until hidden with Ctrl-KH. Hiding a marked block suppresses highlighting which is often distracting. The ability to reestablish or find block markers (see Module 31) in the most recently marked block of text is useful. For example, you may need to return to a passage that is being repeated several places within a document. One handy use is to mark and copy the headings of a multiple-page table.

TYPICAL OPERATION

In this activity, begin at the EDIT menu with the MYLTR document displayed. Next, mark and unmark a passage of text.

1. Open the document MYLTR.
2. Mark the first sentence of the letter paragraph with **Ctrl-KB** at the beginning and **Ctrl-KK** at the first character of the second sentence.
3. Hide and display this block by pressing **Ctrl-KH** several times.
4. Press **Ctrl-KQ** to abandon the document without saving.
5. Turn to Module 20 to continue the learning sequence.

Module 7
BLOCK MATH

> Classic: ^KM
> Pull-Down: Alt-O, select "Block math (add numbers)"

DESCRIPTION

The block math function is used to mark a group of numbers as a block and then sum the numbers within the block. Usually, one or more columns or rows of numbers are included in a marked block using WordStar's standard block markers (Ctrl-KB and Ctrl-KK). When marking columns, the column mode must be turned on with Ctrl-KN. Pressing Ctrl-KM sums the numbers within the marked block. Pressing Esc and typing = or $ inserts the resulting number. The = sign inserts the value as a decimal fraction. You may use Esc $ for dollars and cents or to round a number to two decimal places.

If you use Tab to advance the cursor to a decimal tab, the Esc = or Esc $ sequences position the decimal point at the decimal tab location.

Look at the following rows and columns of numbers. Several are negative, designated by the minus sign. Numbers within parentheses are also treated as negative values. Negative values are subtracted from the series of numbers.

Part No.	Mon	Tues	Wed	Totals
CD-0987	123.45	121.50	454.12	699.07
EG-7232	-95.25	45.67	89.95	40.37
MT-2121	68.50	-34.59	-29.05	4.86
PR-4556	345.45	232.20	12.34	589.99
RT-0908	75.00	-11.18	218.55	282.37
Totals	517.15	353.60	745.91	1616.66

Marking the first column of numbers (using Ctrl-KN to activate the column mode) and then pressing Ctrl-KM displays the answer in a window at the top of your screen. Each row and column can be summed individually. In addition, you can mark the entire matrix to sum all entries within the marked block. However, do not include the part numbers, as any number within the block is automatically included. Accidentally marking part numbers or dates yields the wrong result.

Module 7

APPLICATIONS

Block math lets you use WordStar to enter and compute the values of rows and columns of numbers (or numerical tables) almost as you would manipulate numbers within an electronic spreadsheet. This is an excellent tool for computing (or checking) the results of financial data, expense statements, and similar documents.

TYPICAL OPERATION

In this activity, you enter the table of numbers contained in the example in the Description section of this module. Then you use block math to compute the row and column totals. Begin at the OPENING menu.

1. Open a new document named TEMP.
2. Reset your tabs by typing the following dot command at the left margin.

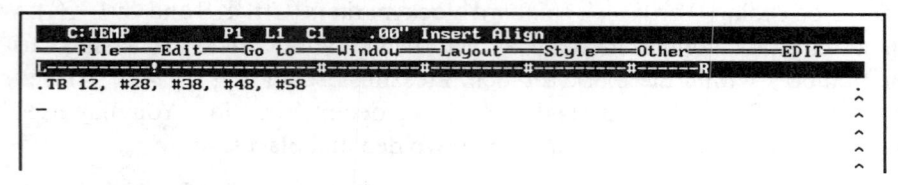

```
 C:TEMP          P1 L1 C1    .00" Insert Align
====File====Edit====Go to====Window====Layout====Style====Other====         ====EDIT====
L----------!------------------#----------#----------#----------#-----R
.TB 12, #28, #38, #48, #58
_
```

3. Enter the following numbers using the Tab key to advance to each column.

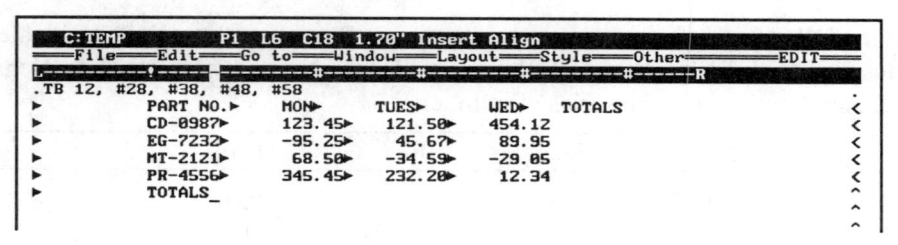

```
 C:TEMP          P1 L6 C18  1.70" Insert Align
====File====Edit====Go to====Window====Layout====Style====Other====         ====EDIT====
L----------!------------------#----------#----------#----------#-----R
.TB 12, #28, #38, #48, #58
►       PART NO.►   MON►     TUES►    WED►    TOTALS              <
►       CD-0987►    123.45►  121.50►  454.12                      <
►       EG-7232►    -95.25►   45.67►   89.95                      <
►       MT-2121►     68.50►  -34.59►  -29.05                      <
►       PR-4556►    345.45►  232.20►   12.34                      <
►       TOTALS_
```

4. Press **Ctrl-KN** to set the column mode on.
5. Block mark the Monday column and press **Ctrl-KM** to compute the column total. (Be sure to include all negative signs and numbers within the block.) Notice the screen. Press **Esc** at the prompt.

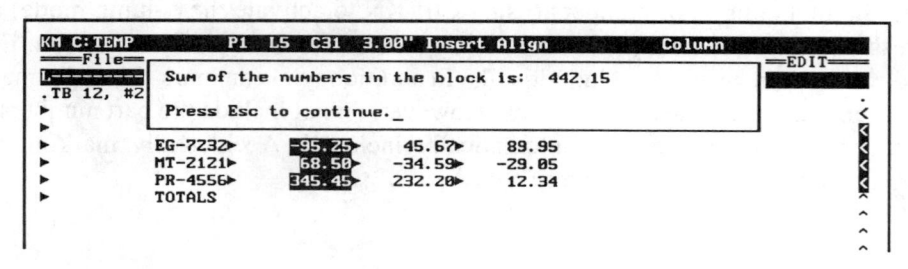

```
KM C:TEMP          P1 L5 C31  3.00" Insert Align         Column
====File====
L---------- Sum of the numbers in the block is:   442.15           ====EDIT====
.TB 12, #2
►           Press Esc to continue._
►                                                                         <
►       EG-7232►   -95.25   45.67►   89.95                                <
►       MT-2121►    68.50  -34.59►  -29.05                                <
►       PR-4556►   345.45  232.20►   12.34                                <
►       TOTALS
```

6. Place the cursor on the Totals row and tab to the decimal tab in the Monday column.
7. Press **Esc $** to insert the column total.
8. Repeat steps 5, 6, and 7 for the Tuesday and Wednesday columns.
9. Block mark the numbers on the first row (Part No. CD-0987) and press **Ctrl-KM** to compute the row total; then press **Esc**. Do not include the part number.
10. Tab to the Totals column decimal tab for row CD-0987 and press **Esc $** to insert the row total.
11. Repeat steps 9 and 10 for the rest of the rows, including the Totals row. Your table should now resemble the following example.

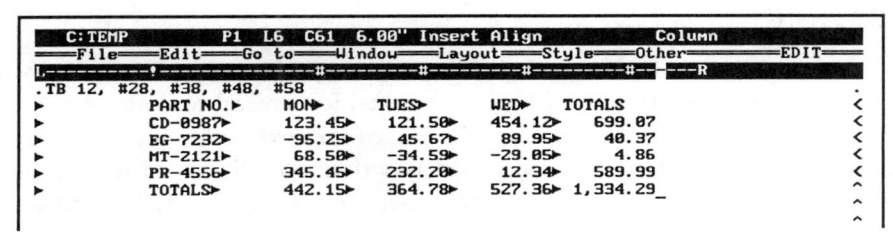

```
   C:TEMP            P1  L6  C61  6.00"  Insert Align        Column
====File====Edit====Go to====Window====Layout====Style====Other========EDIT====
L-----------!----------------#---------#---------#---------#--+---R
.TB 12, #28, #38, #48, #58
 ►          PART NO.►    MON►      TUES►     WED►    TOTALS                <
 ►          CD-0987►    123.45►   121.50►   454.12►   699.07               <
 ►          EG-7232►    -95.25►    45.67►    89.95►    40.37               <
 ►          MT-2121►     68.50►   -34.59►   -29.85►     4.86               <
 ►          PR-4556►    345.45►   232.20►    12.34►   589.99               <
 ►          TOTALS►     442.15►   364.78►   527.36► 1,334.29_              ^
                                                                           ^
```

12. Abandon the document by pressing **Ctrl-KQ** and typing **Y**.
13. Turn to Module 9 to continue the learning sequence.

Module 8
BLOCK SELECTION

> Classic: ^KB, ^KK
> Pull-Down: Alt-E, select "Begin block," "End block"

DESCRIPTION

A block of text is any continuous passage. This can vary from a single word to several paragraphs or even pages. Blocks of text are marked for several reasons. When text is marked, it is identified, or set apart, from the rest of the text within a document. Once marked, the text can be deleted, moved, copied, or written to a disk as a file. You can also change the block of text to all uppercase or all lowercase, using Ctrl-K ' or Ctrl-K ".

When marked, most microcomputers *highlight* the text in some way. Marked text may be half intensity, reversed (black on white background), or an alternate color, also depending on how you installed your screen display. The highlighting lets you see precisely which text is marked. If it is hard to distinguish marked text, you can change your display with WSCHANGE.

Marking text is achieved with the classic BLOCK & SAVE menu or the pull-down EDIT menu. With the cursor at the first character of the block of text to be marked, press Ctrl-KB and notice the beginning marker <B>. Next, move the cursor to the character following the passage you want to mark. Press Ctrl-KK and the block is marked. Remember that B and K are the first and last letters in the word *block*.

The right margin displays a highlighted vertical bar indicating the area of the block.

If you make a mistake, you can extend the beginning or end of the marked block or move it to another area of the document. Just reposition the cursor and repeat the block marking process. You can turn block markers on and off by repeating the block marker key sequence. Press Ctrl-KB to turn on the block beginning marker. Without moving the cursor, press Ctrl-KB again to turn it off.

APPLICATIONS

Block operations affect areas of text ranging from a character to an entire document file. In addition to continuous blocks of text, columns of text can also be moved, copied, or deleted through use of the column editing procedures described in Module 12. Once marked, a block is ready to be moved, copied, written to a file, or deleted. WordStar lets you perform a number of other operations with marked blocks including math, sorting, changing case, and counting characters.

TYPICAL OPERATION

Begin this activity with MYLTR displayed. Then mark a block of text.

1. Open the document MYLTR and place the cursor at the first character of the first word of the letter paragraph. (L9 C1).
2. Press **Ctrl-KB** and notice that the block marker <B> is displayed.
3. Position the cursor at the beginning of the line following the last line of text in the paragraph. Press **Ctrl-KK** and notice that the block is highlighted.

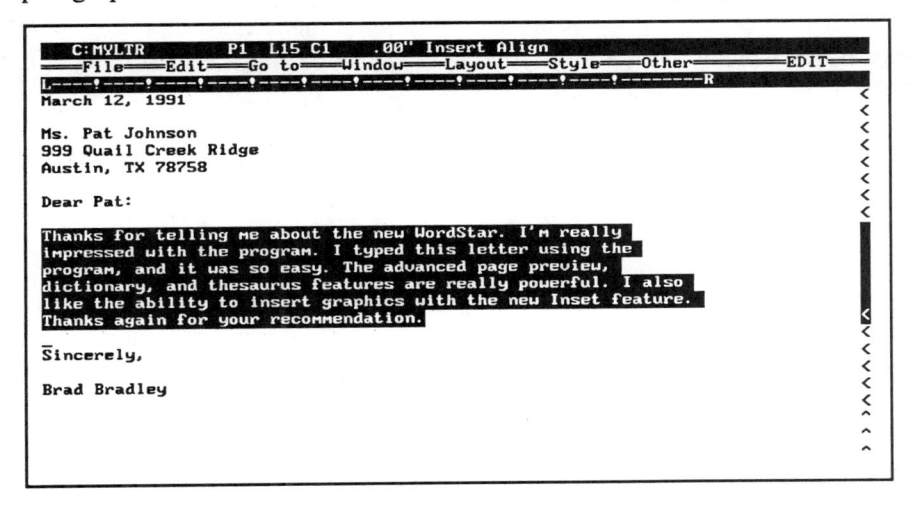

```
C:MYLTR         P1   L15 C1     .00" Insert Align
=====File======Edit======Go to======Window======Layout======Style======Other=======EDIT=====
L----!----!----!----!----!----!----!----!----!----R
March 12, 1991                                                  <
                                                                <
Ms. Pat Johnson                                                 <
999 Quail Creek Ridge                                           <
Austin, TX 78758                                                <
                                                                <
Dear Pat:                                                       <
                                                                <
Thanks for telling me about the new WordStar. I'm really
impressed with the program. I typed this letter using the
program, and it was so easy. The advanced page preview,
dictionary, and thesaurus features are really powerful. I also
like the ability to insert graphics with the new Inset feature.
Thanks again for your recommendation.                           <
                                                                <
Sincerely,                                                      <
                                                                <
Brad Bradley                                                    <
```

NOTE

The marked block can now be deleted, moved, or copied within the document or written to a new file. However, when a document is abandoned, the block markers are canceled.

4. Press **Ctrl-KQ** to abandon the document without saving it.
5. Turn to Module 6 to continue the learning sequence.

Module 9
CALCULATOR (QUICK MATH)

> Classic: ^QM
> Pull-Down: Alt-O, select "Calculator..."

DESCRIPTION

The quick math function provides you with a "pop-up" equation solver. Pressing Ctrl-QM displays a MATH menu at the top of your screen. The prompt "Type a math equation" and a table of mathematical operators are included. The operators are:

+	add	int	integer	atn	arc tangent
–	subtract	ln	base e log	sin	sine
^	exponentiate	log	base 10 log	cos	cosine
*	multiply	exp	e^x	tan	tangent
/	divide	sqr	square root		
%	percent				

Some examples of equations are presented so that you might understand the use of WordStar's quick math function. Pressing Return displays the answer to the right of "Last result."

Equation	Result
35.6+11.3	46.9
5*((23–7)/2)	15
4^3	64
sqr(200)	14.1421356237
9.95*8%	.796
sin(45)	.707106781187
cos(15)	.965925826289
tan(135)	–1
log(3)	.47712125472
ln(3)	1.09861228867
int(24.555)	24
1000*1000000000	1.e11

You can use up to 76 characters in an equation. You can recall the last equation used by pressing Ctrl-R. Once recalled, you can edit it and press Return to get a new result. The last result is inserted into the body of a document by positioning the cursor at the point of insertion and then pressing Esc and typing =. You can use Esc $ for dollars and cents or to display (truncate) the results with two decimal places.

A maximum of 12 digits is displayed. Larger numbers are expressed in scientific notation (as a power of ten). For example, the expression 1.e11 is the same as 1 X 10 raised to the 11th power.

APPLICATIONS

The quick math function is convenient for performing most common mathematical calculations. You can use quick math as an advanced calculator, because the added mathematical and trigonometric operators give you the ability to perform many scientific calculations.

The ability to use the Esc = key sequence to insert the last result into the body of a document eliminates the need for you to remember and retype the last result. If you intend to add a long column or row of numbers, you may find that the block math function is more convenient than the quick math calculator.

TYPICAL OPERATION

In this activity, a temporary document is opened and the quick math function is used to perform a calculation. Next, the result of the calculation is inserted into the document. Begin at WordStar's OPENING menu.

1. Open a new document named TEMP and type **The total purchase price is**. Press the **Spacebar**, press **Ctrl-QM**, and notice the following screen:

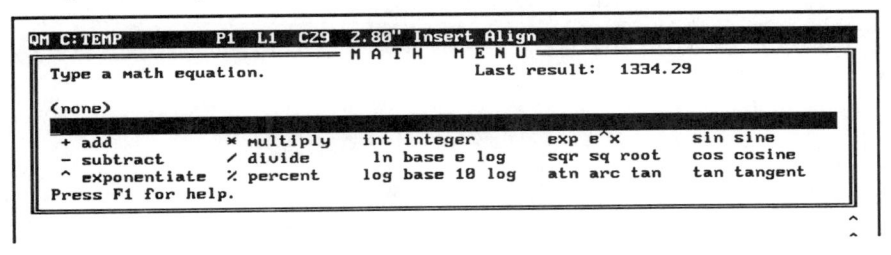

```
QM C:TEMP             P1  L1  C29  2.80" Insert Align
================================ MATH  MENU ================================
 Type a math equation.                   Last result:  1334.29

 (none)

   + add              * multiply    int integer    exp e^x       sin sine
   - subtract         / divide      ln base e log  sqr sq root   cos cosine
   ^ exponentiate     % percent     log base 10 log  atn arc tan  tan tangent
 Press F1 for help.
```

2. Type the equation **49.95*1.0625** and press **Return**. Notice the answer 53.071875 following "Last result:."
3. Press **Ctrl-U** to redisplay the document.

33

Module 9

4. Press **Esc** and type **$**. Notice that the last result is rounded to two decimal places and inserted at the cursor position.

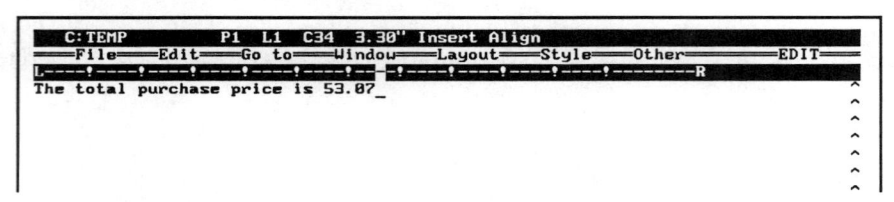

```
 C:TEMP            P1  L1  C34   3.30"  Insert Align
═══File═══Edit═══Go to═══Window═══Layout═══Style═══Other═══════EDIT═══
L----!----!----!----!----!----!--!----!----!----!---------R
The total purchase price is 53.07_
```

5. Type a period to end the sentence.
6. Type **Ctrl-KQ** and type **Y** to abandon the practice document.
7. Turn to Module 25 to continue the learning sequence.

Module 10
CENTERING TEXT ON A LINE OR PAGE

>   Classic: ^OC, ^OV, .OC on/off
>   Pull-Down: Alt-L, select "Center line"

DESCRIPTION

WordStar has an automatic line-centering function that lets you place a character, word, or series of words, such as a title, centered between the left and right margins. WordStar also has vertical centering, which centers one or more lines of text vertically on a page.

Text centering is accomplished by positioning the cursor on the line containing the text you want to center. The precise position of the cursor is not critical, as long as it is on the proper line. The line may already exist, or it may be one that you have just created, with the cursor still located at the end of the line.

With the cursor on the line, press Ctrl-OC to center the text between the left and right margins. If you want to move text that is centered on a line back to the left margin, move the cursor to the left margin (column 01) and press Ctrl-T to delete the spaces between the cursor and the text.

To move vertically centered text back to the top of a page, you must delete each blank line preceding the text. This is achieved with the line delete function (Ctrl-Y) or by marking the blank lines as a block and deleting the lines with Ctrl-KY.

If you have several lines to center, insert the dot command .OC ON at the left margin. When align is on, typed text is automatically centered for you. When you are ready to cancel centering, enter the .OC OFF dot command.

APPLICATIONS

Line centering is often used to position document headings. Without automatic centering, it is necessary to center text manually. This requires character counting and the insertion of spaces to attain an even amount of space on each side of the centered text. This is time-consuming, and errors are easily made.

There are times when you want a document ragged right and left. The center function lets you center a series of lines, like the ones in the following illustration.

Module 10

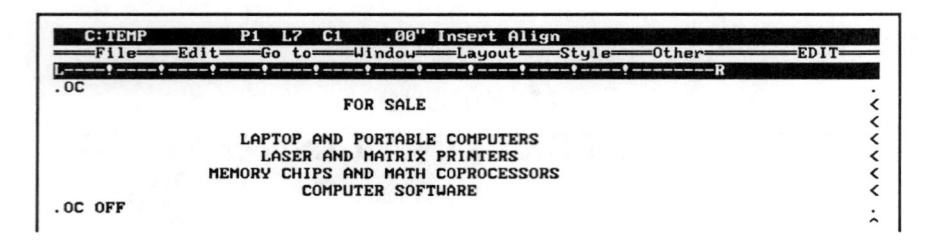

```
 C:TEMP         P1  L7  C1     .00" Insert Align
====File====Edit====Go to====Window====Layout====Style====Other========EDIT====
L----!----!----!----!----!----!----!----!----!----!----!--------R
.OC
                          FOR SALE                                    <
                                                                      <
                 LAPTOP AND PORTABLE COMPUTERS                        <
                   LASER AND MATRIX PRINTERS                          <
                MEMORY CHIPS AND MATH COPROCESSORS                    <
                       COMPUTER SOFTWARE                              <
.OC OFF                                                               .
                                                                      ^
```

Vertical centering is often used to center one or more lines on a title page. If you have several lines, you can first center each line of text with Ctrl-OC. Then place the cursor on the first line and press Ctrl-OV to center the lines on the page.

TYPICAL OPERATION

In this activity, you begin by opening a document named TEMP. Type two centered lines using the center line function. Then center the lines vertically on the page.

1. Open a document named TEMP.
2. Type **BIG COMPUTER**, press **Ctrl-OC**, then press **Return** twice.
3. Type **REFERENCE MANUAL** and press **Ctrl-OC**.
4. Move the cursor to the first centered line (the one containing "BIG COMPUTER") and press **Ctrl-OV**. Examine the resulting page. Refer to the status line to determine the position of the vertically centered text.

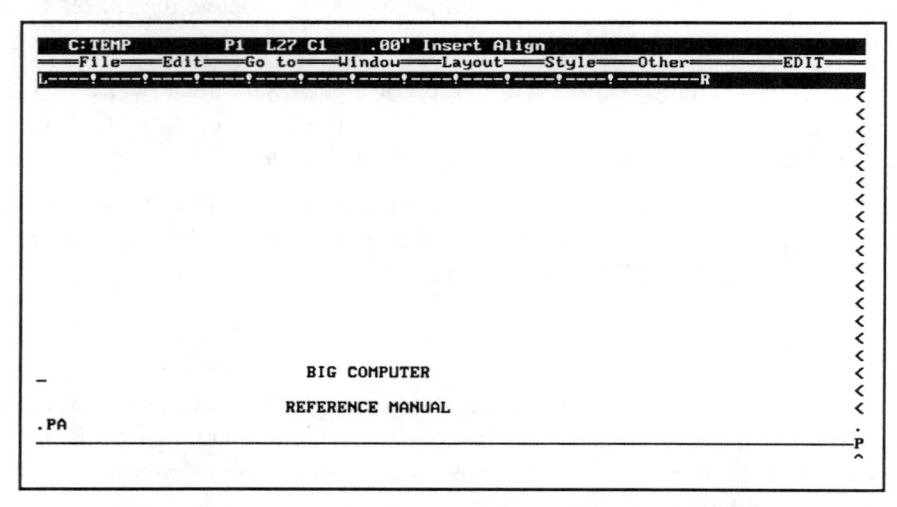

```
 C:TEMP         P1  L27 C1     .00" Insert Align
====File====Edit====Go to====Window====Layout====Style====Other========EDIT====
L----!----!----!----!----!----!----!----!----!----!----!--------R
                                                                      <
                                                                      <
                                                                      <
                                                                      <
                                                                      <
                                                                      <
                                                                      <
                                                                      <
                                                                      <
                                                                      <
                                                                      <
                                                                      <
                                                                      <
                                                                      <
_                       BIG COMPUTER                                  <
                      REFERENCE MANUAL                                <
.PA                                                                   .
                                                                     -P
                                                                      ^
```

5. Continue to experiment with the center functions until you are comfortable with their operation.
6. Press **Ctrl-KQ** and type **Y** to abandon the document without saving.
7. Turn to Module 45 to continue the learning sequence.

Module 11
CHARACTER COUNT

> ^Q?

DESCRIPTION

WordStar lets you count the number of characters that are in a file. You can press Ctrl-Q? while editing to get a character count from the beginning of the document to the cursor position. A screen similar to the following is displayed.

```
Character count at cursor:  596
Press Esc to continue._
```

APPLICATIONS

Some jobs require a character count to determine the service charges or productivity rates. An author might find this utility useful for evaluating article or chapter sizes. A publisher can use it to determine author payments that are based on a fixed rate per character.

TYPICAL OPERATION

In this activity, you determine the character count of the document MYLTR. Open the document, move the cursor to the bottom, and use Ctrl-Q? to display the number of characters.

1. Open the document MYLTR.
2. Press **Ctrl-QC** to move the cursor to the bottom of the document.
3. Press **Ctrl-Q?** and check the display.

```
Character count at cursor:  598
Press Esc to continue._
```

The character count indicates the number of characters, including spaces, in the document.

4. Press **Esc** to return to the document.
5. Press **Ctrl-KQ** to abandon the document.
6. Turn to Module 88 to continue the learning sequence.

Module 12
COLUMNAR EDITING

> Classic: ^KN, ^KI, .cc, .cb, .co
> Pull-Down: Alt-E, select "Column block mode," "Column replace mode"

DESCRIPTION

Block marking and editing operations are presented in the following modules.

Block Operation	Module Number
Mark beginning/end	8
Hide/display	6
Delete	20
Move	51
Copy	14
Copy block to file	13
Copy file into document	16

You should have an understanding of a marked block before you can fully appreciate the meaning of a marked column.

MARKING AND EDITING COLUMNS A block affects text from margin to margin. A column affects only a vertical strip, or column, of text. Tables use columns of text. To delete, move, or copy a column of text, turn on WordStar's column mode by pressing Ctrl-KN. The word Column appears on the status line. Mark the beginning of a column (upper left-hand corner) with Ctrl-KB. Then mark the end of the column (lower right-hand corner) with Ctrl-KK. The marked column is highlighted. If you change your mind, you can move either marker. You can also alternate between column and block marking with Ctrl-KN. When you insert or move a column, text is displaced to the right.

If you want to replace (or write over) text instead of displace it, you can turn on the column replace mode by pressing Ctrl-KI. When column replace is turned on, ColRepl is displayed on the status line. Column replace is turned off by pressing Ctrl-KI again. Column replace only takes effect when in the column mode, although it stays in effect during column editing until you turn it off.

The following sequences are used to delete, move, copy, or write a marked column.

Operation	Key Sequence
Delete Column	Ctrl-KY
Move Column	Ctrl-KV
Copy Column	Ctrl-KC
Write Column to file	Ctrl-KW

NEWSPAPER-STYLE COLUMNS WordStar gives you the ability to prepare and print newspaper-style columns using Ctrl-OU or choosing Set up columns from the Layout pull-down menu and answering the prompts in the Column Layout dialog box.

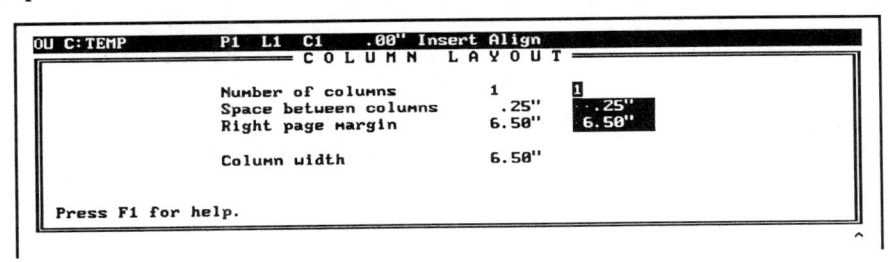

```
OU C:TEMP          P1 L1 C1    .00" Insert Align
                   ═══ C O L U M N   L A Y O U T ═══
        Number of columns        1       1
        Space between columns   .25"    .25"
        Right page margin      6.50"   6.50"

        Column width           6.50"

   Press F1 for help.
```

Another way is to use column dot commands. These dot commands are described here.

.co n1,n2 — Establishes the number of columns to print and the space between each column, where n1 is the number of columns and n2 is the space (in columns or inches) between columns. The value of n1 is a number from 1 to 8.
Examples:
   .co 4,5   (4 columns separated by 5 spaces)
   .co 3,.5" (3 columns separated by 1/2 inch)

.cc — Following columnar text is kept together during subsequent editing.

.cb — Starts a new column before the end of the page. If entered in the last column, it starts a column on a new page.

When typing a column, begin by entering the column width by setting the right margin. For example, if you want a 2-inch-wide column, enter the dot command .rm 2". Now you can specify the number of columns and the space between columns with the .co dot command. For example, if you want 3 columns separated by a .5" separation, use .co 3,.5". Now you can type your text. The page length adjusts automatically to correspond to the three columns. After the first column is filled with text, the second column starts. The dot commands take care of the text. You can use the page preview function (Ctrl-OP) to view the page before it is printed. This shows you how the page will look when it is printed.

Module 12

APPLICATIONS

Without the column-editing function, columns of text are manipulated a line at a time. The ability to move, copy, or delete columns of text saves the time that would otherwise be spent "fixing" a document a character or line at a time. In operations where heavy tabular work is produced, the columnar-editing function is invaluable.

For example, columns are easily switched with the move function. A vertical line is often used to draw a vertical rule in a table. Rules are often marked and copied with column copy. This eliminates the need to hand type each rule a character at a time.

Vertical columns of spaces are often marked and either moved, copied, or deleted to shift entire passages of text to the left or right. When using multiple columns, you can set the left and right margins to match a column width and insert new text in the columns. Adjacent text moves down with your progress. When done, reset the margins and move the adjacent columns back to their original positions.

The newspaper-style columns, which are controlled with the .co, .cc, and .cb dot commands, are used for newsletters and other documents that typically use multiple columns. The control provided by the dot commands lets you type your text as a single column without being concerned about moving text from one column to the next.

TYPICAL OPERATION

In this activity, begin by opening a new document named MYCOL. Then prepare a simple table and use the column function to make adjustments.

1. Open a new document named MYCOL.
2. Create the following simple table. Use the **Spacebar** to advance the cursor between columns.

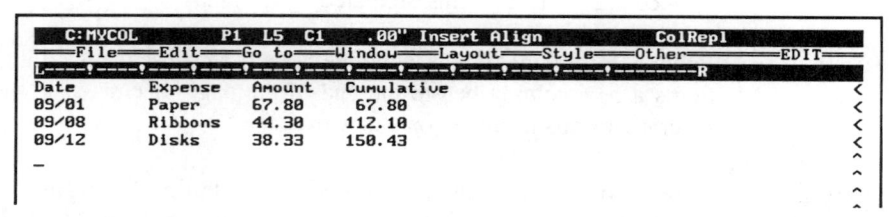

```
  C:MYCOL          P1  L5  C1      .00" Insert Align           ColRepl
====File======Edit======Go to======Window======Layout======Style======Other==========EDIT====
L----!----?----!----?----!----?----!----?----!----?----!----?----!--------R
Date           Expense       Amount     Cumulative                                        <
09/01          Paper         67.80        67.80                                           <
09/08          Ribbons       44.30       112.10                                           <
09/12          Disks         38.33       150.43                                           <
-                                                                                         ^
                                                                                          ^
                                                                                          ^
```

3. Use **Alt-F1** to draw a vertical rule on column 8 as shown.

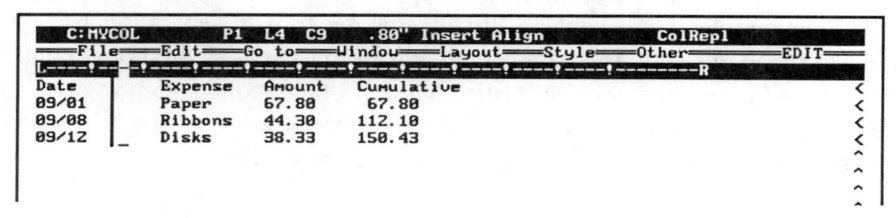

```
  C:MYCOL          P1  L4  C9      .80" Insert Align           ColRepl
====File======Edit======Go to======Window======Layout======Style======Other==========EDIT====
L----!----?----!----?----!----?----!----?----!----?----!----?----!--------R
Date       |   Expense       Amount     Cumulative                                        <
09/01      |   Paper         67.80        67.80                                           <
09/08      |   Ribbons       44.30       112.10                                           <
09/12      |_  Disks         38.33       150.43                                           <
           |                                                                              ^
                                                                                          ^
                                                                                          ^
```

Columnar Editing

4. Press **Ctrl-KN** to turn on the column editing mode.
5. Press **Ctrl-KI** to turn on column replace mode.
6. Move the cursor to the top of the vertical rule (L1 C8).
7. Press **Ctrl-KB** to mark the beginning of the column. Check the position of the block marker. (Text is shifted to the right by the block marker.)

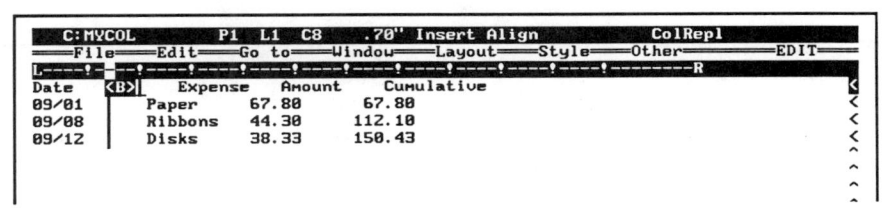

```
   C:MYCOL        P1  L1  C8    .70" Insert Align        ColRepl
 ===File====Edit====Go to====Window====Layout====Style====Other====   ==EDIT==
 L----!----!----!----!----!----!----!----!----!----!---------R
 Date   <B>|  Expense    Amount   Cumulative                              <
 09/01       Paper       67.80      67.80                                 <
 09/08       Ribbons     44.30     112.10                                 <
 09/12       Disks       38.33     150.43                                 <
                                                                          ^
                                                                          ^
                                                                          ^
```

8. Move the cursor to the right of the bottom rule (L5 C9).
9. Press **Ctrl-KK** to mark the end of the column. Check the marked column.

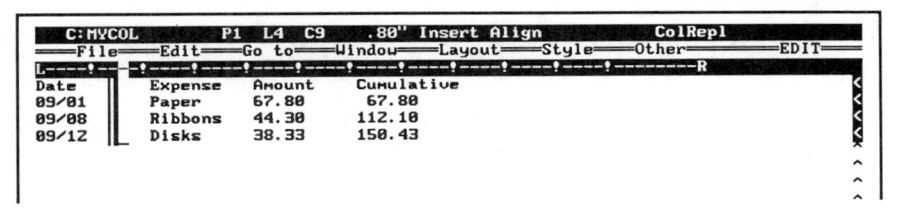

```
   C:MYCOL        P1  L4  C9    .80" Insert Align        ColRepl
 ===File====Edit====Go to====Window====Layout====Style====Other====   ==EDIT==
 L----!----!----!----!----!----!----!----!----!----!---------R
 Date        Expense    Amount   Cumulative                              <
 09/01       Paper       67.80      67.80                                 <
 09/08       Ribbons     44.30     112.10                                 <
 09/12    |  Disks       38.33     150.43                                 <
                                                                          ^
                                                                          ^
                                                                          ^
```

10. Move the cursor to line 1, column 19 and press **Ctrl-KC**.
11. Move the cursor to line 1, column 30 and press **Ctrl-KC**. Your table should resemble the following screen illustration.

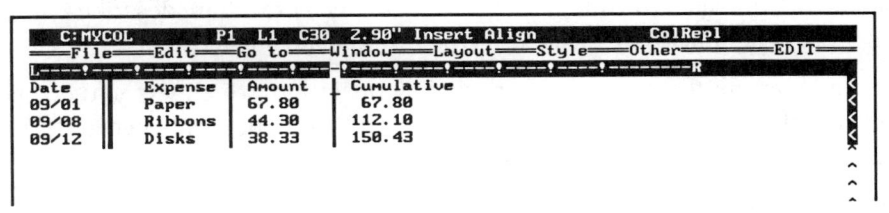

```
   C:MYCOL        P1  L1  C30  2.90" Insert Align        ColRepl
 ===File====Edit====Go to====Window====Layout====Style====Other====   ==EDIT==
 L----!----!----!----!----!----!----!----!----!----!---------R
 Date     | Expense  | Amount  | Cumulative                              <
 09/01    | Paper    |  67.80  |   67.80                                 <
 09/08    | Ribbons  |  44.30  |  112.10                                 <
 09/12    | Disks    |  38.33  |  150.43                                 <
                                                                          ^
                                                                          ^
                                                                          ^
```

12. Press **Ctrl-KQ** and type **Y** to abandon the document without saving.
13. Turn to Module 81 to continue the learning sequence.

Module 13
COPY BLOCK TO FILE (WRITE BLOCK)

```
Classic:     ^KW
Pull-Down:   Alt-E, "Write block to file..."
```

DESCRIPTION

A marked block of text can be copied (or written) to a disk file by marking a block and then pressing Ctrl-KW, where W represents "write." Next, WordStar prompts you for a filename.

Respond by typing a filename and pressing Return. If the filename already exists, WordStar presents the message: "File already exits. Overwrite (Y/N) or append (A)?"

Type Y to overwrite the existing file. Type N to select another filename. Type A to add (or append) the block to the bottom of the designated file.

APPLICATIONS

The ability to write a block of text to a file lets you transfer text from one document to another. You can write a block of text to an intermediate file, display a second document, and read the intermediate file into it using the block read procedure described in Module 16. This process eliminates the need to retype text that already exists.

You should be aware that the WordStar window operation, which lets you display two documents at the same time, also lets you mark and move blocks between documents. The window operation is described in Module 91.

It is useful to create a series of small boilerplate files that contain frequently used passages, such as paragraph-length clauses in legal documents. This allows the material to be assembled later into a new document. The document assembly process is performed with either the block read function or by running merge print (Module 50).

Similarly, the append option lets you assemble a document using excerpts from existing files. This eliminates the need to write blocks to intermediate files before assembling them into a final document.

TYPICAL OPERATION

In this activity, begin with the MYLTR document displayed. Then mark a block and write it to a file.

1. Open the document MYLTR.
2. Mark the paragraph as a block as shown in the following screen illustration.

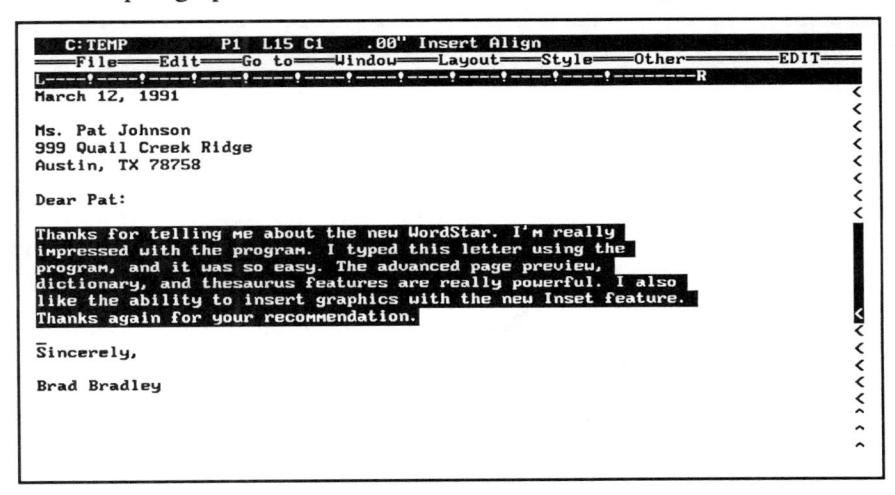

```
═════C:TEMP═════════P1  L15 C1═══════.00" Insert Align═══════════════
════File════Edit════Go to════Window════Layout════Style════Other════════EDIT═══
L────!────!────!────!────!────!────!────!────!────!─────────R
March 12, 1991                                                              <
                                                                            <
Ms. Pat Johnson                                                             <
999 Quail Creek Ridge                                                       <
Austin, TX 78758                                                            <
                                                                            <
Dear Pat:                                                                   <
Thanks for telling me about the new WordStar. I'm really
impressed with the program. I typed this letter using the
program, and it was so easy. The advanced page preview,
dictionary, and thesaurus features are really powerful. I also
like the ability to insert graphics with the new Inset feature.
Thanks again for your recommendation.                                       <
                                                                            <
Sincerely,                                                                  <
                                                                            <
Brad Bradley                                                                <
                                                                            >
                                                                            ^
                                                                            ^
```

3. Press **Ctrl-KW**, type **PARA1** as the filename, and press **Return**.
4. Press **Ctrl-KQ** to abandon the document without saving. Notice that the file directory now includes the file PARA1.

NOTE
Save the document PARA1 as it is used in the next activity.

5. Turn to Module 16 to continue the learning sequence.

Module 14
COPY BLOCKS OF TEXT

> Classic: ^KC
> Pull-Down: Alt-E, select "Copy block"

DESCRIPTION

Marking and copying a passage of text is accomplished by marking the selected passage, moving the cursor to the chosen location within the document, and copying the marked block by pressing Ctrl-KC.

The marked block is duplicated following the cursor position. The copied text displaces any following text to the right and down. The marked block remains in its original location.

The block marking and copying process is presented for your review:

1. Mark the beginning of the block with Ctrl-KB.
2. Mark the end of the block with Ctrl-KK.
3. Position the cursor at the new location.
4. Copy the marked block with Ctrl-KC.

APPLICATIONS

The block copy operation is used to copy words, sentences, paragraphs, and even entire pages. You can copy these elements once or many more times within a document. Often, "boilerplate" material is used many times within a document. Where multiple-page tables are used, the block copy operation is used to reproduce the headings accurately, saving the time that would otherwise be used to retype the material. The copy function can save hours of typing time.

TYPICAL OPERATION

Begin this activity at the EDIT menu with the MYLTR document displayed. Mark a block and copy it to the end of the document.

1. Open the document MYLTR.
2. Move the cursor to the first character in the paragraph on line 9 and press **Ctrl-KB** to mark the beginning of the block.

3. Move the cursor one line below the paragraph. Press **Ctrl-KK** to mark the end of the block. Your screen should resemble the following illustration.

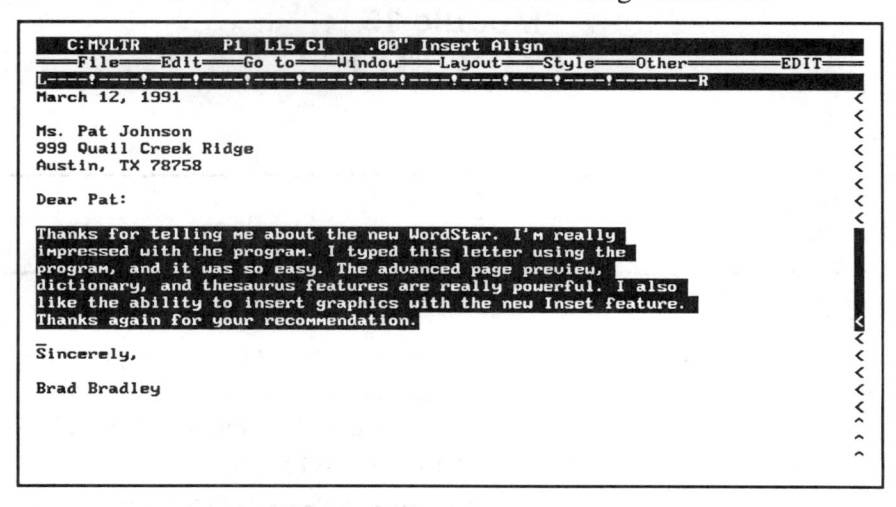

```
C:MYLTR          P1  L15 C1      .00" Insert Align
═══File════Edit════Go to════Window════Layout════Style════Other══════════EDIT═══
L----!----!----!----!----!----!----!----!----!----!----!--------R
March 12, 1991                                                           <
                                                                         <
Ms. Pat Johnson                                                          <
999 Quail Creek Ridge                                                    <
Austin, TX 78758                                                         <
                                                                         <
Dear Pat:                                                                <
                                                                         <
Thanks for telling me about the new WordStar. I'm really
impressed with the program. I typed this letter using the
program, and it was so easy. The advanced page preview,
dictionary, and thesaurus features are really powerful. I also
like the ability to insert graphics with the new Inset feature.
Thanks again for your recommendation.                                    <
                                                                         <
Sincerely,                                                               <
                                                                         <
Brad Bradley                                                             <
                                                                         <
                                                                         ^
                                                                         ^
```

4. Move the cursor to the "S" in Sincerely. If necessary, press **Return** to advance the cursor.

5. Press **Ctrl-KC** to copy the paragraph. Your document now should resemble the following screen illustration.

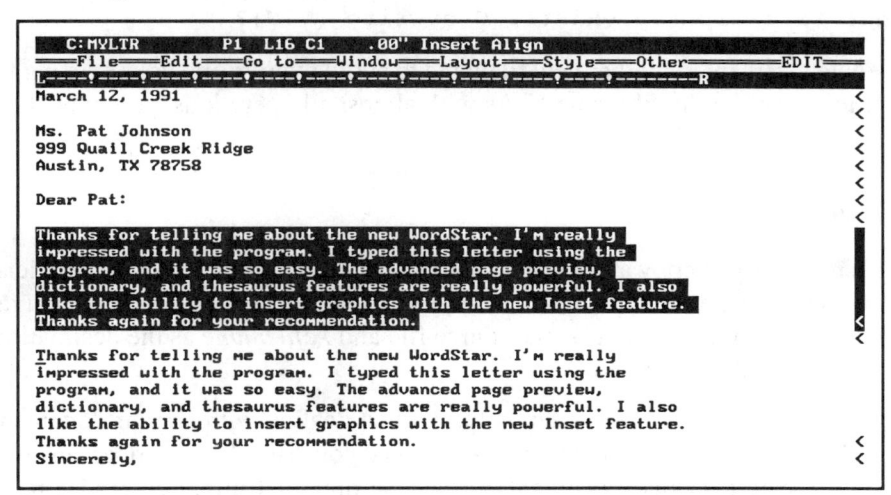

```
C:MYLTR          P1  L16 C1      .00" Insert Align
═══File════Edit════Go to════Window════Layout════Style════Other══════════EDIT═══
L----!----!----!----!----!----!----!----!----!----!----!--------R
March 12, 1991                                                           <
                                                                         <
Ms. Pat Johnson                                                          <
999 Quail Creek Ridge                                                    <
Austin, TX 78758                                                         <
                                                                         <
Dear Pat:                                                                <
                                                                         <
Thanks for telling me about the new WordStar. I'm really
impressed with the program. I typed this letter using the
program, and it was so easy. The advanced page preview,
dictionary, and thesaurus features are really powerful. I also
like the ability to insert graphics with the new Inset feature.
Thanks again for your recommendation.                                    <
                                                                         <
Thanks for telling me about the new WordStar. I'm really
impressed with the program. I typed this letter using the
program, and it was so easy. The advanced page preview,
dictionary, and thesaurus features are really powerful. I also
like the ability to insert graphics with the new Inset feature.
Thanks again for your recommendation.                                    <
Sincerely,                                                               <
```

6. Press **Ctrl-KQ** and type **Y** to abandon the document without saving.
7. Turn to Module 12 to continue the learning sequence.

Module 15
COPY FILE

> Classic:　O, ^KO
> Pull-Down:　F (or Alt-F), select "Copy a file..."

DESCRIPTION

You can copy a file when the OPENING menu is displayed by typing FO for "Copy a file." You are prompted for the source filename and the name of the copy. You can use your cursor keys to point to a displayed filename within the directory display. Next, type the "Name of copy" and press Return to complete the copy operation.

The same operation is achieved from the EDIT menu by pressing Ctrl-KO (or press Alt-F and select "Copy a file...").

If you enter the name of a file that already exists, WordStar prevents you from overwriting the file. The following message tells you that the typed filename exists.

```
That file already exists. Overwrite (Y?N)?
```

Pressing N lets you enter another new filename to avoid overwriting your existing file. If you want to overwrite the file, type Y. As with almost all operations, you may abort the copy process with Ctrl-U.

APPLICATIONS

Often, it is necessary to copy a file from one disk to another. The copy command lets you do this by prefixing the filename with the appropriate disk drive or directory designator. For example, specify C:*filename* as the source file and A:*filename* as the destination file to copy a file from disk C to disk A.

Copying the contents of a file is often helpful when dealing with similar documents or using "boilerplate" files. The copy command lets you use all or part of an existing document to create a second document, saving the time that might otherwise be spent typing the second document from scratch.

Copy File

TYPICAL OPERATION

In this activity, begin with the OPENING menu displayed. Create and save a small document named MYDOC. Then make a copy of MYDOC as MYDOC1.

1. Type **FD**, then type **MYDOC,** and press **Return**. Type **Y** to answer the prompt and create a new file.
2. Type your name on the first line.
3. Press **Ctrl-KD** to save your new document.
4. Type **FO**; MYDOC appears on the file line since it was the last file used. Press **Return**.
5. Type **MYDOC1** as the "Name of copy" and press **Return**.
6. Check the file directory for MYDOC and MYDOC1. Leave them on your practice disk for later exercises.
7. Turn to Module 22 to continue the learning sequence.

Module 16
COPY FILE INTO DOCUMENT
(READ FILE)

> Classic: ^KR
> Pull-Down: Alt-E, select "Insert a file..."

DESCRIPTION

WordStar's BLOCK & SAVE menu lets you copy (or read) a file into an open document. This is done by positioning the cursor to the desired point within the open document and then pressing Ctrl-KR, where R represents "read." WordStar prompts you for a filename.

Respond by typing the filename and pressing Return. The selected file is read into the open document beginning at the cursor position. Following text is displaced to the right and down.

You can read a variety of files from other programs. For example, you can read Lotus 1-2-3, Symphony, and Quattro spreadsheets, and dBASE and FoxPro database files.

When reading a spreadsheet, WordStar gives you the upper left and lower right coordinates. You can change the coordinate values to read a selected portion of the spreadsheet. If a series of cells within a spreadsheet has a name, you can specify the name to be read into the open document.

APPLICATIONS

The ability to copy files into an open document lets you transfer files from one document to another. In addition, you can perform document assembly operations by creating a new document from existing files. This eliminates the need to retype passages of text that are already in other documents.

TYPICAL OPERATION

In this activity, begin at the EDIT menu with the MYLTR document open. Read the file PARA1 into the open document.

1. Open the document MYLTR.

Copy File into Document (Read File)

2. Move the cursor to an empty line beneath the letter paragraph. Press **Return** if necessary to move the cursor two lines below the paragraph. (This should be line 16, column 1.)

3. Press **Ctrl-KR**, type **PARA1** and press **Return**. Notice that the file PARA1 is read into the open document.

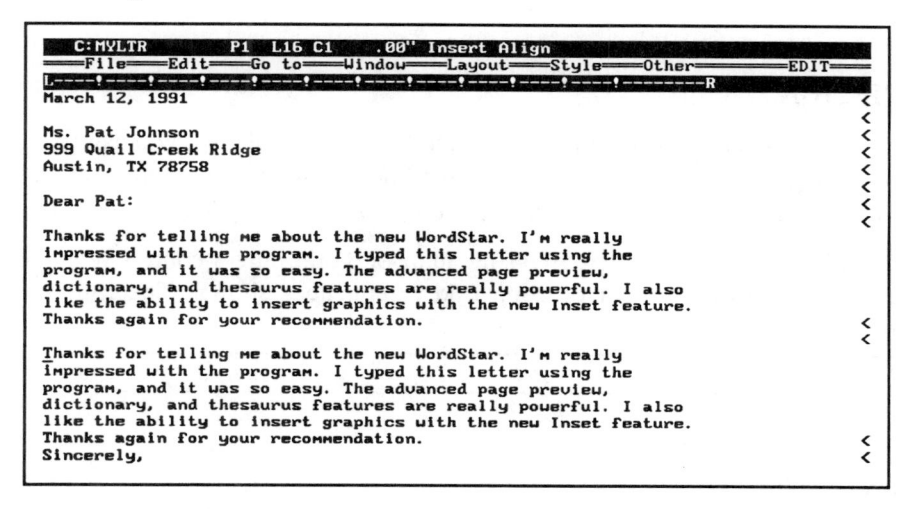

```
  C:MYLTR           P1  L16 C1     .00" Insert Align
====File====Edit====Go to====Window====Layout====Style====Other====        ====EDIT====
L----!----!----!----!----!----!----!----!----!----!--------R
March 12, 1991                                                                <
                                                                              <
Ms. Pat Johnson                                                               <
999 Quail Creek Ridge                                                         <
Austin, TX 78758                                                              <
                                                                              <
Dear Pat:                                                                     <
                                                                              <
Thanks for telling me about the new WordStar. I'm really
impressed with the program. I typed this letter using the
program, and it was so easy. The advanced page preview,
dictionary, and thesaurus features are really powerful. I also
like the ability to insert graphics with the new Inset feature.
Thanks again for your recommendation.                                         <
                                                                              <
Thanks for telling me about the new WordStar. I'm really
impressed with the program. I typed this letter using the
program, and it was so easy. The advanced page preview,
dictionary, and thesaurus features are really powerful. I also
like the ability to insert graphics with the new Inset feature.
Thanks again for your recommendation.                                         <
Sincerely,                                                                    <
```

4. Press **Ctrl-KQ** and type **Y** to abandon without saving the document.

5. Turn to Module 90 to continue the learning sequence.

Module 17
CURSOR CONTROL

DESCRIPTION

Once you have opened a document and the EDIT menu is displayed, you can begin your word processing task. First, however, you must know how to control movement of the *cursor*, the flashing bar that points to the spot on the screen at which text entry occurs.

The left-hand column of the classic EDIT menu displays the cursor control keys. You can use your arrow keys or the cursor control key sequences shown. The following list summarizes these.

Cursor Movement	*Ctrl-*	*Alternate*
One character left	S	← (4)
One character right	D	→ (6)
Jump one word left	A	^← (4)
Jump one word right	F	^→ (6)
One line up	E	↑ (8)
One line down	X	↓ (2)
Previous screen	R	Page up
Scroll up	W	^Page up
Next screen	C	Page down
Scroll down	Z	^Page down
Jump to upper left corner of screen	QE	Home (7)
Beginning of file	QR	^Home
Jump to lower left corner of screen	QX	End (1)
End of end of file	QC	^End

NOTE

Numbers ( ) designate numeric keypad keys on the PC-type numeric keypad.

The circumflex (^) symbol represents a Ctrl key sequence, i.e., ^Home is the same as Ctrl-Home.

You can press Alt-G to review "Go to" commands. Several of these commands are used to jump the cursor to a new position in the document. These are discussed in more detail in Module 18.

The following diagram shows the correlation between the standard WordStar cursor control keys and direction of movement.

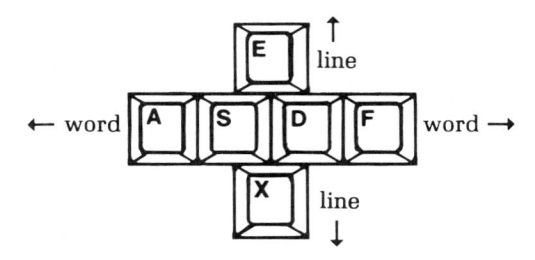

Figure 17-1   Correlation between Keyboard Layout and Standard Cursor Movement

The correlation between the PC-type numeric keypad and cursor movement is shown in the keypad illustration.

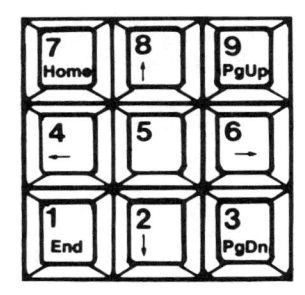

Figure 17-2   Correlation between PC-type Numeric Keypad and Cursor Movement

In addition to using the control key sequences shown in the previous list, there are a number of other keys that cause cursor movement. These are described in the following list.

Key	*Cursor Movement*
Spacebar	One space right
Backspace	One character left
Tab	Jump right one tab
Enter (or Return)	One line down

It is not possible to move the cursor to areas of the screen that are void of text. You can only move the cursor into areas containing text and/or spaces.

In blank documents, you can advance the cursor by typing text or by pressing the Spacebar, Tab key, or Return key.

Module 17

APPLICATIONS

The ability to move the cursor in any direction within a document is vital to word processing efficiency. This separates a word processor, which is often referred to as a *full-screen editor*, from what are called *line editors*. Line editors restrict cursor movement to one line at a time. An example of a line editor is the DOS EDLIN utility. To move to a different line, you must type the line number and press Return. Inserting and deleting interior text is a difficult process.

TYPICAL OPERATION

In this activity, begin at the EDIT menu with the MYLTR document displayed. Move the cursor from line 1, column 1 (the original position) of the displayed document to line 9, column 20.

1. Open the document MYLTR. Your display should resemble the following screen illustration.

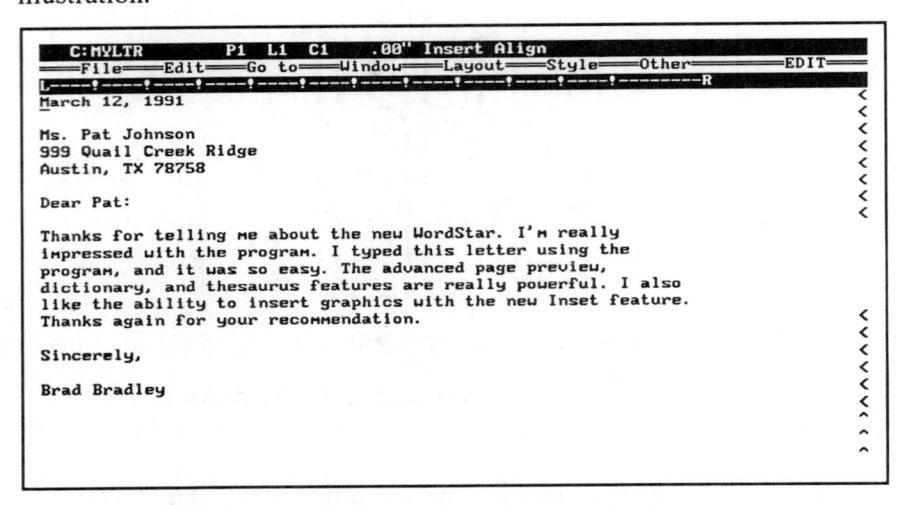

    ```
    C:MYLTR          P1  L1  C1    .00" Insert Align
    =File==Edit==Go to==Window==Layout==Style==Other==       ==EDIT==
    L----!----!----!----!----!----!----!----!----!----!---------R
    March 12, 1991                                                    <
                                                                      <
    Ms. Pat Johnson                                                   <
    999 Quail Creek Ridge                                             <
    Austin, TX 78758                                                  <
                                                                      <
    Dear Pat:                                                         <

    Thanks for telling me about the new WordStar. I'm really
    impressed with the program. I typed this letter using the
    program, and it was so easy. The advanced page preview,
    dictionary, and thesaurus features are really powerful. I also
    like the ability to insert graphics with the new Inset feature.
    Thanks again for your recommendation.                             <
                                                                      <
    Sincerely,                                                        <
                                                                      <
    Brad Bradley                                                      <
                                                                      <
                                                                      <
                                                                      ^
                                                                      ^
    ```

2. Press **Ctrl-X** (or Down Arrow) until the cursor is at the left margin of the first line of the letter, line 9. (See the status line for L9 C1.)
3. Press **Ctrl-F** three times until the cursor is on the "m" in the word "me." (Notice how Ctrl-F jumps the cursor one word at a time.)
4. Check the status line. The cursor is now at line 9, column 20.
5. Press **Ctrl-KQ** to abandon the document without saving.
6. Turn to Module 18 to continue the learning sequence.

Module 18
CURSOR MOVEMENT, QUICK

DESCRIPTION

You learned how to navigate with the cursor in Module 17. This module describes *quick cursor movements*, ways to jump the cursor from margin to margin, to the top and bottom of the screen, and to the top and bottom of the document. These operations use sequences displayed in and controlled by WordStar's classic QUICK menu, or by use of the Go to pull-down menu, accessed with Alt-G.

The classic QUICK menu is displayed with Ctrl-Q.

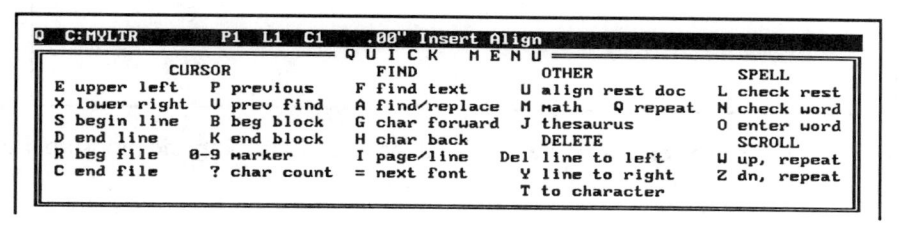

```
Q  C:MYLTR         P1  L1  C1     .00" Insert Align
                       Q U I C K   M E N U
        CURSOR              FIND              OTHER              SPELL
 E upper left    P previous      F find text      U align rest doc   L check rest
 X lower right   U prev find     A find/replace   M math    Q repeat N check word
 S begin line    B beg block     G char forward   J thesaurus        O enter word
 D end line      K end block     H char back         DELETE          SCROLL
 R beg file      0-9 marker      I page/line      Del line to left   W up, repeat
 C end file      ? char count    = next font      Y line to right    Z dn, repeat
                                                  T to character
```

The QUICK menu displays the control characters used for quick cursor movement in the left-hand section. In this module, the use of the first six are described. These are summarized in the following list.

Cursor Movement	Ctrl-Q+
Jump cursor to top left of screen	E or Up Arrow
Jump cursor to bottom right of screen	X or Down Arrow
Jump cursor to left margin of text	S or Left Arrow
Jump cursor to right margin of text	D or Right Arrow
Jump cursor to end of paragraph	G Return
Jump cursor to top of file	R or Ctrl-Home
Jump cursor to bottom of file	C or Ctrl-End
Jump cursor to page n	I (type page number and press Return)
Jump cursor n pages forward	I +n Return
Jump cursor n pages back	I −n Return
Jump cursor to next font	=

Notice that the first four keys E, X, S, and D are the same keys used for cursor up, down, left, and right described in Module 17. Pressing Ctrl-Q with the corresponding arrow key achieves the same result. This means that once you learn the direction keys, you need only to remember to use the Ctrl-Q key sequence to take advantage of the "longer reach" of WordStar's quick movement operations.

Pressing Alt-G displays the following Go to menu:

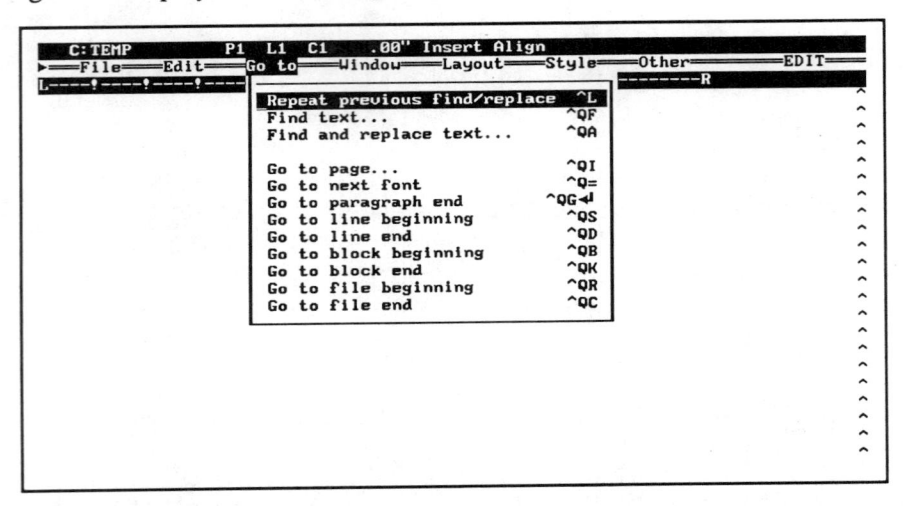

```
  C:TEMP          P1  L1  C1     .00"  Insert Align
 ══File══════Edit══════Go to══════Window══════Layout══════Style══════Other══════════EDIT══
 L────!────!────!────┌─────────────────────────────────────┐────────R
                     │ Repeat previous find/replace    ^L  │
                     │ Find text...                    ^QF │
                     │ Find and replace text...        ^QA │
                     │                                     │
                     │ Go to page...                   ^QI │
                     │ Go to next font                 ^Q= │
                     │ Go to paragraph end            ^QG↵ │
                     │ Go to line beginning            ^QS │
                     │ Go to line end                  ^QD │
                     │ Go to block beginning           ^QB │
                     │ Go to block end                 ^QK │
                     │ Go to file beginning            ^QR │
                     │ Go to file end                  ^QC │
                     └─────────────────────────────────────┘
```

There are other quick movement sequences used for screen scrolling and block operations. These are described in other modules.

APPLICATIONS

The ability to move the cursor long distances within a document saves the time required to move one character or line per keystroke. Being able to "jump" to the top of a file by pressing Ctrl-QR or to the bottom by pressing Ctrl-QC can save many minutes and reduce operator fatigue during the course of a day's word processing.

TYPICAL OPERATION

In this activity, begin at the EDIT menu with the document MYLTR displayed. Next, jump the cursor to the end of the displayed document.

1. Open the MYLTR document.
2. Press **Ctrl-QC** to jump the cursor to the end of the document.

Notice that the cursor is positioned at the bottom of the displayed document.

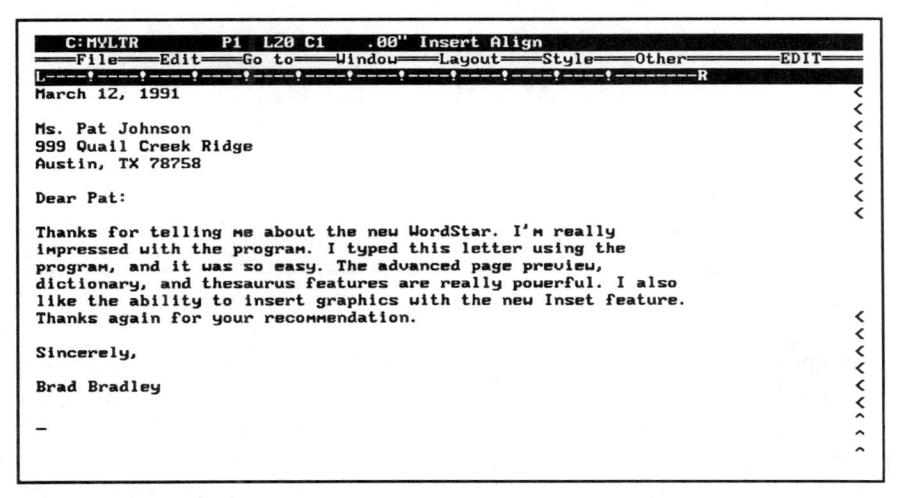

```
      C:MYLTR           P1  LZ0 C1    .00" Insert Align
====File====Edit====Go to====Window====Layout====Style====Other====      ====EDIT====
L----!----!----!----!----!----!----!----!----!----!----!--------R
March 12, 1991                                                           <
                                                                         <
Ms. Pat Johnson                                                          <
999 Quail Creek Ridge                                                    <
Austin, TX 78758                                                         <
                                                                         <
Dear Pat:                                                                <
                                                                         <
Thanks for telling me about the new WordStar. I'm really
impressed with the program. I typed this letter using the
program, and it was so easy. The advanced page preview,
dictionary, and thesaurus features are really powerful. I also
like the ability to insert graphics with the new Inset feature.
Thanks again for your recommendation.                                    <
                                                                         <
Sincerely,                                                               <
                                                                         <
Brad Bradley                                                             <
                                                                         <
_                                                                        ^
                                                                         ^
```

3. Try other quick cursor operations, using the key sequences contained in the cursor movement list.
4. Press **Ctrl-KQ** to abandon the document without saving.
5. Turn to Module 78 to continue the learning sequence.

Module 19
CUSTOM PRINT CODES

> Classic: ^PA, ^PN, ^PQ, ^PW, ^PE, ^PR, ^P!

DESCRIPTION

WordStar lets you establish character width and font values in three ways. First, you can use WSCHANGE to set a normal and alternate print *font*. You can also embed dot commands that define the values issued by the print control sequences Ctrl-PQ, Ctrl-PW, Ctrl-PE, and Ctrl-PR. Finally, you can define print control sequences independently using Ctrl-P! which displays a USER PRINT CONTROL menu. Then enter a printer control value, a displayed control character, and a printer indent value (if needed).

Before modifying printer control characters, you should know that WordStar has built-in printer drivers that anticipate the capabilities of many brands of printers. If your printer is listed on the WSCHANGE (or PRCHANGE) print menus, it is probably configured to take advantage of normal and alternate printing features. You can verify the values by using the WSCHANGE utility to view the Printer Installation menu settings.

TYPE FONTS A font, which is a different type style, is a different type design or size. For example, if you have a simple dot matrix printer, an alternate print style may simply be a change in print width, i.e., changing from 10 to 12 pitch (characters per inch) and back. This is like changing a typewriter font from pica to elite. You can also select type fonts using Ctrl-P=. Then pick a font from the displayed list by typing the font name or pointing to the name and pressing Return. The font name is displayed in the document within double angle brackets as in <<DRAFT 17.1>>.

If you have a printer equipped with downloadable type fonts, such as a laser printer, you may be able to select a variety of type styles. These styles have names like Roman, Dutch, or Swiss. Some printers even offer type fonts that resemble those offered by typesetters. Common type styles include Helvetica, Univers, Times Roman, and many more.

NORMAL AND ALTERNATE PRINT FONTS If you want to set up normal and alternate printing default values that are called with Ctrl-PA (alternate) and Ctrl-PN (normal), use the WSCHANGE utility. Typing WSCHANGE WS and pressing Return displays the WSCHANGE Main Menu. Next, use selection B of the WSCHANGE Main

Custom Print Codes

Menu. Then use "Printing defaults" (selection C of the Printer Menu) to set the default character and line settings. The following Printer Defaults menu is displayed.

```
                    Printing Defaults Menu #1
   A  Print nondocument as default.................OFF      PNODOC
   B  Bidirectional printing........................ON      .bp
   C  Letter quality printing (NLQ)................DIS      .lq
   D  Microjustification...........................DIS      .uj
   E  Underline blanks.............................OFF      .ul
   F  Proportional spacing.........................DIS      .ps
   G  Normal character font...................No font name
   H  Alternate character font................No font name
   I  Strikeout character..........................."-"     STKCHR
   J  Line height (1440ths/inch)...................240      INIEDT+40
   K  Sub/superscript roll (1440ths/inch)..........90       .sr

   Z  Printing Defaults Menu #2
   X  Finished with this menu


   Enter your menu selection..._          F1 = Help
```

```
                    Printing Defaults Menu #2
   A  Print page numbers............................ON      .op
   B  Kerning.......................................ON      .kr
   C  Load Inset at print-time......................ON      IINSET

   1  Printing Defaults Menu #1
   X  Finished with this menu



   Enter your menu selection..._          F1 = Help
```

Now you can use selections G and H to establish your normal and alternate character font. Displayed choices correspond to the current default printer.

When you press Ctrl-PA during editing, an <ALTERNATE> type style flag is displayed. This tells you that following text is printed in the alternate font. Pressing Ctrl-PN restores the normal print value.

You can insert the dot commands at the left margin to achieve the same results. The .CW value (12, 8, etc.) adjusts the character width in 120ths of an inch. For example, 10/120ths is 12 pitch; 12/120ths is 10 pitch. Descriptions of each WordStar dot command are included in Module 24.

57

Module 19

CUSTOM PRINT FONTS ^PQ, ^PW, ^PE, AND ^PR In addition to alternate and normal print controls, there are four additional print control characters that give you control of other capabilities that may be offered by your printer. For example, many printers have several pitch capabilities, plus near-letter-quality, italic, wide, and enhanced print.

Notice the "Q W E R ! custom" entry in the following PRINT CONTROLS menu illustration.

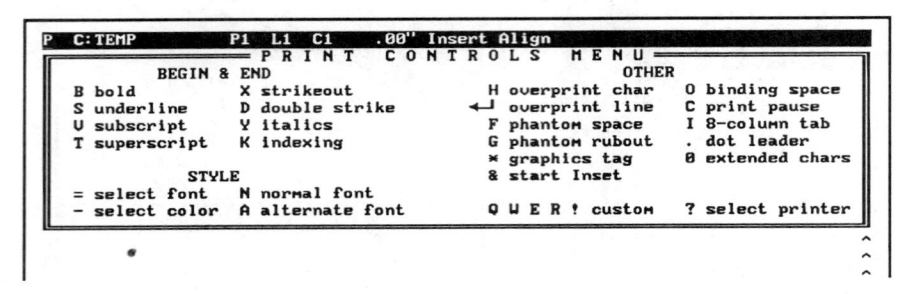

```
P  C:TEMP              P1  L1  C1      .00" Insert Align
                      ═PRINT    CONTROLS    MENU═
           BEGIN & END                        OTHER
      B bold          X strikeout      H overprint char    O binding space
      S underline     D double strike  ↵ overprint line    C print pause
      U subscript     Y italics        F phantom space     I 8-column tab
      T superscript   K indexing       G phantom rubout    . dot leader
                                       ¤ graphics tag      0 extended chars
               STYLE                   & start Inset
      = select font   N normal font
      - select color  A alternate font Q W E R ! custom    ? select printer
```

These values are set using four simple dot commands followed by the values used by your printer. These values are typically included in a table near the end of your printer manual. They are control characters used to reset print width, type style, line spacing, and other characteristics offered by your printer.

The dot commands are .xq, .xw, .xe, and .xr corresponding to the custom print control characters. Each custom print dot command is followed by up to 24 hexadecimal values. Each hex value is separated by a space.

For example, the common hexadecimal value used for compressed print is 0F. The common hex value for normal print is 12. If you want to call compressed print with Ctrl-PQ, use .xq 0F. To establish normal printing with Ctrl-PR, use .xr 12.

The following list includes four common values used on Epson dot-matrix printers.

Description	Dot Code	Command key
Compressed Print	.xq 0F	Ctrl-PQ
Normal Print	.xr 12	Ctrl-PR
Wide Print	.xw 1B 0E	Ctrl-PW
Cancel Wide Print	.xe 14	Ctrl-PE

The codes used to turn wide printing on and off are included in the following line of text as viewed on WordStar's editing screen.

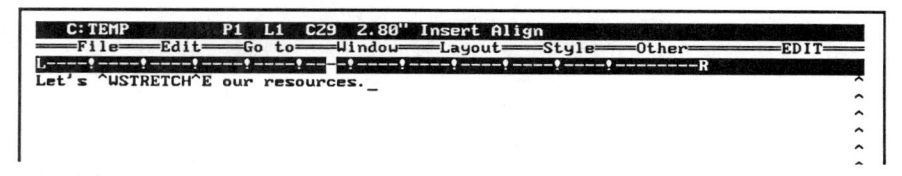

```
  C:TEMP         P1  L1  C29   2.80" Insert Align
====File====Edit====Go to====Window====Layout====Style====Other====EDIT====
L----!----!----!----!----!----!----!----!----!--------R
Let's ^WSTRETCH^E our resources._
```

Using one of the custom print dot commands without hex codes cancels the setting. The custom print dot commands override any previously installed values that may have been established using the WSCHANGE program.

EMBEDDING A SINGLE USER PRINT CONTROL WITH CTRL-P! You can embed a single print control character at the cursor position using the USER PRINT CONTROL menu. Pressing Ctrl-P! displays the USER PRINT CONTROL menu which resembles the following menu illustration.

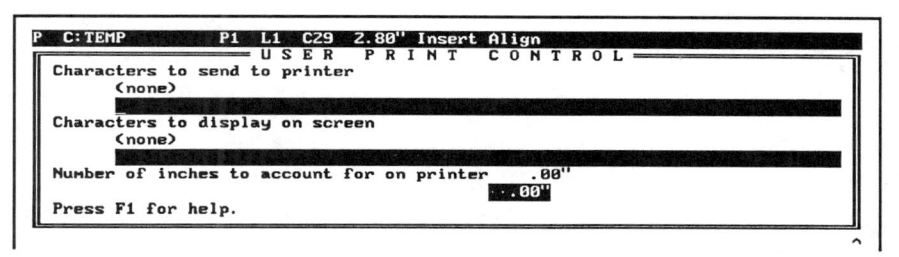

```
P  C:TEMP         P1  L1  C29   2.80" Insert Align
=====================U S E R   P R I N T   C O N T R O L=====================
Characters to send to printer
   <none>

Characters to display on screen
   <none>

Number of inches to account for on printer    .00"
                                           ...00"
Press F1 for help.
```

There are several special characters that are used to define control characters. These are summarized in the following table.

Character	Definition
^	The circumflex character is used in front of a control character. For example, ^C sends a Ctrl-C. An escape is sent with ^[.
%	The percent character is used to accept the following character literally. For example, %^ sends a circumflex; %% sends a percent sign.
%x	The %x combination defines the following value as hexadecimal. For example, %x0A sends 0A hex.

If you decide to send the cancel compressed printing control sequence 12 hex to your printer, type %x12 as "Characters to send to printer" and press Return. Then type "C off" as the "Characters to display on screen" and press Return. Press Return a final time to accept the .00" value and the control code <%x12> is displayed at the cursor position.

The "C off" notation is displayed when print control codes are suppressed with Ctrl-OD. Otherwise, <%x12> is displayed.

Module 19

APPLICATIONS

The ability to control your printer setup while printing lets you mix type styles within a document. Many printers offer a variety of type styles and sizes. If you choose a large, open type style, you may want to use 10 pitch as your standard pitch. If you want to pack a lot of type on a page or compress a passage, use a 12-, 15- or 17-pitch font.

Using the text-embedded dot command (.CW) provides even more flexibility for those using micro-justifying, letter-quality printers. The character width (.CW) dot command, which is always placed at the left margin, is used to change the printed output as often as necessary. When used, you may want to use a printer pause (Ctrl-PC) to let you change print wheels.

Finally, the USER PRINT CONTROLS feature lets you send any set of printer control values to your printer. It is normally used when a unique, little-used control character is needed. Otherwise, you may want to predefine control characters using the .XQ, W, E, or R dot commands.

TYPICAL OPERATION

In this session, you define and use two custom print control codes within a short document.

1. Open a new document named TEMP.
2. Define the custom print controls W and R and type the text shown in the following screen illustration. Press **Ctrl-PW** to insert the ^W and **Ctrl-PR** to insert ^R within the following document.

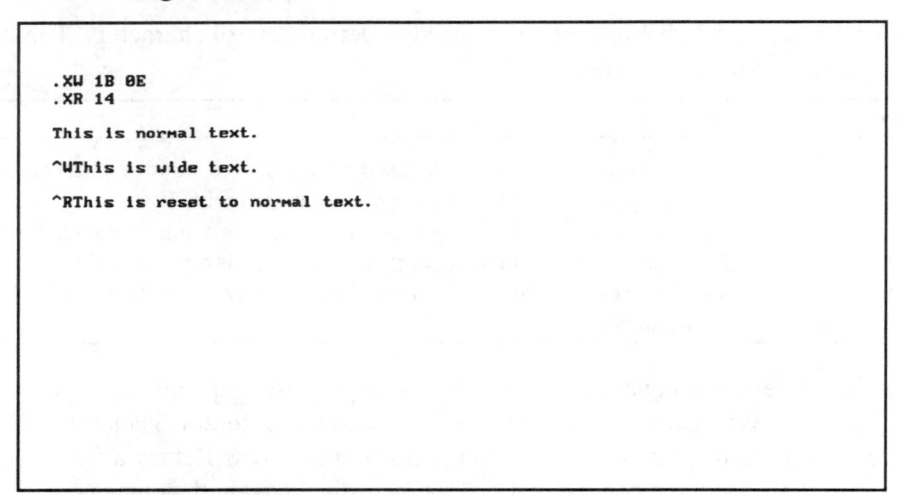

```
.XW 1B 0E
.XR 14

This is normal text.

^WThis is wide text.

^RThis is reset to normal text.
```

NOTE
The dot commands .XW and .XR must begin at the left margin. The periods (or dots) are located in column 1. Check your printer manual for the values that correspond to wide and normal print control. Although common values are used in the example, they may not match those used by your printer.

3. Prepare your printer for printing.
4. Press **Ctrl-PrtSc** to save the document and **F10** to accept the defaults and print.
5. Check the printout to see how the custom print controls worked.
6. Type **FY**, type **TEMP**, and then type **Y** to delete the exercise file.
7. Turn to Module 86 to continue the learning sequence.

Module 20
DELETE BLOCKS OF TEXT

> Classic: ^KY
> Pull-Down: Alt-E, select "Delete block"

DESCRIPTION

You can delete a marked block of text by pressing Ctrl-KY. The entire block disappears from the document and any following text fills in the vacated space. You can recall (or "unerase") the deleted block with Ctrl-U if the block is smaller than 500 characters and was the last one erased. WordStar warns you in the Ctrl-KY procedure if the block is too large to unerase.

Lost or deleted blocks of text can also be recovered by abandoning the document without saving the changes or by renaming and using the corresponding .BAK (backup) file.

The block marking and deleting process is presented for your review:

1. Mark the beginning of the block with Ctrl-KB.
2. Mark the end of the block with Ctrl-KK.
3. Delete the marked block with Ctrl-KY.

APPLICATIONS

The ability to delete an entire block of text saves keystrokes that would otherwise be required to delete either a character, word, or line at a time. Block delete is an efficient, time-saving device used by experienced word processing users.

TYPICAL OPERATION

In this activity, begin at the EDIT menu with the document MYLTR displayed. Mark a block and delete it.

1. Open the document MYLTR.
2. Mark the first sentence of the letter by pressing **Ctrl-KB** at the beginning and **Ctrl-KK** at the first character of the second sentence.

3. Press **Ctrl-KY** to delete the block. Notice the results.

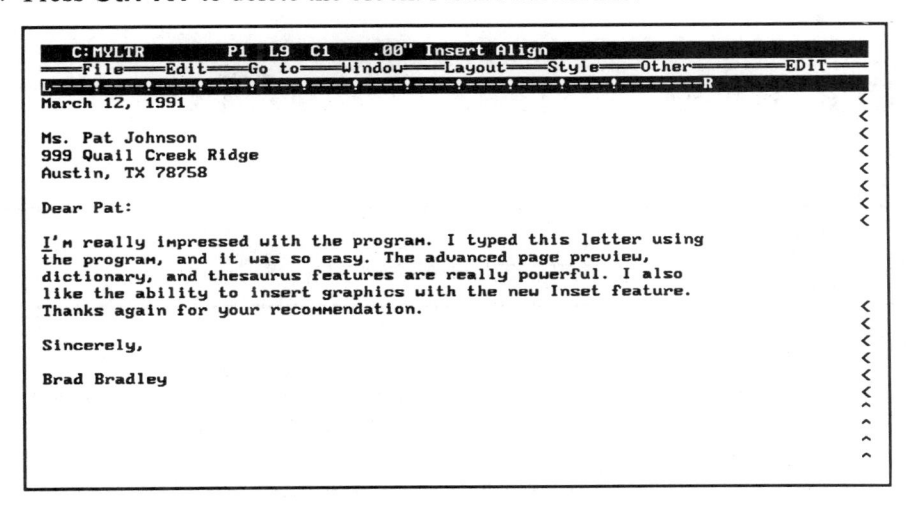

```
  C:MYLTR          P1  L9  C1    .00" Insert Align
 ==File====Edit====Go to====Window====Layout====Style====Other========EDIT==
 L----!----!----!----!----!----!----!----!----!----!--------R
 March 12, 1991                                                       <
                                                                      <
 Ms. Pat Johnson                                                      <
 999 Quail Creek Ridge                                                <
 Austin, TX 78758                                                     <
                                                                      <
 Dear Pat:                                                            <
                                                                      <
 I'm really impressed with the program. I typed this letter using
 the program, and it was so easy. The advanced page preview,
 dictionary, and thesaurus features are really powerful. I also
 like the ability to insert graphics with the new Inset feature.
 Thanks again for your recommendation.                                <
                                                                      <
 Sincerely,                                                           <
                                                                      <
 Brad Bradley                                                         <
                                                                      <
                                                                      ^
                                                                      ^
                                                                      ^
```

Notice that the marked sentence disappears and the paragraph is reformatted.

4. Press **Ctrl-KQ** and type **Y** to abandon the document without saving.
5. Turn to Module 51 to continue the learning sequence.

Module 21
DELETE CHARACTERS, WORDS, AND LINES

> Classic: ^G, Backspace, ^T, ^Y, ^QY, ^Q Del, ^QT char
> Pull-Down: Alt-E, select the appropriate delete operation

DESCRIPTION

WordStar offers a large range of delete (or erase) operations. The specific delete operation is selected based upon how much text you want to eliminate. The following list defines WordStar's classic delete operations:

Operation	Key Sequence
Delete character at cursor	Ctrl-G or Del
Delete character left of cursor	Ctrl-H or Backspace
Delete next word	Ctrl-T
Delete line	Ctrl-Y
Delete to end of line	Ctrl-QY
Delete to beginning of line	Ctrl-Q Del
Delete to next specified character	Ctrl-QT and type the character
Delete sentence	Ctrl-QT and a period (.)
Delete paragraph	Ctrl-QT and a Return

NOTE
Ctrl-U restores the last text deleted except for single characters.

The standard WordStar destructive Backspace moves the cursor to the left, deleting characters in its path. As it moves to the left, following text moves with it, or "closes up." A true delete function, which is performed by pressing Del or Ctrl-G, deletes the character located at the cursor.

APPLICATIONS

The delete function is used to erase text. It is used during text creation or to edit (revise) an existing document. The ability to delete characters, words, lines, and paragraphs makes WordStar's delete function extremely flexible. You can also mark and delete large passages (or blocks) of text. The procedure for doing this is presented in Module 20.

The Ctrl-QT. (period) sequence is convenient for quickly deleting text to the end of a sentence.

TYPICAL OPERATION

In this activity, begin at the EDIT menu with the TEMP document displayed. Then practice several methods for deleting text.

1. Open the document TEMP.
2. Move the cursor to the character "l" in the word "large."

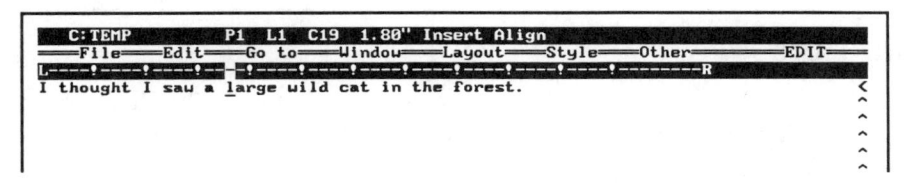

```
C:TEMP            P1  L1  C19  1.80" Insert Align
===File====Edit====Go to====Window====Layout====Style====Other====EDIT===
L----!----!----!----!----!----!----!----!----!--------R
I thought I saw a large wild cat in the forest.
```

3. Press **Ctrl-T**; notice that the word large is erased and the words to the right fill the vacated space.
4. Move the cursor to the character "c" in the word "cat." Press **Ctrl-G** (or **Del**) four times to delete the word cat and the space that follows it.
5. Press **Ctrl-QY** to delete all text from the cursor position to the end of the line.
6. Press **Backspace** twice to delete a space and a character to the left.
7. Press **Ctrl-Y** to delete the entire line.
8. Press **Ctrl-U** to restore the deleted text and period, then move the cursor to the first word in the sentence.
9. Press **Ctrl-QT** and answer the prompt "Delete forward to what character" by typing **.** (period) to delete the entire sentence.
10. Press **Ctrl-KQ** and type **Y** to abandon the document without saving the changes.
11. Type **FY TEMP** and press **Return**. At the prompt, type **Y** to delete the file TEMP.
12. Turn to Module 8 to continue the learning sequence.

Module 22
DELETE FILE

```
Classic:    Y, ^KJ
Pull-Down:  F (or Alt-F), select "Delete a file..."
```

DESCRIPTION

You can delete files from any disk on your computer by typing FY at the OPENING menu. Then type the filename and press Return. If you are at a help level above one, an "Are you sure (Y/N)?" prompt is displayed.

You can use the disk drive prefix in the form A:*filename* if the file to delete is on a different drive than is currently logged. You may also use the wild card (*) or (?) to delete several files in one delete operation (for example, *.BAK).

If your help level is set at two, three, or four, the prompt "Are you sure (Y/N)?" is displayed and you must answer Y to complete the operation. This step is skipped when help levels one or zero are active.

You can also delete files during text editing operations. This is done by typing Ctrl-KJ from the EDIT menu. Proceed as before to delete a file.

APPLICATIONS

The delete operation is used to erase files that are no longer needed. This restores disk space for use with new files. If you attempt to save a document and get a "Disk full" message, you can use the Ctrl-KJ sequence to delete unneeded files to recover disk space.

The ability to use the wild card symbols, such as *.BAK, lets you delete all BAK files from your disk to recover large amounts of disk space.

TYPICAL OPERATION

In this activity, you delete the file MYDOC1 copied in Module 15. Begin with the OPENING menu displayed.

1. Type **FY** and notice the following prompt.

Delete File

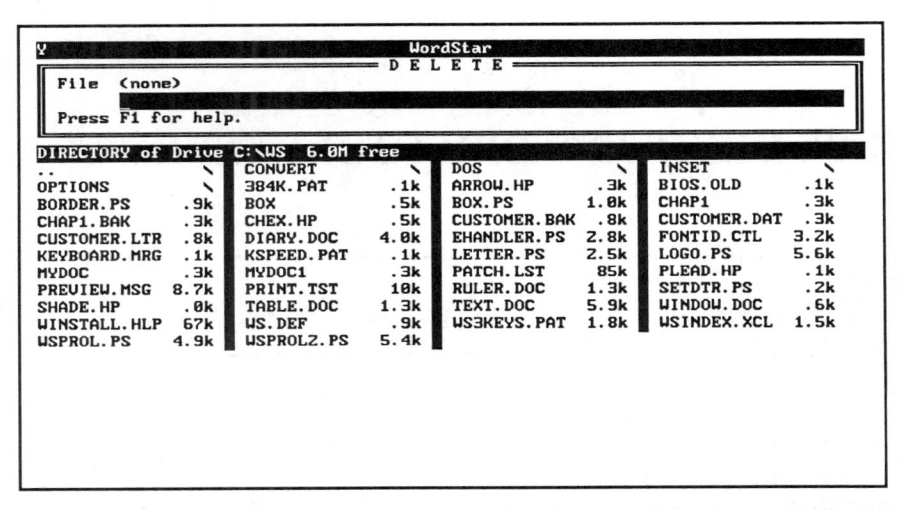

```
                          WordStar
                        = D E L E T E =
  File  (none)

  Press F1 for help.

 DIRECTORY of Drive C:\WS  6.0M free
 ..               \    CONVERT         \    DOS              \    INSET            \
 OPTIONS          \    384K.PAT       .1k   ARROW.HP        .3k   BIOS.OLD        .1k
 BORDER.PS       .9k   BOX            .5k   BOX.PS         1.0k   CHAP1           .3k
 CHAP1.BAK       .3k   CHEX.HP        .5k   CUSTOMER.BAK   .8k    CUSTOMER.DAT    .3k
 CUSTOMER.LTR    .8k   DIARY.DOC     4.0k   EHANDLER.PS   2.8k    FONTID.CTL     3.2k
 KEYBOARD.MRG    .1k   KSPEED.PAT    .1k    LETTER.PS     2.5k    LOGO.PS        5.6k
 MYDOC           .3k   MYDOC1         .3k   PATCH.LST      85k    PLEAD.HP        .1k
 PREVIEW.MSG    8.7k   PRINT.TST     10k    RULER.DOC     1.3k    SETDTR.PS       .2k
 SHADE.HP        .0k   TABLE.DOC     1.3k   TEXT.DOC      5.9k    WINDOW.DOC      .6k
 WINSTALL.HLP    67k   WS.DEF         .9k   WS3KEYS.PAT   1.8k    WSINDEX.XCL    1.5k
 WSPROL.PS      4.9k   WSPROL2.PS    5.4k
```

2. Respond to the prompt by typing **MYDOC1,** pressing **Return**, and typing **Y** at the "Are you sure (Y/N)?" prompt. Notice that the filename MYDOC1 disappears from the file directory.

3. Turn to Module 71 to continue the learning sequence.

Module 23
DISK DRIVE AND DIRECTORY SELECTION

Classic: ^KL
Pull-Down: Alt-F, select "Change drive/directory..."

DESCRIPTION

You have a variety of available options when WordStar's OPENING menu is displayed. Many of these perform DOS operations, like renaming, deleting, and copying files. One of the OPENING menu options lets you change the logged drive or directory from the current selection to another. Selection of the drive or directory depends on the number of disk drives supported by your computer and the available directory paths.

Notice that the logged disk drive is displayed in conjunction with the OPENING menu. When you type FL from the OPENING menu or Ctrl-KL from the EDIT menu, WordStar displays a LOG screen which displays available drive designators and the currently logged (or active) drive and directory. The cursor rests on a line where you can type a different drive/directory designation. Once typed, press Return to finish the process. The directory of the newly logged disk drive is displayed. Now WordStar automatically operates with files on the logged disk. You may abort this process at any point before pressing Return by pressing Ctrl-U (Undo).

APPLICATIONS

Changing the logged disk drive and directory lets WordStar access, edit, and save files on any disk drive or file directory (or filepath) on your system. However, the WordStar program itself should reside on the drive and directory for which it was installed. This is usually drive A:\WS on floppy disk systems and C:\WS on fixed (hard) disk systems.

To prevent having your document files on the same directory as your WordStar program files, it is common to create subdirectories for letters (\WS\LETTER), administrative information (\WS\ADMIN), miscellaneous information (\WS\MISC), and so on. If you have a two-floppy-drive system, you may want to have your DOS system and WordStar on drive A and word processing document files on the disk in drive B. After starting WordStar, use the Change drive/directory operation to log the appropriate drive or directory. This process becomes habitual after using it a few times.

Disk Drive and Directory Selection

Another common use for the Change drive/directory operation is when you exchange diskettes. For example, if your logged disk drive is B, the file directory of the disk in drive B is displayed. After you exchange the diskette in the logged drive, type F L B and press Return. The new disk directory is displayed.

It is not necessary to use the Change drive/directory function to operate with files on different drives or directories. You can specify the drive and directory as part of the filename.

TYPICAL OPERATION

In this activity, you change the logged drive from C to A (or A to B if you have a floppy drive system). Be sure that a formatted diskette is in drive A (or B) before attempting to log drive A or B. Begin at the OPENING menu.

1. Type **FL** and notice the LOG screen.

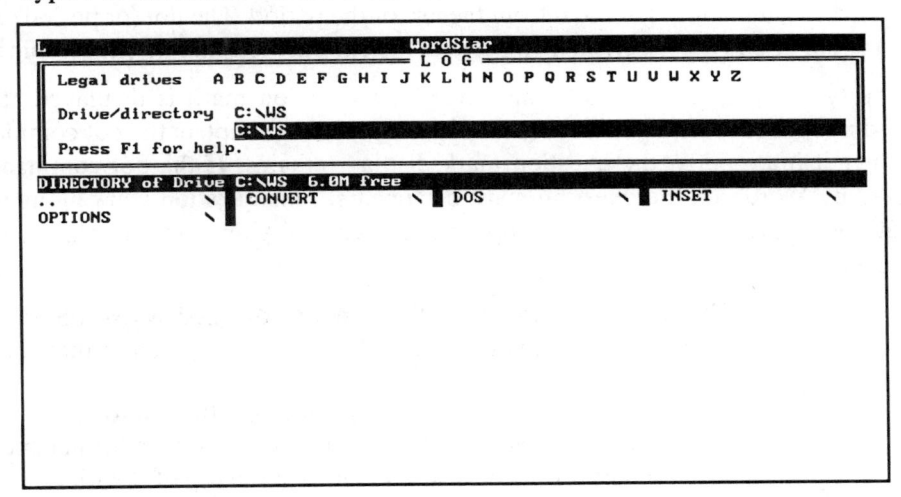

```
L                          WordStar
                            L O G
  Legal drives   A B C D E F G H I J K L M N O P Q R S T U V W X Y Z

  Drive/directory   C:\WS
                    C:\WS
  Press F1 for help.

 DIRECTORY of Drive C:\WS   6.0M free
 ..              \ | CONVERT      \ | DOS          \ | INSET         \
 OPTIONS         \ |
```

2. Type **A** and press **Return**. Notice that the directory of drive A is displayed.
3. Type **FL C** and press **Return** to change back to the original setting.
4. Turn to Module 28 to continue the learning sequence.

Module 24
DOT COMMANDS
(PRINT AND FORMAT CONTROL CODES)

DESCRIPTION

Embedded print control codes are explained in Modules 56 through 63. WordStar has another set of print control codes called *dot commands*. These dot commands offer an extra dimension of format control. Dot commands contain a period and a two-character code that specifies the dot command function.

The name "dot command" is derived from the use of the period. The dot (or period) used to begin the command must *always* be located at the extreme left margin (in column 01).

When you type a period at the left-hand margin, a question mark is displayed at the right-hand margin. This is WordStar's way of asking you to complete the dot command. If you enter it improperly, the question mark display remains. If the dot command is recognized by WordStar, the question mark disappears. This question mark along with other dot command "flags" that may appear at the end of a line are explained in the following list.

?	The dot command on this line is not recognized by WordStar.
.	The dot command on this line changes the onscreen format and the printout.
:	The dot command on this line changes only the printout.
1	The dot command on this line changes the onscreen format and the printout and works best when placed at the top of the file.

Dot commands are entered in either uppercase or lowercase like other WordStar commands. They are often used at the beginning of a document to establish format control for:

Left-hand margin indent (or page offset)	.PO
Headers and footers	.HE and .FO
Top and bottom margin spacing	.MT and .MB

When a "1" is displayed at the right edge of the line, you know that the dot command should be placed at the top of your document for best results.

The line occupied by a dot command is not printed; therefore, it is not counted by WordStar as a line when computing the number of lines per page.

Dot Commands (Print and Format Control Codes)

Dot commands are summarized in the following table. Once you've reviewed this table, you can review some typical examples of dot commands in the Applications section of this module. Of course, examples showing the use of all dot commands would almost fill a book. However, you can experiment on your own to check the effect of each dot command.

Dot Command	Description
.aw on/off	Turns word wrap and align on/off during reformatting of a document with Ctrl-QU.
.bn n	Selects sheet feeder bin 1 through 4, where n = 1-4.
.bp on/off	Turns bidirectional printing on/off.
.cb	Inserts a column break causing following text to print in next column.
.cc n	Starts a new column if less than n lines remain.
.co n	Prints a specified number (n) of columns.
.co n,n	Prints n columns, n spaces or inches (n") apart.
.cp n	Starts a new page if less than n lines remain.
.cs	Clears the screen during printing; often followed by the .dm command used to display a message.
.cv c>e	Prints a comment as an endnote.
.cv c>f	Prints a comment as a footnote.
.cv f>e	Prints a footnote as an endnote.
.cw n	Sets character width to n/120 inch. The default value is 12/120, which is 10 pitch (10 characters per inch).
.dm text	Displays "text" as a message during printing.
.e# n	Sets a starting number or symbol for endnotes.
.f1 text	Prints "text" on footer line 1.
.fo text	Same as .f1, i.e., prints "text" on first footer line.
.f2 text	Prints "text" on footer line 2.
.f3 text	Prints "text" on footer line 3.
.fm n	Prints footer n lines (n") below text, where fm represents footer margin. The default value is 2 lines, or .33".
.fn e/o	Causes footer n to print on even or odd pages only.
.f# n	Sets a starting number or symbol for footnotes.
.hn e/o	Causes header n to print on even or odd pages only.
.h1 text	Prints "text" on header line 1.
.he text	Same as .h1, i.e., prints "text" on header line 1.
.h2 text	Prints "text" on header line 2.
.h3 text	Prints "text" on header line 3.
.hm n	Prints header n lines (n") above text, where hm represents header margin. The default value is 2 lines, or .33".
.ig text	Displays following "text" as nonprinting comment.
.. text	Same as .ig.
.ix text	Uses "text" as index entry.
.lh n	Sets line height in n/48ths of an inch. The default value is 8/48ths, or 6 lines per inch.

Module 24

Dot Command	Description
.lm n	Sets left margin at column n or n". The default is 1 (0").
.lq on/off/dis	Turns near-letter-quality printing on/off/discretionary.
.ls n	Sets line spacing to n (1-9).
.l# 0	Turns line numbering off.
.l# d	Causes line numbering to print throughout document.
.l# d/p 1	Causes continuous line numbers to be single-spaced.
.l# d/p 1/2, n	Prints line numbers n columns to the left of column 1.
.l# d/p 2	Prints line numbers double-spaced.
.l# p	Restarts line numbering at the top of each page.
.mb n	Sets bottom margin to n lines (n"). The default value is 8 lines, or 1.33".
.mt n	Sets top margin to n lines (n"). The default value is 3 lines, or .5".
.oc on/off	Turns line centering on/off.
.oj on/off	Turns justification on/off.
.op	Omits page numbering (turns page numbering off).
.pa	Inserts a page break.
.pc n	Sets the page number column to n (n"); zero centers the page number.
.pe	Prints endnotes immediately following the dot command.
.pg	Restores the default page numbers.
.pl n	Sets page length to n lines (n"). The default value is 66 lines, or 11".
.pm n	Starts the first line of each new paragraph at column n or n".
.pn n	Starts page numbering at n.
.po n	Sets page offset (or indent) at n columns (n") from the left edge of the paper. The default is 8, or .7"; a value of 10, or 1", is recommended for 10-pitch printing.
.po e/o n	Sets even/odd page offset to n cols (n").
.ps on/off	Turns proportional spacing on/off.
.p# n	Sets the starting paragraph number, where n is a value like 1.1.1.
.p# n,s	Sets the starting paragraph number and style, where n is a nuumber like 1.1.1 and s is a value like A.9.a.
.rm n	Sets the right margin to column n (n"). The default value is 65, or 6.4".
.rp n	Repeats printing of the file n times.
.rr text	Used to initiate ruler line embedded in the document.
.rr n	Inserts a preformatted ruler line, where n is a value from 0 to 9.
.sr n	Sets superscript/subscript roll n/48ths of an inch. The default value is 3.
.tb n n n	Sets regular or decimal (#) tabs. For example, the dot command .tb 5 #30 #40 sets a standard tab at column 5 and decimal tabs at columns 30 and 40.
.tb n" n" n"	Sets tabs in inches.
.tc text	Used to identify "text" as a table of contents entry.
.tc n text	Used to identify "text" as a table of contents entry, where n is a number from 1 to 9 corresponding to the TOC 1-9 file.
.uj on/off/dis	Turns microjustification on/off/discretionary.
.ul on/off	Turns underline between words on/off.
.xe	Redefines custom print control ^PE.
.xl	Redefines form feed character.

Dot Commands (Print and Format Control Codes)

Dot Command	Description
.xq	Redefines custom print control ^PQ.
.xr	Redefines custom print control ^PR.
.xw	Redefines custom print control ^PW.
.xx	Redefines strikeout character ^PX.

MERGE PRINT DOT COMMANDS:

.av text,v	Display "text" and asks for variable input from keyboard (known as an ask variable).
.df filename	Defines data or spreadsheet file for read variables (.rv).
.ei	Ends conditional merge print statement.
.el	Do if last .if is not true.
.go top/bot	Go to top/bottom of document.
.if text	Conditional print control.
.ma v= e	Let variable "v" store result of equation "e".
.pf on/off/dis	Align to established margins while printing variables.
.rv v1,v2,...	Read these variables from the data file (.df).
.rv*	Read dBASE file using dBASE field names.
.rv* $x,$y	Read columns (or rows) x,y from spreadsheet.
.rv* xy	Read cell xy from spreadsheet.
.sv v,data	Replace variable with "data".

To print a document exactly as displayed, including dot commands and print controls, answer Y to the print option prompt, "Nondocument?"

APPLICATIONS

As mentioned at the beginning of this module, dot commands are powerful formatting tools. The summary table describes the effect of each dot command. Here, a few common uses are explored.

PAGE OFFSET   It is often desirable to adjust the left-hand margin so that it begins one inch from the left edge of the paper. You can use the page offset command to do this. If you are using 10-pitch type, use .PO 10 at the beginning of your document. If you are using 12 pitch, use .PO 12.

SUPPRESS PAGE NUMBERING   If you don't want page numbers to print on your document, enter .OP at the beginning of your document. Turn page numbering on with .PN n, where n is the current page number.

PRINT LEGAL SIZE (14-INCH) PAGE LENGTH   WordStar's default page length is 66 lines, or 11 inches (six lines per inch). To set a 14-inch legal page length (84 lines), use .PL 84. Using the default top and bottom margins, a page break is displayed

Module 24

automatically every 73 lines. The number of lines used for the top and bottom margins is controlled using the .MT and .MB commands.

DISCRETIONARY PAGE BREAK You can use a dot command to cause an immediate page break at any point within a document using the .PA dot command.

PAGE FOOTER WITH AN EMBEDDED PAGE NUMBER If you want to type a prefixed page number as a footer at the bottom of the page in the form "Page #," where # is the page number, you can use the .FO command. The command line used to position this number at the bottom center of your page is .FO page # and must be inserted at the beginning of the document.

The number sign is replaced by the actual document page number when printed. The .PN n dot command is used to adjust the page number if necessary.

POSITION PAGE NUMBER You can position the printed page number with the .PC n dot command, where n is the page number column. If you want the page number to appear at the bottom right-hand corner of the page, and the right margin is at column 65, you can type .PC 65 at the top of the document.

ALTER PAGE NUMBERS FOR PRINTING The .PN n dot command is used to change the default page number value within a document. Here is a typical application. You have three files that you want to print as a single document. The first contains pages 1 through 6; the second contains 7 through 15; and the third 16 through 22. Enter .PN 7 at the beginning of the second document. Enter .PN 16 at the beginning of the third document. When the three documents are printed, they are numbered continuously from 1 to 22.

TYPICAL OPERATION

In this activity, begin by opening a new document named DOTS. Use dot commands to set the page offset to 10. Create a header that prints "ABC REPORT" at the top of each page. Move the page number to column 65.

1. Open a new document named DOTS.
2. Type **.PO 10** and press **Return**.
3. Type **.HE ABC REPORT** and press **Return**.
4. Type **.PC 65** and press **Return**.

Dot Commands (Print and Format Control Codes)

5. Compare your document to the following illustration.

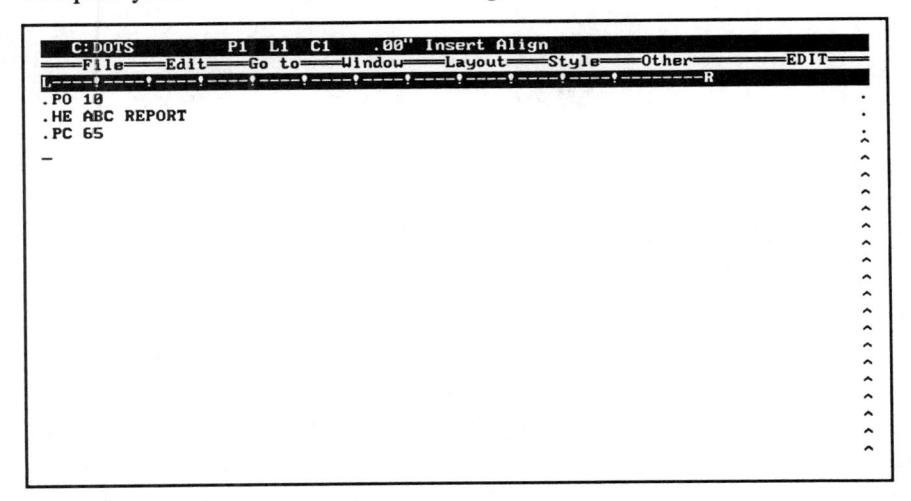

```
    C:DOTS           P1  L1  C1     .00"  Insert Align
====File====Edit====Go to====Window====Layout====Style====Other====EDIT====
L----!----!----!----!----!----!----!----!----!--------R
.PO 10
.HE ABC REPORT
.PC 65
_
```

6. Press **Ctrl-KQ** and type **Y** to abandon the document without saving.
7. Turn to Module 19 to continue the learning sequence.

Module 25
DOT LEADER

> ^P. (Ctrl-P period)

DESCRIPTION

A dot leader is a series of periods, or *dots*. The dot leader is inserted within a document from the cursor position to the next tab setting. Pressing Ctrl-P. inserts the dots. The example in the Typical Operation section of this module illustrates the use of the dot leader command.

APPLICATIONS

The most common use of the dot leader is in tables of contents, parts lists, and catalog listings. The dot leader guides the reader's eye across a page from one entry to another. This ensures easy alignment of entries on opposite sides of a page.

TYPICAL OPERATION

In this activity, you create a temporary document, set a tab at column 60, and enter several lines of a table of contents, using the dot leader command to link the title entry to the page number.

1. Open a new document named TEMP.
2. Type the following lines; begin by typing the dot code **.TB 5"** and pressing **Return** on the first line to set a tab at column 60. Press **Ctrl-P.** and type the page number after each title. Press **Return** after the page number.

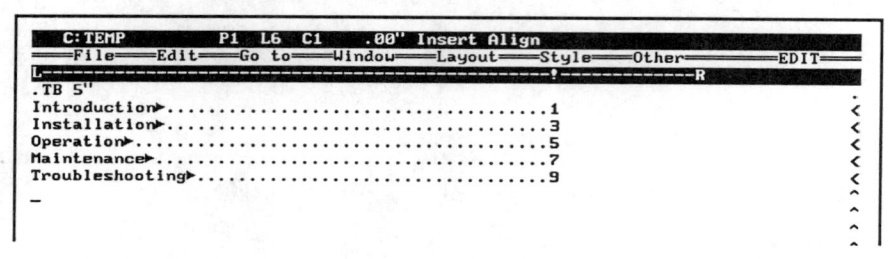

```
 C:TEMP          P1  L6  C1    .00" Insert Align
====File====Edit====Go to====Window====Layout====Style====Other========EDIT====
L---------------------------------------------!-------------R
.TB 5"
Introduction►........................................1                    <
Installation►........................................3                    <
Operation►...........................................5                    <
Maintenance►.........................................7                    <
Troubleshooting►.....................................9                    <
_                                                                         ^
                                                                          ^
                                                                          ^
```

3. Continue experimenting with the dot leader command until you are comfortable with its operation.
4. Press **Ctrl-KQ** and type **Y** to abandon the document.
5. Turn to Module 62 to continue the learning sequence.

Module 26
DRAWING LINES AND BOXES

> Alt-F1 through Alt-F10

DESCRIPTION

WordStar uses function keys F1 through F10 in combination with the Alt key to create certain characters. These characters are lines and corners that are combined to draw boxes. The exact character that is produced depends on your printer. If your printer can't draw the graphics character, WordStar substitutes the one most similar to it.

The predefined characters are shown in the following list. You can use WSCHANGE to select alternate characters to those shown in the list.

Alt-F1	│	Alt-F2	─
Alt-F3	┌	Alt-F4	┐
Alt-F5	└	Alt-F6	┘
Alt-F7	┬	Alt-F8	┴
Alt-F9	├	Alt-F10	┤

APPLICATIONS

Boxes can be drawn around titles or tabular text and used in illustrations such as block diagrams and organization charts. Once they are created, boxes can be stored as files and read into documents as needed. They are easily adjusted in size to accommodate various tables, lists, or charts. You may prefer to program a shorthand character that is defined to insert a stored box file. Module 84 explains shorthand or *macro substitution*.

If you are drawing a chart, it is often best to draw a standard box and save it as a box element. Next, copy the box into your chart document using the copy block command (Ctrl-KR). You may want to modify its size to accommodate interior text. You can copy the box as many times as necessary. You may also want to use WordStar's column editing features to copy boxes within the document.

TYPICAL OPERATION

In this activity, you use the Alt key in combination with function keys to draw a box 50 characters wide and 10 lines deep. You can save the results for later use if desired.

Drawing Lines and Boxes

1. Open a new document named BOX2.
2. Press **Alt-F3** to create the top left corner of a box.
3. Press **Alt-F2** until the top line of the box reaches column 49 (watch the status line).
4. Press **Alt-F4** to draw the right corner and press **Return**.
5. Press **Alt-F1** to begin the vertical left side of the box. Move the cursor under the right corner and press **Alt-F1** again for the right vertical. Press **Return**.
6. Mark the line across both vertical characters as a block with **Ctrl-KB** at the beginning and **Ctrl-KK** at the end of the line (include the return).
7. Copy to the next line with **Ctrl-KC**. Repeat this step six times to create both vertical lines of the box 9 lines deep. Your drawing should resemble the following.

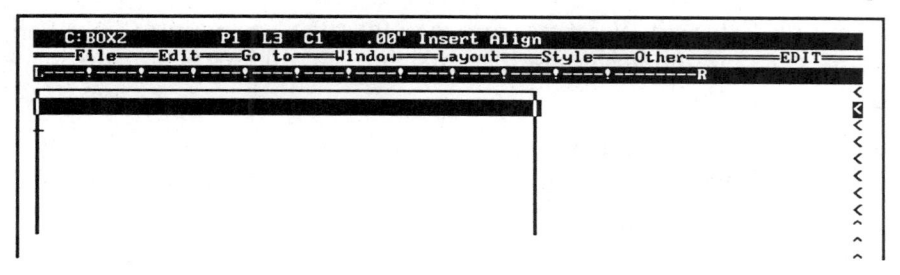

```
 C:BOX2        P1  L3  C1     .00"  Insert Align
═File════Edit════Go to════Window════Layout════Style════Other════════EDIT═
```

8. Press **Alt-F5** at line 10 to draw the bottom left corner.
9. Press and hold **Alt-F2** to draw the line across the bottom. Then press **Alt-F6** to draw the bottom right corner.
10. Experiment with the box drawing and add text to the box. Turn insert off so that text can be entered without disturbing the outline of the box. Use arrow keys and Spacebar to move the cursor, and avoid the use of Backspace and Del.
11. Press **Ctrl-KQ** and **Y** to abandon without saving, or press Ctrl-KD to save the box.
12. Turn to Module 29 to continue the learning sequence.

Module 27
EXIT WORDSTAR

> Classic: X, ^KX
> Pull-Down: F, select "Exit WordStar"

DESCRIPTION

When you are ready to exit WordStar from the OPENING menu, type FX. WordStar returns you to Disk Operating System (DOS) control, and the DOS prompt symbol is displayed (like A> or C>).

If you are editing a document and want to save the document and exit directly to the operating system prompt, press Ctrl-KX. Again, the DOS prompt is displayed.

APPLICATIONS

You should always exit WordStar before turning off your computer. Although the WordStar program is not affected when you remove it from your computer before exiting, your data (text) files can be. You should never remove a diskette from your computer without first saving your files. Once your files are saved, it is a good habit always to exit to DOS and remove your diskettes before turning off your computer. This is true regardless of what computer or program you are using.

TYPICAL OPERATION

In this activity you save and exit WordStar, returning to the DOS prompt. Begin at the EDIT menu with CHAP1 open from the previous module in the learning sequence.

1. Type **Ctrl-KX**. The message "Saving" appears and the DOS prompt of the system disk drive is displayed.
2. Turn to Module 89 to continue the learning sequence.

Module 28
FILE DIRECTORY DISPLAY

> Classic: F
> Pull-Down: Not available

DESCRIPTION

When the OPENING menu is displayed, a file directory of the logged disk and file path is normally displayed. If you want to turn the directory display off, you may do so by changing to help levels 0 through 3 (type OJJ and then type 0, 1, 2, or 3 when the pull down menus are active). Then type F to turn off the directory display.

Once off, you can recall the directory by typing F again. WordStar asks for a specification of files to display. This lets you "filter" your directory to display specific categories of files. By using a wild card (*), for example, you can display only those filenames with the .LTR extension using *.LTR as the file specification.

The file directory is also displayed during text editing whenever a file function (such as copy, rename, erase, print, run a program) is called from the BLOCK & SAVE menu.

APPLICATIONS

One reason for toggling the file directory off is to hide filenames for security purposes. The ability to display the disk directory while word processing lets you examine which files are available on the logged disk. You may want to read (copy) one or more of the files into your open document. Reviewing the file directory lets you see the exact filename to use. The read function is described in Module 16.

The ability to filter the file directory lets you remove unwanted filenames from your directory list. This makes it easier to locate files of interest.

TYPICAL OPERATION

In this activity, you change the help level, then turn the file directory display off and back on. Begin at the OPENING menu.

1. Type **O**, highlight Change help level and press **Return**. Type **3** to set help level 3.

Module 28

2. Type **F**; notice that the file directory and pull down menu display disappear and the classic OPENING menu appears.
3. Type **F** again. Look at the following screen.

```
F                           WordStar
                    ═ F I L E   D I R E C T O R Y ═
 Type *.* and press ↵ to see all files.  Use wild-cards for selected files.

 Display filenames  ????????.???   You can use wild-card characters * and ?.
                    ????????.???
 Press F1 for help.
```

4. Press **Return** to display the unchanged directory.
5. Type **J J** and **4** to restore the help level to 4.
6. Turn to Module 15 to continue the learning sequence.

Module 29
FILE OPERATIONS DURING WORD PROCESSING

> Classic: ^KO, ^KJ, ^KE, ^KL, ^KPP, ^KPM, ^KF
> Pull-Down: Alt-F, select "Copy a file..., Delete a file...,
> Rename a file..., Change drive/directory...
> Print a file..., Merge print a file..."
> Alt-O, select "Run a DOS command"

DESCRIPTION

A number of file operations are available from the OPENING and EDIT menus. WordStar lets you copy, rename, delete, and print files without having to return to DOS. You can even run programs without leaving WordStar.

WordStar's ability to perform file operations while word processing makes it an extremely attractive word processing package when compared to systems having limited file manipulation capabilities.

Modules 13 and 16 describe two file operations. The information in Module 13 describes the process for marking and writing a block. Module 16 describes how to read a file into an open (displayed) document.

The following list includes additional file operations and corresponding key sequences that are used while word processing an open document.

Description	Key Sequence
Copy a file	Ctrl-KO
Delete a file	Ctrl-KJ
Rename a file	Ctrl-KE
Print a file	Ctrl-KPP
Merge print a file	Ctrl-KPM
Change drive/directory	Ctrl-KL
Run a program or DOS command	Ctrl-KF

Module 29

The listed key sequences perform the described file operations and return you to the displayed document so that you can continue your word processing tasks. When the print function is chosen, the selected document is printed while you word process, allowing what is called "concurrent" or "simultaneous" printing and word processing. If you choose to print the active document, you can use the save and print operation by pressing Ctrl-PrtSc.

The print and merge print operations are described in detail in their respective modules.

APPLICATIONS

The ability to perform file operations while word processing lets you execute system-level functions without having to return to either WordStar's OPENING menu or DOS. For example, you can display a file directory, look up a filename, copy, rename, or delete a file, and resume word processing. This saves the time and associated inconvenience of having to exit word processing to perform any one of these tasks.

Concurrent printing lets you enter and edit text while a document is being printed. This eliminates the need to wait for a document to print before you can continue editing tasks.

TYPICAL OPERATION

In this activity, begin at the EDIT menu with the MYLTR document displayed. Display the file directory, copy a file, rename it, and then delete it.

1. Open the document MYLTR.
2. Press **Ctrl-KO** to copy a file. You are prompted to enter the filename and the name of the copy.
3. Type **PARA1** as the File and press **Return**.
4. Type **PARA2** as the Name of copy and press **Return**. The file is copied.
5. Press **Ctrl-KE** to rename a file.
6. Type **PARA2** as the Current name and press **Return**.
7. Type **PARA3** as the New name and press **Return**.
8. Press **Ctrl-KJ** to delete a file.
9. Type **PARA3** as the File and press **Return**. Type **Y** in response to the "Are you sure (Y/N)?" prompt.
10. Press **Ctrl-KQ** and type **Y** to abandon the file without saving.
11. Turn to Module 49 to continue the learning sequence.

Module 30
FIND AND FIND-REPLACE AGAIN

```
                    ^L
```

DESCRIPTION

Modules 34, 35, and 36 describe WordStar's find and find-replace operations. The find and find-replace again operation repeats the last find or find-replace sequence automatically. It is performed by positioning the cursor above the find area within the displayed document and pressing Ctrl-L.

Once you've found the first find string and dealt with it, you can execute the find or find-replace sequence again by repeating Ctrl-L. This jumps the cursor to the next occurrence of the find string. You may continue this process as many times as you like, and in as many documents as you like, until you turn off your computer or leave WordStar.

WordStar always "remembers" the last find, replace, and option string, even after you complete a find-replace operation. This process eliminates the need to retype it in the "Find what?" prompt area.

APPLICATIONS

The ability to automatically repeat an established find or find-replace operation saves time. It eliminates the need to enter an entire find or find-replace definition by letting you use a previous find or find-replace operation. In addition to recalling find and replace strings, the options are also recalled.

You can use find or find-replace again to replace a common character string with another in several document files. For example, if you want to replace June 30 with July 30 in three document files, you can set up the find-replace string and options in the first and use it. Then you can open subsequent documents and continue the find-replace process using Ctrl-L. All previous parameters are used automatically.

Module 30

TYPICAL OPERATION

In this example, you use find and replace again to continue the operation begun in the previous module in the learning sequence.

1. Open the document MYLTR.
2. Press **Ctrl-L** and notice that the cursor jumps to the first occurrence of "the" in the document and replaces it with "that."
3. Press **Ctrl-L** to repeat the find-replace operation. Notice that the cursor jumps to the next instance of "the" and replaces it with "that."
4. Continue experimenting with find-replace using alternate find-replace strings and options until you are comfortable with its operation.
5. Press **Ctrl-KQ** and type **Y** to abandon the document without saving.
6. Turn to Module 35 to continue the learning sequence.

Module 31
FIND BLOCK MARKER

> Classic: ^QB, ^QK
> Pull-Down: Alt-G, select "Go to block beginning"
> Alt-G, select "Go to block end"

DESCRIPTION

Place markers are described in Module 32. They are used to set and find specific locations within a document. It is also possible to jump the cursor directly to the beginning or end of a marked block of text. The beginning and ending block markers are used in the same way as place markers.

You should recall from Module 8 that a beginning block marker is set using Ctrl-KB. The ending block marker is set using Ctrl-KK. The markers are turned on and off with the same control characters. You can jump to the beginning block marker with Ctrl-QB. Similarly, the ending block marker is found with Ctrl-QK.

Marked blocks of text are hidden or redisplayed with Ctrl-KH.

If a block of text is moved or copied to another location within a document, you can return to the beginning of the previous block position with Ctrl-QB. This is convenient for returning directly to an area from which text has been moved, particularly if you want to do some "cleanup" such as changing wording or format. If the block is deleted, the cursor returns to the position of the deleted text.

APPLICATIONS

The ability to jump to the beginning or the end of a marked block is a time-saving device for managing blocks of text. After copying a block to another location within a document, it is often necessary to return to the marked block to make changes. Jumping to either the beginning or end of the block is an easy matter with Ctrl-QB or Ctrl-QK.

TYPICAL OPERATION

In this activity, you mark the body of the letter as a block, hide the block, and then find the beginning and end of the block.

1. Open the document MYLTR.

Module 31

2. Mark the letter paragraph as a block (see Module 8 if required).
3. Hide the block with **Ctrl-KH**.
4. Press **Ctrl-QB** to jump to the beginning of the hidden block.

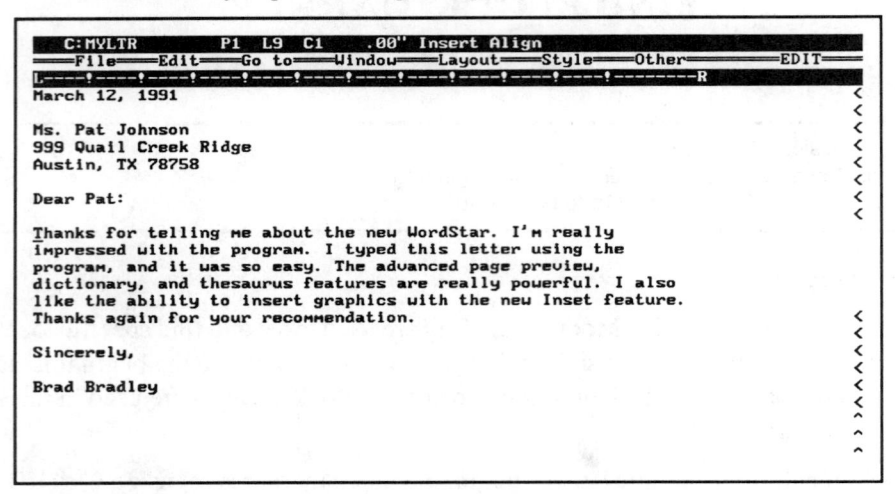

```
   C:MYLTR         P1  L9  C1     .00"  Insert Align
  ═══File═══Edit═══Go to═══Window═══Layout═══Style═══Other═══════════EDIT══
  L----!----!----!----!----!----!----!----!----!----!--------R
  March 12, 1991                                                  <
                                                                  <
  Ms. Pat Johnson                                                 <
  999 Quail Creek Ridge                                           <
  Austin, TX 78758                                                <
                                                                  <
  Dear Pat:                                                       <
                                                                  <
  Thanks for telling me about the new WordStar. I'm really
  impressed with the program. I typed this letter using the
  program, and it was so easy. The advanced page preview,
  dictionary, and thesaurus features are really powerful. I also
  like the ability to insert graphics with the new Inset feature.
  Thanks again for your recommendation.                           <
                                                                  <
  Sincerely,                                                      <
                                                                  <
  Brad Bradley                                                    <
                                                                  <
                                                                  ^
                                                                  ^
                                                                  ^
```

5. Jump to the end of the block with **Ctrl-QK**.
6. Continue experimenting with find block marker until you are comfortable with its operation.
7. Press **Ctrl-KQ** to abandon the document without saving.
8. Turn to Module 36 to continue the learning sequence.

Module 32
FIND PLACE MARKER

> ^K0 through ^K9, then ^Q0 through ^Q9

DESCRIPTION

Up to ten place markers, numbered 0 through 9, are available as reference points within a document. Place marker number 2 is set by positioning the cursor to the desired location and pressing Ctrl-K2. A highlighted 2 is displayed to mark the spot.

Once the place marker is set, you can find it by pressing Ctrl-Q2. The cursor jumps to the place marker.

You can move a place marker by resetting it at a new location within the displayed document. You can turn off a place marker, such as place marker number 2, by either moving to the marker and pressing Ctrl-K2 or by pressing Ctrl-K2 twice at any location within the document. Place markers disappear when the document is saved or abandoned.

Another convenient find function lets you visit a marker and then return to the previous cursor position. If you want to move to place marker number 3, press Ctrl-Q3. Then press Ctrl-QP to jump the cursor back to the previous position.

APPLICATIONS

Those who use place markers consider them important tools when creating large, multiple-page documents. Being able to move directly to selected passages eliminates the need to move through a document a screen at a time in search of a particular passage. The ability to jump to the previous cursor position is also a convenient function.

TYPICAL OPERATION

In this activity, you set two place markers and find them with find place marker commands.

1. Open the document MYLTR.
2. Press **Ctrl-K2** to set place marker number 2 on the first word in the document.
3. Move the cursor down ten lines and press **Ctrl-QD** to jump to the right margin.

Module 32

4. Press **Ctrl-K3** to set place marker number 3. Your document should resemble the following screen illustration.

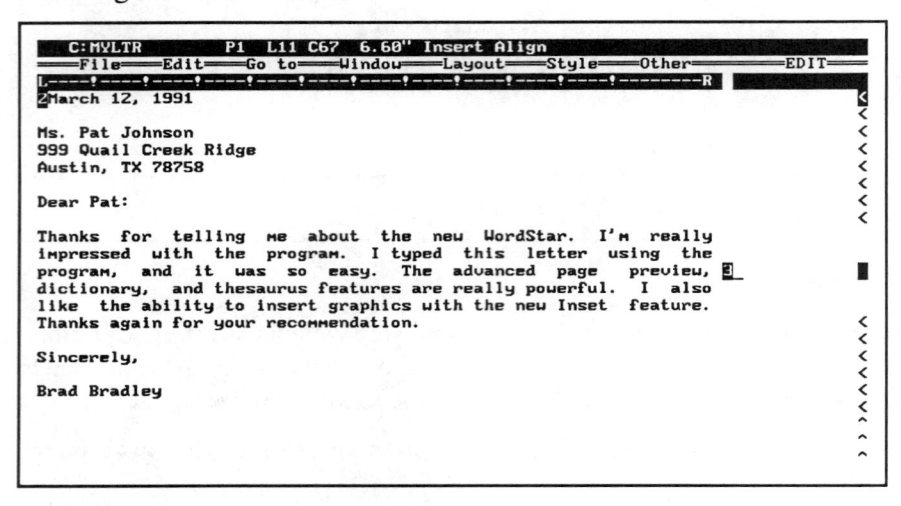

```
 C:MYLTR        P1   L11  C67   6.60" Insert Align
===File======Edit======Go to======Window======Layout======Style======Other=================EDIT===
L----!----!----!----!----!----!----!----!----!----!--------R
2March 12, 1991                                                                              <
                                                                                             <
Ms. Pat Johnson                                                                              <
999 Quail Creek Ridge                                                                        <
Austin, TX 78758                                                                             <
                                                                                             <
Dear Pat:                                                                                    <

Thanks for telling me about the new WordStar. I'm really
impressed with the program. I typed this letter using the
program, and it was so easy. The advanced page  preview, 3_      ▮
dictionary, and thesaurus features are really powerful. I also
like the ability to insert graphics with the new Inset feature.
Thanks again for your recommendation.                                                        <
                                                                                             <
Sincerely,                                                                                   <
                                                                                             <
Brad Bradley                                                                                 <
                                                                                             <
                                                                                             ^
                                                                                             ^
```

5. Press **Ctrl-Q2** to find place marker 2.
6. Press **Ctrl-QP** to jump the cursor to the previous cursor position.
7. Continue experimenting with place markers until you are comfortable with the operation.
8. Press **Ctrl-KQ** to abandon the document without saving.
9. Turn to Module 31 to continue the learning sequence.

Module 33
FIND-REPLACE

> Classic: ^QA
> Pull-Down: Alt-G, select "Find and replace text..."

DESCRIPTION

The process for finding a text string within a document is described in Module 36. WordStar also lets you find and replace a text string with another. As with the find operation, several options are available.

FIND AND REPLACE PROCEDURE   You can find and replace the first occurrence of a text string following the present cursor position with this simple procedure:

1. Press Ctrl-QA to display the FIND & REPLACE menu.

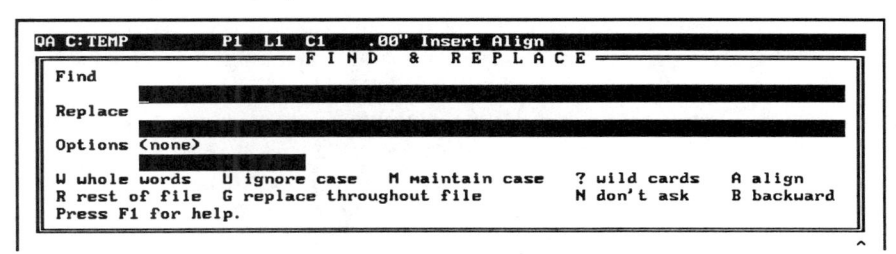

```
QA C:TEMP          P1  L1  C1     .00" Insert Align
═══════════════════ F I N D  &  R E P L A C E ═══════════════════
Find
Replace
Options <none>

W whole words    U ignore case    M maintain case    ? wild cards    A align
R rest of file   G replace throughout file           N don't ask     B backward
Press F1 for help.
```

2. Type the "Find" text string and press Return.
3. Type the "Replace" text string and press Return twice.
4. Notice that the cursor jumps to the first find text string and "Replace Y/N" is displayed at the upper right-hand corner of the screen.
5. Type Y to replace; type N to leave the string unchanged.
6. Press Ctrl-L to find-replace again.

Find and replace strings are limited to a maximum of 68 characters.

OPTIONS   Many of the options for find and replace are identical to those for find (Module 36). When used, the option designators are typed after typing the replace string and pressing Return.

Module 33

Option	Description
?	Wild cards — allows a ? character in the search string to be treated as a wild card representing any character in that position. Otherwise a ? is treated as a literal character in the search string.
B	Search backward — find the specified word by using the B option to search from the cursor backward through the document. If the G option is also used with B, the search begins at the end of the document.
W	Whole words only — specifies that the string to be found must be a whole word. For example, if "THE" is the string to be found, the string faTHEr will be ignored.
U	Ignore case — either uppercase or lowercase forms of the specified string will be found.
M	Maintain case — maintain uppercase and lowercase values of a replaced string. For example, if the string is the first word in a sentence, the first letter remains capitalized.
G	Begin at top of file (or bottom if used with B) — if used with the find-replace operation described in Module 34, searches globally for every occurrence of string.
N	Replace without asking (no ask) — used with the find-replace operation described in this module and Module 34. Replaces all instances of encountered text string automatically. The alternative is to choose each replacement one at a time.
A	Align paragraph — reformats paragraph during find and replace operation to adjust for character count difference between the find string and the replacement. Returns to replacement spot in paragraph after reaching the end of the paragraph unless options G or R are also used.
R	Rest of document — searches globally from where cursor rests when search and replace begins to the end of the document.
3	Find and replace next 3 occurrences — finds and replaces the number of occurrences specified by the number.

You can search and replace an entire document from beginning to end using the G (global) option or backward adding the B (backward). Global find-replace is described in Module 34. You can search and replace from the cursor through the rest of the document with R (rest). You can use the A (align) option to realign or reformat paragraphs affected by replacing strings of text. You can use ? as a wild card option to allow the character string to use the wild card ? to match any character in that position in the search string. Using option N completes the search and replace procedure without stopping to ask "Replace Y/N" at each occurrence. You can use a number as an option to indicate which or how many occurrences you wish to replace.

SPECIAL FIND AND REPLACE STRINGS You can include returns, line feeds, and print control characters in your find and replace strings. For example, if you want to replace single returns with double, you can use Ctrl-P Ctrl-M Ctrl-P Ctrl-J (displayed ^M^J) as the find string. Then use Ctrl-P Ctrl-M Ctrl-P Ctrl-J twice (displayed ^M^J^M^J) as the replace string. To automatically replace every hard return with two, use the GN (global, no-ask) options.

Many of the print control codes are preceded with Ctrl-P. For example, the underline print code is entered in the search string with Ctrl-P Ctrl-S and the bold print code is entered with Ctrl-P Ctrl-B.

HARD AND SOFT RETURNS Hard returns are indicated by < at the right side of the screen. Soft returns, created with automatic word wrap, are indicated by a blank space at the right side of the screen. Hard returns are manually replaced with soft returns by moving to the end of a line and pressing Ctrl-6. (Use the 6 above the keyboard.) Soft returns are replaced with hard returns by pressing Return at the end of a line (with Insert on) and then deleting the blank line. You can replace all soft returns with hard returns by opening a document as a nondocument file and pressing Ctrl-QU. This also "strips" all formatting codes from the document to produce a clean ASCII file.

FINDING OTHER SPECIAL CHARACTERS A list of entries used to find (or find and replace) several special characters follows.

Find	Use
Hard carriage return	^QF^P^M ^P^J
Soft hyphens (within line)	^QF^P^6
Soft hyphen (end of line)	^QF^P^-
Next font change	^Q=

Footnotes, endnotes, comments, and annotations are found by pressing Ctrl-ON and typing G.

APPLICATIONS

The find-replace function is a powerful, time-saving word processing tool. It lets you replace one or more occurrences of a unique text string with another automatically. Although it is most often used to replace one text string with another, it can also be used to replace commonly misspelled words or typing errors with the correctly spelled word.

Module 33

TYPICAL OPERATION

In this activity, you find and replace single returns with double returns using the GN (global no-ask) options.

1. Open the document MYLTR.
2. Move the cursor to the beginning of the document (L1 C1).
3. Press **Ctrl-QA** and notice the FIND & REPLACE menu.
4. Press **Ctrl-P Ctrl-M Ctrl-P Ctrl-J** as the Find string and press **Return**.
5. Press **Ctrl-P Ctrl-M Ctrl-P Ctrl-J Ctrl-P Ctrl-M Ctrl-P Ctrl-J** as the Replace string and press **Return**.
6. Type **GN** as options and press **Return**.
7. Notice that all single returns are replaced with two returns. Press **Esc** at the prompt.
8. Continue experimenting with the find-replace operation by replacing one word with another until you are comfortable with this operation.
9. Press **Ctrl-KQ** and type **Y** to abandon the document without saving.
10. Turn to Module 34 to continue the learning sequence.

Module 34
FIND-REPLACE, GLOBAL

> Classic: ^QA (G option)
> Pull-Down: Alt-G, select "Find and replace text..." (G option)

DESCRIPTION

The find-replace operation, described in Module 33, is greatly enhanced when using the global (G) and don't ask (N) options. The global option lets you find and replace all occurrences of a text string within a document automatically. If you do not use the N option, each find-replace is done selectively, because WordStar prompts you with the message "Replace Y/N."

Typing Y replaces the find string and the cursor jumps to the next occurrence. Typing N tells WordStar not to replace the find string and jumps the cursor to the next find-replace location.

Using the no-ask option (N) replaces every find string with the replace string without stopping and without asking.

If you watch the screen during a global, don't-ask find-replace operation, you can see the cursor jumping from find string to find string, replacing each one with the replace string as it is encountered. If you want to speed up the process without watching the replacement activity, press a cursor key. The screen remains stationary until all find strings are replaced. Once the string is replaced, the cursor is positioned at the bottom of the document. If you used the search backward option (B), the cursor rests at the top of the document. If you wish to interrupt the global find-replace operation, press Ctrl-U.

Review the following examples of the global find-replace options.

Option	Description
G	Find all occurrences of the string beginning at the top of the document. Display the prompt "Replace Y/N" to replace selectively.
GN	Find and replace all occurrences of the string beginning at the top of the document without asking for a replacement decision. (Press a cursor key to speed up the process.)
GNW	Find and replace all occurrences of the find string as a whole word beginning at the top of the document without asking for a replacement decision.

Option	Description
GNMA	Find and replace all occurrences of the find string. Maintain upper and lower case. Align the format to comply with established margins and indent levels.
GB	Find all occurrences of the find string beginning at the end of the document and searching backward. Display the prompt "Replace Y/N" to allow a replacement decision.
GBN	Find and replace all occurrences of the string beginning at the end of the document and searching backward without asking for a replacement decision.
GBNW	Find and replace all occurrences of the find string as a whole word beginning at the end of the document and searching backward without asking for a replacement decision.
R	Find and replace all occurrences of the find string beginning at the present position of the cursor and searching through the rest of the document. Display the prompt "Replace Y/N" to allow a replacement decision.
RN	Find and replace all occurrences of the find string beginning at the present position of the cursor and searching the rest of the document without stopping to ask for a replacement decision.
RNW	Find and replace all occurrences of the find string as a whole word beginning at the present position of the cursor and searching the rest of the document without asking for a replacement decision.
RB	Find all occurrences of the find string beginning at the present position of the cursor and searching backward through the rest of the document. Display the prompt "Replace Y/N" to allow a replacement decision.
RBN	Find and replace all occurrences of the string beginning at the present cursor position and searching backward through the rest of the document without asking for a replacement decision.
RBNW	Find and replace all occurrences of the find string as a whole word beginning at the present cursor position and searching backward through the rest of the document without asking for a replacement decision.

APPLICATIONS

The global find-replace operation is a powerful word processing tool that lets you replace every occurrence of a selected text string with another. It is often used to replace one name with another in standard form letters. If you discover that you make a common typographical error, use find-replace with the GN (global, no-ask) options to replace the typo with the correct word form. A major advantage is that the quality resulting from global find-replace reduces the potential for typographical errors, unless you make a typo when entering the find or replace strings.

Find-Replace, Global

TYPICAL OPERATION

In this example, you use the find and replace GN option to replace "the" with "that" without asking.

1. Open the document MYLTR.
2. Press **Ctrl-QA** and notice that the FIND & REPLACE menu is displayed.
3. Type **the** and press **Return**.
4. Type **that** and press **Return**.
5. Type **GN** as options; check for the following display.

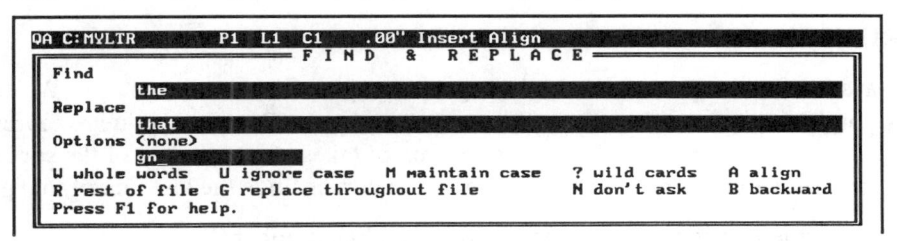

```
QA C:MYLTR         P1 L1 C1   .00" Insert Align
======================= F I N D   &   R E P L A C E =======================
 Find
       the
 Replace
       that
 Options <none>
       gn
 W whole words    U ignore case   M maintain case   ? wild cards   A align
 R rest of file   G replace throughout file         N don't ask    B backward
 Press F1 for help.
```

6. Press **Return** to begin the find-replace operation and **Esc** when complete. Notice that every "the" is replaced with "that." Also notice that without the whole word option (W) in effect, the "the" in "thesaurus" was replaced with "that."

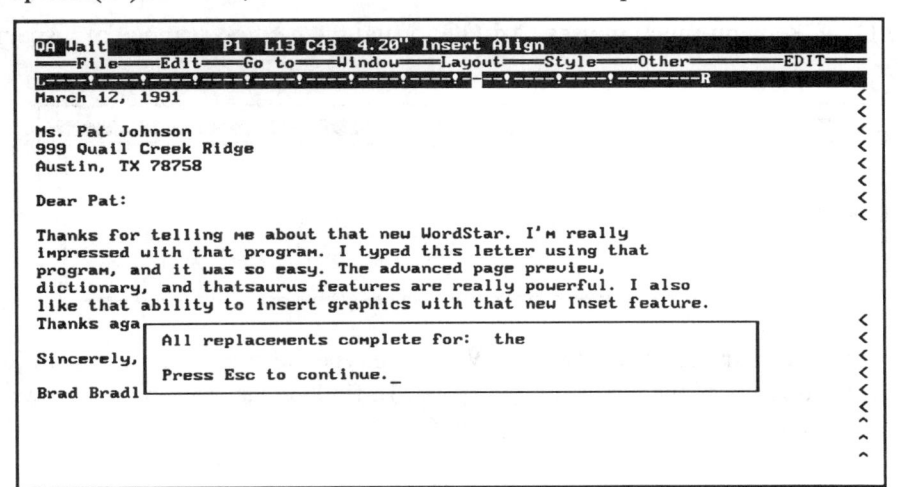

```
QA Wait           P1 L13 C43  4.20" Insert Align
==File==Edit==Go to==Window==Layout==Style==Other========EDIT==
L----!----!----!----!----!----!----!--!----!----!---------R
March 12, 1991                                              <
                                                            <
Ms. Pat Johnson                                             <
999 Quail Creek Ridge                                       <
Austin, TX 78758                                            <
                                                            <
Dear Pat:                                                   <

Thanks for telling me about that new WordStar. I'm really
impressed with that program. I typed this letter using that
program, and it was so easy. The advanced page preview,
dictionary, and thatsaurus features are really powerful. I also
like that ability to insert graphics with that new Inset feature.
Thanks aga┌─────────────────────────────────────┐           <
         │ All replacements complete for:  the │           <
Sincerely,│                                     │          <
         │ Press Esc to continue._             │           <
Brad Bradl└─────────────────────────────────────┘           <
                                                            <
                                                            ^
                                                            ^
```

7. Press **Ctrl-KQ** and type **Y** to abandon the document without saving.
8. Turn to Module 30 to continue the learning sequence.

Module 35
FIND SPECIFIED PAGE, CHARACTER

> Classic: ^QI page no., ^QG char
> Pull-Down: Alt-G, select "Go to page..."

DESCRIPTION

To find a specified page in a multiple-page document file, press Ctrl-QI. WordStar prompts you for a page number. Type the number and press Return. If you are searching for a higher page number in the document, the cursor takes you to the top of the specified page. If you are searching backward for a page, the cursor finds the last line of that page.

In the nondocument mode, you can find a specified line number.

You can also advance or back up a specified number of pages by pressing Ctrl-QI and entering +n or −n, where n is a number. For example, if you want to advance three pages, type +3 and press Return.

Another QUICK menu function uses Ctrl-QG to find the next occurrence of a specified character.

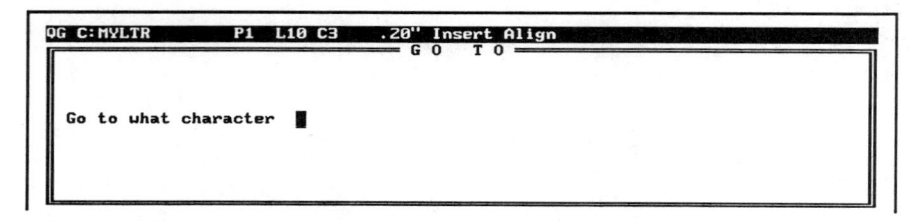

```
QG C:MYLTR           P1  L10 C3      .20" Insert Align
                              = G O    T O =

  Go to what character  ▮

```

The prompt asks for the character to find. When you type the character, the cursor jumps to the next occurrence of the character you typed. To find the last previous occurrence of a specified character, begin the sequence with Ctrl-QH.

APPLICATIONS

As with other quick cursor movements, the advantages of these procedures are in the ability to move about in your document and perform word processing steps quickly and efficiently. Being able to jump directly to a specific page without having to scan screen after screen is a significant time saver.

You can press Ctrl-QG or Ctrl-QH and type a period to jump to the end or beginning of a sentence.

TYPICAL OPERATION

In this activity, you experiment with finding specified characters and page numbers.

1. Open the document MYLTR.
2. Press **Ctrl-QG** and type **p** in response to the "Go to what character" prompt. Notice that the cursor jumps to the "p" in "impressed."
3. Press **Ctrl-QH** and type **h**. Notice that the cursor jumps to the "h" in "the."
4. Move the cursor to the last line of the file. Type **.pa** and press **Return** several times to create pages of blank lines. Repeat this process until you have four page breaks on your screen as in the following illustration.

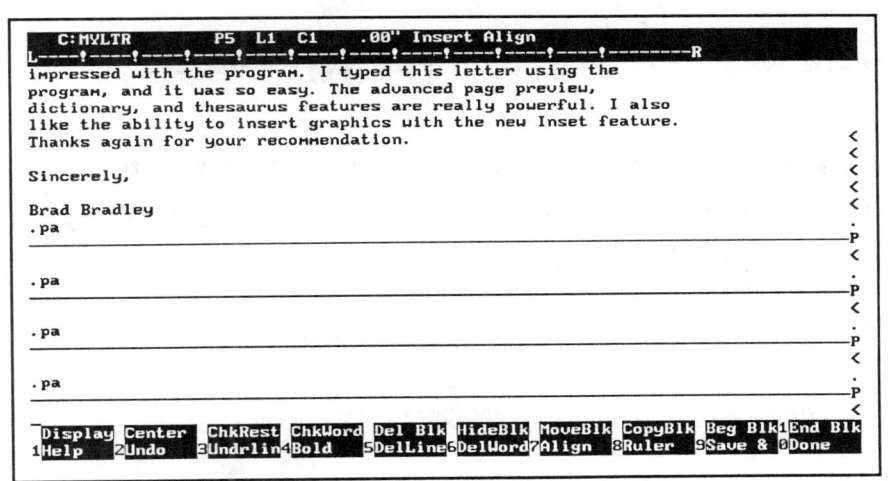

5. Press **Ctrl-QR** to move the cursor to the top of the file.
6. Press **Ctrl-QI**, type **3**, and press **Return**.
7. Notice that the cursor is at the top of page three. (See the status line.)
8. Press **Ctrl-QI**, type **−1**, and press **Return**.
9. Notice that the cursor is at the top of page two.
10. Press **Ctrl-KQ** and type **Y** to abandon the document.
11. Turn to Module 7 to continue the learning sequence.

Module 36
FIND TEXT STRING

> Classic: ^QF
> Pull-Down: Alt-G, select "Find text..."

DESCRIPTION

WordStar's find (or search) command is used to locate a specified character, word, or group of words ranging from 1 to 68 characters within the displayed document. This character, word, or group of words is called a *text string*.

FIND STRINGS   To start the find operation, press Ctrl-QF. WordStar displays a FIND screen, which resembles the following illustration.

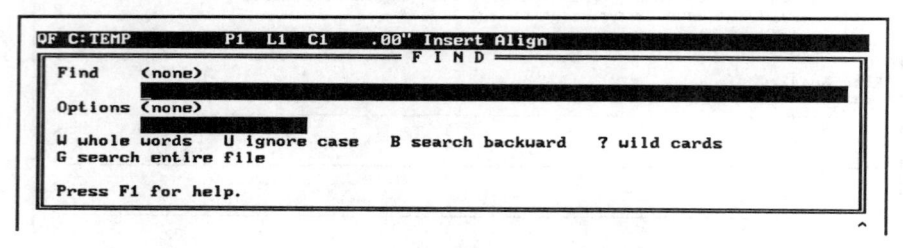

```
QF C:TEMP          P1  L1  C1    .00" Insert Align
                              = F I N D =
 Find      (none)

 Options  (none)

 W whole words     U ignore case    B search backward    ? wild cards
 G search entire file

 Press F1 for help.
```

Respond by typing the text string you want to find and then press Return. You should be aware that you can find some special control characters within a document. For example, you can include a hard return (^M^J) in a find string by pressing Ctrl-P Ctrl-M Ctrl-P Ctrl-J. You can also find print control characters by preceding them with a Ctrl-P. For example, if you want to find ^S, use Ctrl-P Ctrl-S. A ^S is displayed as part of the find string.

OPTIONS   Several options are available. You may elect one or more options or ignore them by pressing Return. Pressing Return finds the first occurrence of the selected text string.

The displayed options are described in more detail in the following list:

Option	Description
?	Wild cards — allows a ? character in the search string to be treated as a wild card representing any character in that position. Otherwise a ? is treated as a literal character in the search string.
B	Search backward — find the specified word by using the B option to search from the cursor backward through the document. If the G option is also used with B, the search begins at the end of the document.
W	Whole words only — specifies that the string to be found must be a whole word. For example, if "THE" is the string to be found, the string faTHEr will be ignored.
U	Ignore case — either uppercase or lowercase forms of the specified string will be found.
G	Begin at top of file (or bottom if used with B) — if used with the find-replace operation described in Module 34, searches globally for every occurrence of string.

To search for a specific word from the cursor position backward, use the BW options. These tell WordStar to search backward for whole words.

If you want to find several occurrences of the same text string, you can repeat the last find sequence by pressing Ctrl-L. This repeats the most recent find command. For example, if you are looking for the name JONES, you would find the first occurrence with "Ctrl-QF JONES Return Return." The cursor jumps to the first letter of the first occurrence of the string JONES. To find the next JONES, press Ctrl-L. The cursor jumps to the next JONES.

APPLICATIONS

The find operation is a powerful word processing tool that lets you find every occurrence of a unique text string within a document. You can use it to find known misspellings or to locate specific information within a document. The automatic find operation saves the time that would otherwise be used to scan a document visually.

TYPICAL OPERATION

In this activity, you use the find operation to find the word "the."

1. Open the document MYLTR. Begin at the top of the document.
2. Press **Ctrl-QF**, type **the**, then press **Return** twice. Notice that the cursor jumps to the first occurrence of "the."
3. Press **Ctrl-L** to jump to the next occurrence.
4. Continue using **Ctrl-L** and notice how "the" is found in the word "thesaurus."

Module 36

5. Go back to the top of the document, press **Ctrl-QF**, press **Return**, type **W** to find whole words, and press **Return**.
6. Continue pressing **Ctrl-L** until you reach the bottom of the document. Press **Esc** at the prompt.

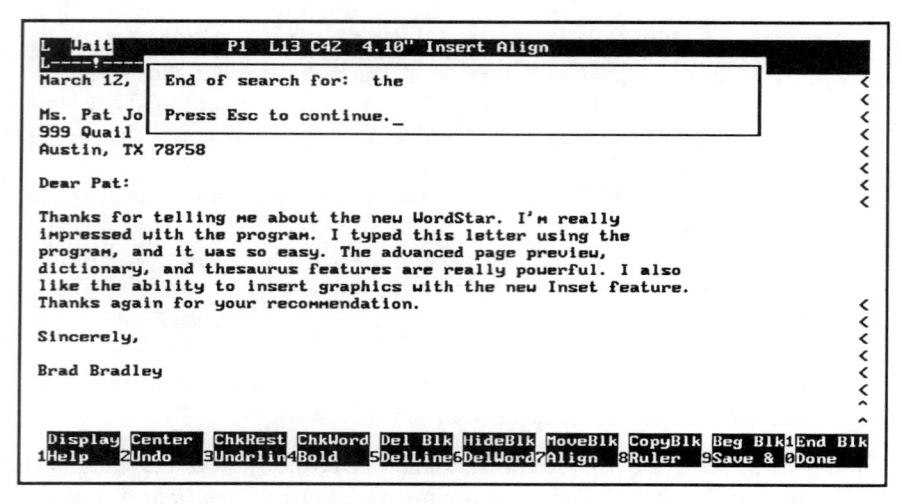

```
L  Wait              P1  L13 C42  4.10"  Insert Align
L----!----
March 12,   ┌─────────────────────────────┐
            │ End of search for:  the     │                <
Ms. Pat Jo  │ Press Esc to continue._     │                <
999 Quail   └─────────────────────────────┘                <
Austin, TX 78758                                           <
                                                           <
Dear Pat:                                                  <
                                                           <
Thanks for telling me about the new WordStar. I'm really
impressed with the program. I typed this letter using the
program, and it was so easy. The advanced page preview,
dictionary, and thesaurus features are really powerful. I also
like the ability to insert graphics with the new Inset feature.
Thanks again for your recommendation.                      <
                                                           <
Sincerely,                                                 <
                                                           <
Brad Bradley                                               <
                                                           <
                                                           ^
                                                           ^
 Display Center  ChkRest ChkWord Del Blk HideBlk MoveBlk CopyBlk Beg Blk End Blk
1Help   2Undo   3Undrlin4Bold   5DelLine6DelWord7Align  8Ruler  9Save & 0Done
```

Notice that this time the find operation ignores "the" within the word "thesaurus."

7. Continue experimenting with the find text string operation until you are comfortable with it.
8. Press **Ctrl-KQ** to abandon the document without saving.
9. Turn to Module 33 to continue the learning sequence.

Module 37
FOOTNOTES, ENDNOTES, ANNOTATIONS, AND COMMENTS

```
Classic:    ^ON
Pull-Down:  Alt-O, select "Footnote/endnote..."
```

DESCRIPTION

A *footnote* is a referenced entry, or note, located at the bottom of the page on which the footnote is referenced. An *endnote* is a referenced entry located on the last page of a document. WordStar lets you enter footnote and endnote references and places corresponding text in the appropriate location.

The footnote/endnote operation also lets you enter *annotations* and *comments*. An annotation is a footnote that is referenced from several locations on a page, as in a chart or table. A comment is a note that is displayed but not printed; comments, as well as footnotes and endnotes, are hidden and redisplayed with Ctrl-OD, which is also used to hide and display print control codes.

THE NOTES MENU   When you press Ctrl-ON, the following NOTES menu is displayed.

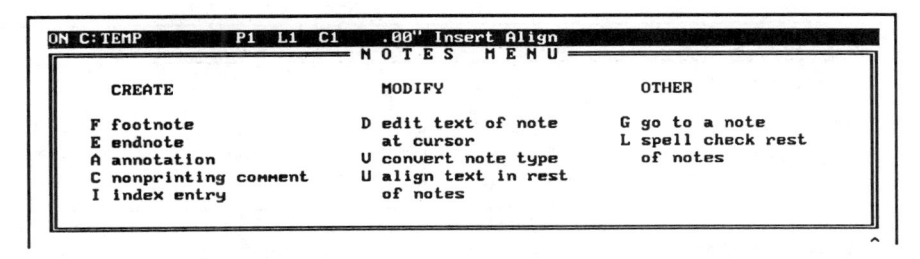

```
ON C:TEMP          P1  L1  C1    .00" Insert Align
                       = N O T E S    M E N U =

       CREATE                MODIFY              OTHER

  F footnote            D edit text of note   G go to a note
  E endnote               at cursor           L spell check rest
  A annotation          U convert note type     of notes
  C nonprinting comment U align text in rest
  I index entry           of notes
```

The key sequences for entering and editing footnotes, endnotes, annotations, and comments are:

Description	Key Sequence
Footnote	Ctrl-ON F
Endnote	Ctrl-ON E
Annotation	Ctrl-ON A
Comment	Ctrl-ON C

Description	Key Sequence
Convert note type	Ctrl-ON V
Align text in notes	Ctrl-ON U
Go to a note	Ctrl-ON G
Spell check notes	Ctrl-ON L

Once you select the type of note you wish to create by typing the appropriate letter when the NOTES menu is displayed, a window is displayed at the bottom half of your screen for text entry. WordStar assigns and "remembers" the note number, beginning with note number 1 and incrementing the number by one with each subsequent note entry.

Once your note entry is typed, press Ctrl-KD to save the note and close the note window. Press Ctrl-KQ if you wish to abandon the note without saving. The first 15 characters of footnotes, endnotes, and comments are displayed as print control codes in your document. When control code displays are hidden with Ctrl-OD, the numbers of footnotes and endnotes are displayed as control codes. The note numbers are printed as superscripts.

NOTES AND PAGE LENGTHS Multiple-line notes are counted by WordStar in order to leave enough room at the bottom of each page for their insertion. Therefore, do not be alarmed if your page lengths seem to vary from page to page. You can adjust the number of lines used for note margins in WordStar's WSCHANGE utility.

NOTE NUMBERS You can modify the note numbering system, which defaults to numbers beginning with 1, to a higher number value, an uppercase or lowercase letter, or asterisks. This is accomplished with the dot command .F# for footnotes and .E# for endnotes. The dot commands are followed by the appropriate value. Look at the following list.

Starting Note Character	Dot Command
Begin with capital A	.F# A or .E# A
Begin with lowercase aa	.F# aa or .E# aa
Begin with number 21	.F# 21 or .E# 21
Begin with an asterisk	.F# * or .E# *

The asterisk format begins with a single asterisk. Subsequent footnotes or endnotes are assigned an increasing number of asterisks, such as **, ***, and so on.

EDITING NOTES Footnotes, endnotes, and comments are edited, spell-checked, and reformatted (or auto-aligned) in the same manner as normal text. To edit a note, place the cursor on the note reference within your document, press Ctrl-ON, and type D. The note window is displayed at the bottom of your screen. Proceed by editing the note using regular WordStar editing commands.

FINDING NOTES   You can jump the cursor to a note by pressing Ctrl-ON and typing G. The following screen is displayed.

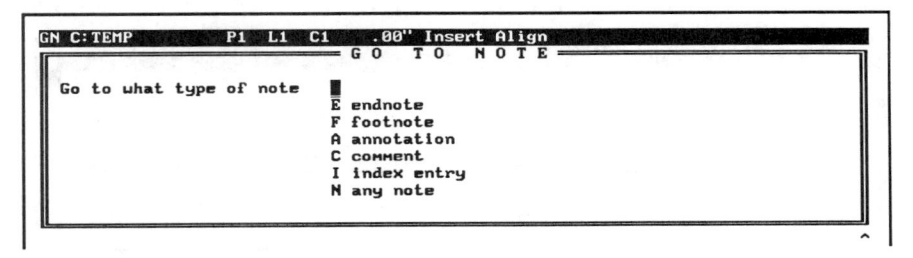

```
GN C:TEMP         P1  L1  C1     .00" Insert Align
                         G O   T O   N O T E
  Go to what type of note
                             E  endnote
                             F  footnote
                             A  annotation
                             C  comment
                             I  index entry
                             N  any note
```

Type the character corresponding to the type of note that you want to find. The cursor locates the next note within the document according to your entry.

CHANGING NOTE TYPES AT PRINTING   You can also change a note from one type to another by positioning the cursor at the beginning of the note, pressing Ctrl-ON, and typing V. The following screen is displayed.

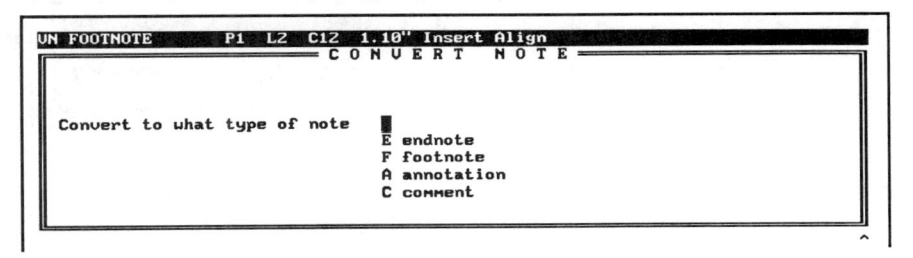

```
UN FOOTNOTE       P1  L2  C12  1.10" Insert Align
                         C O N V E R T   N O T E
  Convert to what type of note
                             E  endnote
                             F  footnote
                             A  annotation
                             C  comment
```

Convert the selected note by typing the appropriate letter. You can also use dot commands to convert from one type of note to another. The dot commands used to do this are:

Print comments as footnotes	.CV cf
Print comments as endnotes	.CV ce
Print endnotes as footnotes	.CV ef
Print footnotes as endnotes	.CV fe

When a note is converted, the note assumes the proper sequence number when printed.

PRINTING ENDNOTES ON A SPECIFIED PAGE   When you wish to print preceding endnotes on some page other than the last page within a document, you can enter the dot command .PE. The command tells WordStar to print all preceding endnotes on the current page. If you use .PE on two different pages within a document, only the unprinted endnotes following the first dot command are printed at the second dot command.

Module 37

ANNOTATION MARKS AND TEXT References to annotations are entered as a mark within a table or chart. A special screen, which is displayed by pressing Ctrl-ON and typing A, is used to enter annotation marks. The ANNOTATION MARK screen follows.

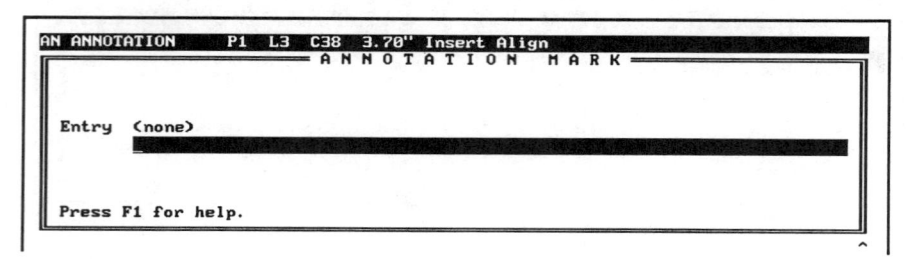

```
AN ANNOTATION      P1  L3  C38  3.70" Insert Align
                   = A N N O T A T I O N   M A R K =

    Entry  <none>
    ▓▓▓▓▓▓▓▓▓▓▓▓▓▓▓▓▓▓▓▓▓▓▓▓▓▓▓▓▓▓▓▓▓▓▓▓▓▓▓▓▓▓▓▓

    Press F1 for help.
```

Once typed, the annotation text is entered within a window like the footnote and endnote screens. Press Ctrl-KD to save the annotation text.

INDEX ENTRY The NOTES menu also lets you embed index entries within a document. This is done by pressing Ctrl-ON and typing I. An INDEX menu is displayed.

```
IN C:TEMP          P1  L3  C38  3.70" Insert Align
                   = I N D E X =
    Entry  <none>
    ▓▓▓▓▓▓▓▓▓▓▓▓▓▓▓▓▓▓▓▓▓▓▓▓▓▓▓▓▓▓▓▓▓▓▓▓▓▓▓▓▓▓▓▓
    Press F1 for help.
```

Type the index entry and press Return. The entry is displayed as a print control code within braces. However, it is not printed on the page. It is printed as an entry within an index. The page number on which the index entry occurs is included in the index. A second alternative to marking an index word or phrase with the INDEX menu is to enclose the word or phrase within Ctrl-PKs. Another is to use the dot command .IX followed by the index text. Module 42 explains indexing in more detail.

APPLICATIONS

Many documents require footnotes, endnotes, annotations, and comments. Footnotes are used as clarifying comments or references to other information sources. Endnotes are typically used as numbered bibliographies, which are ordinarily placed at the end of a document.

Comments are displayed but not printed. Comments are notes to yourself, which serve as reminders about document format, passages to be added later, or printing information.

Annotations are typically used in charts and tables to clarify certain entries. Annotation marks vary. They are often symbols, such as asterisks and daggers.

Footnotes, Endnotes, Annotations, and Comments

The ability to convert from one type of annotation to another lets you experiment with the printed format in order to select the one offering the clearest meaning. The conversion eliminates the need to retype all numbers and notes.

Being able to insert index entries within a line of text eliminates the need to place index entries on separate lines with the .IX dot command.

TYPICAL OPERATION

In this activity, you open a new document named TEMP and enter several footnotes. Next, the document is printed. Finally, the document is deleted at the OPENING menu.

1. Open a new document named TEMP.
2. Carefully perform steps a through c to create the following document. (Note that footnote 1 is at the end of the first sentence and that footnote 2 is at the end of the second sentence.)
   a. Type the text up to the point of the first footnote.
   b. Enter each footnote as encountered by pressing **Ctrl-ON**, typing **F**, entering the footnote text, and pressing **Ctrl-KD**.
   c. Alternately press **Ctrl-OD** to display the footnote number rather than the first 15 characters of the note.

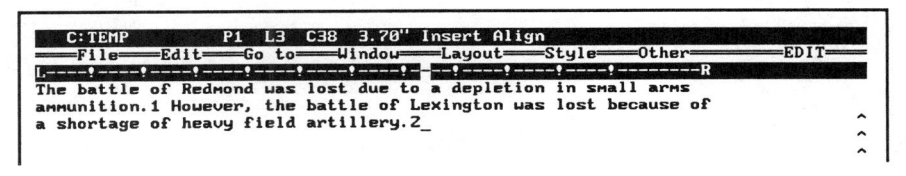

```
 C:TEMP         P1  L3   C38  3.70"  Insert Align
====File====Edit====Go to====Window====Layout====Style====Other====        ====EDIT====
L----!----!----!----!----!----!--!----!----!----R
The battle of Redmond was lost due to a depletion in small arms
ammunition.1 However, the battle of Lexington was lost because of
a shortage of heavy field artillery.2_
```

The footnote text is:

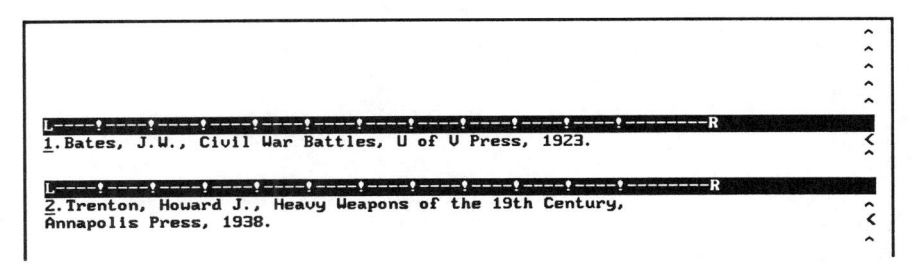

```
L----!----!----!----!----!----!----!----!----!--------R
1.Bates, J.W., Civil War Battles, U of V Press, 1923.
```

```
L----!----!----!----!----!----!----!----!----!--------R
2.Trenton, Howard J., Heavy Weapons of the 19th Century,
Annapolis Press, 1938.
```

3. Press **Ctrl-QR** to move to the beginning of the document.

107

Module 37

4. Press **Ctrl-ON**, type **G**, then type **F** and notice the following screen.

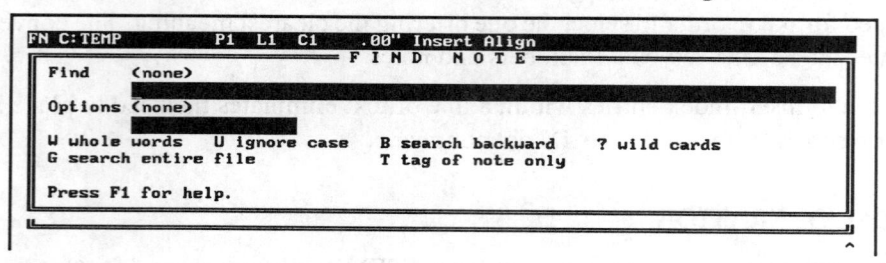

```
FN C:TEMP           P1  L1  C1    .00" Insert Align
                           F I N D   N O T E
 Find    (none)
 Options (none)
 W whole words    U ignore case   B search backward    ? wild cards
 G search entire file             T tag of note only
 Press F1 for help.
```

5. Type **1** and press **Return** on the Find prompt line. Then type **T** and press **Return** at the Options prompt. Notice that the cursor jumps to footnote tag 1.
6. Press **Ctrl-KD** to save the TEMP document.
7. From the OPENING menu, type **FP** and press **Return**.
8. Press **F10** to print the document. After printing, examine the footnotes.
9. Delete the TEMP document from the OPENING menu.
10. Turn to Module 54 to continue to learning sequence.

Module 38
FORMAT RULER

DESCRIPTION

The format ruler displays the position of margins, tabs, and the cursor. The format ruler occupies a line on the screen. If you want to use the line occupied by the format ruler to display one more line of your document, you can suppress the format ruler by pressing Ctrl-OT. You can turn it back on by pressing Ctrl-OT again.

The presence or absence of the format ruler has no effect on margin or tab locations. Text is typed in a normal manner. Although format ruler information is suppressed, WordStar continues to use established margins and tabs.

CHARACTERS ON THE FORMAT RULER There are several characters used on the format ruler to represent, or control, document format characteristics. These are summarized in the following table.

Character	Meaning	Default Setting
L	Left margin	0.00"
P	Paragraph margin	Stored at 0.00" in .RR 2
R	Right margin	6.50"
V	Temporary indent	Set with Ctrl-OG
!	Tab stop	Set every .5"
#	Decimal tab stop	Set with # in front of tab value
-	Columns between margins	

CHANGING THE FORMAT RULER You can change the format ruler display by changing the margin and tab settings as described in Modules 49, 84, and 85 using the MARGINS & TABS menu or with dot codes.

You can type a new ruler line in the document and read it into the top format ruler with Ctrl-OF. The cursor must rest on the created ruler when Ctrl-OF is pressed. If the cursor is on a line of text rather than a typed ruler line, left and right margins are adjusted to correspond to the length of the line of text. The changed format ruler is saved with the document. You can enter two periods at the left margin of the ruler line to convert it to a comment line that does not print.

Module 38

You can copy the current ruler into your text using Ctrl-OO and then edit the current settings to fit your needs. The changes are reflected in text that follows and in the format ruler at the top of the screen.

A new format ruler is created using the .RR dot command and typing in the desired settings. The original format ruler at the top of your screen is erased and the new one is mirrored when you end the line with a right margin setting. The ruler takes effect immediately and remains in effect until a new ruler is entered or the document is saved or abandoned.

Using these techniques, you can create any number of format rulers and store them with your documents.

The following example shows a typed format ruler within a document.

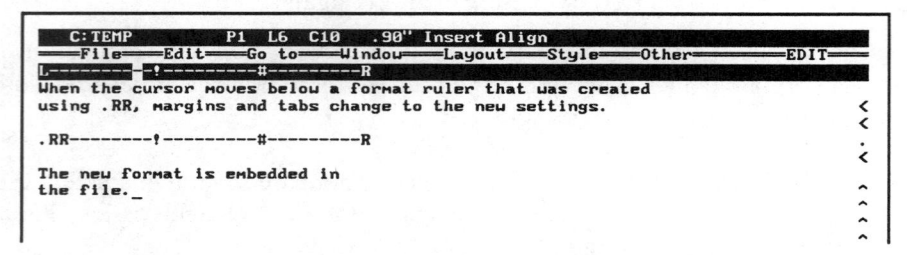

```
     C:TEMP          P1  L6  C10   .90" Insert Align
=====File====Edit====Go to====Window====Layout====Style====Other=========EDIT===
L--------!---------#---------R
When the cursor moves below a format ruler that was created
using .RR, margins and tabs change to the new settings.          <
                                                                 <
.RR--------!---------#---------R                                 .
                                                                 <
The new format is embedded in
the file._                                                       ^
                                                                 ^
                                                                 ^
                                                                 >
```

STORED FORMAT RULERS (PARAGRAPH STYLE GUIDES) WordStar lets you store up to ten format rulers, including the default ruler. These rulers are called with the .RR n dot command, where n is a number between 0 and 9. Rulers 0 through 2 are predefined. However, all rulers are easily modified with the WordStar Page Layout menu of the WSCHANGE utility.

Ruler number 0 (.RR 0) is WordStar's default ruler. The left margin is at 0.00" and the right margin is at 6.50". If .RR is used without a number, a value of 0 is assumed.

```
     C:TEMP          P1  L1  C1    .00" Insert Align
=====File====Edit====Go to====Window====Layout====Style====Other=========EDIT===
L----!----!----!----!----!----!----!----!----!----!--------R
.RR 0
_                                                                .
                                                                 ^
                                                                 ^
                                                                 ^
```

Ruler number 1 (.RR 1) indents the left and right margin by one tab.

```
     C:TEMP          P1  L1  C6         Insert Align
=====File====Edit====Go to====Window====Layout====Style====Other=========EDIT===
     L----!----!----!----!----!----!----!----!----!----!----R
.RR 1_
                                                                 .
                                                                 ^
                                                                 ^
                                                                 ^
                                                                 .
```

Format Ruler

Ruler number 2 provides a *hanging indent*. This format leaves the first line of a paragraph against the left margin and subsequent lines are indented to the first tab stop.

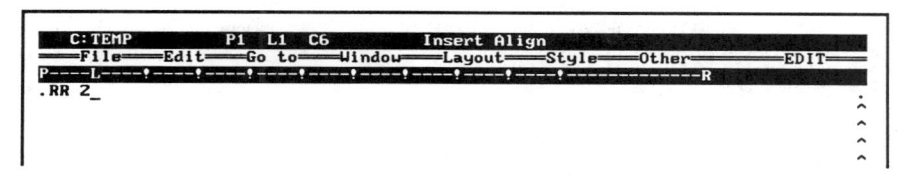

```
    C:TEMP            P1  L1  C6         Insert Align
======File=====Edit=====Go to=====Window=====Layout=====Style=====Other=============EDIT===
P----L----!----!----!----!----!----!----!----!--------------R
.RR 2_
```

Ruler numbers 3 through 9 are set to the default ruler values. This serves as a guideline during modification with WSCHANGE.

APPLICATIONS

Making format changes in a document, using various format rulers, lets you view the format changes as you create your document. The convenience of being able to store the appropriate formats within each document saves the time and effort of redefining the formats settings, such as tabs, margins, paragraph indents, and temporary indents each time you reopen the file.

Having the ability to create, store, and call up to seven format rulers is an extremely productive tool, letting you change the format of your document by typing the .RR dot command followed by the appropriate number.

Some experienced WordStar users prefer to suppress the format ruler in order to display more lines of text. After you have used WordStar for several weeks, you may want to set the menu help level to 0 or 1 and suppress the ruler with Ctrl-OT. However, most users continue to display the format ruler in order to check the position of margins, tabs, and the cursor.

TYPICAL OPERATION

In this activity, you use the predefined hanging indent format. Then you create your own format ruler with the .RR command.

1. Open the document MYLTR.
2. Type **.RR2** at the top of the document. With the cursor on Thanks press **Ctrl-B** to reformat the paragraph. Notice the following results.

Module 38

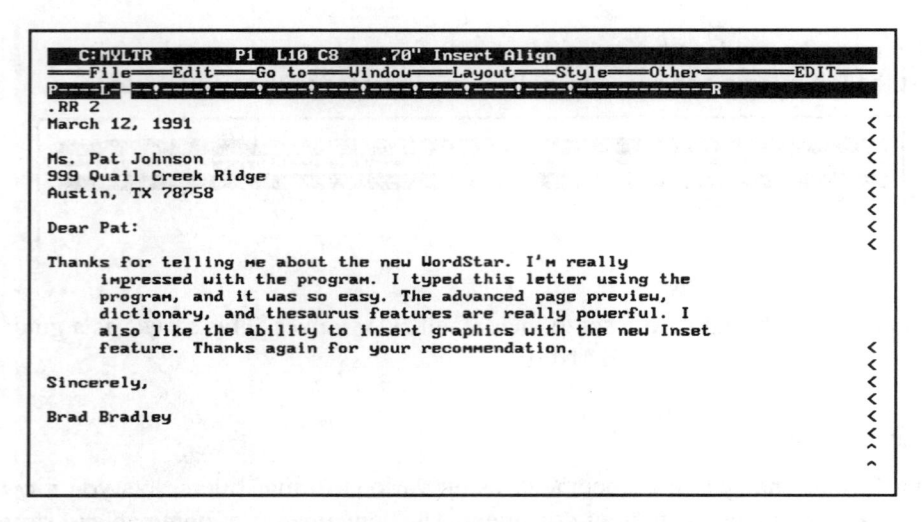

```
  C:MYLTR        P1  L10 C8    .70" Insert Align
====File====Edit====Go to====Window====Layout====Style====Other=========EDIT===
P----L--!----!----!----!----!----!----!----!--------------R
.RR 2
March 12, 1991

Ms. Pat Johnson
999 Quail Creek Ridge
Austin, TX 78758

Dear Pat:

Thanks for telling me about the new WordStar. I'm really
    impressed with the program. I typed this letter using the
    program, and it was so easy. The advanced page preview,
    dictionary, and thesaurus features are really powerful. I
    also like the ability to insert graphics with the new Inset
    feature. Thanks again for your recommendation.

Sincerely,

Brad Bradley
```

3. Press **Ctrl-R** to move the cursor to the top of the file.
4. Type **.RR** and create a new format ruler with new tab settings. Notice the new settings in the format ruler at the top of your screen.

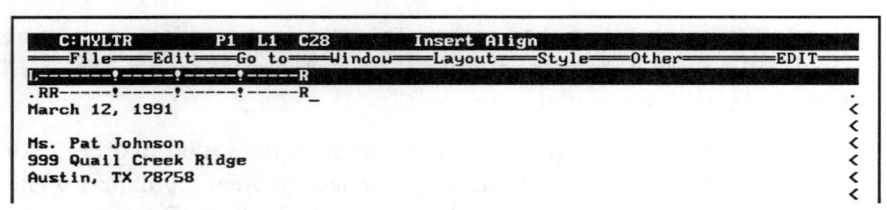

```
  C:MYLTR        P1  L1  C28      Insert Align
====File====Edit====Go to====Window====Layout====Style====Other=========EDIT===
L-------!-----!-----!-----R
.RR-----!-----!-----!-----R_
March 12, 1991

Ms. Pat Johnson
999 Quail Creek Ridge
Austin, TX 78758
```

5. Press **Ctrl-KQ** and type **Y** to abandon the document without saving.
6. Turn to Module 92 to continue the learning sequence.

Module 39
HELP AND HELP LEVELS

> Classic: ^JJ
> Pull-Down: Alt-O, select "Change help level..."

DESCRIPTION

Help is text that is displayed on the screen. The text provides information about a word processing operation. The operation may be in progress, or you may elect to display information about some specific area of interest.

On the other hand, help levels are set to provide different amounts of information about WordStar operations and prompts. These are designed to help you remember which keys to press or what to type when performing a specific word processing operation.

You can display help information about an operation being performed by pressing F1 from either the OPENING or EDIT menus. You can change the help level to display either less or more onscreen help information. A default help level exists when you start WordStar. You can change the default level using WordStar's WSCHANGE utility.

MENUS WordStar menus are described in detail in Module 2. Both pull-down and onscreen help menus are available. These menu systems are designed to assist you with word processing procedures. There are five possible help level settings, numbered 0 through 4. Help level 4 works in conjunction with the pull-down menus; 1 through 3 work with four levels of WordStar's classic menu system. Help level 0 suppresses onscreen key labels and allows hidden block changes. WordStar operates fastest at level 0.

As you become familiar with WordStar, you may want to use a low level of the classic menu system, which suppresses the display of menus, reduces the keystrokes involved in word processing operations, and speeds up WordStar's response time. When either the pull-down system is used or the classic menus are suppressed, more screen area is available to view your document. Some prompts such as "Are you sure?" are also suppressed with the level 0 help setting.

The classic help levels (1 through 3) are familiar to users experienced with earlier versions of WordStar. Level 3 provides maximum help information. During text entry operations, Level 2 suppresses the EDIT menu to provide a larger working screen. However, subordinate help menus are displayed when performing such things as block or onscreen format operations. Level 1 suppresses all menus and confirmation prompts; this level and level 0 are usually selected by experienced WordStar users.

Help levels are selected from the OPENING menu by typing OJJ; from the classic EDIT menu by pressing F1 twice or Ctrl-JJ. You can change help levels when the pull-down EDIT menu is in use by pressing Alt-O and typing JJ or selecting "Change help level..." and pressing Return.

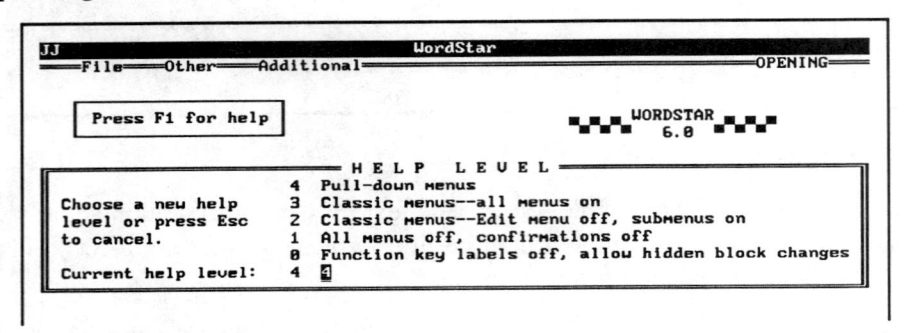

```
JJ                              WordStar
=File===Other===Additional=================================OPENING=

  Press F1 for help                      ▪▪▪ WORDSTAR ▪▪▪
                                         ▪▪▪   6.0    ▪▪▪
                          ═ H E L P    L E V E L ═
                       4  Pull-down menus
  Choose a new help    3  Classic menus--all menus on
  level or press Esc   2  Classic menus--Edit menu off, submenus on
  to cancel.           1  All menus off, confirmations off
                       0  Function key labels off, allow hidden block changes
  Current help level:  4  4
```

HELP INFORMATION WordStar has a comprehensive set of help information which is accessed by pressing F1 (or Ctrl-J using the classic menu). The help information is "context sensitive," i.e., pressing F1 during an operation often displays information about the operation in progress. Otherwise, you are prompted to type a letter that corresponds to the item about which you need help.

APPLICATIONS

Beginning WordStar users as well as seasoned users that need information on infrequently used commands can benefit from the onscreen help available with the F1 function key or Ctrl-J. With these help keys, you have answers to questions about every command.

Setting certain help levels frees up screen space and lets you view a larger portion of the document being edited. Suppressing help menus also increases the operational speed of WordStar, as word processing operations are delayed while WordStar writes the subordinate menus to the screen. You may want to use levels 1 or 0 to increase operational speed. If you need some help, you can restore the help level. Once you've checked your help menu, you can return to level 1 or 0.

TYPICAL OPERATION

In this activity, you display help information and then change the help level to 2. The activity assumes that your system is set to help level 4, which is the normal default value. Begin at the OPENING menu.

Help and Help Levels

1. Type **F** and then press **F1**. Notice that help information is displayed about the Speed Write selection since that is where the highlighted bar is resting. This is context sensitive help.

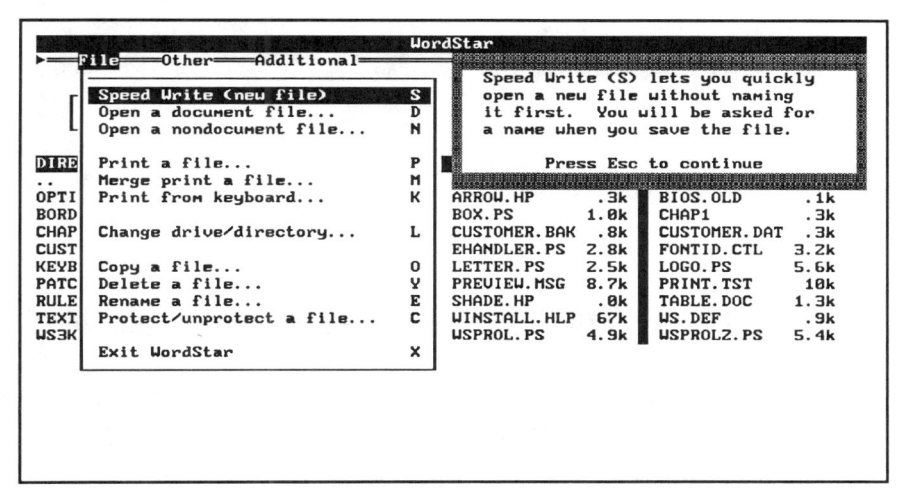

```
                              WordStar
  ╒══File═══Other═══Additional═╕
  │ Speed Write (new file)    S │  Speed Write (S) lets you quickly
  │ Open a document file...   D │  open a new file without naming
  │ Open a nondocument file...N │  it first. You will be asked for
DIRE                              a name when you save the file.
..    Print a file...        P
OPTI  Merge print a file...  M
BORD  Print from keyboard... K    ARROW.HP    .3k   BIOS.OLD    .1k
CHAP                              BOX.PS     1.0k   CHAP1       .3k
CUST  Change drive/directory...L  CUSTOMER.BAK .8k  CUSTOMER.DAT .3k
KEYB                              EHANDLER.PS 2.8k  FONTID.CTL  3.2k
PATC  Copy a file...         O    LETTER.PS   2.5k  LOGO.PS     5.6k
RULE  Delete a file...       Y    PREVIEW.MSG 8.7k  PRINT.TST   10k
TEXT  Rename a file...       E    SHADE.HP    .0k   TABLE.DOC   1.3k
WS3K  Protect/unprotect a file...C WINSTALL.HLP 67k WS.DEF      .9k
                                  WSPROL.PS   4.9k  WSPROL2.PS  5.4k
      Exit WordStar           X
```

2. Press **Esc** to lose the help display.
3. Type **D TEMP**, press **Return**, and type **Y** to display a new document file named TEMP.
4. Press **Alt-O** and use the arrow keys to highlight the Change help level selection from the pull-down menu. Press **Return** and notice the following screen.

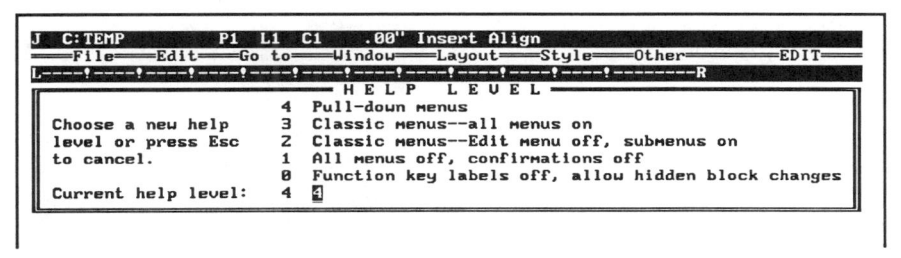

```
J  C:TEMP        P1 L1 C1    .00" Insert Align
  ═══File═══Edit═══Go to═══Window═══Layout═══Style═══Other═════════EDIT═
  L----!----!----!----!----!----!----!----!---------R
                         ── H E L P   L E V E L ──
                       4  Pull-down menus
  Choose a new help    3  Classic menus--all menus on
  level or press Esc   2  Classic menus--Edit menu off, submenus on
  to cancel.           1  All menus off, confirmations off
                       0  Function key labels off, allow hidden block changes
  Current help level:  4  4
```

5. Type **2**; WordStar returns to the word processing mode. Notice that the pull-down menu bar is suppressed, giving you an additional line for text.
6. Press **F1** and notice the HELP screen.

115

Module 39

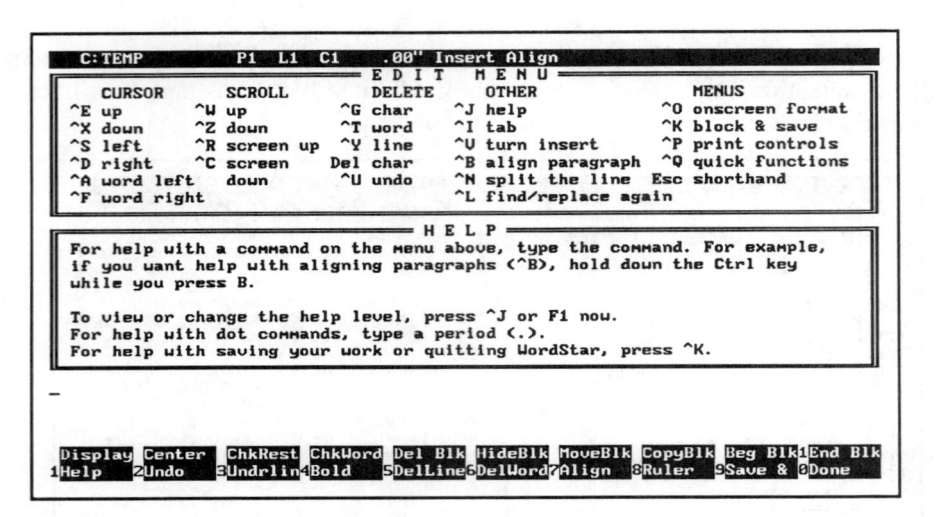

```
 C:TEMP          P1  L1  C1     .00" Insert Align
================================ E D I T   M E N U ================================
    CURSOR          SCROLL          DELETE       OTHER              MENUS
 ^E up           ^W up           ^G char      ^J help           ^O onscreen format
 ^X down         ^Z down         ^T word      ^I tab            ^K block & save
 ^S left         ^R screen up    ^Y line      ^U turn insert    ^P print controls
 ^D right        ^C screen       Del char     ^B align paragraph ^Q quick functions
 ^A word left       down         ^U undo      ^N split the line  Esc shorthand
 ^F word right                                ^L find/replace again
================================== H E L P ==================================
 For help with a command on the menu above, type the command. For example,
 if you want help with aligning paragraphs (^B), hold down the Ctrl key
 while you press B.

 To view or change the help level, press ^J or F1 now.
 For help with dot commands, type a period (.).
 For help with saving your work or quitting WordStar, press ^K.




 Display Center  ChkRest ChkWord Del Blk HideBlk MoveBlk CopyBlk Beg Blk End Blk
 1Help   2Undo   3Undrlin4Bold   5DelLine6DelWord7Align  8Ruler  9Save & 0Done
```

You may want to experiment with the display of help information by typing an EDIT menu key or a period. Press **Spacebar** to redisplay the editing screen.

7. Press **F1** twice and type **4** to reestablish help level 4.
8. Press **Ctrl-KQ** to abandon the document without saving changes.
9. Turn to Module 23 to continue the learning sequence.

Module 40
HYPHENATION

```
Classic:    ^OH
Pull-Down:  Not applicable
```

DESCRIPTION

WordStar's auto-hyphenation function automatically finds those words that fall at the end of a line and contain too many characters to fit. This is done by using reformat described in Module 70 with auto-hyphenation turned on. Auto-hyphenation is turned off and on with Ctrl-OH.

You can check to see if auto-hyphenation is on or off by displaying the ONSCREEN FORMAT menu with Ctrl-O. If auto-hyphenation is off, type H to turn it on. If you are satisfied with the status, press the Spacebar to leave it unchanged.

When auto-hyphenation is on, reformatting a paragraph automatically inserts hyphens at the appropriate locations within words.

You can also insert hyphens manually. Just move the cursor to the desired hyphenation break point within a word and press Ctrl-OE. WordStar inserts a *soft hyphen* and wraps the portion of the word to the right of the hyphen to the next line. The soft hyphen is ignored at print time if the word is moved from the end of the line as the result of subsequent reformatting. When this happens, the soft hyphen appears as an equal sign (=). You can insert a soft hyphen anywhere within a document by pressing Ctrl-OE.

APPLICATIONS

The auto-hyphenation function is another powerful word processing tool that saves time. It lets you type your text without being concerned about line endings and hyphenation decisions. Once typing is completed, you can move through your document and let WordStar help with hyphenation decisions by using auto-hyphenation and reformat. This is much faster than visually scanning each line ending to find hyphenation decisions.

TYPICAL OPERATION

In this activity, you turn on auto-hyphenation and reformat the paragraph. Then you abandon the document without saving it.

Module 40

1. Open the document MYLTR.
2. Press **Ctrl-OH** to turn auto-hyphenation on. Verify that it is on by displaying the ONSCREEN FORMAT menu.
3. Check that the cursor is at the beginning of the paragraph (line 9, column 1).
4. Press **Ctrl-B** to reformat with auto-hyphenation and notice that the word "impressed" is automatically hyphenated.

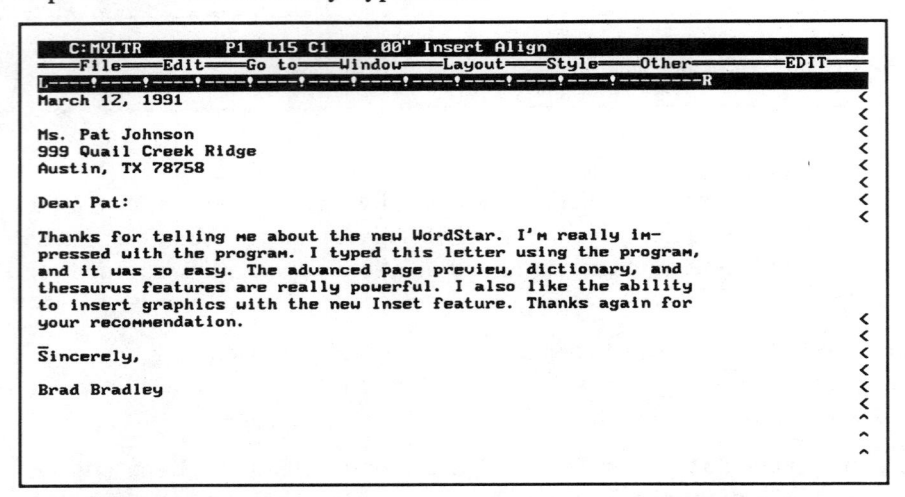

```
╔════════════════════════════════════════════════════════════╗
║ C:MYLTR        P1  L15 C1    .00" Insert Align             ║
║====File====Edit====Go to====Window====Layout====Style====Other====        ====EDIT====║
║L----!----!----!----!----!----!----!----!----!--------R                    ║
║March 12, 1991                                         <   ║
║                                                       <   ║
║Ms. Pat Johnson                                        <   ║
║999 Quail Creek Ridge                                  <   ║
║Austin, TX 78758                                       <   ║
║                                                       <   ║
║Dear Pat:                                              <   ║
║                                                           ║
║Thanks for telling me about the new WordStar. I'm really im-║
║pressed with the program. I typed this letter using the program,║
║and it was so easy. The advanced page preview, dictionary, and║
║thesaurus features are really powerful. I also like the ability║
║to insert graphics with the new Inset feature. Thanks again for║
║your recommendation.                                   <   ║
║                                                       <   ║
║Sincerely,                                             <   ║
║                                                       <   ║
║Brad Bradley                                           <   ║
║                                                       <   ║
║                                                       ^   ║
║                                                       ^   ║
╚════════════════════════════════════════════════════════════╝
```

5. Press **Ctrl-KQ** and type **Y** to abandon the document without saving.
6. Turn to Module 32 to continue the learning sequence.

Module 41
INDENT (PARAGRAPH TABS)

> ^OG

DESCRIPTION

Setting, using, and ending paragraph tabs, frequently called "indent tabs," are useful formatting tools provided by WordStar. You can establish a temporary left margin by indenting to any tab setting. Tab settings appear on the format ruler as exclamation marks (!).

To indent to the first tab, press Ctrl-OG. As you type text, the left margin adjusts to the first tab. The indent level remains in effect until you press Return (with the insert mode on), align the paragraph with Ctrl-B, or change the left margin with Ctrl-OL. Pressing Ctrl-OG twice advances the indent to the second tab. Pressing it three times advances it to the third tab, and so on. The indent level is indicated by a "V" in the format ruler.

You can adjust the position of an indent by setting the tab position. Using the classic menu system, this is done by pressing Ctrl-OI, typing the tab position (like 12), and pressing Return. Tabs are cleared by pressing Ctrl-ON, typing A for all, or a number for an individual tab. In the pull-down menu system, first press Ctrl-OI; then enter or clear each tab position (in inches) on the "Tabs" line, and press F10 to resume editing. Standard (or typewriter) tabs are described in more detail in Module 85.

Another related function is the paragraph margin (Module 49) where first lines of paragraphs are indented automatically. Paragraph tabs are set with .PM n, where n is a column number. A paragraph tab remains in effect until canceled with .PM 0 or .PM Return.

APPLICATIONS

Indent tabs are used when you have to move the left margin from left to right to indicate text subordination. This is a common practice in technical specifications and Roman-style outlines. Without the ability to indent paragraphs, it would be necessary to tab each line individually or adjust the left margin to each indent level.

Module 41

TYPICAL OPERATION

In this activity, you open a new document and practice using WordStar's indent function.

1. Open a new document named INDENT.
2. Press **Ctrl-OG** twice; notice the V in the format ruler that indicates the tab setting.

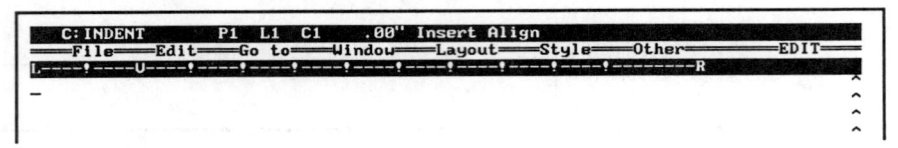

   ```
   C:INDENT       P1  L1  C1    .00" Insert Align
   ====File====Edit====Go to====Window====Layout====Style====Other====        =EDIT=
   L----!----U----!----!----!----!----!----!----!----!--------R
   ```

3. Type the following sentence and end it by pressing **Return**.

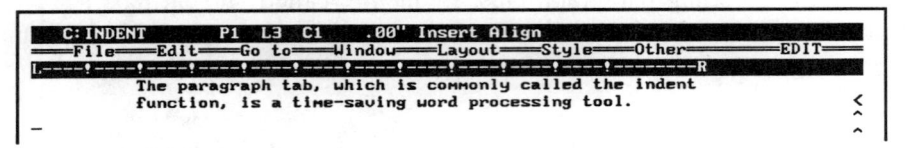

   ```
   C:INDENT       P1  L3  C1    .00" Insert Align
   ====File====Edit====Go to====Window====Layout====Style====Other====        =EDIT=
   L----!----!----!----!----!----!----!----!----!----!--------R
              The paragraph tab, which is commonly called the indent
              function, is a time-saving word processing tool.
   ```

Notice that the left margin is aligned with the second tab. Also notice how pressing Return moved the cursor to the left margin and removed the "V" in the format ruler.

4. Press **Ctrl-OG** three times and type the next two lines of text.

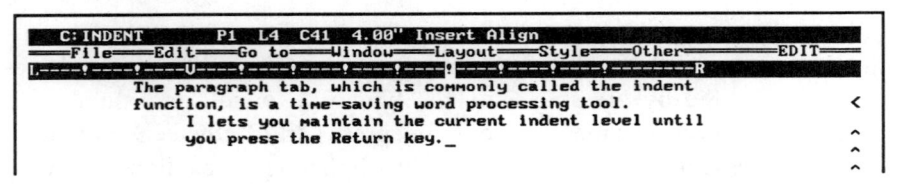

   ```
   C:INDENT       P1  L4  C41  4.00" Insert Align
   ====File====Edit====Go to====Window====Layout====Style====Other====        =EDIT=
   L----!----U----!----!----!----!----!----!----!----!--------R
              The paragraph tab, which is commonly called the indent
              function, is a time-saving word processing tool.
                   I lets you maintain the current indent level until
                   you press the Return key._
   ```

5. Check the indent alignment. It should correspond to the third tab.
6. Experiment with the indent tab until you are satisfied that you understand how it works.
7. Press **Ctrl-KQ** and type **Y** to abandon the document without saving.
8. Turn to Module 70 to continue the learning sequence.

Module 42
INDEXING

> Classic: ^PK, ^ON I, .IX
> Pull-Down: Alt-O, select "Index entry..."

DESCRIPTION

WordStar provides the ability to create an index file automatically. Indexes contain a list of selected (or key) words and the corresponding page numbers. Words are marked within a document in three ways. They are entered on a line using the .IX dot command, enclosed within Ctrl-PK control codes, or entered using the I option of the NOTES menu (see Module 37).

Once index entries are marked within a document, the document is saved. Next, OI is typed from WordStar's OPENING menu. The following Index prompts are displayed:

```
                          WordStar
                           INDEX
  File   C:\WS\TEMP.BAK

  Index every word    N    N
  Page numbers        All  A
  All/even/odd        All  A

  Press F1 for help.
```

Notice that in addition to marking specific words, you can index every word in the document. The prompt also lets you restrict indexing to certain pages. Pressing Return to each prompt indexes selected words only, uses all pages, and begins the indexing process. This process creates an index file. The filename is the same as the indexed document with the extension IDX. The contents of the .IDX file resemble the following:

```
Command, 3
Create,
  document, 1
  file, 2
Drought, 2
Dearth, 3
Echo, 1
Example, 2
```

Module 42

MARKING WORDS WITH CTRL-PK　You can mark specific words by pressing Ctrl-PK before and after the word. For example, to index Holland, press Ctrl-PK, type Holland, and press Ctrl-PK again. The word is displayed as ^KHolland^K within the line of text.

MARKING WORDS WITH CTRL-ON I　You can also use the NOTES menu to insert words within a document. While editing, press Ctrl-ON to display the NOTES menu (see Module 37 for more information about the NOTES menu). Then type I to display the INDEX menu.

```
IN C:TEMP           P1  L1  C1    .00" Insert Align
======================== I N D E X ========================
Entry  (none)
Press F1 for help.
```

Type the word or phrase to be indexed and press Return. The word is displayed like a print code, except that it is within braces. The index entry does not print, as it is for reference only.

MARKING A LINE OF WORDS　A line of text, or series of words, is marked using the .IX dot command. The words on dot command lines are suppressed during document printing and are only entered for index compilation purposes. The entry

```
.IX Sycamore trees
```

adds an entry to your index file that resembles the following:

```
Sycamore trees, 14
```

Because the text following .IX does not print during normal printing, you can enter a paragraph heading, block copy it, and then insert .IX at the left margin of the copied paragraph heading line. You can also enter a word or phrase followed by a comma and a modifier. For example, the entries

```
.IX Sycamore trees, bark
.IX Sycamore trees, leaves
```

are printed in the index file as follows:

```
Sycamore trees
  bark, 14
  leaves, 14
```

You can boldface the page numbers by placing a + sign in front of the entry. Following is an example of this technique.

```
.IX + Menu, Main
```

Indexing

If you want to refer the reader to another word without printing the current page number, you can precede the entry with a minus sign.

    .IX - CPU, see Central Processing Unit

APPLICATIONS

It is important to include a good subject and word index in large documents such as books and reports. The ability to let WordStar automatically compile an index saves hours of time that would otherwise be spent writing and sorting the words by hand. The ability to use .IX lets you mark paragraph headings or an entire expression or thought.

TYPICAL OPERATION

In this activity, you create a small document named TEMP and embed a series of index codes. Then you index the document, which creates the file TEMP.IDX. Finally, you open the index file to examine its contents.

1. Create and save the following document named TEMP. Place the indicated words within ^K's (produced with Ctrl-PK).

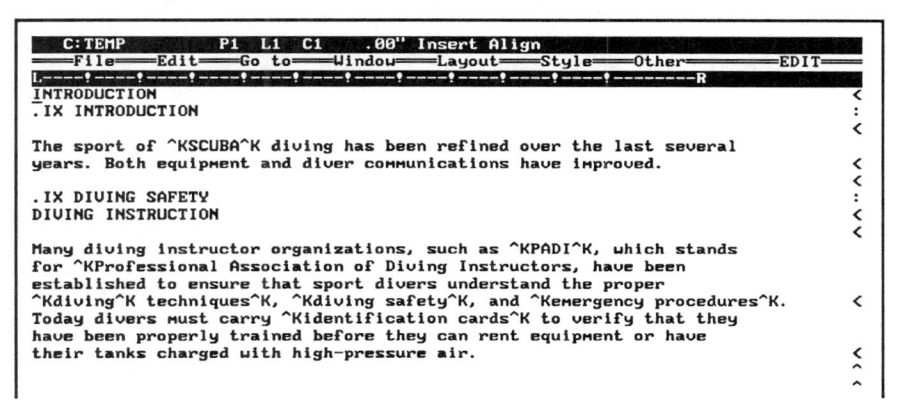

```
  C:TEMP          P1 L1 C1    .00" Insert Align
======File======Edit======Go to======Window======Layout======Style======Other==========EDIT====
L----!----!----!----!----!----!----!----!----!----!----!---------R
INTRODUCTION                                                                    <
.IX INTRODUCTION                                                                :
                                                                                <
The sport of ^KSCUBA^K diving has been refined over the last several
years. Both equipment and diver communications have improved.                   <
                                                                                <
.IX DIVING SAFETY                                                               :
DIVING INSTRUCTION                                                              <
                                                                                <
Many diving instructor organizations, such as ^KPADI^K, which stands
for ^KProfessional Association of Diving Instructors, have been
established to ensure that sport divers understand the proper
^Kdiving^K techniques^K, ^Kdiving safety^K, and ^Kemergency procedures^K.      <
Today divers must carry ^Kidentification cards^K to verify that they
have been properly trained before they can rent equipment or have
their tanks charged with high-pressure air.                                     <
                                                                                ^
                                                                                ^
```

2. At the OPENING menu, type **OI**, enter **TEMP**, and press **Return**. Press **F10** to accept all prompt default values.

3. Open the TEMP.IDX file after the indexing activity ceases and examine its contents.

123

Module 42

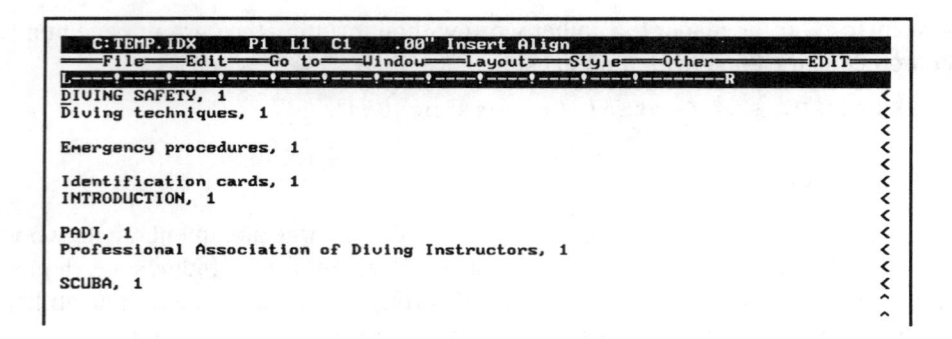

```
 C:TEMP.IDX      P1  L1  C1      .00" Insert Align
===File====Edit====Go to====Window====Layout====Style====Other====EDIT===
L----!----!----!----!----!----!----!----!----!--------R
DIVING SAFETY, 1                                              <
Diving techniques, 1                                          <
                                                              <
Emergency procedures, 1                                       <
                                                              <
Identification cards, 1                                       <
INTRODUCTION, 1                                               <
                                                              <
PADI, 1                                                       <
Professional Association of Diving Instructors, 1             <
                                                              <
SCUBA, 1                                                      <
                                                              ^
                                                              ^
```

4. Press **Ctrl-KQ** to abandon the document.
5. Erase the files TEMP and TEMP.IDX to recover disk space.
6. Turn to Module 73 to continue the learning sequence.

Module 43
INSERT ON/OFF

> ^V, Ins

DESCRIPTION

Now that you know how to open a document and move around in it, it's a simple matter to master the use of the insert function. Unless changed during the installation process, WordStar normally displays "Insert" on the status line when the program is first used. When insert is on, all typed text is inserted, pushing following text to the right and down as new material is entered.

Press Ctrl-V (or Ins) to turn insert off. Now the Insert display disappears and typed text replaces any text at the cursor position. This is called *strikeover*. Press Ctrl-V (or Ins) again to turn Insert on again.

If you are typing in a new, blank area of a document, the status of the insert function is unimportant. You can enter new text in either the insert or strikeover mode.

APPLICATIONS

The insert function is normally used to insert new text within an existing document, although it can be on when a new document is created. Many WordStar users leave Insert on. Others like to use it only when an insertion is required.

The strikeover mode (Insert off) is used to enter text and spaces in place of existing characters, words, sentences, or paragraphs. Otherwise, the superseded text must be eliminated with a delete operation.

If you are editing boxed text or multi-column tables, it is best to turn Insert off. This avoids misalignment of text or rules to the right or the cursor.

TYPICAL OPERATION

In this activity, you create a document called TEMP and use insert and strikeover to edit the text.

1. Create a document named TEMP.

Module 43

2. Type **I thought I saw a wild dog in the forest.** Your screen should resemble the following illustration.

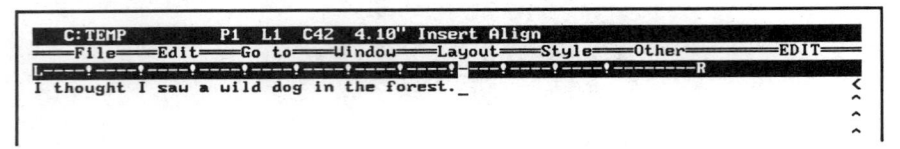

```
 C:TEMP           P1  L1  C42  4.10"  Insert Align
===File====Edit====Go to====Window====Layout====Style====Other=======EDIT===
L----!----!----!----!----!----!-!----!----!----!--------R
I thought I saw a wild dog in the forest._
```

3. Move the cursor to the "w" in the word "wild."
4. With Insert on, type **large** followed by a space.
5. Move the cursor to the "d" in the word "dog."
6. Turn off the insert function by pressing **Ctrl-V** or **Ins**.
7. Type **cat** over the word dog. The line now reads:

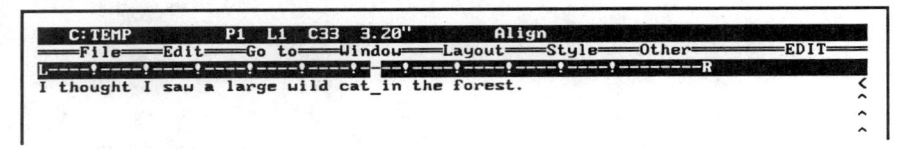

```
 C:TEMP           P1  L1  C33  3.20"         Align
===File====Edit====Go to====Window====Layout====Style====Other=======EDIT===
L----!----!----!----!----!-!--!----!----!----!--------R
I thought I saw a large wild cat_in the forest.
```

8. Spend a minute or so experimenting with insert and strikeover, then restore the document as shown in step 7. Press **Ctrl-KD** to save the document for later use.
9. Turn to Module 21 to continue the learning sequence.

Module 44
INSET (MERGING GRAPHICS)

> Start Inset
>   Classic: ^P&
>   Pull-Down: Alt-O, select "Start Inset..."
> Insert graphics tag
>   Classic: ^P*
>   Pull-Down: Alt-O, select "Insert graphics tag..."

DESCRIPTION

WordStar's graphic Inset program is used to produce documents that have text and computer graphics. Graphics can be placed on the same page as text or on a separate page, depending on your needs. Computer graphics are typically pictures or charts used to convey your written ideas more clearly.

The Inset program is installed initially using the WordStar WINSTALL program. Mark the Inset program for inclusion in WordStar and the installation routine automatically copies the necessary files into an INSET subdirectory.

STARTING AND STOPPING INSET Once installed, INSET can be started from within WordStar while editing a document (press Ctrl-P&), or you can run it as a separate program outside of the WordStar program. This is done by logging the \WS\INSET directory, typing INSET from the DOS prompt, and pressing Return. When Inset is started from within WordStar, it is terminated automatically when you exit WordStar. If started directly from the DOS prompt, you can type RI and press Return to remove Inset from your computer's memory.

The first time you use Inset, Inset's installation program, called Setup, runs automatically. This causes a menu to be displayed. Here, you select a monitor and printer that are compatible with your computer. If you change your monitor or printer, use Inset's SETUP program to reconfigure Inset for your new equipment. It is critical that Inset, WordStar, and your graphic program be installed for identical monitors for proper operation.

Once properly installed and running, the Inset program resides in memory as a popup, or terminate-stay-ready (TSR), program. Once Inset is loaded into memory, you can display a graphic screen, start Inset by pressing a hot key (Ctrl-left Shift or Alt-left Shift) and then capture, name, and save the displayed picture. The saved picture file assumes the extension .PIX. Make a habit of saving your graphic files to either the \INSET subdirectory or to a subdirectory set up especially for .PIX files. This makes finding your picture files easier when you are ready to insert them into a document.

Graphic Tags Once all necessary graphic screens have been displayed, captured, and saved, you can begin editing a document using WordStar. To insert a picture, press (Ctrl-P*), type a .PIX filename, and press Enter. A graphic tag is inserted within your document at the current cursor position. The graphic tag contains the name of the graphic file within square brackets. This is the name you gave the picture when you captured and saved it.

To view the graphic on the page of a document being edited, use WordStar's Advanced Page Preview. Press Ctrl-OP to view the page with the displayed graphic in place. You can also pop up the Inset program while editing a document to view or modify a graphic on the screen. This is achieved by either pressing Ctrl-P& to load and run Inset, or by pressing the Inset hot keys (Ctrl-left Shift or Alt-left Shift) if you have already loaded Inset into memory. Use the Esc key to back out of Inset program menus and to return to WordStar editing.

Inset and Your Computer's Memory When a file containing a picture is printed, Wordstar automatically loads Inset into memory to accomplish output of the picture. During printing, you cannot run other memory-intensive operations, such as performing spelling checks or opening second document windows. When printing is completed, you can resume normal use of all WordStar features.

THE INSET MENU When the Inset program is active, menu options are displayed at the bottom left corner of the screen.

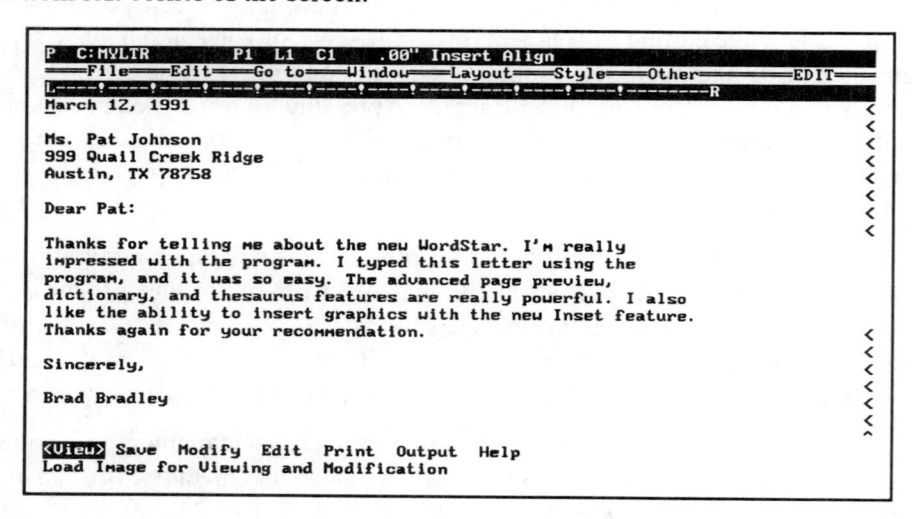

```
P C:MYLTR         P1 L1 C1    .00" Insert Align
====File====Edit====Go to====Window====Layout====Style====Other====    ====EDIT====
L----!----!----!----!----!----!----!----!----!----!----!--------R
March 12, 1991                                                        <
                                                                      <
Ms. Pat Johnson                                                       <
999 Quail Creek Ridge                                                 <
Austin, TX 78758                                                      <
                                                                      <
Dear Pat:                                                             <

Thanks for telling me about the new WordStar. I'm really
impressed with the program. I typed this letter using the
program, and it was so easy. The advanced page preview,
dictionary, and thesaurus features are really powerful. I also
like the ability to insert graphics with the new Inset feature.
Thanks again for your recommendation.                                 <
                                                                      <
Sincerely,                                                            <
                                                                      <
Brad Bradley                                                          <
                                                                      ^
<View> Save  Modify  Edit  Print  Output  Help
Load Image for Viewing and Modification
```

Each of the menu selections performs a different operation. These are described in the following list.

View (Load Image for Viewing and Modification)—Displays a filename prompt. Type \WS\INSET* and press Return to see a list of PIX files.

Save (Save Screen Image and Modifications)—Displays a filename prompt. Type a new name or use the existing name to replace the viewed file.

Modify—Used to change the viewed graphic. Selections are:

> *Image*—Used to modify the viewed graphic as follows:
>
>> Clip—Isolate (or clip) and save part of a displayed graphic screen. Use your cursor keys to place a border around the desired area. You can also use the Home and PgDn keys for diagonal border movement. Pressing Return moves from the upper left border to the lower right border. Pressing Return a second time exits the Clip operation. Use the Shift key with the cursor keys for faster movement.
>>
>> Rotate—You may rotate the image Left (90 degrees counter-clockwise), Horizontal (no rotation), Right (90 degrees clockwise).
>>
>> Expand—Expand as a multiple (1x through 6x), in proportion to text size (Col/Row), or in inches (width and height).
>>
>> Ink—Prints graphic as selected: Std prints standard inks and gray scales; Invert is the same as Std where black and white prints exactly as displayed; B&W causes black to print white and white to print black. Table lets you pick 0 (if screen color is black) or 1 (if screen color is light white); Contrast lets you select between Random (original patterns), Gray (halftone patterns for gray images), and High (for high-contrast patterns, such as text). The Display option displays color palette control as 0 (default) or 1 for CGA two-color and black and white (or additional colors depending on your system monitor and the way you last responded to Inset's Setup menu).
>>
>> Pass—This selection controls the number of passes used by the printer at print time. This includes a single or double pass.
>>
>> Border—Lets you add a border around the picture at print time.
>>
>> Status—Displays statistical and dimensional information about the currently viewed graphic.
>>
>> NoMenu—Suppresses Inset menu for full screen display of graphic.

Module 44

ReSize—Resizes the image by modifying its outline. You can use the cursor keys to adjust the left and bottom edges of the graphic; the gray + and gray – keys are used to move the right edge of the graphic right or left. Two selections, Natural and Scale, show printer size or screen size, respectively. Scale gives you finer adjustment.

PreView—Displays the text and graphics layout on the screen as last resized.

Edit—Used to modify a viewed graphic or to draw additional elements such as lines, circles, and boxes.

Line—Line draws a line at the cross hair position. Press Return to start a line, move the crosshair, and press Return again to end the line. You may change color and line width by pressing F2. The color selection corresponds to how Inset was last setup. Typically, black = 0, white = 1, and width numbers use a range from 1 to 8.

Rect—Draws a box. You may fill with or without one of 16 stored patterns. As with Line, press Return to start the rectangle, move the cursor keys to draw the rectangle, and press Return again to end the rectangle.

Circle—Draws a circle or oval; uses the same control keys as Line and Rect.

Dots—Used to draw freehand. Ideal for signature entry.

Magnify—Zooms in for closeup work; similar to "fat bit" editing used by drawing programs.

Text—Used to enter, accept (making it permanent), undo, and select a direction (Right, Down, Left, or Up), height, width, italics (on or off), and a text font. (Text fonts may be 8 X 7 dots for an IBM Graphics printer or you can load your fonts from disk.)

Block—Copies or moves a blocked area from one location to another. You can also import a clipped image into the currently displayed graphic.

Fill—Fills an enclosed area with a color.

Erase—Erases a selected element from a dot to a rectangular area.

Options—Sets colors and line width; also accessed by pressing F2 during graphic editing.

Print—Used for direct control over your printer.

Go—Starts printing operation.

Margins—Sets left margin for printed output.

Formfeed—Sends a form feed command to the printer.

Down—Sends a line feed command to the printer.

Up—Sends a reverse line feed command to the printer.

TOF—Sets the top of form for proper vertical printer alignment.

Inset (Merging Graphics)

Output—Sets up printing parameters. Changes here are also made to the Inset Setup parameters.

Offset—Enter a column number that corresponds to the desired left-margin offset for the current graphic (.PIX) element.

Pitch—Sets the column width corresponding to the selected pitch (characters per inch). Examples of common pitch settings are 10, 12, 15, and 17.

Quality—Lets you select between draft and letter quality. Draft quality prints fastest on most printers; letter quality produces the highest quality and normally makes multiple passes to ensure dark copy.

Fast—Creates a .FST file which causes fast printing. Response to this option is Yes or No.

Help (Help - Overview)—Provides help for the Inset Help utility. Pressing F1 during an Inset operation displays help about that operation.

MIXING GRAPHICS AND COLUMNAR TEXT   WordStar lets you place graphics and text on the same line. However, you must perform a few simple operations to ensure that the text portion does not overwrite the graphics. First, reset the margins to keep text out of the graphics area. Then turn on absolute leading (auto-leading must be off).

Picture to the Left of Text   Follow these simple steps to position a picture to the left of a column of text:

1. Set the paragraph margin at the left side of the picture.
2. Set the left margin at the left edge of text.
3. Also set a tab stop at the left edge of the text (left margin and tab stop at the same column position).
4. Insert the picture (press Ctrl-P*, type .PIX filename, and press Enter).
5. Press Tab to move to the left margin; type your text.
6. Use Advanced Page Preview to view your page (Ctrl-OP). If your image is too wide, press Ctrl-P& and use the Modify-Resize-Natural option (use the cursor keys) to adjust the picture size to fit. Then review the page and use Zoom as necessary to ensure the picture and text fit properly.

Picture to the Right of Text   You can also adjust the picture to fit to the right of a column of text. Follow these simple steps.

1. Set your margins and type the column of text that will be printed to the left of the picture.
2. Check that Auto Align (Ctrl-OA) is turned off.
3. Move your cursor to the end of the first line of text.
4. Use the Spacebar to move to the left edge of the picture.

5. Press **Ctrl-P***, the .PIX filename, and press Enter.
6. Use Advanced Page Preview and Zoom as necessary to check your page layout. You may wish to use Inset to resize the picture if it is too wide (see previous step 6).

APPLICATIONS

The Inset program lets you capture computer-displayed pictures, modify them as necessary for inclusion into a document, insert them at the desired location, and then print them in place. The ability to modify pictures using Inset's Modify and Edit features lets you create high-quality business documents that include graphs, charts, logos, and even cursive signatures.

Inset lets you add text, lines, boxes, circles, and patterns; resize pictures to fit page areas; touch up fuzzy areas; change colors; and even control the way your printer operates. You can also clip portions of pictures and assemble them in the desired orientation. All of these capabilities make WordStar and Inset an ideal commercial publishing tool.

TYPICAL OPERATION

In this activity you use Inset to prepare a document containing both text and graphics. Be sure that Inset has been properly set up for your computer's display system.

1. Open a new document named TEXTPIC.
2. Type **.RM 3"** and press **Return**. Ensure that the period is at column 1.
3. Check that Auto Align (Ctrl-OA) is turned off.
4. Type the following text as shown.

   The illustration to the right is one that is supplied with WordStar 6.0. It is ideal for showing how to mix text and pictures on the same page.

5. Move the cursor back to the line containing .RM 3" and press **Ctrl-Y** to delete the line containing the dot command. Notice that the margin settings return to normal.
6. Press **Ctrl-QD** to move to the end of the first line. Then press the **Spacebar** until the cursor is at column 36 (check the status line).
7. Press **Ctrl-P***, point to the supplied file named MAN.PIX, and press **Return**. Notice that the file tag is inserted at the current cursor position.

Inset (Merging Graphics)

```
 C:TEXTPIC        P1  L1  C1    .00"  Insert Align
===File====Edit====Go to====Window====Layout====Style====Other========EDIT===
L----!----!----!----!----!----!----!----!----!----!--------R
                                                                          <
The illustration to the right      [C:\WS\INSET\MAN.PIX]
is one that is supplied with
WordStar 6.0. It is ideal for
showing how to mix text and
pictures on the same page.                                                <
                                                                          ^
                                                                          ^
                                                                          ^
```

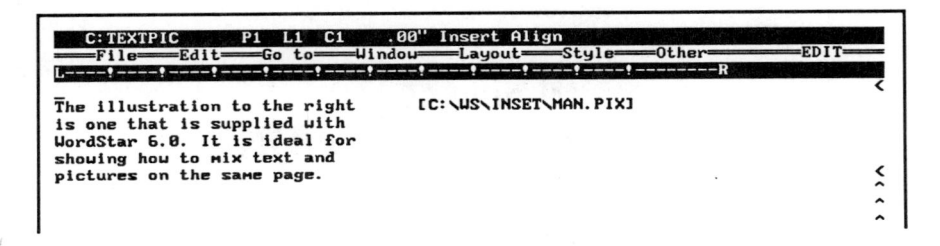

8. Press **Ctrl-OP** to use Advanced Page Preview. Type **V2** for a 2X zoom and a closer look at the page.
9. Type **RC** to return to the current page.
10. Press **Ctrl-KQ** and type **Y** in response to the "Abandon anyway..." prompt.
11. Turn to Module 61 to continue the learning sequence.

Module 45
JUSTIFICATION OFF/ON

```
Classic:     ^OJ
Pull-Down:   Alt-L, select "Right-justify text"
```

DESCRIPTION

Justification produces a smooth right-hand margin. WordStar justifies the right-hand margin of each line of text by inserting extra spaces between words. When right-hand justification is on, the end of each line of text is aligned at the right margin.

Justification is turned off and on with Ctrl-OJ. You can check to see if justification is on or off by displaying the ONSCREEN FORMAT menu with Ctrl-O. If you want to leave your modes unchanged, press the Spacebar.

If a document is created with justification off (with a "ragged" right-hand margin), you can justify the right margin by turning justification on and reformatting each paragraph of text. Conversely, if a document is created with justification on, you can make it ragged right by turning justification off and reformatting each paragraph. You can use a convenient shortcut to reformat all paragraphs. Place the cursor at the top of the document and press Ctrl-QU (see Module 70).

You can set justification on or off within a file using the dot command .OJ on/off. Simply type ".OJ on" at the left margin on a line preceding the text you want to justify. Type ".OJ off" at the left margin when you want to end justification. These settings are saved and stored as a part of your document (see Module 24, Dot Commands).

When a document is printed, what you see is what you get. If the document is displayed justified, it prints justified. The same is true for unjustified text. WordStar's default condition is to have justification on. Many users prefer justification off, and they set the justification default to off at WordStar installation with WSCHANGE. You can use WordStar's preview function by pressing Ctrl-OP to examine the appearance of a full page (see Module 54).

APPLICATIONS

Right-hand justification is usually used for appearance. Many people prefer a smooth right-hand margin to a ragged one. Others believe that the extra spaces make the text too loose. In addition, gapped text is often harder to read.

Justification Off/On

TYPICAL OPERATION

In this activity, you turn justification on and reformat the text in the document MYLTR. Then you abandon the document without saving.

1. Open the document MYLTR.
2. Turn justification on with **Ctrl-OJ**. Verify the justification status by looking for RgtJust on the status line at the top of the screen and notice the dot command added at the top of the file.
3. Move the cursor to the beginning of the paragraph (line 9, column 1) and press **Ctrl-B** to reformat the paragraph as justified.

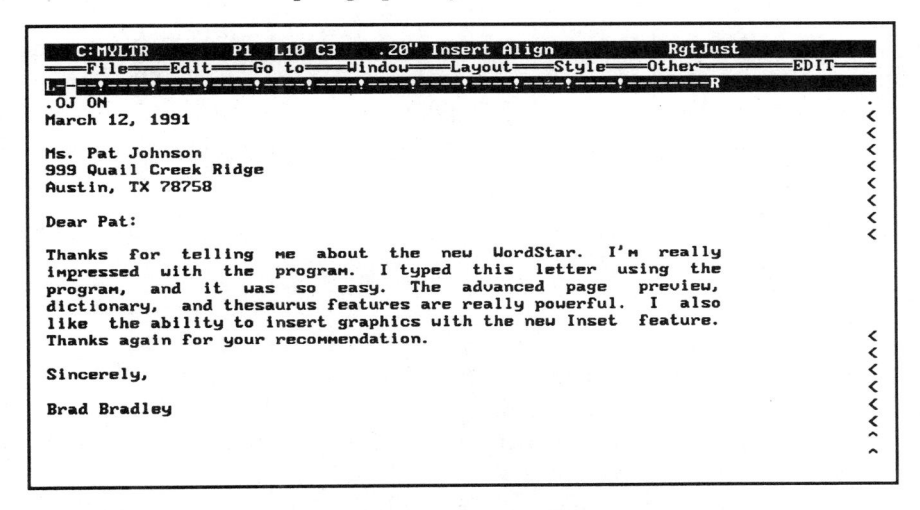

```
  C:MYLTR         P1  L10 C3    .20" Insert Align          RgtJust
=====File====Edit====Go to====Window====Layout====Style====Other====EDIT====
L--!----!----!----!----!----!----!----!----!----!----!---------R
.OJ ON                                                              .
March 12, 1991                                                      <
                                                                    <
Ms. Pat Johnson                                                     <
999 Quail Creek Ridge                                               <
Austin, TX 78758                                                    <
                                                                    <
Dear Pat:                                                           <
                                                                    <
Thanks for telling  me about  the new WordStar.  I'm really
impressed with  the  program.  I typed this  letter  using the
program,  and  it  was  so  easy.  The  advanced  page   preview,
dictionary,  and thesaurus features are really powerful.  I also
like  the  ability to  insert graphics with the  new Inset  feature.
Thanks again for your recommendation.                               <
                                                                    <
Sincerely,                                                          <
                                                                    <
Brad Bradley                                                        <
                                                                    <
                                                                    ^
                                                                    ^
```

4. Press **Ctrl-KQ** and type **Y** to abandon the document without saving.
5. Turn to Module 40 to continue the learning sequence.

135

Module 46
LINE NUMBERING

> .l# ss,c

DESCRIPTION

You can print line numbers in the left margin at a specified column using the line number dot command. The line numbers are not displayed in the document, but they are printed. The format is .l# ss,c where ss is spacing (single or double) and style (d for continuous or p for starting over on each page) and ,c is the column number where the line numbers will print.

You can print line numbers beginning 1 on each page or number continuously throughout the document. Here are a few examples that illustrate ways to use the line numbering dot command.

.l# p1,5	Prints line numbers beginning with 1 on each page, single spaced; the line numbers are located 5 columns to the left of column 1.
.l# d2,3	Prints continuous line numbers throughout the document, double spaced; line numbers are positioned 3 columns (the default) to the left of column 1.
.l# 0	Turns off line numbering.

If you place the line number dot command to start or stop in the middle of a page, the command takes effect on the following page. If your page offset is not wide enough to accommodate the line numbers, WordStar automatically increases the page offset to provide sufficient space for line numbering.

APPLICATIONS

You may want to number lines on the draft of a document so that reviewers can suggest changes by line number. If you are printing computer program source code for a language such as Pascal, C, dBASE, or Quick BASIC, line numbers can serve as reference tools for people who check the code.

TYPICAL OPERATION

In this activity, you create a document named TEMP and print it to see the effect of the line number dot command.

1. Open a new document named TEMP.
2. Type the dot command **.l# p1,4** at the left margin on the line above the first line of the document.
3. Type a few paragraphs of text.
4. Press **Ctrl-KD** to save the document.
5. Type **FP**, enter TEMP as the File, and press **F10** to print the document.
6. Check the line numbers on the printed document. The line numbers should appear similar to the following illustration.

```
 1   |This is a sample few paragraphs to demonstrate the results of
 2   |using line numbering in a file.
 3   |
 4   |This is a sample few paragraphs to demonstrate the results of
 5   |using line numbering in a file.
 6   |
 7   |This is a sample few paragraphs to demonstrate the results of
 8   |using line numbering in a file.
 9   |
10   |
11   |
12   |
13   |
14   |
15   |
```

7. Type **FY** and **TEMP**, press **Return**, and type **Y** to delete the TEMP document.
8. Turn to Module 26 to continue the learning sequence.

Module 47
LINE SPACING

```
Classic:    ^OS
Pull-Down:  Alt-L, select "Single/double spacing..."
```

DESCRIPTION

WordStar's normal (or default) line spacing setting is single space. However, you can use the ONSCREEN FORMAT menu to set the line spacing to a value of 1 to 9. This is done at the EDIT menu by pressing Ctrl-OS and then typing the desired number. For example, typing 2 gives double spacing (one blank line between each line of text). A value of 3 provides two spaces between each line of text, and so on.

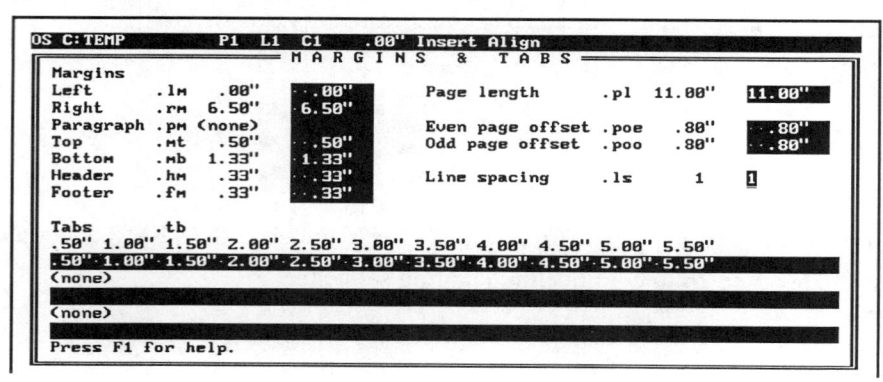

```
OS C:TEMP           P1 L1 C1    .00" Insert Align
═══════════════════ M A R G I N S   &   T A B S ═══════════════════
Margins
 Left        .lm    .00"     .00"
 Right       .rm   6.50"    6.50"   Page length       .pl  11.00"   11.00"
 Paragraph   .pm  (none)
 Top         .mt    .50"     .50"   Even page offset  .poe   .80"     .80"
 Bottom      .mb   1.33"    1.33"   Odd page offset   .poo   .80"     .80"
 Header      .hm    .33"     .33"
 Footer      .fm    .33"     .33"   Line spacing      .ls     1       1

Tabs         .tb
 .50" 1.00" 1.50" 2.00" 2.50" 3.00" 3.50" 4.00" 4.50" 5.00" 5.50"
 .50" 1.00" 1.50" 2.00" 2.50" 3.00" 3.50" 4.00" 4.50" 5.00" 5.50"
(none)

(none)

Press F1 for help.
```

You can also use the .LS dot command followed by a number that corresponds to the line spacing. For example, .LS 2 sets double spacing.

WordStar indicates the selected line spacing on the screen in two places. First, your document is displayed in the selected line spacing. In addition, the right-hand side of the status line displays the line spacing value when it is greater than 1. A "LinSp-2" designates double spacing.

The selected line spacing takes effect during automatic word wrap as text is created. Existing text is reformatted or realigned to a changed line spacing with Ctrl-B for a paragraph or Ctrl-QU for the entire document, beginning at the cursor position.

You can select the line space setting and make it a part of your file by using the dot command .LS followed by the number to indicate the spacing. This method eliminates having to reset the default value line spacing every time the file is opened.

APPLICATIONS

Being able to specify line spacing eliminates the need to insert blank lines by manually inserting *hard returns* between each line. (A hard return is inserted by pressing the Return key with Insert on.) Double spacing is normally used for draft copies and manuscripts, which are subject to copy editing marks. Once the editorial marks are incorporated into the final document, it is normally reformatted in single space and printed.

Another benefit of WordStar's automatic line spacing function is being able to visualize a double- or triple-spaced document on the screen, which is helpful when positioning page breaks within a multiple-page document.

TYPICAL OPERATION

In this activity, you open a file, set the line spacing to 2, and type a few lines of text.

1. Open a new document named TEMP.
2. Press **Ctrl-OS**, type **2** and press **F10**.
3. Check the status line for the line spacing value and type the following text.

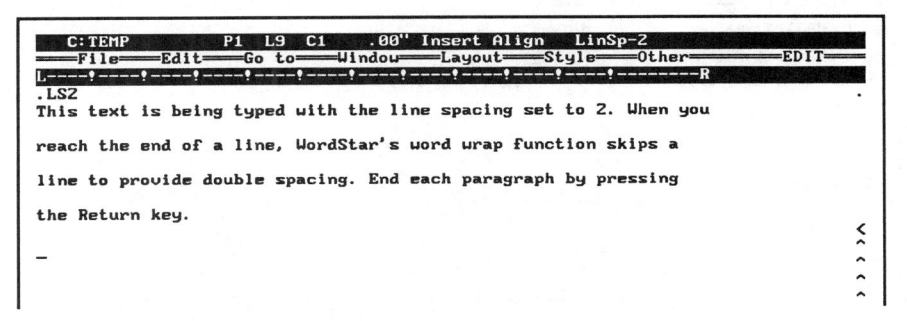

```
    C:TEMP          P1  L9  C1      .00" Insert Align    LinSp-2
====File====Edit====Go to====Window====Layout====Style====Other====        =EDIT=
L----!----!----!----!----!----!----!----!----!----!----!--------R
.LS2
This text is being typed with the line spacing set to 2. When you

reach the end of a line, WordStar's word wrap function skips a

line to provide double spacing. End each paragraph by pressing

the Return key.
                                                                    <
                                                                    ^
  _                                                                 ^
                                                                    >
                                                                    >
                                                                    >
                                                                    ^
```

4. Press **Ctrl-KQ** and type **Y** to abandon without saving.
5. Turn to Module 41 to continue the learning sequence.

Module 48
MAILLIST

```
Classic:     A, then M from Classic OPENING menu
Pull-Down:   A, select "MailList..." from the OPENING menu
DOS prompt:  Type WSLIST and press Return
```

DESCRIPTION

The WordStar MailList program is supplied with two prepared forms, or *template* files. One has the filename WSLIST.DEF, the other is INVNTORY.DEF. With these two forms are companion data files having the same name with the extension DTA. These are data files that contain information entered, edited, and rearranged (or sorted) using MailList. Sorted versions of the data files are given new names and saved.

The MailList program is started by running the program WSLIST from the DOS prompt or by selecting MailList using the OPENING menu's Additional selection.

The MAILLIST menu display offers a number of options.

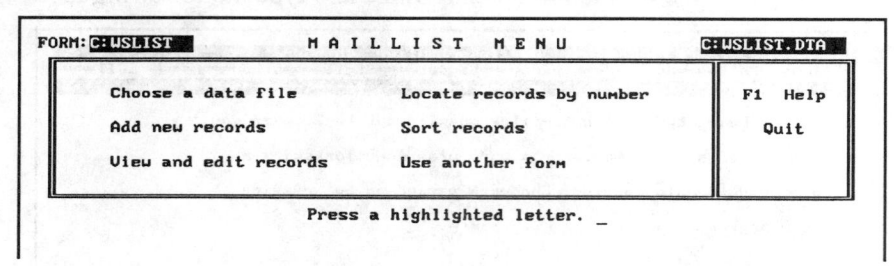

```
FORM: C:WSLIST           M A I L L I S T   M E N U        C:WSLIST.DTA

       Choose a data file       Locate records by number     F1  Help
       Add new records          Sort records                     Quit
       View and edit records    Use another form

                      Press a highlighted letter. _
```

The WSLIST.DEF (definition) file is the default form file used by the MailList program. You can choose a data file with the MAILLIST menu C option, or another directory and form using the U option. This lets you choose the INVNTORY.DEF form file.

Following is a list of the MAILLIST menu options and brief descriptions of each.

MailList

Option	Description
C	Places either the WSLIST or INVNTORY file in use.
A	Adds a new record to the end of the selected file.
V	Lets you view and edit the data file.
L	Locates a record by record number.
S	Rearranges records in either ascending or descending order using one or more selected fields as a basis for the sort. Sorted records are saved in a new data file.
U	Lets you put another form in use.

THE WSLIST AND INVNTORY FILES The WSLIST and INVNTORY forms are illustrated for your review.

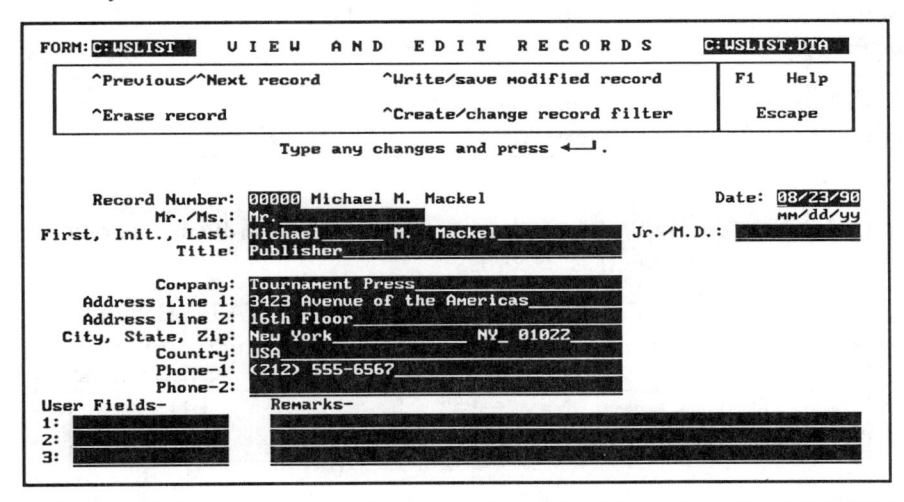

```
FORM: C:WSLIST       VIEW  AND  EDIT  RECORDS        C:WSLIST.DTA
   ^Previous/^Next record      ^Write/save modified record    F1   Help
   ^Erase record               ^Create/change record filter   Escape
               Type any changes and press ↵.

   Record Number: 00000 Michael M. Mackel         Date: 08/23/90
         Mr./Ms.: Mr.                                   MM/dd/yy
First, Init., Last: Michael    M.    Mackel       Jr./M.D.:
          Title: Publisher
        Company: Tournament Press
  Address Line 1: 3423 Avenue of the Americas
  Address Line 2: 16th Floor
  City, State, Zip: New York          NY_ 01022
        Country: USA
        Phone-1: (212) 555-6567
        Phone-2:
User Fields-      Remarks-
1:
2:
3:
```

```
FORM: C:INVNTORY       ADD  NEW  RECORDS           C:INVNTORY.DTA
   ^Copy from previous record   ^Write/save record in file   F1   Help
                                                             Escape
               Type data and press ↵.

   Record Number: 00000                     Date: 00/00/00 MM/dd/yy
           Item:             Code:        Status:
    Description:

        Account:
       Quantity:
          Price:
User Fields-      Remarks-
1:
2:
3:
```

MAILLIST CONTROL KEYS The control keys associated with editing and moving between *fields* and *records* within a MailList data file are described in the following table. A few definitions are in order for clarification. A field is a single entry within the displayed screen, such as an Address or Country. The entire display screen and all information associated with it comprise a record. Records are numbered sequentially, and the record number is displayed at the top of the screen. MailList menus are displayed that correspond to the current operation. The keys used to perform specific operations that correspond to the selected menu are displayed in the menu. Common control keys used to move between and within fields of a displayed record are contained in the following list.

Keys	Use
Backspace	Rub out previous character
Ctrl-T or Home	Top of record (first field)
Ctrl-L or End	End of record (last field)
Ctrl-S or ←	Previous character
Ctrl-D or →	Next character
Ctrl-A or Ctrl ←	Previous field
Ctrl-F or Ctrl →	Next field

MAILLIST OPERATIONS The following paragraphs describe the operations used to add, view, locate, and sort MailList records.

Choose A Data File Type C to display the CHOOSE A DATA FILE menu.

```
FORM: C:USLIST        C H O O S E   A   D A T A   F I L E      C:USLIST.DTA
     ┌──────────────────────────────────────────────┬─────────────┐
     │ Type or highlight a name. Press ←┘.          │ F1   Help   │
     │ Move highlighting with cursor keys.          │             │
     │ Erase errors with Backspace.                 │ Escape      │
     └──────────────────────────────────────────────┴─────────────┘

     Data file or directory to use? _
```

Then choose a data file that corresponds to the selected form file. If you have used the sort operation to create new data files, they are listed for your selection. Type the filename or point to it using the cursor keys. This option also lets you choose a different directory if necessary. To select the INVNTORY form file, use the MAILLIST menu U option.

Adding Records Records are added to the selected data file by first typing A to display the ADD NEW RECORDS menu shown below.

```
FORM: C:USLIST         A D D   N E W   R E C O R D S      C:USLIST.DTA
     ┌──────────────────────────────────────────────┬─────────────┐
     │ ^Copy from previous record   ^Write/save record in file │ F1   Help   │
     │                                              │ Escape      │
     └──────────────────────────────────────────────┴─────────────┘
                       Type data and press ←┘.
```

Information is added by typing it in the appropriate field. Pressing Ctrl-W and Return saves the record and advances you to the next one. When adding multiple records, you can copy information from the previous record by positioning the cursor in the desired field and pressing Ctrl-C. When you are finished adding records, press Esc to redisplay the MAILLIST menu.

Viewing Records   To view records, type V from the MAILLIST menu to display the VIEW AND EDIT RECORDS menu.

```
FORM: C:USLIST    V I E W   A N D   E D I T   R E C O R D S   C:USLIST.DTA
  ^Previous/^Next record      ^Write/save modified record    F1   Help
  ^Erase record               ^Create/change record filter        Escape
                Type any changes and press ←┘.
```

Use Ctrl-P and Ctrl-N to move between records. Press Ctrl-E to erase a record. If you change a record, press Ctrl-W to save the changes. If you want to restrict viewing and editing to records containing a common element, such as those in a certain city, press Ctrl-C to display the filter screen. Then type characters in the appropriate field(s) that match the records you want to view or edit.

Locate Records By Number   Typing L displays the following menu.

```
FORM: C:USLIST    L O C A T E   R E C O R D S   B Y   N U M B E R  C:USLIST.DTA
  ^Previous/^Next number      ^Write/save modified record    F1   Help
  ^Erase record                                                    Escape
              Type the record number and press ←┘.
```

Type a record number and press Return to display a specific record. Move between records with Ctrl-P (previous) and Ctrl-N (next). Erase records with Ctrl-E. If you modify a record, save it with Ctrl-W. Press Esc to redisplay the MAILLIST menu.

Sort Records   Type S to display the SORT RECORDS menu.

```
SORT ORDER RECORDNO      S O R T   R E C O R D S        C:USLIST.DTA
  ^Erase order         ^Use this order              F1   Help
  ^Key field           Ascend/Descend
  ^Save sort order     ^Choose/Create sort order         Escape
              Press a highlighted letter or number.
```

The sort process lets you rearrange the data file using one or more key fields to control the sort. Select a key field with the cursor (use Ctrl-F and Ctrl-A to move between fields). Press Ctrl-K to designate the field for sort control. A series of numbers within the field shows the precedence. For example, if the Company field is filled with 1s, it becomes the first key field.

Typing A or D at the end of the field changes between ascend and descend. Point to the next field, such as Last name, and press Ctrl-K to make it the second key field. This sorts records by company and last name within the company.

Press Ctrl-U to save and sort the list to the named file; press Ctrl-S to save the sort order without actually sorting the data file. The sort order can be chosen at a later time; then use Ctrl-U to sort the data.

Remember that leading spaces are significant to a sort. If a field contains leading spaces, they will have a lower sort value than numbers or letters. Also, if you plan to sort by date, use the date displayed at the lower right-hand corner of your screen, which sorts by year, month, and date (yymmdd) rather than by month, day, and year.

Choose A Form You can choose another form by typing U to display the CHOOSE A FORM menu.

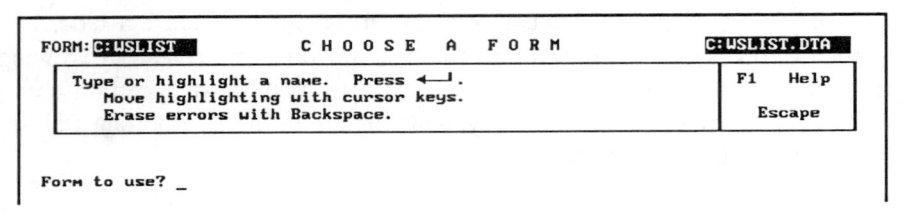

```
FORM: C:WSLIST          C H O O S E   A   F O R M          C:WSLIST.DTA
    Type or highlight a name. Press ←┘.              F1    Help
        Move highlighting with cursor keys.
        Erase errors with Backspace.                       Escape


   Form to use? _
```

This menu lets you select another form menu. For example, if you are using the WSLIST form and wish to switch to the INVNTORY form, type U, type or highlight the INVNTORY.DEF form name, and press Return.

USING THE DATA FILE WITH MERGE PRINT You can use the information within a data file with merge print. If you use the nondocument editing mode to examine the records and fields within a data file, you determine the file structure and its organization. You quickly see that each record is on a line. The fields are separated by commas. By assigning a variable name to each field on the read variable line (.RV) of a merge print master document, you can prepare directories, mail labels, and a number of other documents that use the information within the MailList data file.

APPLICATIONS

The MailList program provides two ready-to-use template files for maintaining mail lists and inventory information. The mail list (WSLIST) is ideal for managing customer, personnel, or membership information. The ability to use the WSLIST.DTA file with Merge Print means you can prepare and print a variety of form letters to the listed people with little effort. The ability to sort and filter by category lets you manipulate and organize your data files to satisfy specific requirements.

The INVNTORY form and corresponding data file are ideal for maintaining inventory information. The User Fields, which are available in both the WSLIST and INVNTORY files, give you a great deal of flexibility. You can use these fields for additional information or for added control of sorts and filters.

TYPICAL OPERATION

In this activity, you use the WSLIST form and add three records. Then you sort these records in last name order. Begin at the DOS prompt of the directory containing the WSLIST program, definition, and data files. (If you installed your WordStar program using WSSETUP, you may find MailList in your OPTIONS subdirectory.)

1. Type **WSLIST** and press **Return**. Notice that the MAILLIST menu is displayed.

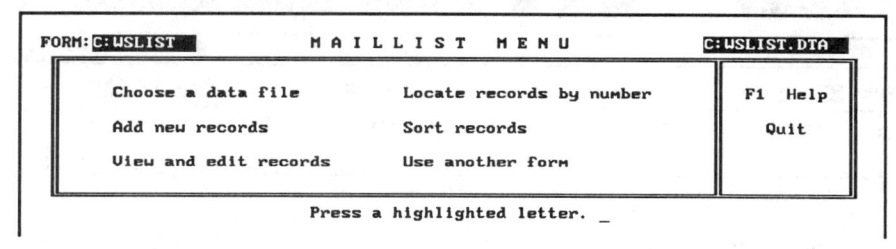

```
FORM: C:WSLIST              M A I L L I S T   M E N U              C:WSLIST.DTA

        Choose a data file          Locate records by number      F1  Help
        Add new records             Sort records                  Quit
        View and edit records       Use another form

                        Press a highlighted letter. _
```

2. Type **C**, select WSLIST.DTA as the data file, and press **Return**.
3. Type **A** to add new records.
4. Enter the following three records. Press **Ctrl-W** and press **Return** as each record is completed. Press **Esc** after the third record is saved.

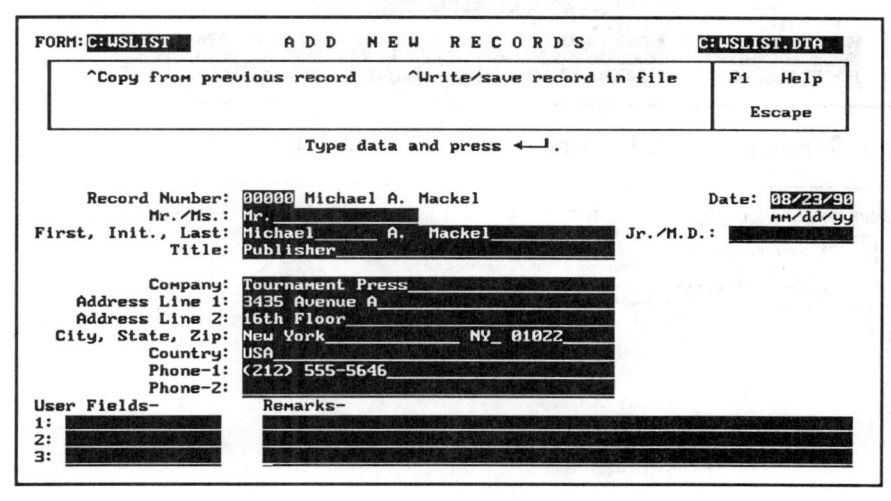

```
FORM: C:WSLIST              A D D   N E W   R E C O R D S          C:WSLIST.DTA
        ^Copy from previous record    ^Write/save record in file   F1  Help
                                                                   Escape
                        Type data and press ↵ .

        Record Number: 00000 Michael A. Mackel          Date: 08/23/90
              Mr./Ms.: Mr.                                    mm/dd/yy
    First, Init., Last: Michael      A.   Mackel      Jr./M.D.:
                Title: Publisher
              Company: Tournament Press
        Address Line 1: 3435 Avenue A
        Address Line 2: 16th Floor
      City, State, Zip: New York              NY  01022
              Country: USA
              Phone-1: (212) 555-5646
              Phone-2:
        User Fields-        Remarks-
        1:
        2:
        3:
```

145

Module 48

```
FORM: C:WSLIST         ADD  NEW  RECORDS           C:WSLIST.DTA
     ^Copy from previous record     ^Write/save record in file    F1   Help
                                                                  Escape
                       Type data and press <─┘.

       Record Number: 00001 Daniel M. Dansford              Date: 08/23/90
             Mr./Ms.: Mr.                                         mm/dd/yy
  First, Init., Last: Daniel      M.    Dansford    Jr./M.D.:
               Title: Operations Manager
             Company: Crandal Auto Supply
      Address Line 1: 35 Wrecker Road
      Address Line 2: P.O. Box 377
    City, State, Zip: Princetown            TX_  75099
             Country: USA
             Phone-1: (214) 445-5565
             Phone-2:
 User Fields-              Remarks-
 1:
 2:
 3:
```

```
FORM: C:WSLIST         ADD  NEW  RECORDS           C:WSLIST.DTA
     ^Copy from previous record     ^Write/save record in file    F1   Help
                                                                  Escape
                       Type data and press <─┘.

       Record Number: 00002 Dorothy L. Graskey             Date: 08/23/90
             Mr./Ms.: Ms.                                        mm/dd/yy
  First, Init., Last: Dorothy     L.    Graskey     Jr./M.D.:
               Title: Vice President
             Company: Trans Trucking
      Address Line 1: 8998 Highway Drive
      Address Line 2: P.O. Box 3838
    City, State, Zip: Naples                FL_  33937
             Country: USA
             Phone-1: (817) 644-7824
             Phone-2:
 User Fields-              Remarks-
 1:
 2:
 3:
```

5. Type **S** from the MAILLIST menu to display the Sort Records menu.

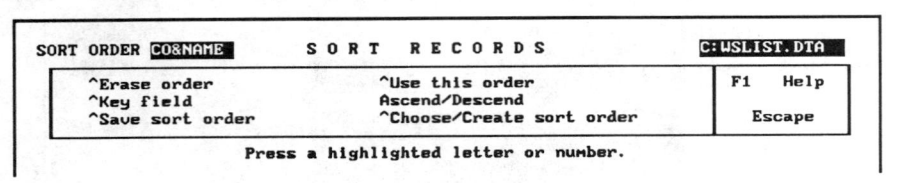

```
SORT ORDER CO&NAME       SORT  RECORDS            C:WSLIST.DTA
       ^Erase order           ^Use this order          F1   Help
       ^Key field             Ascend/Descend
       ^Save sort order       ^Choose/Create sort order     Escape
                  Press a highlighted letter or number.
```

6. Press **Ctrl-C**; then type **CO&NAME** as a new data file name and press **Return**.
7. Using Ctrl-F and Ctrl-A to move between fields, move to the Company field and press **Ctrl-K**; then move to the Last name field and press **Ctrl-K**. Your screen should resemble the following illustration.

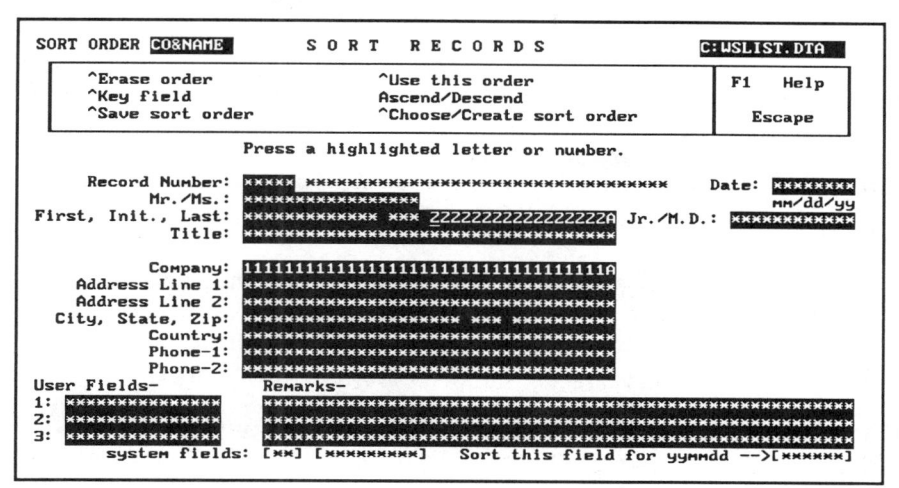

```
┌─────────────────────────────────────────────────────────────────────────┐
│ SORT ORDER CO&NAME      S O R T   R E C O R D S        C:USLIST.DTA    │
│    ┌─────────────────────────────────────────────────┐  ┌────────────┐  │
│    │ ^Erase order          ^Use this order           │  │ F1   Help  │  │
│    │ ^Key field            Ascend/Descend            │  │            │  │
│    │ ^Save sort order      ^Choose/Create sort order │  │    Escape  │  │
│    └─────────────────────────────────────────────────┘  └────────────┘  │
│              Press a highlighted letter or number.                      │
│     Record Number: xxxxx xxxxxxxxxxxxxxxxxxxxxxxxxxxxx   Date: xxxxxxxx │
│           Mr./Ms.: xxxxxxxxxxxxxxxx                           mm/dd/yy  │
│  First, Init., Last: xxxxxxxxxxx xxx 2222222222222222A Jr./M.D.: xxxxxxx│
│             Title: xxxxxxxxxxxxxxxxxxxxxxxxxxxxx                        │
│           Company: 1111111111111111111111111111111A                     │
│    Address Line 1: xxxxxxxxxxxxxxxxxxxxxxxxxxxxx                        │
│    Address Line 2: xxxxxxxxxxxxxxxxxxxxxxxxxxxxx                        │
│   City, State, Zip: xxxxxxxxxxxxxxxxxxxxxx xxx xxxxxxxxx                │
│           Country: xxxxxxxxxxxxxxxxxxxxxxxxxxxxx                        │
│           Phone-1: xxxxxxxxxxxxxxxxxxxxxxxxxxxxx                        │
│           Phone-2: xxxxxxxxxxxxxxxxxxxxxxxxxxxxx                        │
│ User Fields─       Remarks─                                             │
│ 1: xxxxxxxxxxxxxxx  xxxxxxxxxxxxxxxxxxxxxxxxxxxxxxxxxxxxxxxxxxxxxxxx    │
│ 2: xxxxxxxxxxxxxxx  xxxxxxxxxxxxxxxxxxxxxxxxxxxxxxxxxxxxxxxxxxxxxxxx    │
│ 3: xxxxxxxxxxxxxxx  xxxxxxxxxxxxxxxxxxxxxxxxxxxxxxxxxxxxxxxxxxxxxxxx    │
│       system fields: [xx] [xxxxxxxxx]  Sort this field for yymmdd -->[xxxxxx] │
└─────────────────────────────────────────────────────────────────────────┘
```

8. Press **Ctrl-U** to use the selected order. This sorts the data file.
9. Upon completion, press **Esc** to return to the MAILLIST menu and type **V** to view the sorted file.
10. Move between records and notice how they are now in Company order. If more than one name existed per company, the names would be alphabetized within the company records.
11. Press **Esc** and type **Q** to quit.
12. Turn to Module 57 to continue the learning sequence.

Module 49
MARGIN SETTINGS

> Classic: ^OR, ^OL
> Pull-Down: Alt-L, select "Margins and tabs..."

DESCRIPTION

If you look at your format ruler when you first open a document for word processing, you notice that WordStar has a set of default margins. These are either those that are supplied with your new copy of the WordStar program, or those that are established during installation. The margin values are adjusted with WordStar's WSCHANGE program.

You can temporarily alter margin settings to suit your word processing job. When you press Ctrl-OR or Ctrl-OL (where R and L stand for "right" and "left"), WordStar 6.0 displays a MARGINS & TABS screen. This screen lets you set margins, page length, tab positions, and line spacing. This screen is shown in the following illustration.

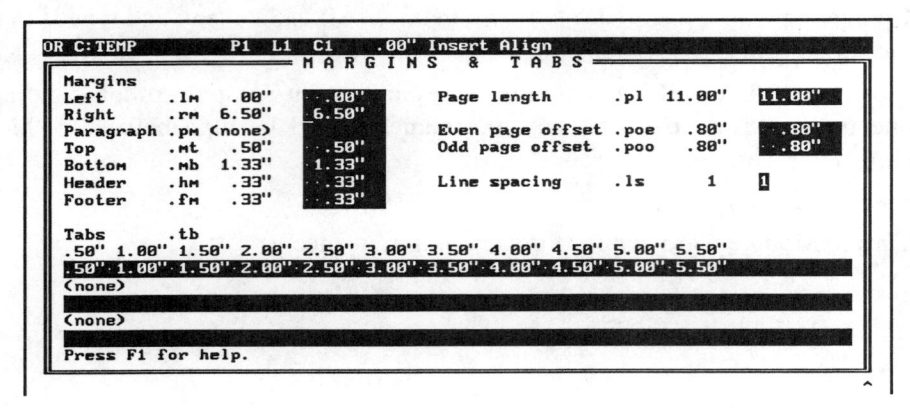

```
OR C:TEMP          P1  L1  C1    .00" Insert Align
                  ═══════ M A R G I N S  &  T A B S ═══════
 Margins
 Left        .lm    .00"      ..00"    Page length      .pl  11.00"   11.00"
 Right       .rm   6.50"      .6.50"
 Paragraph   .pm  (none)               Even page offset .poe   .80"     .80"
 Top         .mt    .50"      ..50"    Odd page offset  .poo   .80"     .80"
 Bottom      .mb   1.33"      1.33"
 Header      .hm    .33"      ..33"    Line spacing     .ls    1        1
 Footer      .fm    .33"      ..33"

 Tabs        .tb
  .50"  1.00"  1.50"  2.00"  2.50"  3.00"  3.50"  4.00"  4.50"  5.00"  5.50"
  .50"  1.00"  1.50"  2.00"  2.50"  3.00"  3.50"  4.00"  4.50"  5.00"  5.50"
 (none)

 (none)

 Press F1 for help.
```

Margins are set by typing the position of the right or left margin in inches. For example, a right margin value of 7.5" sets the right margin at 7.5 inches. Once the value is typed, press F10 to accept the value and resume editing.

DOT COMMANDS Notice the dot commands, .lm (left margin), .rm (right margin), through .ls (line spacing). These codes are entered at the left margin (the period must be in column 1) and take effect immediately. Dot commands are described in detail in

Margin Settings

Module 24. Users who are familiar with dot commands often enter dot commands directly into the text rather than displaying the MARGINS & TABS screen to enter values.

Margin settings established with dot commands .LM or .RM are followed by either the number of the margin column, or by an inch value. These are easily inserted wherever margin changes are required and are saved as a part of the file.

For example, if you wish to indent both margins 15 characters and the current left and right margins are 1 and 65, you can use .LM 15 and .RM 50. After the indented material is typed, return to the original margin values with .LM 1 and .RM 65. This is a time-saving shortcut.

If you wish to indent the left margin 1 inch, you can use .LM 1".

THE EFFECT OF MARGIN AND TAB SETTINGS The left and right margin settings control the way a document is displayed on the screen and, ultimately, the way it is printed. Before you set your margins, you should be familiar with a few important concepts.

Looking at the MARGINS & TABS screen, notice the Margin and Page length columns. The margins control the line length. These settings work in conjunction with the format ruler. The default left margin setting is 0.00", which is at column 1. The right margin tells you how many inches long the line is from column 1. If WordStar is installed to use your printer and its fonts, the line length should be given in inches. Then, regardless of the print font (or pitch) used, WordStar takes care of the character count for you. If you are using a draft printer that uses 10 pitch as its primary text font, you may have to do some manual conversions when you use compressed print (17 pitch) as your alternate font. This is done with the .RM dot command. For example, if you set right margin to 65 characters for the 10-pitch font, you can adjust it to 110 with .RM 110 for compressed (17 pitch) printing. This is normally selected using Ctrl-PA. The alternate font tag, ALTERNATE, is displayed. Return to normal printing with Ctrl-PN.

PAGE OFFSET VALUES The Even and Odd page offset values, which control the white space at the left edge of a printed page, also control your page layout. These page offset values set the position of column 1 on your printed output. An odd page offset refers to right-hand pages; an even page offset controls left-hand pages (or "backs"). For clarification, examine any professionally produced book. Notice how the book always begins with page i or 1 as a right-hand, opening page. (The i page is usually the front cover or title page, which is unnumbered, but still counted in the numbering scheme.) The back side of a right-hand, odd numbered page is always a left-hand, even-numbered page.

WordStar's odd and even page offsets are provided so you can alternate margin settings when printing both sides of a sheet of paper. It is often desirable to leave a wider inside (or *binding*) margin. This makes reading easier for tightly bound books.

Module 49

PUTTING IT ALL TOGETHER Now, some actual values are provided to illustrate the use of the page offset. If you use a page offset of 1.00", which is recommended for 10-pitch printing, a 10-character or one-inch page offset is achieved. This is what typists refer to as the left margin. If you want your printed text to begin one inch from the left edge of the paper, you should use a page offset of 10 (10 characters per inch). If you use 12-pitch printing, your page offset should be 12 (12 characters per inch).

You should normally leave the left margin set to column 1; the right margin should be set to control the printed line length. You should use inch notation, like .rm 6.5" rather than .rm 65. If you have installed WordStar to use the features of your printer, (normal and alternate pitch values), WordStar honors inch settings regardless of the pitch in use. However, if you use column numbers instead of inches, the following table, which includes 10-, 12-, and 15-pitch settings, may be useful. All values assume .LM 1.

Page Offset and Right Margin

Page Offset	Line Length	10 Pitch	12 Pitch	15 Pitch
1 inch	6.5 inches	.po 10 .rm 65	.po 12 .rm 78	.po 15 .rm 98
.5 inch	7.5 inches	.po 5 .rm 75	.po 6 .rm 90	.po 8 .rm 112

ALTERNATE METHODS USING WORDSTAR'S CLASSIC MENU There are alternate methods for setting text boundaries. These operate with WordStar's classic menu system. Once the classic help level is set, you can press Ctrl-OR or Ctrl-OL for right or left margin, enter a margin value, like 6.5", and press Return. Still another method lets you position the cursor to the desired margin column, press Ctrl-OR or Ctrl-OL for right or left margin, and press Esc instead of typing a number and pressing Return. You can verify the new setting by looking at the format ruler, which shows margins and tab settings. Remember, however, that these two approaches operate with the classic menu and are remnants of earlier versions of WordStar.

MARGIN RELEASE It is also possible to release your margins to allow text entry beyond either the left or right margin boundary. The margin release is turned on by pressing Ctrl-OX.

AUTO-ALIGN WordStar's auto-align feature adjusts each paragraph of text as it is typed. This is sometimes undesirable, as it causes centered text to re-align flush left. You can turn auto-align off and on by pressing Ctrl-OA.

PARAGRAPH MARGINS Paragraph margins or indents are set by using either the MARGINS & TABS screen or the dot command .PM followed by a number. The value of the number corresponds to the number of spaces used to indent the first line of each new paragraph. Each subsequent paragraph is indented to the established value until returned to the normal margin with .PM 0 or .PM Return.

APPLICATIONS

Being able to set your margins is necessary to establish a format that is compatible with the document being created. The convenience of being able to change the margin value lets you change line lengths and positions for easy control of your document.

There are times when a narrow column of text is used to set it apart from the regular body text. Use of the left and right margin settings lets you set the new indent levels. You can then enter text without worrying about how each line wraps.

It is often necessary to change the right margin when you change printer pitch. For example, if you're printing in 10 pitch (10 characters per inch) on 8 1/2-inch-wide paper, and you want an inch of white space at both the left- and right-hand margins, your margins should be at 1 and 65 for a 6 1/2-inch line length.

In 12 pitch (12 characters per inch), you'll want to have a 78-character line length. Here, you'll want to set your margins at 1 and 78. Next, you'll have to ensure that your printer is adjusted properly so that the first printed character is 1 inch in from the left edge of the sheet of paper. When using 10 pitch, use the .PO 10 dot command for a page offset of 10 spaces. In 12 pitch, use .PO 12.

Finally, being able to set and save your margin settings with dot commands embedded in your document allows you to preserve them for later uses.

TYPICAL OPERATION

In this activity, you adjust the right margin and reformat a paragraph to see the effect.

1. Open the document MYLTR.
2. Press **Ctrl-OR**, press **Ctrl-Y** to clear the existing value, then type **4.00"**, and press **F10**.
3. Move the cursor to the beginning of the letter paragraph.
4. Press **Ctrl-B** to reformat the paragraph. Notice that the new right margin takes effect.

Module 49

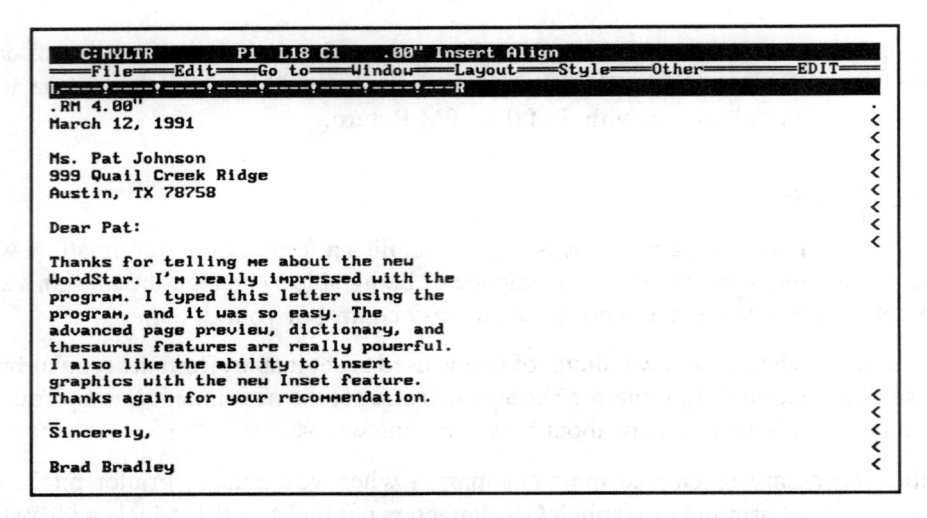

```
 C:MYLTR        P1  L18 C1      .00" Insert Align
===File====Edit====Go to====Window====Layout====Style====Other=========EDIT===
L----!----!----!----!----!----!----!---R
.RM 4.00"
March 12, 1991                                                          <
                                                                        <
Ms. Pat Johnson                                                         <
999 Quail Creek Ridge                                                   <
Austin, TX 78758                                                        <
                                                                        <
Dear Pat:                                                               <

Thanks for telling me about the new
WordStar. I'm really impressed with the
program. I typed this letter using the
program, and it was so easy. The
advanced page preview, dictionary, and
thesaurus features are really powerful.
I also like the ability to insert
graphics with the new Inset feature.
Thanks again for your recommendation.                                   <
                                                                        <
Sincerely,                                                              <
                                                                        <
Brad Bradley                                                            <
```

5. Reset the right margin to 6.5" by typing **.RM 6.50"** (this is the dot code for right margin).
6. Notice that the format ruler is readjusted to the previous setting.
7. Press **Ctrl-KQ** and type **Y** to abandon the document without saving.
8. Turn to Module 47 to continue the learning sequence.

Module 50
MERGE PRINT

DESCRIPTION

WordStar's merge print utility is designed to let you perform a number of powerful printing operations. For example, you can merge a list of variable information, such as a personnel roster or customer list, into the body of a form letter. You can also use merge print to create a control document used to print a stylized data list, such as a telephone directory. Both of these processes are called *list merge*.

Merge print also lets you combine different text files into a single document. Many word processing people call this process *document assembly*.

At the heart of merge print is a set of special merge print dot commands. These dot commands are embedded at the left margin of a control (or *base*) document, just like other dot commands. They are designed to use external information from a data file or directly from the keyboard. Merge print dot commands have a broad range of applications. The following list contains merge print dot commands, a brief definition of each, and an example of how these dot commands might be entered.

Command	Description
.DF	Specifies the name of the data file to use. .DF staff.dta
.RV	Reads a series of variables from the specified data file using the specified variable name. .RV fname,lname,adr1,adr1,city,state,zip,phone
.SV	Sets a variable name and its contents. .SV company,Barton Construction An alternate form that includes leading spaces: .SV company=" Barton Construction"
.AV	Asks for variable contents; enter contents from keyboard. .AV lname An alternate form used to display a user message: .AV "Last name?",lname
.FI	Inserts the named file within the document (similar to block read). .FI para3.txt

Module 50

Command	Description
.CS	Clears the screen, or clears the screen and displays an operator message or prompt. .CS An alternate form used to display a user message: .CS "Please wait during printout"
.DM	Displays an operator message or prompt. .DM "Insert a new sheet of stationery"
.PF on/off/dis	Controls formatting of printed text when the insertion of one or more variables causes a line length to exceed the right margin. .PF *dis* causes lines to wrap at the discretion of merge print when variable insertion causes a line to go beyond the right margin. This is the default setting. .PF *off* prevents discretionary line wrap, keeping lines intact. You can also use the .AW/off dot command to prevent realignment of certain sections. .PF *on* is used to align every paragraph within a document at print time. Use WordStar's .AW on/off dot command to protect areas, such as tables, where reformatting is undesired (see Module 70). You can also use WordStar's conventional dot commands, such as .lm, .rm, .rr, .ls, and .oj on/off for desired settings.
.IF,.EL,.EI	The .IF dot command lets you select specific records within the data file based on some field value. The general form of the .IF dot command is: .IF &variable& operator constant where *variable* is the name of an established read, set, or ask variable. *constant* is the value of the named variable. *operator* is one of the following:

Alpha Operators	Description	Numeric Operators	Description
=	the same as	=	equal to
<	comes before	#<	less than
>	comes after	#>	greater than
<=	comes before or the same as	#<=	less than or equal to
>=	comes after or the same as	#>=	greater than or equal to
<>	not the same as	#<>	not equal to

Look at the following examples.

    .IF &state& = GA
    .FI georgia.doc
    .EI

Command	Description
	This tells merge print to insert the file GEORGIA.DOC if the state field contains the value GA.

Notice the .EI (end if) dot command. For every .IF dot command there must be an .EI (end if) dot command. The if-endif statement can include an internal else (.EL) dot command to provide an alternate response when the .IF condition is false.

The following example uses the .EL dot command in combination with two .IF commands. Examples 1 and 2 accomplish the same result by providing a three-way branch.

Example 1	Example 2
.IF &state& = GA	.IF &state& = GA
.FI georgia.doc	.FI georgia.doc
.IF &state& = AL	.EI
.FI alabama.doc	.IF &state& = AL
.EL	.FI alabama.doc
.FI national.doc	.EL
.EI	.FI national.doc
.EI	.EI

Command	Description
.GO t/b	This dot command sends printing activity to the top or bottom of a file, where printing activity is resumed. Use the letter T or B, or the entire word Top or Bottom.

The following example includes the .GO dot command:

.IF &zip& >= 75000
.GO bottom
.EI

.MA	The .MA (math) dot command is used to sum two or more numeric variables. It is arranged in the form of an equation. The general form of the .MA dot command is

.MA variable=equation

Look at the following examples.

.MA total=&hotel& + &airfare& + &meals& + &auto&

An alternate form substitutes a comma for the equal sign.

.MA total,&hotel& + &airfare& + &meals& + &auto&

The total variable, which takes the form &total& within the base document, is established in three ways. First, it can exist in the named data file (.DF) and be assigned a variable name on the .RV line. It can also be established using the .SV or .AV dot commands.

Command	Description

Using .SV, the lines might be:

 .DF travel.dta
 .RV name,hotel,airfare,meals,auto
 .SV total
 .MA total=&hotel& + &airfare& + &meals& + &auto&

Expense	Amount
Name	&name&
Hotel	&hotel&
Airfare	&airfare&
Meals	&meals&
Auto	&auto&
Total	&total&

The data file might resemble the following:

 Stewart Travis,75.55,350.00,15.07,33.24
 Bonnie Sanchez,80.21,124.00,36.54,24.50

If total is part of the read variable line, the first three lines could be:

 .DF travel.dta
 .RV name,hotel,airfare,meals,auto,total
 .MA total=&hotel& + &airfare& + &meals& + &auto&

The last field of the data file is blank to ensure that the read variable list is consistent with the number of fields in the record. A blank field is added by placing a comma at the end of each line in the data file. This provides for the "total" variable.

 Stewart Travis,75.55,350.00,15.07,33.24,
 Bonnie Sanchez,80.21,124.00,36.54,24.50,

The resulting document would resemble the following:

Name	Stewart Travis
Hotel	75.55
Airfare	350.00
Meals	15.07
Auto	33.24
Total	473.86
Name	Bonnie Sanchez
Hotel	80.21
Airfare	124.00
Meals	36.54
Auto	24.50
Total	265.25

To align the decimals, you can use one of the merge print format variables discussed later in this module.

As you can see in the preceding list, dot commands let you:

- Specify filenames
- Assign one or more variable names
- Clear the screen
- Display custom messages and prompts
- Control the format of printed output
- Perform math operations
- Restrict variables to those that match an established criterion
- Move activity to the top or bottom of the document being used.

THE DATA FILE If you use WordStar to create a data file, use the nondocument mode. This prevents alien format control characters from contaminating the data file. Their presence can interfere with the way merge print operates. Data files are also obtained from other programs, such as database managers and spreadsheets that produce ASCII text files. Each record corresponds to a row of data elements. The data elements within the record (or row) are called fields. Fields contain items such as name, address, city, state, and zip code. Therefore, a data file contains a group of records. Records contain a group of fields. The fields must be consistent in the way they are organized, and each record must contain the same number of fields. The following sample contains three records. Each record contains eight fields.

```
Jones,Lt.,Trudy,Airdale AFB,PO Box 34345,New York,New York,01010
Smith,Mr.,Roger,123 Holland Avenue, ,Tampa,Florida,33456
Stone,Ms.,Vicki,Leland Corp.,4454 Elm Drive, Houston,Texas,76076
```

Notice how each field is *comma delimited*. This means they are separated by commas. Smith has a single line address. Because each record must have the same number of fields, a blank field is substituted.

If a field of information contains a comma, you can surround it with quotation marks. This causes merge print to treat the comma just like any other character. The following example shows a variation of the preceding data file. The city and state fields are combined. Notice how quotes are used to handle the comma character.

```
Jones,Lt.,Trudy,Airdale AFB,PO Box 34345,"New York,New York",01010
Smith,Mr.,Roger,123 Holland Avenue, ,"Tampa,Florida",33456
Stone,Ms.,Vicki,Leland Corp.,4454 Elm Drive,"Houston,Texas",76076
```

THE BASE DOCUMENT A base document can use the variables within a data file to produce a form letter. Each letter uses a record at a time, beginning with the first and finishing with the last. The data file is identified with the .DF dot command. The fields within the records are named using the .RV dot command. The point of insertion within the base document uses the variable name surrounded by ampersands, such as &company&. If a blank field (or variable) is possible, as in a second or third address line, include a /o after the variable name, such as &adr2/o&. An example of a base document using the first data file follows. Notice the /o on the line containing the adr2 variable. This omits a blank variable and the blank line it produces. In the example, assume the data file is named CUSTOMER.DTA.

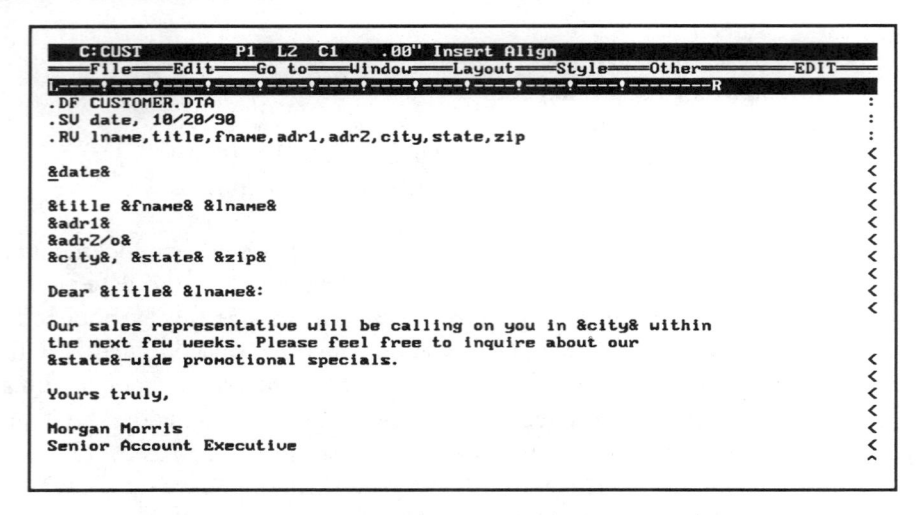

```
  C:CUST         P1  L2  C1    .00" Insert Align
====File====Edit====Go to====Window====Layout====Style====Other====EDIT====
L----!----!----!----!----!----!----!----!----!----!--------R
.DF CUSTOMER.DTA                                                     :
.SU date, 10/20/90                                                   :
.RV lname,title,fname,adr1,adr2,city,state,zip
                                                                     <
&date&                                                               <
                                                                     <
&title& &fname& &lname&                                              <
&adr1&                                                               <
&adr2&/o&                                                            <
&city&, &state& &zip&                                                <
                                                                     <
Dear &title& &lname&:                                                <
                                                                     <
Our sales representative will be calling on you in &city& within
the next few weeks. Please feel free to inquire about our
&state&-wide promotional specials.                                   <
                                                                     <
Yours truly,                                                         <
                                                                     <
Morgan Morris                                                        <
Senior Account Executive                                             <
                                                                     ^
```

The preceding base letter is modified to include a few additional dot commands. Examine the letter and then read how the added dot commands affect it. The note annotation within parentheses, which is for reference, is not part of the letter.

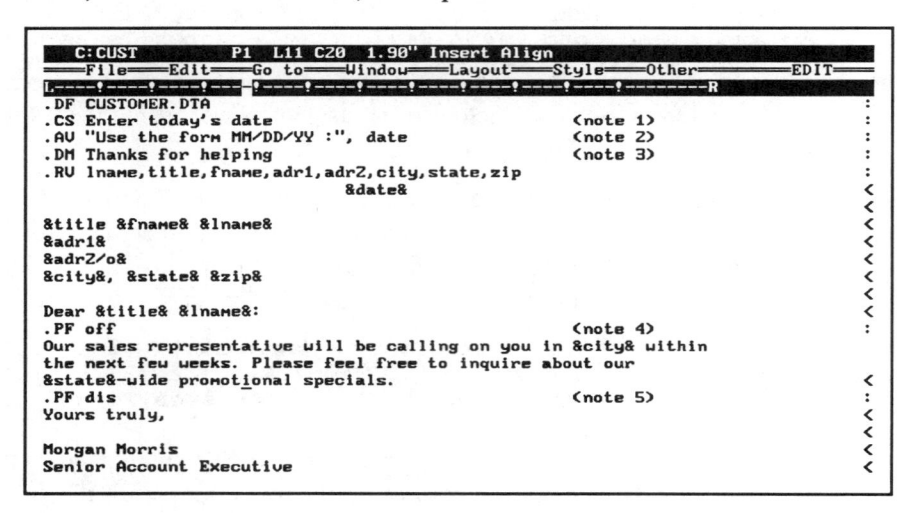

```
  C:CUST         P1  L11 C20  1.90" Insert Align
====File====Edit====Go to====Window====Layout====Style====Other====EDIT====
L----!----!----!----!----!----!----!----!----!----!--------R
.DF CUSTOMER.DTA                                                     :
.CS Enter today's date                        (note 1)               :
.AV "Use the form MM/DD/YY :", date           (note 2)               :
.DM Thanks for helping                        (note 3)               :
.RV lname,title,fname,adr1,adr2,city,state,zip
                         &date&                                      <
                                                                     <
&title& &fname& &lname&                                              <
&adr1&                                                               <
&adr2&/o&                                                            <
&city&, &state& &zip&                                                <
                                                                     <
Dear &title& &lname&:                                                <
.PF off                                       (note 4)               :
Our sales representative will be calling on you in &city& within
the next few weeks. Please feel free to inquire about our
&state&-wide promotional specials.                                   <
.PF dis                                       (note 5)               :
Yours truly,                                                         <
                                                                     <
Morgan Morris                                                        <
Senior Account Executive                                             <
```

Notes:

1. Clears the screen and displays the prompt "Enter today's date."
2. Displays the prompt "Use the form MM/DD/YY :" and accepts entry from the keyboard for the variable date.

3. Displays the message "Thanks for helping."
4. Turns reformatting off to prevent lines from wrapping during printing if text exceeds right margin setting.
5. Turns discretionary (normal) reformatting back on. Lines wrap if inserted variables cause the text to exceed the right margin setting.

Predefined Variables   There are four predefined variables that can be inserted in any base document. These are:

Variable	Value
&#&	page number
&_&	line number
&@&	system date
&!&	system time

Format Variables   Format variables provide format control by assigning a format control variable to a number. You can use the .SV dot command to establish the format variable relationship with a set of merge print format control codes. If .sv1=*format code* is used, the merge variable is entered as &variable/1&. The /1 tells WordStar to apply set variable 1 to the specified data variable. First, a few examples are shown and then a complete list of format control codes are defined.

.sv 3=" RRRR" (two spaces, four characters)
                22334 is printed sp sp 334 sp

.sv 4=$$,$$$.99
                1234.12 is printed $1,234.12

Format variables:

Symbol	Meaning
L, R, C	Set variable flush left (L), flush right (R), or center on line (C); each symbol (L, R, or C) occupies one character space. Placing the symbol and leading or trailing spaces within quotes causes characters to be replaced by the corresponding spaces. .SV 2=LLLLLL Sets the first six characters of the variable flush left.
9	Digits or blanks are replaced by 0's. .SV 3=99999.99 Causes 123.12 to print 00123.12 Causes 12 to print 00012.00
Z	Digits, blanks are replaced by spaces. .SV 4=ZZZZZ.ZZ Causes the number 123.12 to print 123.12 Causes the number 12 to print 12.

Module 50

Symbol	Meaning	
*	Digits or blanks are replaced by asterisks.	
	.SV 5=*****.**	
	Causes 123.12 to print	**123.12
	Causes 12 to print	***12.00
$	Digits or spaces; leading zeros are replaced by spaces.	
	.SV 3=$$$$$.99	
	Causes 123.12 to print	$123.12
	Causes 12 to print	$12.00
–	Places minus sign in front of first digit if value is negative	
	.SV 2=-$$$$$.99	
	Causes –123.12 to print	–$123.12
	Causes –12 to print	–$12.00
( )	Places parentheses around negative value.	
	.SV 7=(*****.99)	
	Causes –123.45 to print	(123.45)
.	Places a decimal point at specified location.	
	.SV 4=99999.99	
	Causes 12.345 to print	00012.34
	Causes 12 to print	00012.00
,	Places a comma within number.	
	.SV 6=99,999	
	Causes 12345 to print	12,345

The .SV dot command example is used in the Typical Operation section of this module to illustrate the use of decimal alignment and to print dollar signs.

APPLICATIONS

WordStar's merge print feature lets you perform many important office operations. Document assembly operations let you assemble clauses or paragraphs to build a contract, statement of work, product specification, or any other document that can benefit from the use of canned information, often referred to as *boilerplate*.

The ability to merge structured lists of information with a base document, which serves as a control file, lets you create a host of form letters and custom lists. Automatic generation of personalized advertising pieces and notifications is possible. You can also create tailored telephone directories and personnel rosters.

With the math and format variable dot commands, you can prepare financial documents such as departmental expense summaries, invoices, and vouchers of all kinds. Here, WordStar performs calculations for you.

The ability to extract *comma-delimited* data lists from database products, such as Ashton Tate's dBASE, gives you the combined power of a database manager and a full-featured word processor. For additional information on how to create a comma-delimited file using dBASE, obtain a copy of one of Wordware's *Illustrated dBASE* books and refer to the COPY module.

TYPICAL OPERATION

In this activity you create a small data file and base document. Then you use merge print to print the document. If you like, you can use the ASCII printer to print to WordStar's ASCII.WS file. Begin at the OPENING menu.

1. Open a new document file named MERGE.DOC.
2. Create and save the following document. Be sure all dot commands begin at column 1 and all lines end with a Return.

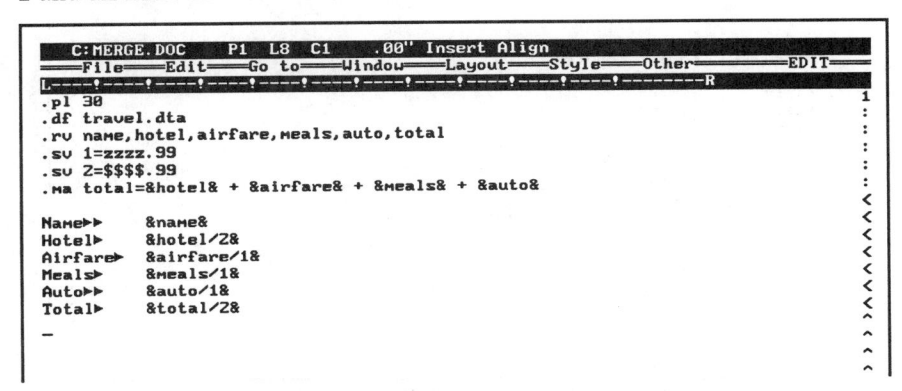

```
C:MERGE.DOC     P1  L8  C1      .00" Insert Align
====File====Edit====Go to====Window====Layout====Style====Other====EDIT====
L----!----!----!----!----!----!----!----!----!----!--------R
.pl 30
.df travel.dta
.rv name,hotel,airfare,meals,auto,total
.sv 1=zzzz.99
.sv 2=$$$$.99
.ma total=&hotel& + &airfare& + &meals& + &auto&

Name►    &name&
Hotel►   &hotel/2&
Airfare► &airfare/1&
Meals►   &meals/1&
Auto►    &auto/1&
Total►   &total/2&
-
```

3. Create and save the following nondocument file named TRAVEL.DTA.

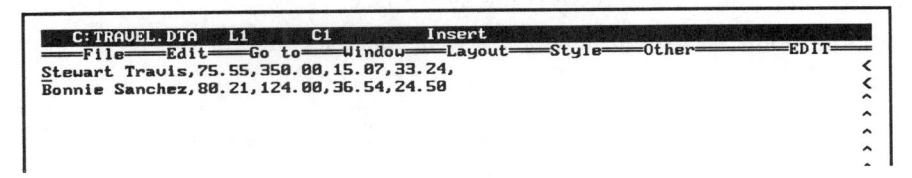

```
C:TRAVEL.DTA    L1    C1        Insert
====File====Edit====Go to====Window====Layout====Style====Other====EDIT====
Steuart Travis,75.55,350.00,15.07,33.24,
Bonnie Sanchez,80.21,124.00,36.54,24.50
```

4. Type **FM** at the OPENING menu. Then respond to the filename prompt by typing **MERGE.DOC** and pressing **Return**.
5. Press **Return** in response to each of the merge print prompts until the cursor is on the Printer name line.

Module 50

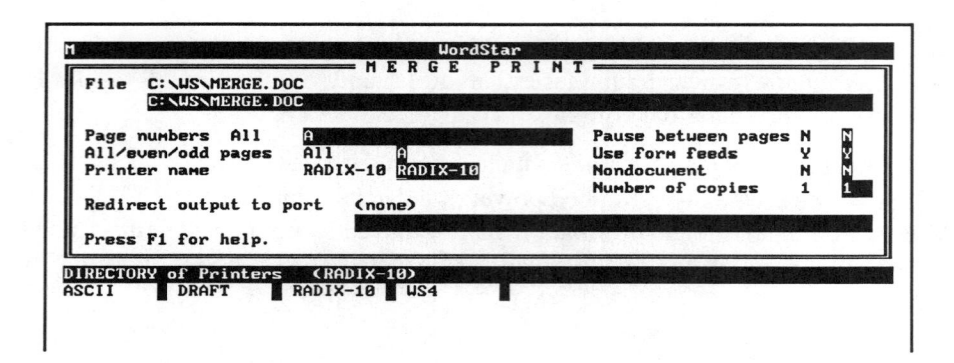

```
M                            WordStar
                        ═══ M E R G E   P R I N T ═══
  File   C:\WS\MERGE.DOC
         C:\WS\MERGE.DOC

  Page numbers    All     A                   Pause between pages  N    N
  All/even/odd pages      All    A            Use form feeds       Y    Y
  Printer name            RADIX-10  RADIX-10  Nondocument          N    N
                                              Number of copies     1    1
  Redirect output to port      (none)

  Press F1 for help.
  ─────────────────────────────────────────────────────────────────
  DIRECTORY of Printers    (RADIX-10)
  ASCII      DRAFT       RADIX-10    WS4
```

6. Type **ASCII** then press **F10** to print to WordStar's ASCII.WS file, or press **F10** to print the document on your printer.

7. Upon completion, examine the document. It should resemble the following. (If you used ASCII, open document ASCII.WS to display the document.)

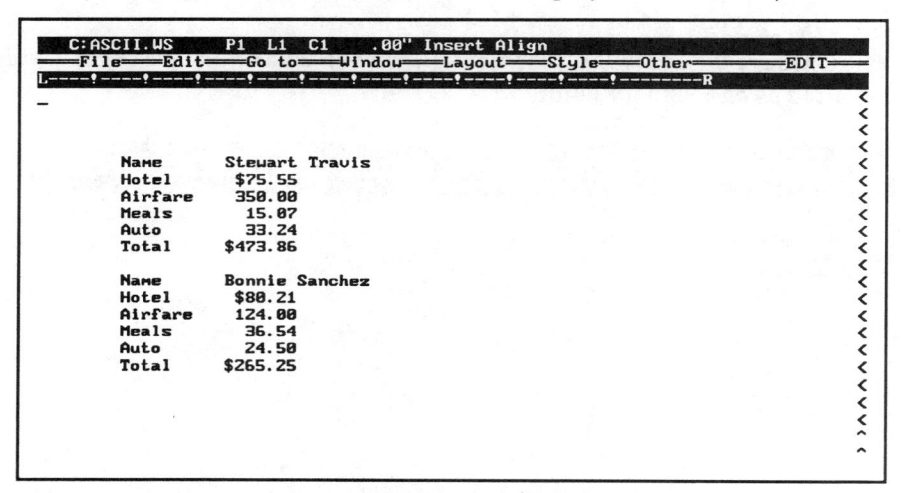

```
  C:ASCII.WS      P1  L1  C1    .00"  Insert Align
  ══File══════Edit══════Go to══════Window══════Layout══════Style══════Other══════════EDIT══
  L────!────!────!────!────!────!────!────!────!────!────!─────────R
  ─
                                                                                        <
                                                                                        <
              Name       Stewart Travis                                                 <
              Hotel      $75.55                                                         <
              Airfare    350.00                                                         <
              Meals      15.07                                                          <
              Auto       33.24                                                          <
              Total      $473.86                                                        <
                                                                                        <
              Name       Bonnie Sanchez                                                 <
              Hotel      $80.21                                                         <
              Airfare    124.00                                                         <
              Meals      36.54                                                          <
              Auto       24.50                                                          <
              Total      $265.25                                                        <
                                                                                        <
                                                                                        <
                                                                                        ^
                                                                                        ^
```

8. If you like, delete the files TRAVEL.DTA, MERGE.DOC, and ASCII.WS (if you used it) from your disk to recover the used space.

9. Turn to Module 48 to continue the learning sequence.

Module 51
MOVE BLOCKS OF TEXT

> Classic: ^KV
> Pull-Down: Alt-E, select "Move block"

DESCRIPTION

To move a passage of text, mark it, move the cursor to the new location, and press Ctrl-KV. The marked block is moved to the current cursor position. Any following text is displaced to the right and down as the moved block is inserted. The space vacated by the moved block is filled by the text that follows.

The block marking and moving process is presented for your review.

1. Mark the beginning of the block with Ctrl-KB.
2. Mark the end of the block with Ctrl-KK.
3. Position the cursor at the new text location.
4. Move the marked block with Ctrl-KV.

APPLICATIONS

The block move operation is used to move words, sentences, paragraphs, and even entire pages within a document. You can use the block move function to transpose (switch) paragraphs of text in a matter of a few seconds. Without the move function, the entire text passage would have to be manually inserted in the new location and deleted from its original spot.

TYPICAL OPERATION

In this activity, begin with the document MYLTR displayed. Mark and move the letter paragraph to the bottom of the file.

1. Open the document MYLTR.
2. Position the cursor at the first character of the letter paragraph and press **Ctrl-KB** to mark the beginning of the block.

Module 51

3. Position the cursor at the line below the paragraph and press **Ctrl-KK** to mark the end of the block. Check that your document resembles the following screen illustration.

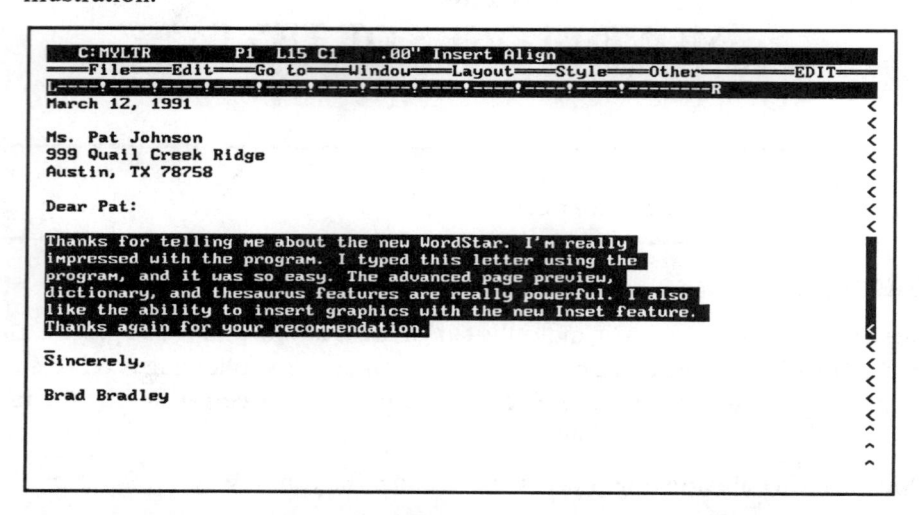

```
 C:MYLTR         P1  L15 C1     .00" Insert Align
====File====Edit====Go to====Window====Layout====Style====Other====       ====EDIT====
L----!----!----!----!----!----!----!----!----!----!--------R
March 12, 1991                                                              <
                                                                            <
Ms. Pat Johnson                                                             <
999 Quail Creek Ridge                                                       <
Austin, TX 78758                                                            <
                                                                            <
Dear Pat:                                                                   <
                                                                            <
Thanks for telling me about the new WordStar. I'm really
impressed with the program. I typed this letter using the
program, and it was so easy. The advanced page preview,
dictionary, and thesaurus features are really powerful. I also
like the ability to insert graphics with the new Inset feature.
Thanks again for your recommendation.                                       <
                                                                            <
Sincerely,                                                                  <
                                                                            <
Brad Bradley                                                                <
                                                                            <
                                                                            ^
                                                                            ^
```

4. Move the cursor to the bottom of the screen and press **Ctrl-KV** to move the block. Compare the results to the following screen illustration.

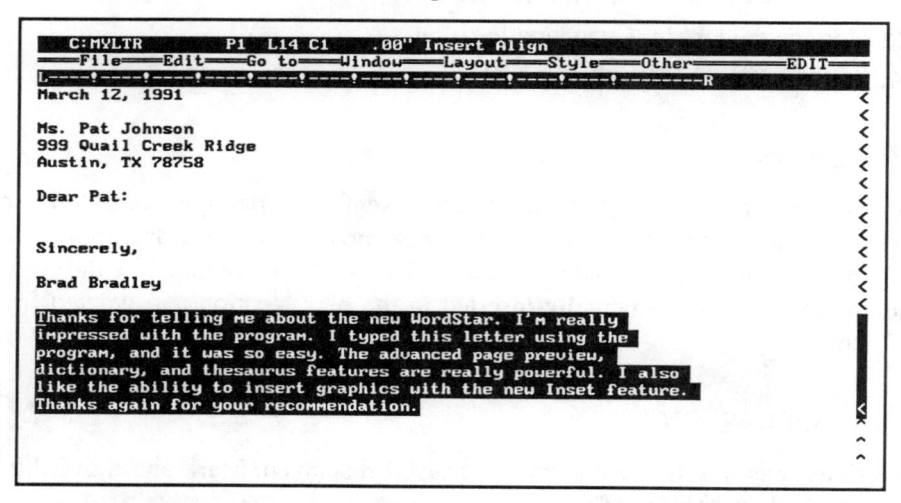

```
 C:MYLTR         P1  L14 C1     .00" Insert Align
====File====Edit====Go to====Window====Layout====Style====Other====       ====EDIT====
L----!----!----!----!----!----!----!----!----!----!--------R
March 12, 1991                                                              <
                                                                            <
Ms. Pat Johnson                                                             <
999 Quail Creek Ridge                                                       <
Austin, TX 78758                                                            <
                                                                            <
Dear Pat:                                                                   <
                                                                            <
Sincerely,                                                                  <
                                                                            <
Brad Bradley                                                                <
                                                                            <
Thanks for telling me about the new WordStar. I'm really
impressed with the program. I typed this letter using the
program, and it was so easy. The advanced page preview,
dictionary, and thesaurus features are really powerful. I also
like the ability to insert graphics with the new Inset feature.
Thanks again for your recommendation.                                       <
                                                                            ^
                                                                            ^
```

5. Press **Ctrl-KQ** and type **Y** to abandon without saving changes.
6. Turn to Module 14 to continue the learning sequence.

Module 52
OPEN A DOCUMENT OR NONDOCUMENT FILE

> OPENING Menu:
>   Classic: S, D, N
>   Pull-Down: F, select "Speed Write (new file)"
>   F, select "Open a document file..."
>   F, select "Open a nondocument file..."

DESCRIPTION

You can open a standard WordStar document or a standard ASCII file (called *nondocument*) when the OPENING menu is displayed. A document file contains special characters that control the placement of text within a document. Nondocument files are often used by programmers to prepare program source files or to exchange the files with other word processors capable of handling ASCII file formats. You should use the nondocument file option when WordStar's format control characters interfere with program operation.

Always type F to "pull down" the File menu. Examine the first 3 menu selections in the following pull-down menu illustration.

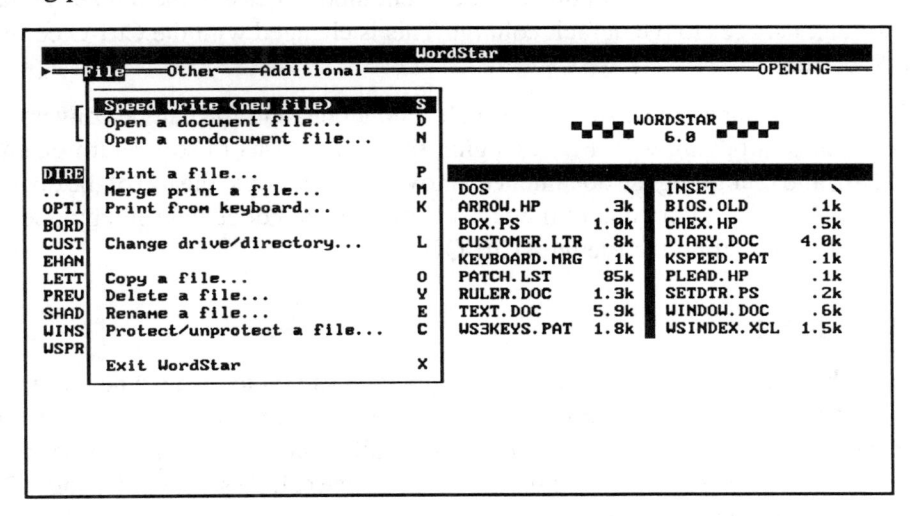

```
                              WordStar
   ═══File═══Other═══Additional═══════════════════════OPENING═══
      ┌─Speed Write (new file)    S ─┐
      │ Open a document file...   D  │      ■■■ WORDSTAR ■■■
      │ Open a nondocument file... N │      ■■■    6.0    ■■■
 DIRE │ Print a file...           P  │
  ..  │ Merge print a file...     M  │  DOS           \  INSET          \
 OPTI │ Print from keyboard...    K  │  ARROW.HP    .3k  BIOS.OLD     .1k
 BORD │                              │  BOX.PS     1.0k  CHEX.HP      .5k
 CUST │ Change drive/directory... L  │  CUSTOMER.LTR .8k DIARY.DOC   4.0k
 EHAN │                              │  KEYBOARD.MRG .1k KSPEED.PAT   .1k
 LETT │ Copy a file...            O  │  PATCH.LST   85k  PLEAD.HP     .1k
 PREV │ Delete a file...          Y  │  RULER.DOC  1.3k  SETDTR.PS    .2k
 SHAD │ Rename a file...          E  │  TEXT.DOC   5.9k  WINDOW.DOC   .6k
 WINS │ Protect/unprotect a file... C│  WS3KEYS.PAT 1.8k WSINDEX.XCL 1.5k
 WSPR │                              │
      │ Exit WordStar             X  │
      └──────────────────────────────┘
```

165

Module 52

Type S to speed write a document file, D to open a document file, or N to open a nondocument file. Typing D or N causes WordStar to display a "File" prompt. Respond by typing a filename and pressing Return. Type Y if you see the prompt

```
Can't find that file. Create a new one (Y/N)?
```

An existing file is opened in either of two ways. Either type the filename and press Return or use the arrow keys to move the cursor to the displayed filename within the directory and press Return. WordStar displays the EDIT menu and you are ready to begin your word processing task.

SPEED WRITE A NEW FILE   You can open a new document file with the "Speed Write (new file)" option. This option skips the File prompt and displays the EDIT menu screen. You are prompted for a filename when you save the document.

NONDOCUMENT FILES   Because this book is primarily about word processing, it sticks to using document files. However, before leaving the subject of nondocument files, please note a few differences about the way WordStar treats nondocument files.

Nondocument files do not display the format ruler with the nondocument EDIT menu. The ONSCREEN menu is never displayed in the nondocument mode. Lines are ended with the Return key. Any attempt to reformat a line of text introduces control characters which contaminate your file. Therefore, never reformat a nondocument file with Ctrl-B.

Some functions, such as variable tabs, word wrap, and page breaks are not operational in the nondocument mode. For example, you can set a tab at character position 3 (column 3) in a standard document file. In the nondocument mode, pressing the tab key advances the cursor eight spaces to the default column. This is changed with the Ctrl-O command to 2, 4, 8, or 16.

Any file can be opened with either FD or FN. A nondocument file can be converted to a document file by opening with FD, changing the hard returns to soft return characters using Ctrl-6, and realigning the document by moving the cursor to the top of the document and pressing Ctrl-QU. A document file is converted to a nondocument file by opening it with FN and reformatting the file with Ctrl-QU.

APPLICATIONS

Opening either a document or a nondocument file allows you to create a new file, revise an existing file, or display a file for examination. Document files let you take advantage of WordStar's many document format controls, while nondocument files produce pure ASCII files. Many WordStar users produce BASIC, Pascal, Assembler, C, and dBASE source files using nondocument.

The Speed Write option is convenient when you are preparing a new memo or note. This eliminates the interruption by the "File" prompt, letting you get on with your text preparation without delay.

TYPICAL OPERATION

The typical operations in this book are intended as "hands-on" practice exercises. You are encouraged to follow the steps with your computer so you can learn by experiencing each of the WordStar operations.

In this example, you open a new document named Chap1. Type WS from the DOS prompt to start WordStar and begin with the OPENING menu displayed.

1. Type **FD** and notice the "File" prompt.
2. Type **CHAP1** and press **Return**. Then type **Y** in response to the "Can't find that file. Create a new one (Y/N)?" prompt. A blank file is opened and the cursor is located at the top left-hand portion of the text entry area.

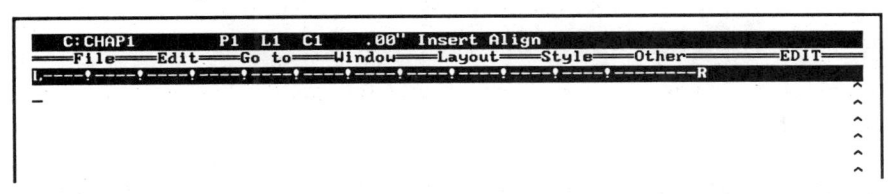

```
    C:CHAP1        P1  L1  C1     .00" Insert Align
   ====File====Edit====Go to====Window====Layout====Style====Other====    ====EDIT====
   L----!----!----!----!----!----!----!----!----!----R
    -                                                                  ^
                                                                       ^
                                                                       ^
                                                                       >
                                                                       >
                                                                       >
                                                                       ^
```

3. Press **Ctrl-KQ** to abandon the document without saving.
4. Turn to Module 27 to continue the learning sequence.

Module 53
PAGE BREAKS, PAGE LENGTH

> Classic: .pa, .pl, .cp
> Pull-Down: Alt-L, select "New page"
> Alt-L, select "Conditional new page..."

DESCRIPTION

When you type a document in the document mode, page breaks occur automatically. The default value is 55 lines of text on each page. When the text is printed, a new sheet of paper is used with each new page. The position of an automatic page break can vary if a different page length is selected during WordStar installation or if the page length dot command, like .PL 60, is used. The default page length is .PL 66.

A page break is designated by a solid horizontal line and a P at the right margin. An automatic page break looks like the following.

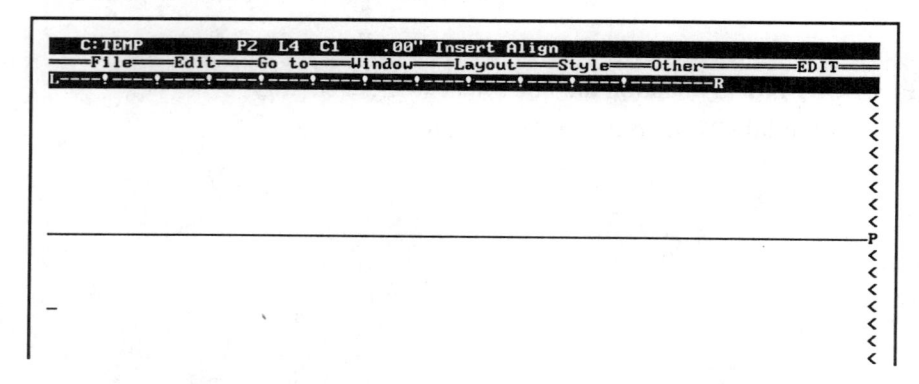

```
 C:TEMP          P2  L4  C1      .00" Insert Align
=File====Edit====Go to====Window====Layout====Style====Other=========EDIT=
L----!----!----!----!----!----!----!----!----!----!----!--------R
                                                                      <
                                                                      <
                                                                      <
                                                                      <
                                                                      <
                                                                      <
                                                                      <
                                                                      <
_____P
                                                                      <
                                                                      <
                                                                      <
                                                                      <
 -                                                                    <
                                                                      <
                                                                      <
```

You can insert a page to break anywhere in your text with the .PA dot command. The .PA is typed at the left margin and followed by Return. Inserted page breaks appear in your file as follows:

```
 C:TEMP          P1  L32 C1          Insert Align
=File====Edit====Go to====Window====Layout====Style====Other=========EDIT=
L----!----!----!----!----!----!----!----!----!----!----!--------R
                                                                      <
                                                                      <
                                                                      <
.pa                                                                   .
_____P
                                                                      <
                                                                      <
```

168

Conditional page breaks are used to keep a specified number of lines together without breaking. This is done with the dot command .CP followed by a number to indicate the number of lines required to stay together. It is entered on the line above the text it controls. For example, .CP 2 ensures that at least two lines of text stay together at the bottom of a page; if only one fits, the passage is moved to the top of the following page.

APPLICATIONS

Being able to insert a page break where you wish gives you control over how your document is printed. A conditional page break lets you keep a specified number of lines together, preventing passages from separating. You may consider using the .CP dot code to keep items like tables, lists, and charts together on the same page. The .CP dot code is excellent for preventing what publications people call *widows* and *orphans*.

TYPICAL OPERATION

In this activity, you begin with the document MYLTR displayed and insert a page break.

1. Open the document MYLTR.
2. Move the cursor to the blank line between the address and the greeting. Then type **.pa** and press **Return**. Notice the following screen.

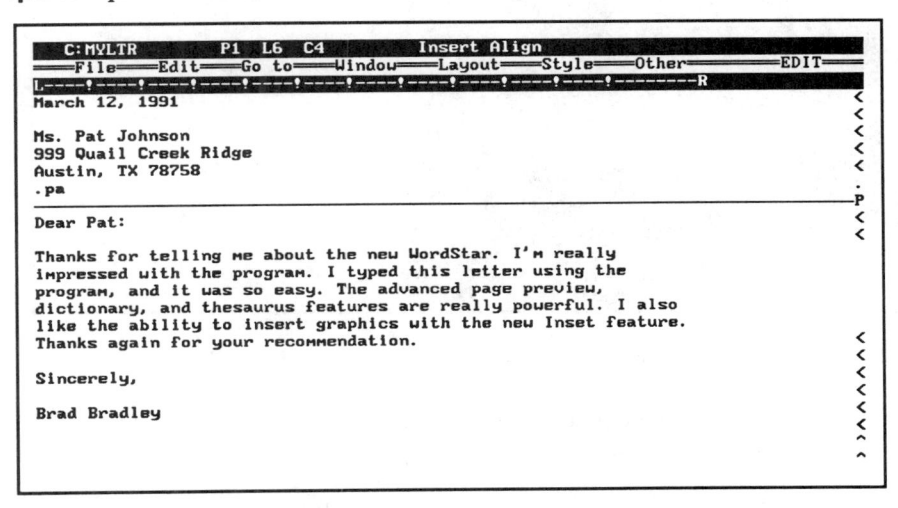

```
   C:MYLTR         P1  L6  C4            Insert Align
====File====Edit====Go to====Window====Layout====Style====Other========EDIT====
L----!----!----!----!----!----!----!----!----!----!----!--------R
March 12, 1991                                                          <
                                                                        <
Ms. Pat Johnson                                                         <
999 Quail Creek Ridge                                                   <
Austin, TX 78758                                                        <
.pa                                                                     .
                                                                        P
Dear Pat:                                                               <
                                                                        <
Thanks for telling me about the new WordStar. I'm really
impressed with the program. I typed this letter using the
program, and it was so easy. The advanced page preview,
dictionary, and thesaurus features are really powerful. I also
like the ability to insert graphics with the new Inset feature.
Thanks again for your recommendation.                                   <
                                                                        <
Sincerely,                                                              <
                                                                        <
Brad Bradley                                                            <
                                                                        <
                                                                        ^
                                                                        ^
```

3. Press **Ctrl-KQ** and type **Y** to abandon the document without saving.
4. Turn to Module 38 to continue the learning sequence.

Module 54
PAGE PREVIEW

```
Classic:      ^OP
Pull-Down:    Alt-L, select "Page preview"
```

DESCRIPTION

WordStar's page preview feature lets you look at a graphic representation of one or more pages. Pressing Ctrl-OP displays an image of the current page, with a menu bar across the top.

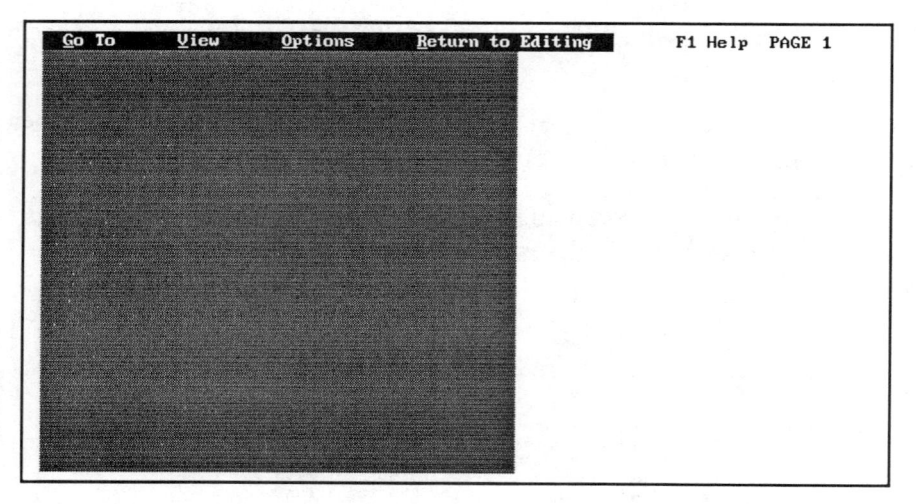

The menu selections are made by typing the first letter of each option.

GO TO   The Go To menu lets you move to different pages within the current document for previewing. Your options are:

Specified page...	Specify a page number
First page	Go to the first page
Last page	Go to the last page
Next page	Go to the next page
Previous page	Go to the previous page

Pressing Alt-1 is a shortcut to return you to the page currently being previewed. Alt-2 returns you to the original page.

VIEW The View selection lets you view one or more pages in different ways. The options are:

Entire page	The default view; displays a full view of the current page.
Facing pages	Displays the current page and the facing page.
Multiple pages	Displays a series of pages.
Thumbnail display	Displays a miniature view of one or multiple pages.
2x zoom	Enlarges the current page by two times.
4x zoom	Enlarges the current page by four times.
Adjust window	Lets you select a portion of the displayed page to enlarge.

You can use the + and − keys as a shortcut to change the magnifications of views. For example, the + key moves progressively larger from thumbnail display to 4x zoom. You can also use the Left or Right Arrow key to move the page number highlighting in the thumbnail display. Once a page number is highlighted, press Alt-1 to return to the selected page.

OPTIONS The Options selection lets you scan pages one after another. It also lets you overlay an 8 1/2 X 11-inch grid over a displayed page. The options are:

Automatic scan	Scans a range of pages in the current document for a quick preview of multiple pages.
Scan range ...	Lets you specify the first and last page to scan.
Grid display On/Off	Turns the overlay grid on and off.

RETURN TO EDITING This selection lets you return to the original page or, if you moved to a different page, the current page.

APPLICATIONS

WordStar's preview page feature is one of the most advanced features available in word processing systems. It lets you see one or more pages in either miniature or enlarged form. The autoscan feature lets you preview an entire document before you print it. This ensures that document pagination and individual page layout is satisfactory before committing the document to paper.

Previewing newspaper-style columns (see Module 12) is indispensable. This is the only way to see a facsimile of the document before it prints, because the original WordStar file is simply a single column of text.

Module 54

Finally, you can preview integrated graphics (or PIX files) which are linked to the page using WordStar's Inset feature.

TYPICAL OPERATION

In this activity, you type a temporary document and then view it using the page preview feature.

1. Open a new document named TEMP.
2. Type two or three paragraphs. You may wish to use *Greeking*, that is, type random characters in order to fill about one half of a page. Be sure to insert spaces every five to ten characters.
3. Press **Ctrl-OP** and look at the graphic representation of the page.
4. Type **V** and **2** to display a 2x zoom view.
5. Type **R** and press **Return** to redisplay the document.
6. Press **Ctrl-KQ** and type **Y** to abandon the document.
7. Turn to Module 44 to continue the learning sequence.

Module 55
PARAGRAPH NUMBERING

```
Classic:    ^OZ
Pull-Down:  Alt-L, select "Paragraph numbering ..."
```

DESCRIPTION

You can insert paragraph numbers in a document by positioning the cursor in the appropriate location and pressing Ctrl-OZ. The following menu is displayed:

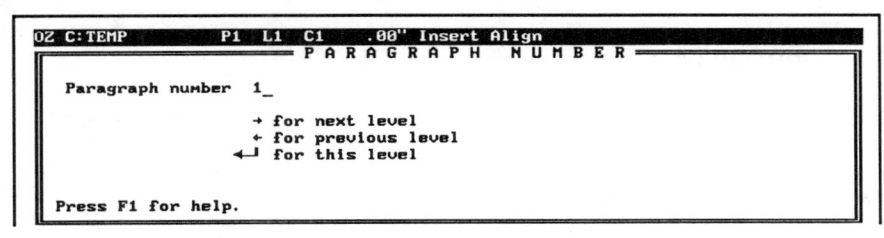

```
OZ C:TEMP              P1  L1  C1    .00" Insert Align
                      ═══PARAGRAPH    NUMBER═══
    Paragraph number  1_
                       → for next level
                       ← for previous level
                       ↵ for this level

    Press F1 for help.
```

Pressing Return inserts the Paragraph number 1 at the cursor position. Notice the Left and Right Arrows let you choose the next and previous levels. Pressing the Right Arrow changes the 1 to 1.1. Pressing Return inserts 1.1 at the cursor position.

WordStar monitors the numbers inserted into a document. If you delete an inserted paragraph number, following numbers are adjusted automatically. If you wish to insert a paragraph number between two existing ones, an appropriate number is displayed for your selection and insertion. Again, following paragraph numbers adjust automatically.

You can adjust the starting number using the dot command .p# n, where n is the starting paragraph number. For example, using .p# 3.2 starts paragraph numbers with 3.2. You can use up to eight levels (1.1.1.1.1.1.1.1). You can also use letters, Roman numerals, or a combination of letters and numbers. This is done with the .p# dot command in combination with Z, z, I, i, and 9. These are defined in the following list.

Character	Description
Z	Uses capital letters
z	Uses lowercase letters
I	Uses uppercase Roman numerals
i	Uses lowercase Roman numerals
9	Uses numbers

Examples:

.p# A.1,Z.9	(Starts numbering with A.1)
.p# A.1.a,Z.9.z	(Starts numbering with A.1.a)
.p# I.1,I.9	(Starts numbering with I.1)
.p# I.1.a,I.9.z	(Starts numbering with I.1.a)
.p# A.1,[Z.9]	(Starts numbering with [A.1])
.p# II.A,I,Z	(Starts numbering with II.A)

APPLICATIONS

WordStar's paragraph numbering feature is ideal for technical specifications and contracts where paragraph numbering is commonly used. The fact that paragraph numbers are adjusted automatically when you insert, add, or delete paragraphs lets you concentrate on the text rather than numbering.

TYPICAL OPERATION

In this activity, you create a document and use WordStar's paragraph numbering feature to insert and modify paragraph numbers.

1. Open a new document named TEMP.
2. Type the dot command **.p# I.A,I.Z** and press **Return**.
3. Create the following document. Press **Ctrl-OZ**, **Return**, and **Spacebar**. Then type the paragraph heading for each entry and press **Return** twice after each heading.

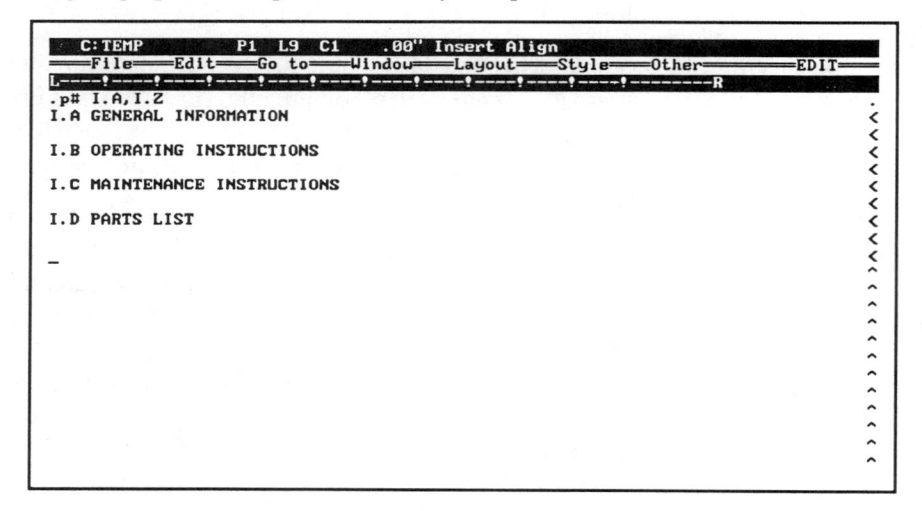

```
   C:TEMP         P1  L9  C1    .00" Insert Align
====File====Edit====Go to====Window====Layout====Style====Other=========EDIT====
L----!----!----!----!----!----!----!----!----!----!----!----R
.p# I.A,I.Z                                                                    .
I.A GENERAL INFORMATION                                                        <
                                                                               <
I.B OPERATING INSTRUCTIONS                                                     <
                                                                               <
I.C MAINTENANCE INSTRUCTIONS                                                   <
                                                                               <
I.D PARTS LIST                                                                 <
                                                                               <
_                                                                              <
```

Paragraph Numbering

4. Move the cursor to the "I" in I.B. With Insert on, press **Ctrl-OZ, Return, Spacebar**, type **INSTALLATION INSTRUCTIONS**, and press **Return** twice. Your document should resemble the following one.

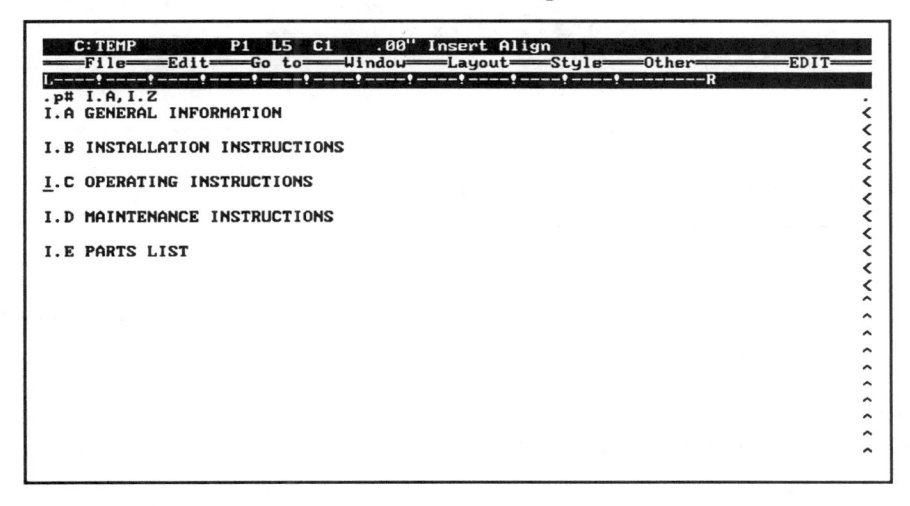

```
      C:TEMP          P1  L5  C1     .00" Insert Align
====File====Edit====Go to====Window====Layout====Style====Other==========EDIT====
L----!----!----!----!----!----!----!----!----!----!----!---------R
.p# I.A,I.Z                                                              .
I.A GENERAL INFORMATION                                                  <
                                                                         <
I.B INSTALLATION INSTRUCTIONS                                            <
                                                                         <
I.C OPERATING INSTRUCTIONS                                               <
                                                                         <
I.D MAINTENANCE INSTRUCTIONS                                             <
                                                                         <
I.E PARTS LIST                                                           <
                                                                         <
                                                                         <
                                                                         ^
                                                                         ^
                                                                         ^
                                                                         ^
                                                                         ^
                                                                         ^
                                                                         ^
```

Notice that the paragraph numbers were automatically adjusted.

5. Press **Ctrl-KQ** and type **Y** to abandon the document.
6. Turn to Module 46 to continue the learning sequence.

Module 56
PARAGRAPH STYLES

> Classic: ^OF
> Pull-Down: Alt-S, select "Paragraph styles"

DESCRIPTION

WordStar's paragraph styles feature lets you use stored styles for different elements of text. Styles are inserted to control the format of headings, body text, and tables. Each paragraph style has a corresponding style sheet. The paragraph style sheet can be displayed and edited at any time. You may edit the text font, margin and tab settings, and a variety of text attributes including boldface, underscore, and color. Once edited, you can save a paragraph style as either local to the current document, or in a library of paragraph styles.

A library-resident style sheet can be used with any document. Local styles are created and retained by the document in which they are created. Local paragraph styles are not available to other documents. However, a local paragraph style can be converted to a library style if it is required by other documents.

The following paragraphs describe each of the Paragraph Style menu options.

USING STYLES The default style is Body Text, which remains in effect until it is changed using the Paragraph Style menu. The Paragraph Style menu is accessed by pressing Ctrl-OF and is shown in the following screen illustration.

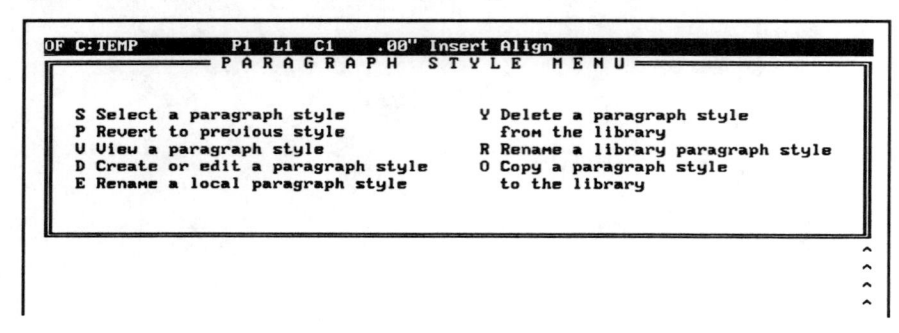

```
OF C:TEMP          P1  L1  C1     .00" Insert Align
                 = P A R A G R A P H    S T Y L E    M E N U =

      S Select a paragraph style          Y Delete a paragraph style
      P Revert to previous style            from the library
      U View a paragraph style           R Rename a library paragraph style
      D Create or edit a paragraph style O Copy a paragraph style
      E Rename a local paragraph style     to the library
```

Paragraph Styles

Select a paragraph style   Typing S from the Paragraph Style menu displays the current style name in addition to other paragraph style names. Use the cursor keys to highlight a new paragraph style and press Return to insert it at the cursor position. The paragraph style name is displayed within angle brackets. Following text assumes the text characteristics, i.e., margins and text attributes of the corresponding style sheet.

Revert to previous style   Type P to insert the previous style sheet at the current cursor location. This saves you the trouble of having to remember the previous paragraph style name.

View a paragraph style   You can view the current paragraph style parameters by typing V from the Paragraph Style menu. The name, font, margins, text attributes, and tab settings are displayed.

Create or edit a paragraph style   Creating or editing paragraph styles is accessed by typing D from the Paragraph Style menu. Next, type the paragraph style name and press Return. Enter or change the margins and text attributes as desired. When finished, press F10 or Ctrl-K to save the changes. When saving the new or edited paragraph style, a dialogue box is displayed. This box lets you save the paragraph style as local to the current document, or you can type Y to save the changes to the library. When saved to the library of paragraph style names, it is available for use in any document. When local, it is saved with the document, but not placed in the library. You can add local paragraph styles to the library whenever desired by opening the document and making the addition.

Rename a local paragraph style   Typing E from the Paragraph Style menu lets you change a local paragraph style name, without changing the paragraph style parameters. A local paragraph style is created and saved with the document without being added to the library of paragraph style names. To save disk space, WordStar deletes local paragraph styles from the library when the current document is closed.

Delete a paragraph style from the library   You can delete a paragraph style from the library by typing Y, the paragraph style name, and then pressing Return. The paragraph style name is deleted from the list.

Rename a library paragraph style   Type R to rename a paragraph style name contained in the library. Type the new name and press Ctrl-K or F10.

Copy a paragraph style to the library   Typing O and a local paragraph style name lets you copy a local paragraph style to the library.

Module 56

APPLICATIONS

Having a variety of preset document formats (or paragraph styles) saves the time that would otherwise be required to reformat each different element of text manually. Paragraph styles are ideal for quickly setting the format characteristics of chapter and paragraph headings, different elements of body text including special passages such as quotations, notes, cautions, warnings, and tables.

TYPICAL OPERATION

In this activity you open a new document, create a paragraph style, and insert it into the document.

1. Open a new document named STYLE.
2. Type **NOTE**, press **Ctrl-OC**, and press **Return** twice.
3. Press **Ctrl-OF**, type **D**, type **Note text**, and press **Return**.
4. Enter paragraph style parameters that correspond to your printer and adjust the paragraph indent as shown.

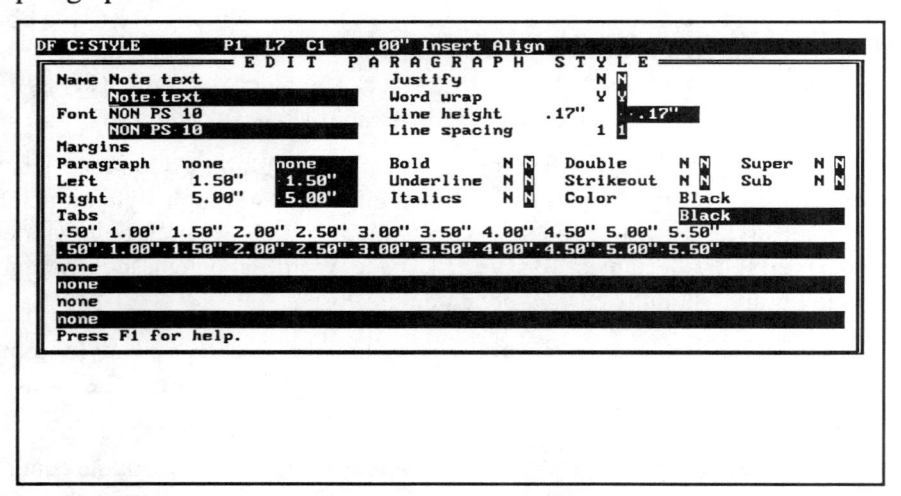

```
DF C:STYLE         P1  L7  C1     .00" Insert Align
═══════════════════ E D I T   P A R A G R A P H   S T Y L E ═══════════════════
         Name Note text               Justify             N N
              Note text               Word wrap           Y Y
         Font NON PS 10                Line height     .17"     .17"
              NON PS 10                Line spacing       1  1
      Margins
      Paragraph      none      none    Bold         N N   Double    N N   Super  N N
      Left           1.50"     1.50"   Underline    N N   Strikeout N N   Sub    N N
      Right          5.00"     5.00"   Italics      N N   Color     Black
      Tabs                                                          Black
      .50" 1.00" 1.50" 2.00" 2.50" 3.00" 3.50" 4.00" 4.50" 5.00" 5.50"
      .50" 1.00" 1.50" 2.00" 2.50" 3.00" 3.50" 4.00" 4.50" 5.00" 5.50"
      none
      none
      none
      none
      Press F1 for help.
```

5. Press **Return** until the dialogue box appears. Save the Note text paragraph style as local by typing **N** in response to the displayed dialogue box.

Paragraph Styles

6. Press **Ctrl-OF** and type **S** to select a paragraph style. Select the Note text paragraph style at the menu prompt. Then type the note shown in the following screen illustration.

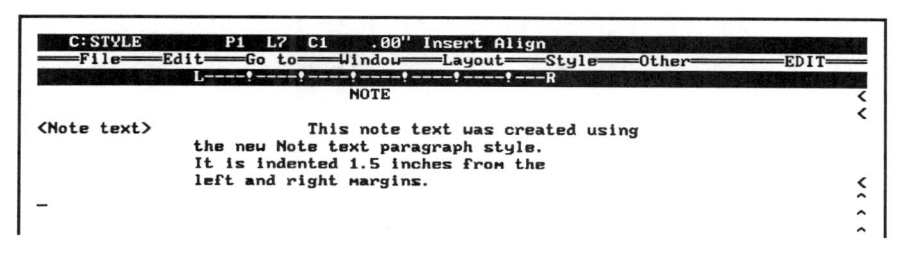

```
   C:STYLE           P1  L7  C1    .00" Insert Align
===File====Edit====Go to====Window====Layout====Style====Other========EDIT===
              L----!----!----!----!----!----!---R
                              NOTE                                          <
                                                                            <
   <Note text>            This note text was created using
                     the new Note text paragraph style.
                     It is indented 1.5 inches from the
                     left and right margins.                                <
                                                                            ^
    -                                                                       ^
                                                                            ^
```

7. Press **Ctrl-OF** and then type **P** to revert to the previous style.
8. Press **Ctrl-KQ** and type **Y** to abandon the document without saving it.
9. Turn to Module 24 to continue the learning sequence.

Module 57
PC-OUTLINE™

DESCRIPTION

The PC-Outline program from Brown Bag Software® is supplied with WordStar as an outlining and list management utility. This module provides an overview of PC-Outline's features and command keys and includes a typical example of its use.

LOADING PC-OUTLINE Before running PC-Outline, you should make a \PCO subdirectory and copy all files from the supplied diskette to this subdirectory. PC-Outline is run by typing PCO and pressing Return. If you want to run it as a memory resident utility, type PCO/R and press Return. Then, press Ctrl-\ to pop up and use PC-Outline. When it is run as a pop-up program, you can work on an outlining task and then return to the original program. Be sure that you have sufficient memory for WordStar, PC-Outline, and any other memory-resident utilities that you use. If your computer has limited memory, you may want to run PC-Outline as a program from the DOS prompt rather than as a pop-up utility.

REMOVING PC-OUTLINE FROM MEMORY To take PC-Outline out of memory, save your outlines and go to the DOS prompt. Be certain that any other memory-resident programs loaded after PC-Outline are removed from memory. Then pop up PC-Outline and display the edit screen. Press Ctrl-Backspace three times to remove PC-Outline from memory.

USING PC-OUTLINE Start PC-Outline as prescribed in the Loading PC-Outline paragraph. The OPENING menu screen lets you:

- Open a new outline
- Load an existing one
- Change the drive/directory
- Quit

The process for opening a new outline includes giving it a filename. Once open, a PCO File screen is displayed. Subsequent uses of PC-Outline go directly to the File screen.

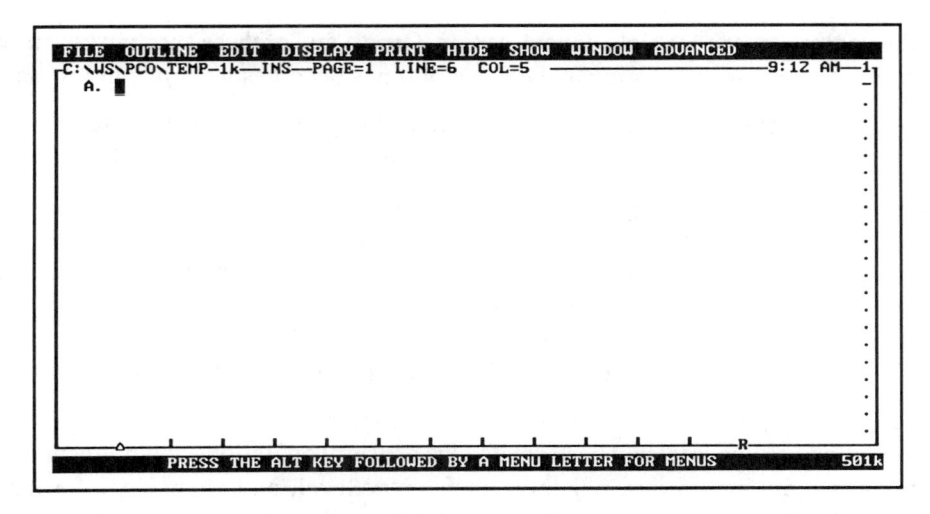

```
┌──FILE  OUTLINE  EDIT  DISPLAY  PRINT  HIDE  SHOW  WINDOW  ADVANCED─────────┐
│ ┌C:\WS\PCO\TEMP-1k──INS──PAGE=1  LINE=6  COL=5 ─────────────9:12 AM──1│
│   A. ▌                                                                      │
│                                                                             │
│                                                                             │
│                                                                             │
│                                                                             │
│                                                                             │
│                                                                          R  │
│         PRESS THE ALT KEY FOLLOWED BY A MENU LETTER FOR MENUS        501k  │
└─────────────────────────────────────────────────────────────────────────────┘
```

You can now type an outline using a special set of control keys. Use the Arrow, PgUp, PgDn, Home, and End keys to move around in the outline. Use Del and Backspace to delete text. Use Esc to leave the current operation. Call help screens with Alt-x, where x is the first letter of the entries across the top of the screen. For example, Alt-F displays the FILE window. You can also press F10 and use the Right or Left Arrow keys to select different menu options.

Choose options within a menu with the Up or Down Arrow keys or by typing the letter in front of the option. Many of the menu selections are called directly from the File screen by pressing a control character or function key. Look at the OUTLINE menu.

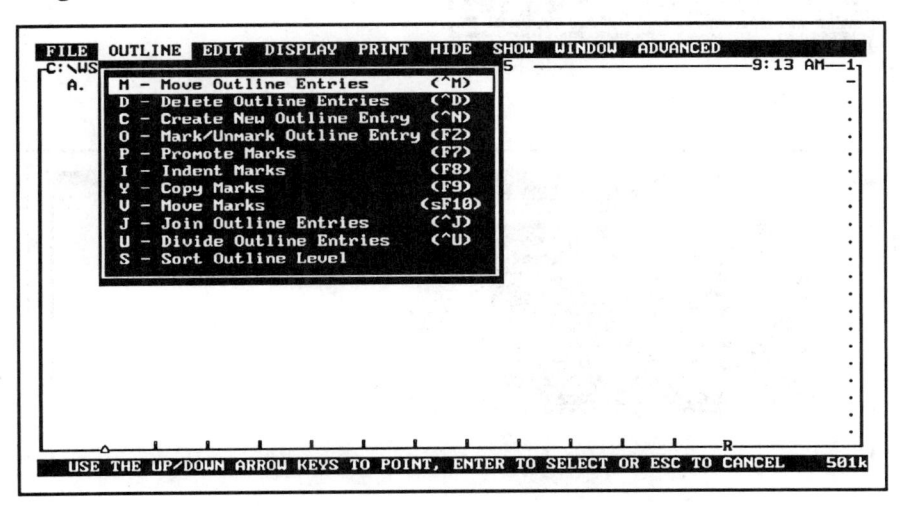

```
┌──FILE  OUTLINE  EDIT  DISPLAY  PRINT  HIDE  SHOW  WINDOW  ADVANCED─────────┐
│ ┌C:\WS┌─────────────────────────────────────┐5 ────────────9:13 AM──1│
│   A.  │ M - Move Outline Entries      (^M)  │                              │
│       │ D - Delete Outline Entries    (^D)  │                              │
│       │ C - Create New Outline Entry  (^N)  │                              │
│       │ O - Mark/Unmark Outline Entry (F2)  │                              │
│       │ P - Promote Marks             (F7)  │                              │
│       │ I - Indent Marks              (F8)  │                              │
│       │ Y - Copy Marks                (F9)  │                              │
│       │ V - Move Marks               (sF10) │                              │
│       │ J - Join Outline Entries      (^J)  │                              │
│       │ U - Divide Outline Entries    (^U)  │                              │
│       │ S - Sort Outline Level              │                              │
│       └─────────────────────────────────────┘                              │
│                                                                          R  │
│    USE THE UP/DOWN ARROW KEYS TO POINT, ENTER TO SELECT OR ESC TO CANCEL  501k│
└─────────────────────────────────────────────────────────────────────────────┘
```

Module 57

Notice the control keys to the right of each option. Once a few of these shortcut keystrokes are committed to memory, creating and editing outlines becomes a simple, quick task.

Outline Terms There are some special terms that you should understand before preparing and editing an outline document. These are summarized in the following list.

Element or Entry	A single grouping within an outline
Text	Descriptive text associated with an outline entry
Family	A top-level outline entry and all associated subentries (or "children" and "grandchildren")
Children	Subelements within a family or subordinate to a parent
Parent	An outline entry that has a set of subelements (or "children")

Menus and Editing Keys PC-Outline is a rich program. The menus as shown below and on the following pages let you perform dozens of useful operations, including marking and moving or copying entries, changing their entry level, and changing information formats. You can also display multiple PC-Outline File screens as small windows. Because the PC-Outline program is so rich in features, complete coverage would require another book. Therefore, this module provides summary information. To get the most out of PC-Outline, perform the Typical Operation and then experiment with the commands.

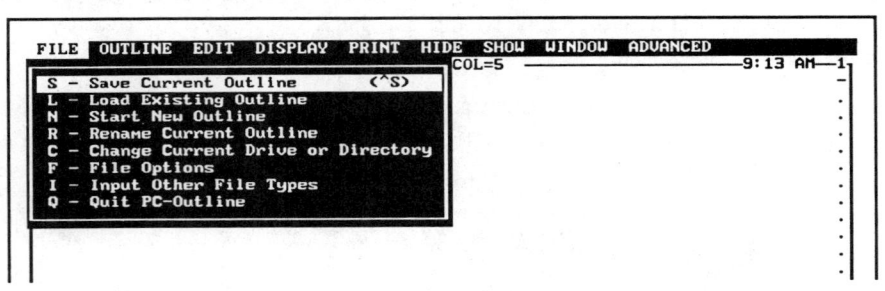

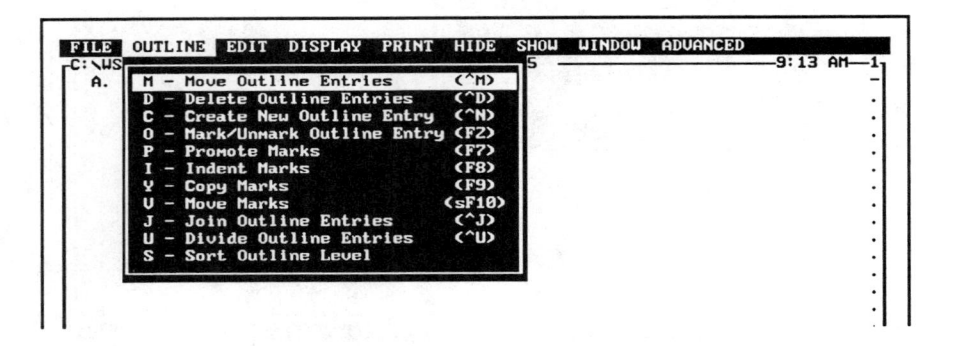

```
FILE OUTLINE EDIT DISPLAY PRINT HIDE SHOW WINDOW ADVANCED
                                    COL=5                    9:13 AM  1
 S - Save Current Outline        (^S)
 L - Load Existing Outline
 N - Start New Outline
 R - Rename Current Outline
 C - Change Current Drive or Directory
 F - File Options
 I - Input Other File Types
 Q - Quit PC-Outline
```

```
     FILE OUTLINE EDIT DISPLAY PRINT HIDE SHOW WINDOW ADVANCED
    C:\WS                         5                    9:13 AM  1
     A.   M - Move Outline Entries       (^M)
          D - Delete Outline Entries     (^D)
          C - Create New Outline Entry   (^N)
          O - Mark/Unmark Outline Entry  (F2)
          P - Promote Marks              (F7)
          I - Indent Marks               (F8)
          Y - Copy Marks                 (F9)
          V - Move Marks                 (sF10)
          J - Join Outline Entries       (^J)
          U - Divide Outline Entries     (^U)
          S - Sort Outline Level
```

NOTE
In general, outline entries are first marked and then manipulated using the commands in the OUTLINE menu.

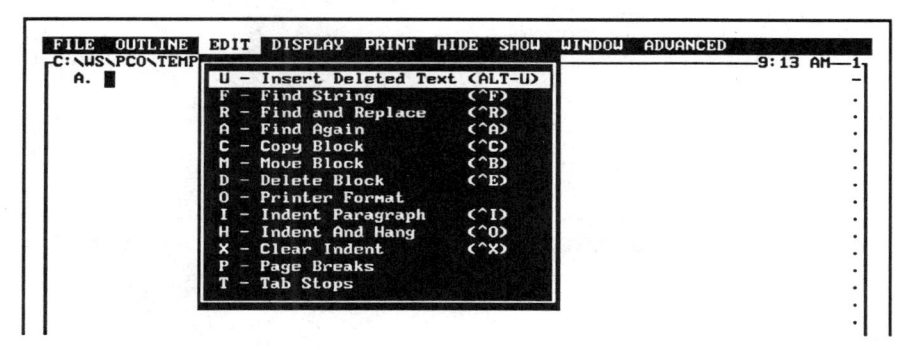

```
FILE OUTLINE EDIT DISPLAY PRINT HIDE SHOW WINDOW ADVANCED
C:\WS\PCO\TEMP                                      9:13 AM—1
A.    U - Insert Deleted Text (ALT-U)
      F - Find String            (^F)
      R - Find and Replace       (^R)
      A - Find Again             (^A)
      C - Copy Block             (^C)
      M - Move Block             (^B)
      D - Delete Block           (^E)
      O - Printer Format
      I - Indent Paragraph       (^I)
      H - Indent And Hang        (^O)
      X - Clear Indent           (^X)
      P - Page Breaks
      T - Tab Stops
```

NOTE
Marking blocks of text is done with the cursor. Finishing a block operation is accomplished by pressing Return.

The Page Break command lets you set hard page breaks with .p or conditional page breaks with .c. Either are set or deleted by placing the cursor at the page break, pressing Alt-E, and typing P.

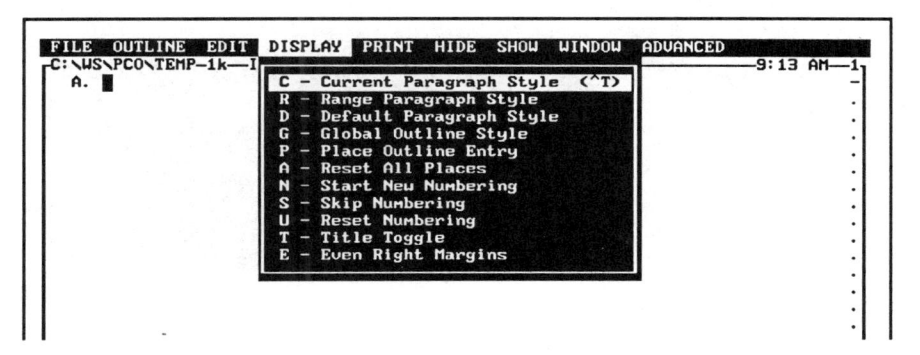

```
FILE OUTLINE EDIT DISPLAY PRINT HIDE SHOW WINDOW ADVANCED
C:\WS\PCO\TEMP-1k—I                                 9:13 AM—1
A.    C - Current Paragraph Style  (^T)
      R - Range Paragraph Style
      D - Default Paragraph Style
      G - Global Outline Style
      P - Place Outline Entry
      A - Reset All Places
      N - Start New Numbering
      S - Skip Numbering
      U - Reset Numbering
      T - Title Toggle
      E - Even Right Margins
```

NOTE
Place Outline Entry and Skip Numbering are used together to enter passages of normal text.

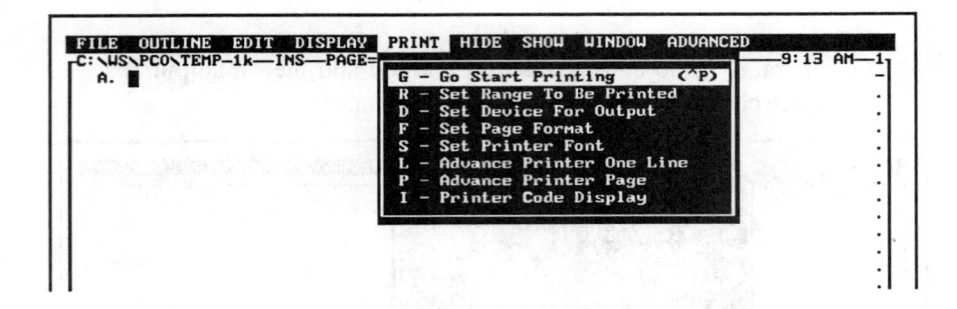

Module 57

```
FILE  OUTLINE  EDIT  DISPLAY  PRINT  HIDE  SHOW  WINDOW  ADVANCED
C:\WS\PCO\TEMP-1k──INS──PAGE=              ┌─────────────────9:13 AM──1┐
 A. ▮         G - Go Start Printing       (^P)
              R - Set Range To Be Printed
              D - Set Device For Output
              F - Set Page Format
              S - Set Printer Font
              L - Advance Printer One Line
              P - Advance Printer Page
              I - Printer Code Display
```

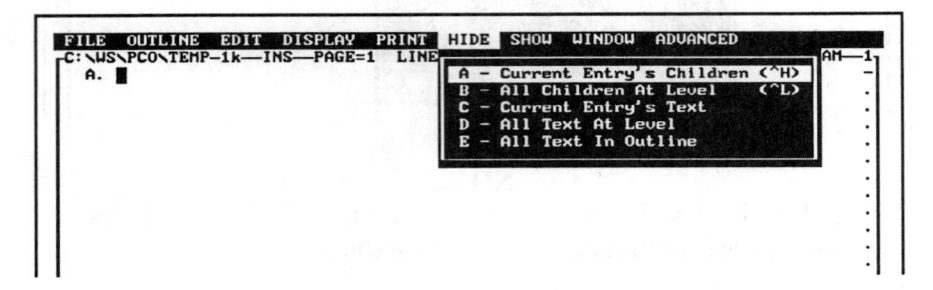

```
FILE  OUTLINE  EDIT  DISPLAY  PRINT  HIDE  SHOW  WINDOW  ADVANCED
C:\WS\PCO\TEMP-1k──INS──PAGE=1  LINE    A - Current Entry's Children (^H)
 A. ▮                                   B - All Children At Level    (^L)
                                        C - Current Entry's Text
                                        D - All Text At Level
                                        E - All Text In Outline
```

NOTE

You can substitute the gray + key for ^H to toggle text on and off.
You can use Ctrl-PgDn for C to toggle text on and off.

```
FILE  OUTLINE  EDIT  DISPLAY  PRINT  HIDE  SHOW  WINDOW  ADVANCED
C:\WS\PCO\TEMP-1k──INS──PAGE=1  LINE=6  CO   A - Current Entry's Children
 A. ▮                                        B - All Children At Level
                                             C - Current Entry's Text
                                             D - All Text At Level
                                             E - All Text In Outline
                                             F - All Children In Outline
                                             G - All Text And Children
                                             H - All Family Children
                                             I - All Family Text
```

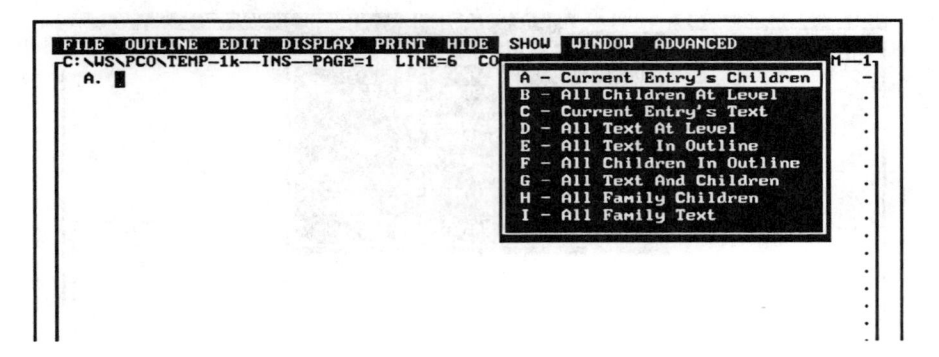

NOTE

Selections F through I redisplay all entries regardless of how hidden.

184

PC-Outline

```
FILE OUTLINE EDIT DISPLAY PRINT HIDE SHOW WINDOW ADVANCED
C:\WS\PCO\TEMP-1k—INS—PAGE=1 LINE=6 COL=5
A. ▌         L - Load Outline New Window
             N - New Outline New Window
             C - Close Window
             M - Move Window
             S - Size Window
             A - Arrange Windows
             T - Transfer Windows (ALT 1-9)
             I - List Windows        (^Z)
             Z - Zoom Window
             Q - Copy Family         (^Q)
             W - Move Family         (^W)
```

```
FILE OUTLINE EDIT DISPLAY PRINT HIDE SHOW WINDOW ADVANCED
C:\WS\PCO\TEMP-1k—INS—PAGE=1 LINE=6 COL=5
A. ▌         C - Config. Settings
             K - Key Definition      (^K)
             O - Key Def. Options
             D - Insert Static Date  (sF1)
             V - Insert Live Date    (sF2)
             T - Insert Static Time  (sF3)
             X - Insert Live Time    (sF4)
             E - Export Block
             P - Export Options
             I - Import Block
             M - Import Options
             H - Key Help            (F1)
             F - Flatten Whole Outline
```

APPLICATIONS

The PC-Outline program lets you create outlines, lists, legal documents, or any other kind of document using numbered entries. PC-Outline lets you concentrate on the content of an outlined document, without being concerned about assigning numbers to new or edited entries or readjusting numbers when entries are moved or deleted.

PC-Outline's ability to load as a memory-resident program makes it a powerful pop-up utility. The ability to import and export screens lets you interchange information between an outline and a program or use PC-Outline as a clipboard to import information from one program and then export that information to a second program.

TYPICAL OPERATION

In this activity, you start PC-Outline to open a new outline named TEMP. You then type an outline and modify it using several PC-Outline control keys.

1. Move to the DOS directory containing the PCO files.
2. Type **PCO** and press **Return**; the PC-Outline OPENING menu is displayed.
3. Select "Open an outline," press **Return**, type **TEMP**, and press **Return** to display the File screen.

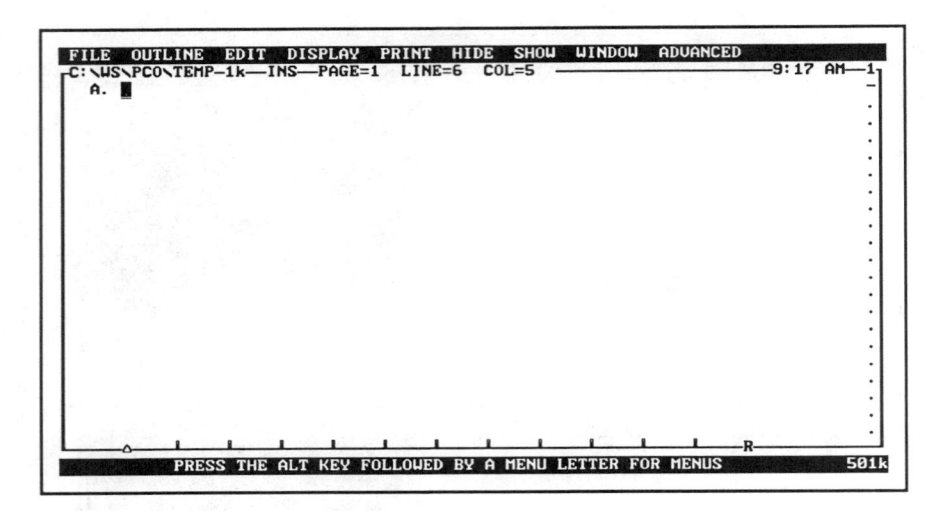

Module 57

```
┌FILE  OUTLINE  EDIT  DISPLAY  PRINT  HIDE  SHOW  WINDOW  ADVANCED─────┐
├C:\WS\PCO\TEMP-1k──INS──PAGE=1  LINE=6  COL=5 ─────────────9:17 AM──1┤
│  A. ▮                                                                │
│                                                                      │
│                                                                      │
│                                                                      │
│                                                                   R  │
│         PRESS THE ALT KEY FOLLOWED BY A MENU LETTER FOR MENUS   501k │
└──────────────────────────────────────────────────────────────────────┘
```

4. Type the following outline, pressing **Ctrl-Return** at the end of each entry.

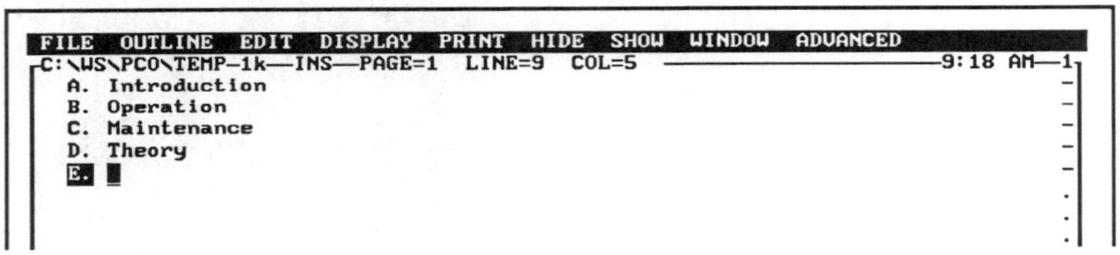

```
┌FILE  OUTLINE  EDIT  DISPLAY  PRINT  HIDE  SHOW  WINDOW  ADVANCED─────┐
├C:\WS\PCO\TEMP-1k──INS──PAGE=1  LINE=9  COL=5 ─────────────9:18 AM──1┤
│    A. Introduction                                                   │
│    B. Operation                                                      │
│    C. Maintenance                                                    │
│    D. Theory                                                         │
│    E. ▮                                                              │
└──────────────────────────────────────────────────────────────────────┘
```

5. Move the cursor to B and type **Installation**. Your list now resembles the following one.

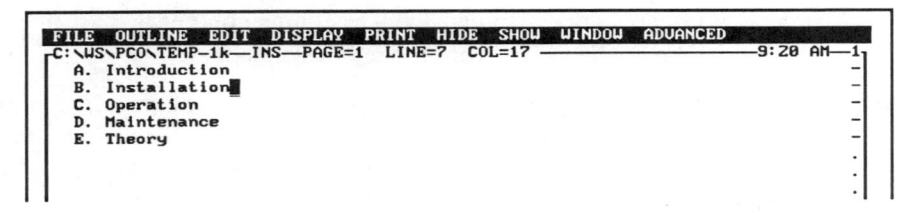

```
┌FILE  OUTLINE  EDIT  DISPLAY  PRINT  HIDE  SHOW  WINDOW  ADVANCED─────┐
├C:\WS\PCO\TEMP-1k──INS──PAGE=1  LINE=7  COL=17 ────────────9:20 AM──1┤
│    A. Introduction                                                   │
│    B. Installation▮                                                  │
│    C. Operation                                                      │
│    D. Maintenance                                                    │
│    E. Theory                                                         │
└──────────────────────────────────────────────────────────────────────┘
```

6. Move cursor under I in Installation to enter a 1. beneath B.
7. Type **Unpacking**, press **Ctrl-Return**, and then type **Assembly**. Your outline document should resemble the following one.

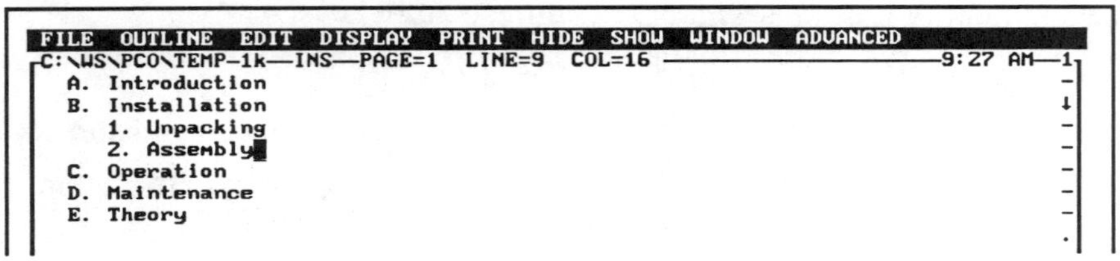

```
┌FILE  OUTLINE  EDIT  DISPLAY  PRINT  HIDE  SHOW  WINDOW  ADVANCED─────┐
├C:\WS\PCO\TEMP-1k──INS──PAGE=1  LINE=9  COL=16 ────────────9:27 AM──1┤
│    A. Introduction                                                   │
│    B. Installation                                                   │
│       1. Unpacking                                                   │
│       2. Assembly▮                                                   │
│    C. Operation                                                      │
│    D. Maintenance                                                    │
│    E. Theory                                                         │
└──────────────────────────────────────────────────────────────────────┘
```

PC-Outline

8. Move the cursor to the Theory line and press **Ctrl-M** to mark and move the entry.
9. Press **Up Arrow** once to move the Theory entry above Maintenance and press **Return**. Notice how the entries are renumbered automatically.

```
FILE  OUTLINE  EDIT  DISPLAY  PRINT  HIDE  SHOW  WINDOW  ADVANCED
C:\WS\PCO\TEMP-1k—INS—PAGE=1  LINE=11 COL=5                9:28 AM—1
   A. Introduction
   B. Installation
      1. Unpacking
      2. Assembly
   C. Operation
   D. Theory
   E. Maintenance
```

10. Press **Alt-A** and type **F** to "flatten" the file, which puts all entries to the first level. Your outline now resembles the following one.

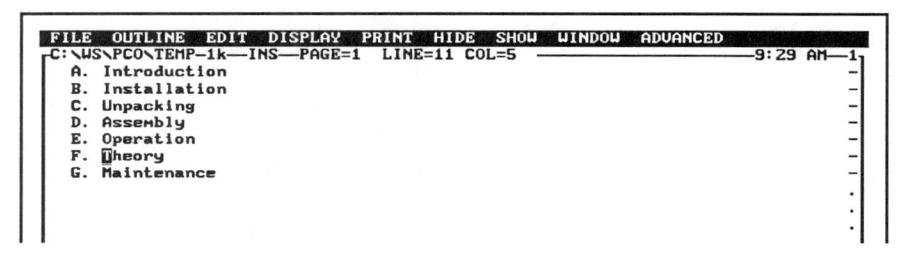

```
FILE  OUTLINE  EDIT  DISPLAY  PRINT  HIDE  SHOW  WINDOW  ADVANCED
C:\WS\PCO\TEMP-1k—INS—PAGE=1  LINE=11 COL=5                9:29 AM—1
   A. Introduction
   B. Installation
   C. Unpacking
   D. Assembly
   E. Operation
   F. Theory
   G. Maintenance
```

11. Experiment with other PC-Outline commands to see how they work.
12. From the File screen, press **Esc** and type **Y** to exit the PC-Outline program.
13. Turn to Module 68 to continue the learning sequence.

Module 58
PRINT ALTERNATE PITCH

```
                ^PA
```

DESCRIPTION

The number of printed characters per inch is expressed in *pitch*. For example, ten characters per inch is called 10 pitch, which is the most common default value. Twelve characters per inch is called 12 pitch. This is WordStar's default alternate pitch. Sixteen to seventeen characters per inch, often called *compressed print*, is also available on most dot matrix and laser printers.

The printer codes that shift your printer from one pitch to another are set using WordStar's WSCHANGE utility. Here, you can select the printer type, the standard pitch value, and the alternate pitch value. The pitch value, expressed in 120ths of an inch, for 10 pitch is 12, or 12/120ths. Twelve pitch is 10/120ths, and 15 pitch is 8/120ths. You can use 7/120ths to obtain compressed print on most dot matrix printers.

Use WSCHANGE to install both alternate and standard pitch values. Alternate pitch can be compressed, 12 pitch, or wide print, depending upon your personal needs. Set the standard pitch value to return your printer to normal printing.

You can alter the character width of alternate pitch in your file by following the Ctrl-PA with .CW and a number you choose on the line below the Ctrl-PA. When you return to normal pitch, you can change the character pitch back with another .CW number.

APPLICATIONS

Alternate pitch is often used to set off passages of text, such as excerpts from articles, books, or quotations. When the alternate pitch is compressed, it is sometimes used to help fit long lines of text within established margins. For example, assume alternate pitch is 17 cpi. You must fit an 80-character line into a document having a right margin setting of 65. You can change to alternate pitch and have space to spare. In fact, 110 17-pitch characters occupy the same space as 65 10-pitch characters.

TYPICAL OPERATION

Before proceeding with this activity, be sure that WordStar is properly installed for your printer. Then open a new document and type a few lines of text with embedded alternate and standard print codes.

1. Open a new document named TEMP.
2. Type the following passage of text, using **Ctrl-PA** to select alternate pitch and **Ctrl-PN** to return to standard pitch as indicated by the <ALTERNATE> and <NORMAL>.

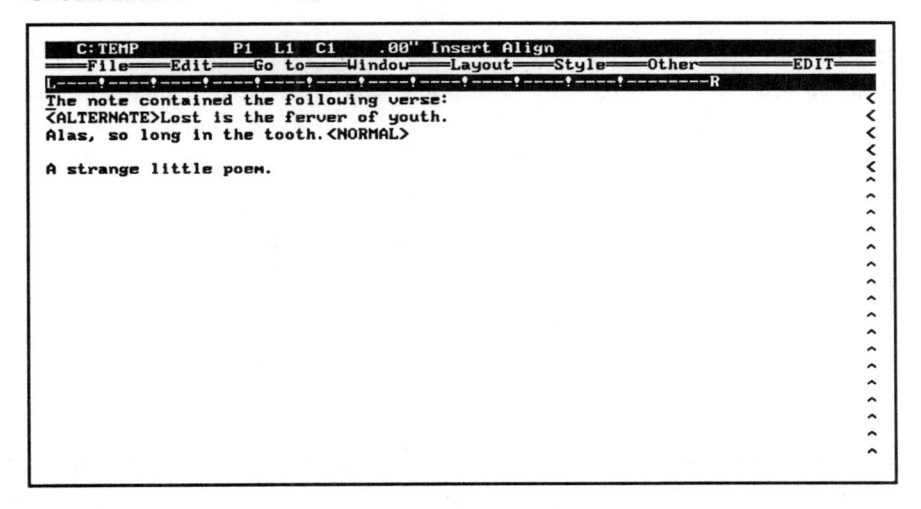

```
    C:TEMP           P1  L1  C1     .00" Insert Align
====File====Edit====Go to====Window====Layout====Style====Other====       EDIT==
L----!----!----!----!----!----!----!----!----!--------R
The note contained the following verse:
<ALTERNATE>Lost is the fervor of youth.
Alas, so long in the tooth.<NORMAL>

A strange little poem.
```

NOTE

If printed, the <ALTERNATE> causes the verse to print in alternate pitch. The <NORMAL> shifts the printer back to standard (or normal) pitch.

3. Press **Ctrl-KQ** and type **Y** to abandon the document without saving.
4. Turn to Module 60 to continue the learning sequence.

Module 59
PRINT BINDING (NON-BREAK) SPACE

> ^PO

DESCRIPTION

The binding, or *non-break*, space is treated like a standard character instead of a space. The automatic word wrap function, described in Module 89, does not break two words bound together with a binding space. The binding space joins the words together as one. A binding space is inserted with Ctrl-PO, where O is a capital oh.

If you put a binding space between the words New and London, it is displayed

New■London

Notice that the binding space is displayed as a solid square block.

APPLICATIONS

The binding space is most often used to prevent proper names or numbers from being broken at the end of a line of text. The New London example is typical of its use.

TYPICAL OPERATION

In this activity, you open a document and type a line of text using the binding space to prevent word wrap from breaking a proper name.

1. Open a new document named TEMP.
2. With the right margin set at 65 (the default value), type the following sentence. Press **Ctrl-PO** between "San" and "Francisco."

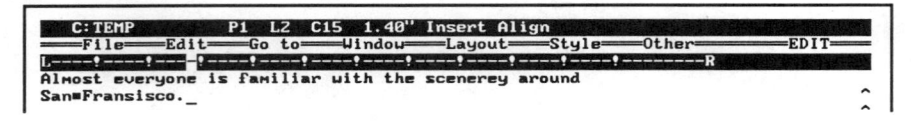

```
  C:TEMP            P1  L2  C15  1.40"  Insert Align
=====File====Edit====Go to====Window====Layout====Style====Other====EDIT====
L----!----!----!----!----!----!----!----!----!----!--------R
Almost everyone is familiar with the scenerey around
San■Fransisco._
```

3. Notice how the entire name "San Francisco" wrapped, rather than breaking between San and Francisco.
4. Press **Ctrl-KQ** and type **Y** to abandon without saving.
5. Turn to Module 65 to continue the learning sequence.

Module 60
PRINT COLOR

```
^P-
```

DESCRIPTION

WordStar incorporates the ability to print in a variety of colors when using a color printer. Use the control sequence Ctrl-P-, where "-" is the hyphen character. The following screen is displayed.

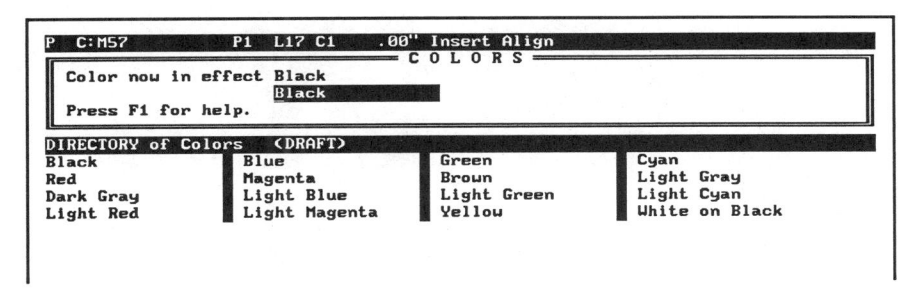

```
P  C:M57         P1  L17 C1     .00" Insert Align
                         C O L O R S
 Color now in effect Black
                     Black
 Press F1 for help.

DIRECTORY of Colors   <DRAFT>
Black           Blue            Green           Cyan
Red             Magenta         Brown           Light Gray
Dark Gray       Light Blue      Light Green     Light Cyan
Light Red       Light Magenta   Yellow          White on Black
```

To select a color, either type a displayed color or point to it using your cursor keys. Then press Return. The color selection is displayed within angle brackets in your document.

APPLICATIONS

Having a color printer and the ability to enter color change codes within your documents lets you highlight passages of text for emphasis. Normally, you should use color sparingly, as the use of too much color tends to diminish its effectiveness.

TYPICAL OPERATION

In this activity, you begin by opening a new document and then type a passage of text containing a color change.

1. Open a new document named TEMP.

Module 60

2. Type the following line of text. Use Ctrl-P-, Red, and Return to insert the first color change; use Ctrl-P-, Black, Return for the second color change.

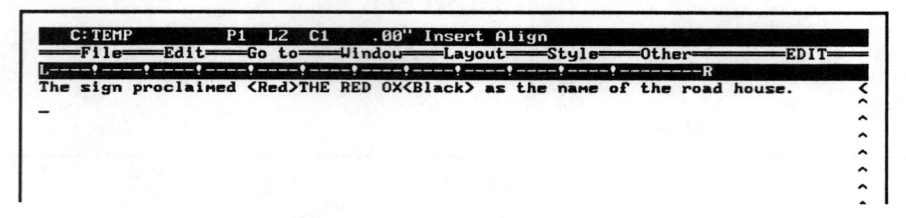

```
 C:TEMP            P1  L2  C1      .00" Insert Align
====File====Edit====Go to====Window====Layout====Style====Other====EDIT====
L----!----!----!----!----!----!----!----!----!----!--------R
The sign proclaimed <Red>THE RED OX<Black> as the name of the road house.
```

3. Press **Ctrl-KQ** and type **Y** to abandon the document without saving.
4. Turn to Module 63 to continue the learning sequence.

Module 61
PRINT DOCUMENT

> Classic: ^KPP
> Pull-Down: Alt-F, select "Print a file..."

DESCRIPTION

A document is printed from either the OPENING menu or the EDIT menu. At the OPENING menu, typing FP displays the PRINT menu. If you are editing, you can press Ctrl-KP and then type P to display the PRINT menu. However, before you print your first document, be sure that WordStar is properly installed to match your printer. Use WSCHANGE (or PRCHANGE) and examine the printer choices. Then select the name of your printer to ensure that WordStar uses the printer driver that matches yours. The WSCHANGE Printer menu lets you specify most popular printers by brand and model.

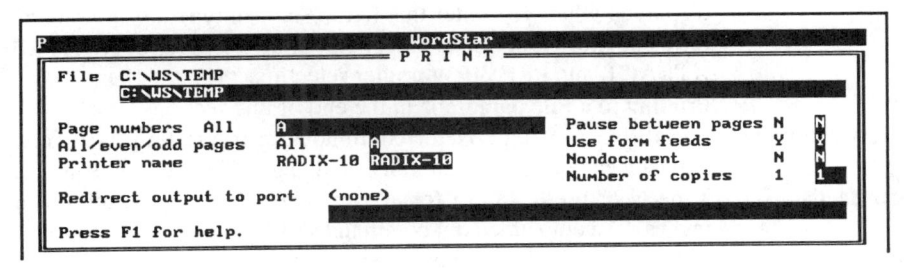

```
P                              WordStar
                              ═ P R I N T ═
 File  C:\WS\TEMP
       C:\WS\TEMP

 Page numbers    All    A                Pause between pages  N    N
 All/even/odd pages     All   A          Use form feeds       Y    Y
 Printer name           RADIX-10 RADIX-10 Nondocument         N    N
                                         Number of copies    1    1
 Redirect output to port   (none)

 Press F1 for help.
```

CUSTOM PRINTERS If a printer selection is not available in the installation menu, you can use the custom printer selection to specify the control codes for underline, boldface, double strike, alternate pitch, and so on. For special printer patches, get a copy of *The WordStar Customizing Guide* from your bookstore or directly from Wordware Publishing, Inc. The address is given in the front of this book.

When properly configured, WordStar has a powerful repertoire of printing commands. If you have a full-featured daisy-wheel or thimble printer, such as a Diablo 630 or NEC 3550, WordStar lets you exercise its full potential. If your printer is a simple, non-backspacing teletype-type unit, WordStar's versatility still lets you perform most printing capabilities by using common "work arounds," such as making multiple passes on a line to achieve underline and bold print.

Module 61

The printing procedures described in this module and in modules 58 through 67 assume that you are using a popular dot matrix or letter-quality printer, although almost every printer on the market is compatible with WordStar's special control features.

STARTING PRINTING   Once a document is properly saved, it is ready to print. There are three ways to print a document. You can print during the text editing process by pressing Ctrl-KP, typing P, and responding to WordStar's print prompts. You are asked if you want to merge print.

You can also press Ctrl-PrtSc to save the file currently being edited and go directly to the PRINT menu.

The most common way to print a document is to type FP and follow the print prompts from WordStar's OPENING menu. The printing prompts are:

Print Prompts	*Description*
File	The name of the file to print.
Page numbers	The pages you wish to print. Enter a single number, a range, or a combination. To print pages 1 and 5 through 9, enter 1,5-9.
All/even/odd pages	Type A, O, or E to print all, odd, or even numbered pages.
Printer name	The default value is the installed printer. A menu of printer drivers is displayed when you enter this field. You can type a printer name or use the cursor keys to select a printer name and press Return. The ASCII, WS4, XTRACT, and PREVIEW printer selections print the file to disk. See the Printing to a File paragraph at the end of this section.
Pause between pages	Press Return or type N for continuous form printing; type Y to pause between each page to feed individual pages. The default is no.
Use form feeds	Type N or press Return for a normal paper advance each 66 lines (11 inches). An embedded dot command (.PL n) is used to change the normal page length. Typing Y suppresses automatic line counting. The default is no.
Nondocument	The default is N. If you say Y for yes, the file will print using page layout defaults. You can print a document in nondocument mode to print all dot commands as displayed instead of executing them.
Number of copies	The default number is 1; you can print more than one copy.
Redirect output to	You can type the name of a file to which the document is printed. You can also print to a printer port other than the one selected with WSCHANGE (normally LPT1:). For example, you can enter LPT2: or COM1: to redirect the output to parallel port 2 or serial communications port 1.

You can press Return or Tab to advance to the next PRINT menu field. Pressing Return in the last PRINT menu field or pressing F10 or Ctrl-K from any field prints the document in accordance with the information entered in the PRINT menu. You may change your mind about printing at any time by pressing Ctrl-U.

SIMULTANEOUS PRINTING WordStar supports simultaneous printing and editing. When you print from a displayed document using the Ctrl-KP, you may resume text editing without leaving the displayed document. The status line includes the word "Printing" as it is occurring or "Print wait" if it stops. If you print from the OPENING menu, you can open a document and edit it during the printing operation. However, simultaneous printing and editing slows the editing response time and also reduces the printing speed.

READYING YOUR PRINTER Prior to printing, be sure that your printer is ready. Power should be on, ribbon installed, and paper loaded and properly aligned. You can control your top, bottom, and left margins by using the proper dot commands, which are control codes that are embedded in the body of your document. Complete descriptions of these powerful print control codes are presented in Module 24.

DEFAULT MARGINS If dot commands are not used, WordStar's default margin settings are:

Top Margin	3 blank lines
Page Offset	8 blank spaces
Bottom Margin	8 blank lines
Header Margin	2 blank lines
Footer Margin	2 blank lines
Left Margin	0.00"
Right Margin	6.50"

INTERRUPTING PRINTING If you decide to stop printing from the OPENING menu, type FP; to stop printing when a document is being edited, press Ctrl-KP. In either case, WordStar displays the Printing screen for the options:

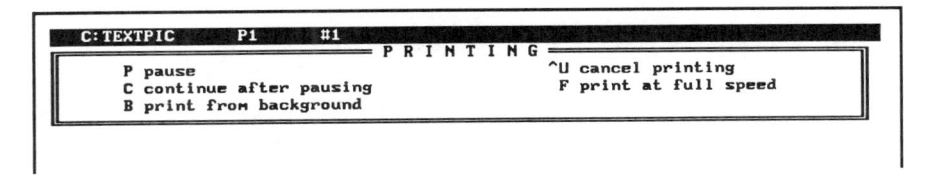

```
 C:TEXTPIC      P1      #1
==================== P R I N T I N G ====================
 P pause                          ^U cancel printing
 C continue after pausing         F print at full speed
 B print from background
```

Responding to the prompt with P pauses the printing temporarily. Ctrl-U cancels the printing operation and returns you to the menu that you left.

PRINTING TO A FILE WordStar has printer drivers that let you print a document to a disk file. The printer drivers let you print a file to disk as an ASCII file, a WordStar Release 4 file, or a file that resembles a printed document. Select one of the following printer names in the Printer name field to convert a file and save it to disk.

Name	Description
ASCII	Converts file to ASCII. Assumes the filename ASCII.WS. Removes all dot commands, control characters, and high-order bits on characters. Places a hard return at the end of each line.
PREVIEW	The preview printer driver provides a document that looks much like the printed document. Includes headers, footers, and page numbers. Merge print master documents include inserted data.
WS4	Converts the file for compatibility with WordStar Release 4. You should search and replace dot commands that control margins and tabs to ensure that the resulting document aligns properly. For example, if you are using a compressed print, reset the right margin to inches rather than columns. A dot command such as .RM 65 is replaced with .RM 6.5". You should also use the font command (Ctrl-P=) for font selection rather than the .CW dot command for best results. The resulting default filename is WS4.WS. You can rename the output document prior to printing.
XTRACT	Produces a document similar to the preview document without headers, footers, or page breaks. You can print a merge print master document containing selected read variable names. The resulting document gives you a list of selected variables. Look at the following master document, which uses a data file named customer.dat. Notice that it prepares a list of customers and their phone numbers. .op .db customer.dat .rv company,adr1,adr2,city,state,zip,phone &company& &phone&

APPLICATIONS

WordStar's print operation is powerful and easy to use. Available format control, which is achieved through dot commands and default settings, makes WordStar an extremely versatile word processing package. Of course, the way you set your margins and line spacing during document creation also controls the way it looks when printed.

TYPICAL OPERATION

In this example, begin with the OPENING menu displayed. Print the document MYLTR.

1. Check your printer to see that it is ready for printing. This includes:
    a. Ribbon installed
    b. Paper loaded
    c. Power turned on
    d. On line indicator lighted (if your printer is equipped with one)

Print Document

2. Type **FP**; notice that the PRINT menu is displayed.
3. Type **MYLTR** on the File line and press **Return**.
4. Review the rest of the fields on the PRINT menu.

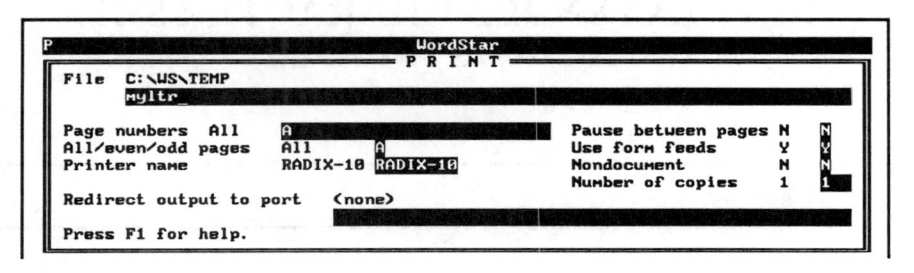

```
P                          WordStar
                         ═ P R I N T ═
 File   C:\WS\TEMP
        myltr_

 Page numbers     All    A                    Pause between pages  N   N
 All/even/odd pages  All     A                Use form feeds       Y   Y
 Printer name        RADIX-10 RADIX-10        Nondocument          N   N
                                              Number of copies     1   1
 Redirect output to port   (none)

 Press F1 for help.
```

5. Press **F10** to accept all the defaults; notice that the document prints.
6. Turn to Module 66 to continue the learning sequence.

Module 62
PRINT EXTENDED CHARACTER SET (SPECIAL SYMBOLS)

> ^P0

DESCRIPTION

Extended characters are those that have ASCII values outside the normal text, number, and punctuation range. For example, the horizontal rule symbol has an ASCII value of 196. Extended characters are normally unavailable through your keyboard unless called by special means. For example, WordStar's Alt-F2 calls a horizontal rule (see Module 26).

WordStar lets you call additional extended characters. This is achieved by pressing Ctrl-P0 (the last character is a zero). The following table of extended characters is displayed in the EXTENDED CHARACTER menu.

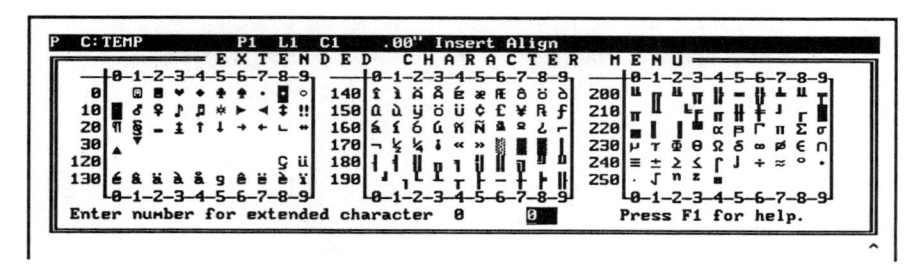

You can look up a character and its number in the EXTENDED CHARACTER menu. For example, the heart symbol is 03. The square root symbol is 251. To place an extended character at the cursor position, type the number and press Return at the menu. It is inserted at the cursor position.

These same characters can be entered using the Alt key in combination with the number on the numeric keypad. For example, press Alt, type 03, and release the Alt key. Upon release, a heart character (ASCII value 03) is inserted.

It is important that you use a graphics printer capable of interpreting and printing those characters having ASCII values from 0 to 255. This is the IBM extended character set. If you do not have a graphics printer, you cannot reproduce extended characters. The best way to find out is to prepare a document that includes extended characters and try to print it.

Print Extended Character Set (Special Symbols)

APPLICATIONS

Extended characters are often used to produce mathematical equations or to insert special symbols. For example, the Return symbol can be produced using characters 17 and 217 in combination to achieve the symbol ⬅┘.

Some other symbols are included for your examination.

ASCII Values	Symbols
171 246 172:	½ ÷ ¼
03 04 05 06:	♥ ♦ ♣ ♠
244: 245:	∫
218 196 196 196: 251:	┌─── └
218 196 196 196: 179: 251:	┌─── │ └

TYPICAL OPERATION

In this activity, you open a temporary document and type a line of text in combination with extended characters.

1. Open a new document named TEMP.
2. Type the following line of text, using Ctrl-P0 17 (Return) and Ctrl-P0 217 (Return) to produce the return symbol.

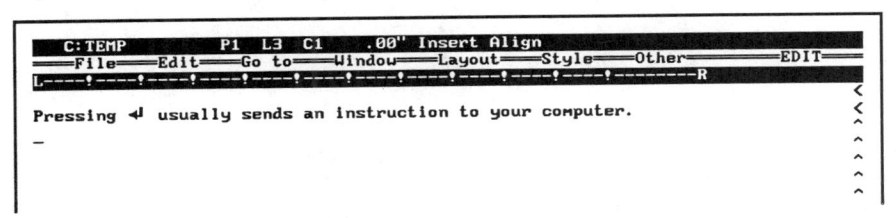

```
 C:TEMP           P1  L3  C1     .00" Insert Align
==File====Edit====Go to====Window====Layout====Style====Other====    =EDIT==
L----!----!----!----!----!----!----!----!----!---------R
Pressing ⬅┘ usually sends an instruction to your computer.
_
```

Module 62

3. Try the following equation using extended characters 171 246 171 and 172. The equal sign is a normal keyboard character.

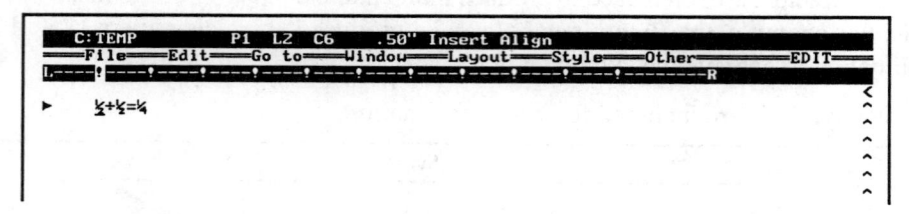

```
 C:TEMP          P1  L2  C6    .50" Insert Align
===File====Edit====Go to====Window====Layout====Style====Other========EDIT===
L---!----!----!----!----!----!----!----!----!----!--------R
  ▶   ½+½=¼
```

4. Reproduce the equation entered in step 3 using the Alt key in combination with the numbers on your numeric key pad. Remember that the characters are displayed as you release the Alt key, not when you type the numbers.
5. Continue experimenting with the extended character set until you understand its use.
6. Press **Ctrl-KQ** and type **Y** to abandon the document without saving.
7. Turn to Module 67 to continue the learning sequence.

Module 63
PRINT FROM KEYBOARD

> From the Opening Menu
>   Classic: K
>   Pull-Down: F, select "Print from keyboard..."
> From the Edit Menu
>   Classic: Ctrl-KP, K

DESCRIPTION

WordStar now has a typewriter mode that lets you use your printer like a typewriter. When you are in the typewriter mode, which is started by typing K from the OPENING menu, each typed line prints when you press Return at the end of the line.

When you first enter the typewriter mode command, a PRINT FROM KEYBOARD menu is displayed, which is shown in the following illustration.

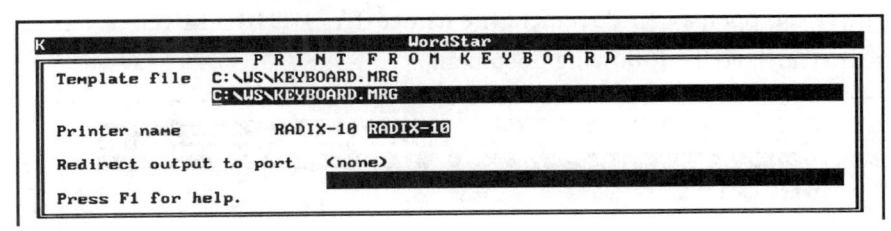

```
K                             WordStar
═══════════════════ P R I N T   F R O M   K E Y B O A R D ═══════════════════
  Template file       C:\WS\KEYBOARD.MRG
                      C:\WS\KEYBOARD.MRG

  Printer name             RADIX-10  RADIX-10

  Redirect output to port   (none)

  Press F1 for help.
```

Notice the template file, C:\WS\KEYBOARD.MRG. This file is supplied with WordStar 6.0 and contains a series of dot commands used to control the way a typed document prints. You can create your own template file to control such parameters as margins, page offset, page numbers, and line spacing. The following dot commands are typical of those found in a template file.

.mt 0, .mb 0	Sets the top and bottom margins to 0
.op	Suppresses page numbers
.cw 10	Sets character width to 12 pitch (10/120 of an inch)
.rp 2	Prints two copies of the typed text
.av input	Asks for a variable input; &input& should also be included as the last line of the template file

Module 63

Look at the following template file.

.rp 2	Make two copies of the typed text
.mt 0	Set the top margin to 0
.op	Omit page numbers
.av date	Ask for the date
&date&	Date variable that corresponds to the .av date command

If your printer only types when the page is full, you may want to type .pa at the bottom of the document to cause a form feed, where .pa is the page break dot command.

APPLICATIONS

The typewriter mode is an excellent way to type a quick note or to address an envelope, post card, or mailing label. You should create your own template file to be sure the output conforms to your needs. In particular, margins and indents may be crucial to your output.

TYPICAL OPERATION

In this activity you create a template file and then use the typewriter mode to produce a note. Begin at the OPENING menu.

1. Type **N** and open a non-document file named TYPETHRU.MRG.
2. Create and save the following document.

```
  C:TYPETHRU.MRG P1  L1   C1            Insert Align
======File======Edit======Go to======Window======Layout======Style======Other======EDIT======
.RP 50
.IF &START& <> 1
.MT 0                                                                               1
.MB 0                                                                               1
.PO 10
.OP
.EI
.SV START,1
.DM Type a line and press Enter.
.AV "",LINE
&LINE&
```

3. From the OPENING menu, type **K**, enter **TYPETHRU.MRG** as the template filename, and press **F10**.

4. Type the following note. Press **Return** where indicated by <CR>. Press **Ctrl-U** after the last <CR>.

   John: <CR>
   <CR>
   Please call Arthur Johnson and set an appointment for next<CR>
   Thursday afternoon in my office. Please obtain an overhead<CR>
   projector for the meeting. Thanks for your assistance.<CR>
   <CR>
   Marie Wood <CR>

5. Note that each line prints when Return is pressed. Also, the Ctrl-U issues a form feed.

6. Turn to Module 56 to continue the learning sequence.

Module 64
PRINT PAUSE (STOP) CODE

> Classic: ^PC

DESCRIPTION

If you want to stop your printer at a specific location within your document, you can insert a printer stop code by pressing Ctrl-PC. When your printer reaches this code, which is displayed as ^C, it stops printing and the message "Print Wait" is displayed.

To restart the printer from the OPENING menu, type PC. From the EDIT menu, press Ctrl-KP, type C to continue after pausing, and respond to menu prompts. You can use the printer pause as many times as you like within a document.

APPLICATIONS

The printer pause, or stop code, is commonly used to pause the printer for print wheel, ribbon, or paper changes. For example, if you use a daisy-wheel printer, you may wish to change from a standard type face to an italic face by pausing the printer with a stop code. You can also use the stop code when filling in a preprinted form having variable line spacing. You can type a line and then enter a stop code. When the printer stops, you can "soft roll" the paper until the next line is properly aligned. Then restart printing by typing P and C (FPC using pull-down menus).

TYPICAL OPERATION

In this activity, begin by opening a document named TEMP. Enter a printer pause before and after the book title *MegaTraits* so that the printer stops before and after the book title. If you are using a daisy-wheel type printer, this procedure lets you change to an italic type wheel for the book title.

1. Open the document TEMP.

2. Type the following line, pressing **Ctrl-PC** before and after the word "MegaTraits."

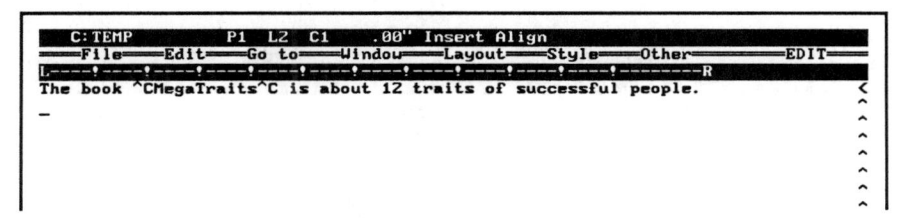

```
  C:TEMP            P1  L2  C1     .00" Insert Align
====File====Edit====Go to====Window====Layout====Style====Other====        ====EDIT====
L----!----!----!----!----!----!----!----!----!----!----!--------R
The book ^CMegaTraits^C is about 12 traits of successful people.
```

NOTE

If the line is printed, the printer stops before the book title. Change to an italic type font and resume printing by typing FP then C for continue. If a document is open, use Ctrl-KP. After the title is printed, the printer pauses again. Change back to the regular type wheel and resume printing by typing FP C or pressing Ctrl-KP and typing C to continue.

3. Press **Ctrl-KQ** and type **Y** to abandon the document without saving.
4. Turn to Module 58 to continue the learning sequence.

Module 65
PRINT PHANTOM SPACE AND RUBOUT (SPECIAL CHARACTERS)

^PF, ^PG

DESCRIPTION

The WordStar PRINT CONTROLS menu displays prompts for printing what are called "phantom space" and "phantom rubout." The effect of these embedded print codes depends upon your printer. If you have a list of control codes for your printer, you can determine which characters correspond to these codes.

The phantom space code is embedded in your document by pressing Ctrl-PF. This sends a hex 06 code to your printer. This may be a printable character or a space, depending upon your printer.

Similarly, the phantom rubout is embedded in your document by pressing Ctrl-PG. This sends a hex 07 code to your printer. Like the phantom space, the effect varies with the type of printer you have. You may want to experiment with these codes to determine what character is printed when using the phantom space and rubout functions. In addition, it is possible to modify the code using WordStar's WSCHANGE (or PRCHANGE) program (used to install and modify the way WordStar operates).

APPLICATIONS

The phantom space and phantom rubout characters are often adjusted using WordStar's installation procedure to be compatible with special printer control codes supported by your printer. For example, you may wish to use the phantom space and phantom rubout codes to print cents, trademark, copyright, or some other special character.

TYPICAL OPERATION

In this activity, you open a new document and type a line of text with embedded phantom space and phantom rubout codes.

Print Phantom Space and Rubout (Special Characters)

1. Open a new document named TEMP.
2. Type the following lines and press **Ctrl-PF** and **Ctrl-PG** at the end of each.

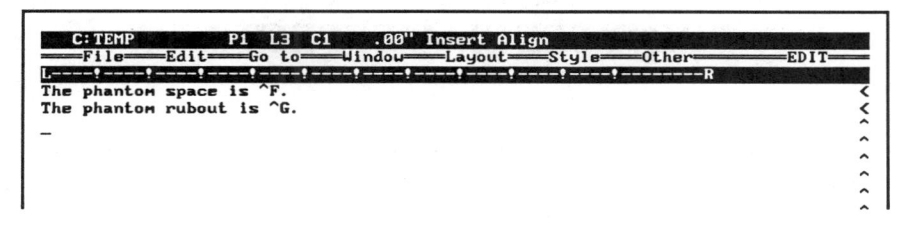

```
C:TEMP            P1  L3  C1    .00" Insert Align
=====File=====Edit=====Go to=====Window=====Layout=====Style=====Other=============EDIT=====
L----!----!----!----!----!----!----!----!----!----!--------R
The phantom space is ^F.                                          <
The phantom rubout is ^G.                                         <
_                                                                 ^
                                                                  ^
                                                                  ^
                                                                  ^
```

NOTE

You may wish to print the document to determine the effect of these codes.

3. Press **Ctrl-KQ** and type **Y** to abandon the document without saving.
4. Turn to Module 64 to continue the learning sequence.

Module 66
PRINT SPECIAL EFFECTS

> Classic: ^PB, ^PS, ^PY, ^PV, ^PT, ^PX, ^P, ^P=, ^OD
> Pull-Down: Alt-S, select desired style or "Hide/display controls"

DESCRIPTION

Module 61 describes the procedure for printing a document. There are a number of printing enhancements available within WordStar. Each is described in the following list.

Style	*Control Sequence*
Bold	Ctrl-PB
Underline	Ctrl-PS
Italic	Ctrl-PY
Subscript	Ctrl-PV
Superscript	Ctrl-PT
Strike out	Ctrl-PX
Double strike	Ctrl-PD
Overstrike (two characters)	Ctrl-PH
Overprint two lines	Ctrl-P
Change font (type face)	Ctrl-P=
Style display on/off	Ctrl-OD

All print styles make use of the PRINT CONTROL menu. To illustrate the way print styles operate, the underline style is described. Underline is typical of the print control codes and serves as a good example.

UNDERLINE To underline a character, word, or entire passage of text, place the cursor at the beginning of the first character to be underlined. Press Ctrl-PS and notice that ^S is inserted in front of the character. Press Ctrl-PS again after the last character to be underlined. The text appears underlined on the screen if you have a monochrome monitor. It is often blue on color monitors. You can change the display characteristics using WSCHANGE.

When the ^S is encountered during printing, an underline control code is sent to your printer. All text is underlined until another ^S is encountered, which turns off the underline mode.

Print Special Effects

Look at the following example. The words Paragraph One are underlined.

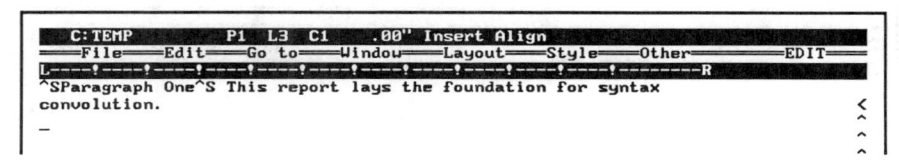

```
  C:TEMP         P1  L3  C1    .00" Insert Align
====File====Edit====Go to====Window====Layout====Style====Other====EDIT====
L----!----!----!----!----!----!----!----!----!----!----!--------R
^SParagraph One^S This report lays the foundation for syntax
convolution.
```

Normally, when printed, spaces between words are not underlined. If you want to underline between words, type the dot command for continuous underline (.UL on) at the left margin above the text to underline. This command is canceled with .UL off. Underline on or off default is set with WSCHANGE.

STRIKEOUT The strikeout code (Ctrl-PX) is entered in the same way as underline. Strikeout types a series of Xes over the included text. The strikeout character can be changed using WSCHANGE.

OVERSTRIKE The overstrike code (Ctrl-PH) causes compatible printers to back up one character and type the next character in line over the previously typed character. The series N Ctrl-PH Y prints Y over N.

DOUBLE STRIKE The double strike code (Ctrl-PD) causes the printer to strike characters twice. This differs from the bold style, as bold usually offsets printing left and right of center to give a bold character effect. Bold (Ctrl-PB) normally uses three strikes.

SUBSCRIPTS AND SUPERSCRIPTS The subscript and superscript functions respectively move characters below and above the text baseline by either a half line space or a full line space, depending on your printer's capability.

An example of a subscript is used in the chemical equation for carbon dioxide, which is

```
  C:TEMP         P1  L2  C14  1.30" Insert Align
====File====Edit====Go to====Window====Layout====Style====Other====EDIT====
L----!----!----!----!----!----!----!----!----!----!---------R
              CO^V2^V_
```

The first Ctrl-PV rolls the printer platen up and prints the 2 below the baseline. The second Ctrl-PV returns the printer platen to its original position.

Superscript operates in the same way as subscript, except that it rolls the printer platen down resulting in characters that are printed above the baseline. The Ctrl-PT key sequence is used to roll the platen down and back up. An example of a superscript is an exponent expression as in ten squared. When printed, it looks like this.

$$10^2$$

Module 66

The key sequence used to generate this expression is displayed:

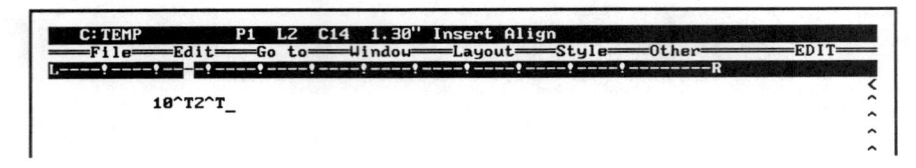

```
  C:TEMP         P1  L2  C14  1.30"  Insert Align
===File===Edit===Go to===Window===Layout===Style===Other======EDIT===
L----!---!---!----!----!----!----!----!----R
            10^T2^T_
                                                              <
                                                              ^
                                                              ^
                                                              ^
                                                              ^
```

Some printers let you change the amount of platen roll using the .SR n dot command, where n is in 48ths of an inch above or below the current text. For example, the dot command .SR 6 rolls the platen 6/48ths of an inch.

OVERPRINT TWO LINES   Overprinting two lines is achieved by pressing Ctrl-P at the end of a line. When printed, this code causes a return without a line feed. The result is that the current and following lines of text are printed on the same line.

CHANGING FONTS   Pressing Ctrl-P= displays a list of fonts that are compatible with your printer. The font selection, such as 10 pitch, 12 pitch, elite, expanded, or Roman, depends on the currently installed printer. If you are using a DRAFT printer, a font list is not displayed.

Scalable fonts were introduced with the release of WordStar 6.0. These fonts can be used with several brands of laser printers. Scalable fonts are measured in points, where a point is approximately 1/72nd of an inch. The maximum scalable font size is 999.9 points.

Some laser printers have a set of internal fonts, while others make use of plug-in cartridges, called cartridge fonts. There are also soft fonts, which are contained in software and downloaded to the printer as needed. Some common font names are:

    Helvetica
    Times Roman
    Century Schoolbook
    Souvenir
    Ding Bats
    Courier

Some fonts have different styles, i.e., bold, italic, and bold-italic. For example, the Times Roman font family may include

    Times Roman Normal
    Times Roman Italic
    Times Roman Bold
    Times Roman Bold-Italic

You can look at available fonts for each installed printer by pressing Ctrl-P? and picking a different printer. Then press Ctrl-P= and check the available fonts. If you decide to select a new set of fonts associated with a different printer, be sure to reformat the document so that all line lengths will conform to the font widths. This is achieved by placing your cursor at the beginning of the document and pressing Ctrl-QU. You can reformat notes with Ctrl-ONU.

Fonts that are sized in points use different width settings for different characters. For example, the width of an i is narrow, while the width of a w is wider. Therefore, character widths are in proportion to the shape of the letters. When you change from a 10- or 12-pitch style font, which is measured in a fixed number of characters per inch, to a font that is measured in points, the new proportional character widths change the line lengths.

You can use page preview to see how your line lengths are affected with different fonts. You should do this before you print your document as character widths vary with font changes. You can search for fonts within a document using Ctrl-Q= (or select Go to next font from the pull-down menu).

HIDE/DISPLAY CONTROLS Embedded print codes cause the right-hand margin to be displaced to the right on the screen. However, this is not the case when printed. The text is properly aligned. You can hide the print control codes by pressing Ctrl-OD. This displays normal line lengths. To recall the display of print control codes, press Ctrl-OD again.

APPLICATIONS

All print styles have important applications. Several common applications are included for your examination.

Underlining is used to highlight or emphasize passages of text. The underline is also used to designate book titles or ship names, where italics are normally used. It is also used to make text prominent, as in table and paragraph titles and in block diagrams. It is frequently used in place of italics for printers that do not feature the italic font.

Bold printing is used to highlight or emphasize passages of text, titles, and paragraph headings. It is also used for visual presentation material, where bold print is desired for legibility.

Double strike is often used to ensure that a passage of text is dark and clear, particularly if the material is to be reproduced on an office copier. Another application of double strike is to increase the impression clarity when carbon copies are being produced.

Strikeout text is used to show passages of deleted material. Legal documents sometimes retain struck out text passages to show changes that can communicate legal intent. When certain legal parameters are struck out but retained in the document, concerned parties to the agreement know what has been removed.

A common use for the overstrike code is to place a slash sign (/) through a zero (0) to differentiate between the zero and capital O. The sequence used to generate a zero symbol is 0^H/, which is printed ∅. Other applications include the generation of accent marks, such as using a lower case A and an apostrophe to print "á."

Subscripts and superscripts are used extensively in mathematical and chemical equations. They are also used to achieve space and one-half printing, where a standard line feed and a subscript is used to achieve a one and one-half line platen roll. Of course, your printer must have half-line capability for effective use of the subscript and superscript functions.

The ability to change font style and size lets you prepare commercial-quality documents. For example, you can change the size of superscript and subscript characters so that they are approximately half the size of the standard text font. If you are using 12-point Helvetica for mathematical equations, you may want to use 6-point Helvetica for superscript and subscript notation.

You can also use a variety of font styles for chapter and paragraph headings in a report or newsletter. You can also use real italic print for items such as book titles and ship names.

TYPICAL OPERATION

In this activity, you open a new document, type a line, and underline the name of the United States submarine *USS Odax*.

1. Open a new document named PRINT.
2. Type the following line, pressing **Ctrl-PS** before and after USS Odax.

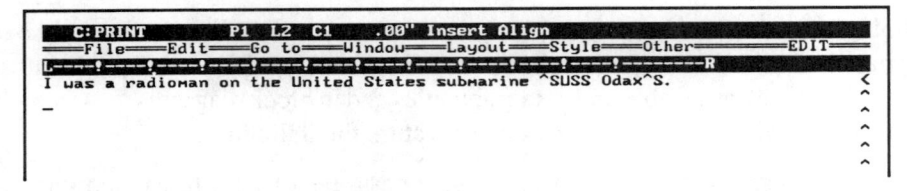

```
 C:PRINT        P1  L2  C1    .00" Insert Align
====File====Edit====Go to====Window====Layout====Style====Other====    ====EDIT====
L----!----!----!----!----!----!----!----!----!----R
I was a radioman on the United States submarine ^SUSS Odax^S.
```

NOTE
When the document is printed, the text *USS Odax* is underlined.

3. Press **Ctrl-KQ** and type **Y** to abandon the document without saving.
4. Turn to Module 59 to continue the learning sequence.

Module 67
PRINTER SELECT

```
^P?
```

DESCRIPTION

You can specify a printer to use for printing the current document by using the select printer function. The printer is selected by pressing Ctrl-P?. A CHANGE PRINTER menu is displayed.

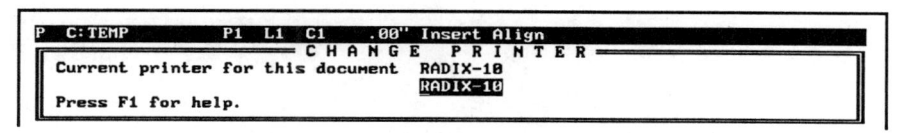

```
P  C:TEMP            P1  L1  C1    .00"  Insert Align
━━━━━━━━━━━━━━━━━━━━ C H A N G E   P R I N T E R ━━━━━━━━━━
│ Current printer for this document   RADIX-10           │
│                                     RADIX-10           │
│ Press F1 for help.                                     │
```

Typing a printer name or pointing to it with the cursor keys and pressing Return completes the selection process.

APPLICATIONS

The ability to associate a specific printer with a document ensures that the selected printer honors all the embedded print controls within the document. It also reminds you which printer to use, as the printer name is displayed in the PRINT menu prior to the printing process.

TYPICAL OPERATION

In this activity, you open a document and then associate the ASCII printer with the document, which prints an image of the document as an ASCII file.

1. Open a new document named TEMP.
2. Press **Ctrl-P?**, use the cursor keys to point to ASCII, and press **Return**.

Module 67

3. Press **Ctrl-P?** again to verify the printer setup.

```
P  C:TEMP          P1  L1  C1     .00" Insert Align
                          CHANGE   PRINTER
  Current printer for this document  ASCII
                                     ASCII
  Press F1 for help.
```

4. Press **Ctrl-P?** again and select your normal printer setup.
5. Press **Ctrl-KQ** to abandon the document without saving.
6. Turn to Module 37 to continue the learning sequence.

Module 68
PROFINDER

```
OPENING Menu:
     Classic:    R, type PF and press Return
     Pull-Down:  O, select "Run a program..." type PF and press Return
```

DESCRIPTION

ProFinder is a file management utility that is supplied with WordStar. ProFinder is a menu-driven file utility that lets you perform a number of file operations. These operations include:

- Displaying files within different disk drives and directories
- Assigning descriptive names or information to filenames
- Tagging files for copy and delete operations
- Sorting displayed filenames by name, extension, date, or size
- Locating files within a directory that include a specified character string (word or phrase)
- Viewing files and locating text within a viewed file
- Starting WordStar or another program from ProFinder
- Printing a selected directory
- Automating a series of often-used keystrokes through macros (or personal menus)

STARTING PROFINDER   ProFinder is started by logging the directory containing the ProFinder program PF.EXE, typing PF, and pressing Return. The ProFinder screen is displayed, which shows those filenames contained within the logged file directory.

Function key tags are displayed at the bottom of the screen. To use any of these commands, press the function key (F1 - F10), an equivalent number key (0 - 9), or press Alt in combination with the first letter of the tag command.

For example, you can change directories by pressing F6, selecting "Directory and mask," and typing the directory and mask (such as C:\WS*.*). Use the Sort function (F7) to manipulate the directory in alphabetical or date order. You can use the period (.) to back up one operation at a time. Esc cancels the entire operation. Esc is also used to take you back to the directory that was first displayed when you started ProFinder. A description of each ProFinder function key is provided later in this module.

Module 68

QUITTING PROFINDER You can quit ProFinder or cancel an operation using the Esc key. Pressing F8 or Alt-Q from the primary ProFinder screen also quits the program.

CHANGING DIRECTORIES OR DISK DRIVES You can change directories or disk drives using the following keys. These display prompts require your response.

Key	Description
\	Change to another directory by typing the directory name.
^\ (or Ctrl-\)	Change to the root directory.
:	Change to another disk drive.
.	Change to another directory by selecting it from a displayed list.

You can use wild cards (*) in your directory names to select certain types of files. For example, if you want to view files ending in DTA in the \WS directory, use \WS*.DTA as the directory name.

MOVING AROUND IN THE DIRECTORY You can use conventional WordStar commands to move within the ProFinder directory display. The following list summarizes these keys.

Key	Description
PgDn or Ctrl-C	Scroll down one screen
PgUp or Ctrl-R	Scroll up one screen
Ctrl-QC	Go to the top of the directory
Ctrl-QR	Go to the bottom of the directory
Up Arrow or Ctrl-E	Move up one line
Down Arrow or Ctrl-X	Move down one line

USING PROFINDER AS A CLIPBOARD You can start ProFinder and then run WordStar under ProFinder by picking a file to edit. This lets you flip back and forth between WordStar and ProFinder using the gray plus key (on the numeric keypad on most keyboards).

When running WordStar under ProFinder, you can flip to ProFinder to view files, mark passages, and copy them into the active WordStar document. This approach lets you use ProFinder like a "pop-up" clipboard. The steps used to open WordStar from ProFinder, view a file, and copy a block from the viewed file into the WordStar document are:

1. Start ProFinder with PF.
2. Point to a WordStar document file and press the gray plus key (the one by the numeric keypad on most keyboards) to start WordStar. The file is displayed in WordStar's EDIT screen.

3. Press the gray plus key to redisplay the ProFinder screen.
4. Point to another WordStar document file and press Alt-V to view it.
5. Mark a block using WordStar's Ctrl-KB and Ctrl-KK keys.
6. Press gray plus to redisplay the WordStar EDIT screen.
7. Move the cursor to the point within your file at which you wish to insert the block you marked in step 5.
8. Press the gray minus key to insert the marked block from the document previously viewed.

TITLES You can assign meaningful names to files at ProFinder's main screen by pointing to a filename, pressing the Right Arrow (or Ctrl-D, Tab, or Ctrl-F), and typing a meaningful title. Press a cursor key or Tab to move the cursor back to the directory listing.

PROFINDER OPERATIONS To start ProFinder, log the ProFinder directory, type PF, and press Return. You may also type *pathname*\PF (where *pathname* is the ProFinder directory). The ProFinder menu resembles the following illustration.

```
C:\WS\*.*                                  Copyright (c) 1988 WordStar International Corp.
..             ◄UPDIR► 12-22-86   3:35p
WINSTALL  OUR    21681  7-25-90   3:44p
WINSTALL  EXE   309504  3-14-90   6:00p
TABLES2   OUR     3670  3-14-90   6:00p
LSRFONTS  COM      818  3-14-90   6:00p
PRCHANGE  COM      818  3-14-90   6:00p
PDFEDIT   COM      818  3-14-90   6:00p
WSCHANGE  COM      818  3-14-90   6:00p
DISPFONT  OUR     4259  3-14-90   6:00p
DISPFONT  COM      562  3-14-90   6:00p
WSCHANGE  OUR    49216  3-14-90   6:00p
CHANGE    OUR    79962  3-14-90   6:00p
384K      PAT      128  3-14-90   6:00p
WS3KEYS   PAT     1792  3-14-90   6:00p
KSPEED    PAT      128  3-14-90   6:00p
WS        DEF      896  3-14-90   6:00p
SWITCH    COM      571  3-14-90   6:00p
README    COM    29212  3-14-90   6:00p
JOHN                58  7-30-90   8:08a
PATCH     LST    84992  3-14-90   6:00p
MOVEPRN   EXE    19697  3-14-90   6:00p
BIOS      OLD       77  3-14-90   6:00p
WS        EXE   187008  7-30-90   9:06a
F1Help F2Locate F3Tag  F4Files F5View F6Option F7Sort F8Exit F9Run 10Menu
```

A series of operation names is displayed at the bottom of the ProFinder screen. These operations are accessed by pressing the displayed function key or pressing Alt in combination with the first letter of the operation name.

F1 Help You can press F1 to display help information about a selected operation. Help information is context sensitive, that is, pressing F1 during an operation displays help information about that operation. Each operation is summarized in the following paragraphs.

Module 68

F2 Locate The Locate operation uses the following menu selections.

```
C:\US\*.*                          Copyright (c) 1988 WordStar International Corp.
..              <UPDIR>  12-22-86  3:35p
WINSTALL OUR    21681    7-25-90   3:44p
WINSTALL EXE   309504    3-14-9  ┌─── Locate ──────────┐
TABLES2  OUR     3670    3-14-9  │ Search files by text│
LSRFONTS COM      818    3-14-9  │ Find files by title │
PRCHANGE COM      818    3-14-9  │ List all files      │
PDFEDIT  COM      818    3-14-9  │ Extensions to skip  │
USCHANGE COM      818    3-14-9  └─────────────────────┘
DISPFONT OUR     4259    3-14-90   6:00p
DISPFONT COM      562    3-14-90   6:00p
USCHANGE OUR    49216    3-14-90   6:00p
CHANGE   OUR    79962    3-14-90   6:00p
384K     PAT      128    3-14-90   6:00p
US3KEYS  PAT     1792    3-14-90   6:00p
KSPEED   PAT      128    3-14-90   6:00p
US       DEF      896    3-14-90   6:00p
SWITCH   COM      571    3-14-90   6:00p
README   COM    29212    3-14-90   6:00p
JOHN               58    7-30-90   8:08a
PATCH    LST    84992    3-14-90   6:00p
MOVEPRN  EXE    19697    3-14-90   6:00p
BIOS     OLD       77    3-14-90   6:00p
US       EXE   187008    7-30-90   9:06a
F1Help F2   F3   F4   F5   F6   F7   F8   F9   10
```

This operation is used to find files quickly by filename, using a tag name that you assigned using ProFinder, or by a text string within one or more files. The "Search files by text" operation lists all files containing a user-entered search string at the top of the screen. You can use as many as three 20-character long search strings. Notice, also, that ProFinder lets you list all files with the "List all files" selection. You can filter out unwanted files with the "Extensions to skip" selection.

F3 Tag The Tag operation lets you mark multiple files for a copy, delete, or move operation. Tagging is accomplished by pointing to a file and pressing F3 or Alt-T. Untagging is accomplished in the same way. You can display a list of tagged files using the "Select tagged files" option in the Files menu. You can tag multiple files using the F4 Files option described next.

F4 Files The Files menu lets you perform a number of operations on files as shown in the following illustration. Notice that you can copy, move, delete, change a file's time/date stamp, print a directory, write the directory to a file, and even display the DOS command prompt. When printing directories, tagged files are underlined. When writing a directory containing tags, only the tagged files are saved.

Other Files operations include working with tagged files. A "Select tagged files" option displays a list of tagged files. "List all files" redisplays all files. You can use the "File tag by wild card" selection to tag a group of files using a wild card. For example, using *.DTA tags all files having the DTA file extension.

"Retag" is used to reset tags that are suppressed after performing a Files operation. "Untag all" eliminates all file tags.

ProFinder

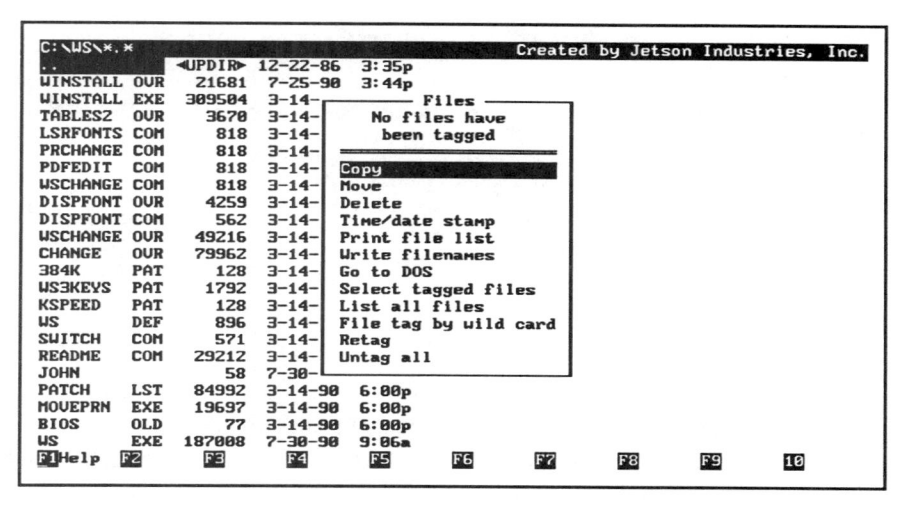

```
C:\WS\*.*                                    Created by Jetson Industries, Inc.
..              <UPDIR> 12-22-86  3:35p
WINSTALL  OUR    21681  7-25-90  3:44p
WINSTALL  EXE   309504  3-14-┌──── Files ────┐
TABLES2   OUR     3670  3-14- │ No files have │
LSRFONTS  COM      818  3-14- │  been tagged  │
PRCHANGE  COM      818  3-14- ├───────────────┤
PDFEDIT   COM      818  3-14- │ Copy          │
WSCHANGE  COM      818  3-14- │ Move          │
DISPFONT  OUR     4259  3-14- │ Delete        │
DISPFONT  COM      562  3-14- │ Time/date stamp│
WSCHANGE  OUR    49216  3-14- │ Print file list│
CHANGE    OUR    79962  3-14- │ Write filenames│
384K      PAT      128  3-14- │ Go to DOS     │
WS3KEYS   PAT     1792  3-14- │ Select tagged files│
KSPEED    PAT      128  3-14- │ List all files│
WS        DEF      896  3-14- │ File tag by wild card│
SWITCH    COM      571  3-14- │ Retag         │
README    COM    29212  3-14- │ Untag all     │
JOHN                58  7-30- └───────────────┘
PATCH     LST    84992  3-14-90  6:00p
MOVEPRN   EXE    19697  3-14-90  6:00p
BIOS      OLD       77  3-14-90  6:00p
WS        EXE   187008  7-30-90  9:06a
F1Help  F2    F3    F4    F5    F6    F7    F8    F9    F10
```

F5 View Use the View option by pointing to a WordStar document file and pressing F5 or Alt-V. Pointing to the filename and pressing Return achieves the same result. Use conventional WordStar keys to move within the displayed document. You can mark blocks and write them to other files using WordStar block commands. Press F1 to view a list of command keys. Press Esc to exit the viewed document.

You can also open and view a second or even a third document using Ctrl-OK or F9. Enter the filename and press Return to display the second or third document. Press Esc or period to redisplay the previous file. The files must be in the current directory (or file list).

While viewing a file, press F8 to display another set of function keys. These keys let you perform the following operations.

Key	Description
F1 Help	Display help information
F2 Locate	Locate a specified text string
F3 Prev	Locate the previously found text string
F4 Next	Locate the next text string
F5 Write	Write to a specified file
F6 Print	Print the displayed file
F7 Begin	Mark the beginning of a block
F8 End	Mark the end of a block
F9 Open	Open and view a second or third file
F10 Auto	Mark lines automatically; continue pressing F10 until the desired block is marked

Module 68

F6 Option The Option operation lets you set ProFinder operational parameters.

```
C:\WS\*.*
..            <UPDIR>  12-22-86   3:35p
WINSTALL  OVR    21681  7-25-90   3:44p
WINSTALL  EXE   309504  3-14-9 ┌─── Options ───────────┐
TABLES2   OVR     3670  3-14-9 │ Resume                │
LSRFONTS  COM      818  3-14-9 │ Directory and mask    │
PRCHANGE  COM      818  3-14-9 │ List all files        │
PDFEDIT   COM      818  3-14-9 │ Programs only    NO   │
WSCHANGE  COM      818  3-14-9 │ Subdirs only     NO   │
DISPFONT  OVR     4259  3-14-9 │ Titles           YES  │
DISPFONT  COM      562  3-14-9 │ Configure             │
WSCHANGE  OVR    49216  3-14-9 └───────────────────────┘
CHANGE    OVR    79962  3-14-90  6:00p
384K      PAT      128  3-14-90  6:00p
WS3KEYS   PAT     1792  3-14-90  6:00p
KSPEED    PAT      128  3-14-90  6:00p
```

F7 Sort Sort lets you control the way that a directory is displayed. You can sort by name, extension, date and time, or file size. You can use "Order of sort" to arrange the directory in either ascending or descending order.

```
C:\WS\*.*
..            <UPDIR>  12-22-86   3:35p
WINSTALL  OVR    21681  7-25-90   3:44p
WINSTALL  EXE   309504  3-14-90   6: ┌──── Sort ────────┐
TABLES2   OVR     3670  3-14-90   6: │ Begin sort       │
LSRFONTS  COM      818  3-14-90   6: │ Order of sort    │
PRCHANGE  COM      818  3-14-90   6: │ Auto sort   NO   │
PDFEDIT   COM      818  3-14-90   6: └──────────────────┘
WSCHANGE  COM      818  3-14-90   6:00p
DISPFONT  OVR     4259 ┌─── Order ───┐ p
DISPFONT  COM      562 │ Extension A │ p
WSCHANGE  OVR    49216 │ Name      A │ p
CHANGE    OVR    79962 │             │ p
384K      PAT      128 │             │ p
WS3KEYS   PAT     1792 └─────────────┘ p
KSPEED    PAT      128  3-14-90   6:00p
WS        DEF      896  3-14-90   6:00p
SWITCH    COM      571  3-14-90   6:00p
```

F8 Exit The Exit operation is used to quit ProFinder and redisplay the DOS prompt.

F9 Run The Run operation is used to run a selected program. This function does not operate when you are flipping between ProFinder and WordStar. You can run an .EXE or .COM file by highlighting the desired file and then pressing F9. This takes you back to DOS and executes the program file.

If you have files that are associated with a program and use a common extension, such as TXT, WKS, PRG, or DAT, you can prepare a control file having the extension .PF. Once created, highlighting the file automatically executes the corresponding program and loads the highlighted file. The following file is an example of a .PF file. These are created using WordStar's nondocument mode.

```
LTR,C:\WS\WS ~d~p~f~e
 pf
```

The contents of this file has the following meaning.

Command	Meaning
LTR,	This is the extension name of files associated with WordStar; the comma is used to separate the extension from the file path and program name.
C:\WS\WS	This is what is typed to start the WordStar program.
~d	Specifies use of the logged disk drive
~p	Specifies use of the logged file path
~f	Specifies use of the highlighted (or selected) filename
~e	Specifies use of the highlighted extension
pf	Restarts ProFinder upon exiting from the program

The tilde (~) commands are also used with menu commands described in the next paragraph.

F10 Menu   You can build your own user menus which combine ProFinder commands with DOS batch files. The resulting menu file receives the name USERMENU.PF. ProFinder looks for this file in the logged directory when you select the Menu operation. The Sample Menu and the corresponding USERMENU.PF file supplied with ProFinder are shown for your examination. Embedded ProFinder control characters plus others that are available are explained following the listing.

```
C:\WS\*.*
..              <UPDIR>  12-22-86   3:35p
WINSTALL  OUR    21681   7-25-90    3:44p
WINSTALL  EXE   309504   3-14-90    6:00p
TABLES2   OUR     3670   3-14-9 ┌──── Sample Menu ────┐
LSRFONTS  COM      818   3-14-9 │ Documents           │
PRCHANGE  COM      818   3-14-9 │ ------ Inset ------ │
PDFEDIT   COM      818   3-14-9 │ Inset               │
WSCHANGE  COM      818   3-14-9 │ Remove Inset        │
DISPFONT  OUR     4259   3-14-9 │ ---- PC Outline --- │
DISPFONT  COM      562   3-14-9 │ Normal version      │
WSCHANGE  OUR    49216   3-14-9 │ Small version       │
CHANGE    OUR    79962   3-14-9 │ ------ Other ------ │
384K      PAT      128   3-14-9 │ Lotus               │
WS3KEYS   PAT     1792   3-14-9 │ Quit                │
KSPEED    PAT      128   3-14-9 └─────────────────────┘
WS        DEF      896   3-14-90   6:00p
SWITCH    COM      571   3-14-90   6:00p
README    COM    29212   3-14-90   6:00p
JOHN                58   7-30-90   8:08a
```

| >Sample Menu | Centers "Sample Menu" on first line of menu. |
| <—— Text —— | Displays following text as a submenu heading; not subject to highlighting for selection. |

Undisplayed commands are indented by one or more spaces.

No menu entry can exceed 30 characters. ProFinder automatically centers text using the longest line as a guide for the left and right margins of the menu. A list of control characters and explanations are included in the following list.

Module 68

Key	Description
,	Used to separate displayed information from commands that follow on the same line.
/k=	Closes the menu and performs following ProFinder keystrokes. An explanation of the second line in the listing follows.
	`Documents, /k=":c{enter}{F3}\doc{enter}{F7}{enter}"`
	"Documents" is printed as text; it is against the left margin.
	The comma separates "Documents" from following commands.
	The /k= closes the menu.
	The ProFinder keystrokes are within quotes.
	:c{enter} are ProFinder commands used to select the C disk drive.
	{F3}\doc{enter} tags the \doc directory.
	{F7}{enter} selects Sort and accepts the default sort.
	The entry
	<——— Other ——-
	Lotus, c:
	cd\lotus
	123
	pf ~d~p
	<——— Other ———- is centered within the menu
	Lotus is displayed as a menu option
	c: chooses drive c:
	cd\lotus changes to the \lotus directory
	123 starts the Lotus 1-2-3 program
	pf restarts ProFinder upon an exit from Lotus 1-2-3
	~d ~p uses the current drive and path letters (see ~d and ~p below)
	The entry
	`Quit, /m=quitmenu.pf`
	Quit is displayed as a menu option
	/m=quitment.pf exits the menu and calls the menu file QUITMENU.PF
/m=	Closes current menu and displays a named menu following the =
~d	Replaced with the current drive letter and a colon
~p	Replaced with the current file path (like \WS\DOC)
Other keys	
~f	Replaced with the current filename
~e	Replaced with the current filename extension (like .TXT)
~h	Replaced with hexadecimal offset value (first location of a file using the Locate operation)
~o	Replaced with decimal offset value (instead of the hexadecimal value obtained with ~h)
{esc}	The Esc key
/f=	Highlights a following filename

APPLICATIONS

When used in conjunction with WordStar, your ProFinder can be used to view a list of filenames and the contents of those files without having to leave the WordStar program. This is particularly important if you do not remember a filename to bring into a WordStar window.

The ability to start ProFinder, select a file to edit with WordStar, and then use ProFinder as a clipboard is especially convenient. You can also perform many common DOS operations without leaving your document.

Tagging multiple files for copying or deleting is also a time-saving feature when comparing the effort required to copy or delete one file at a time.

ProFinder's File-move operation supplies the ability to move a file from one directory to another without having to first copy it and then delete the original file.

TYPICAL OPERATION

In this activity you start ProFinder and then view a series of files using the View option. You may also wish to use the procedure contained in the USING PROFINDER AS A CLIPBOARD paragraph within the Description section of this module, as this is a powerful capability.

This and the clipboard activities assume that the ProFinder and WordStar programs are either in the same directory or that your DOS PATH command includes the paths C:\WS and C:\WS\PF (if ProFinder is in its own directory). To be sure, you may wish to enter the following PATH command from the DOS command prompt.

```
PATH=C:\;C:\DOS;C:\WS;C:\WS\PF
```

1. At the C:\WS DOS prompt type **PF** and press **Return** to start ProFinder.
2. Highlight a text file, such as MYLTR, and press **F5**; notice that the file is displayed and a new series of function keys are displayed at the bottom of the viewing screen.

Module 68

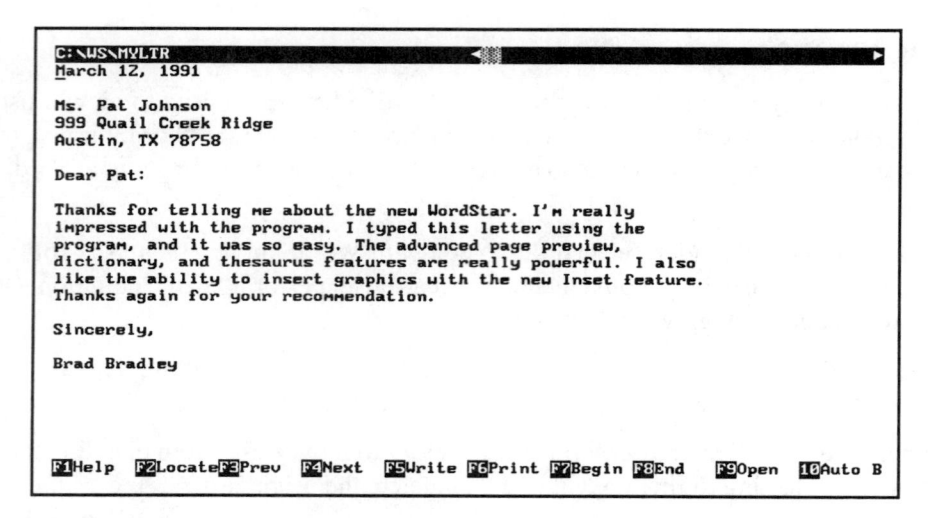

```
C:\WS\MYLTR
March 12, 1991

Ms. Pat Johnson
999 Quail Creek Ridge
Austin, TX 78758

Dear Pat:

Thanks for telling me about the new WordStar. I'm really
impressed with the program. I typed this letter using the
program, and it was so easy. The advanced page preview,
dictionary, and thesaurus features are really powerful. I also
like the ability to insert graphics with the new Inset feature.
Thanks again for your recommendation.

Sincerely,

Brad Bradley




F1Help  F2Locate F3Prev  F4Next  F5Write F6Print F7Begin F8End  F9Open  10Auto B
```

3. Press **F1** and review the Help screen. Then press **Esc** to close the Help screen.

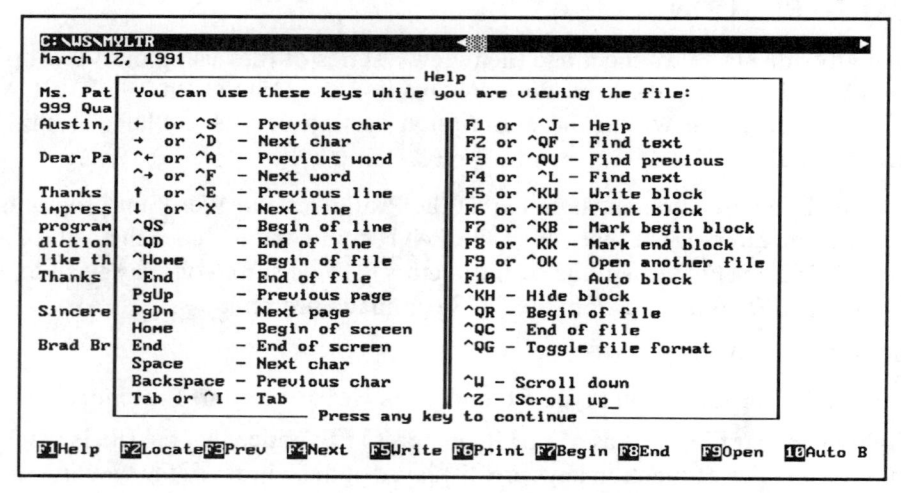

```
C:\WS\MYLTR
March 12, 1991
                          ┌─── Help ───┐
Ms. Pat   You can use these keys while you are viewing the file:
999 Qua
Austin,    ← or ^S  - Previous char    F1 or ^J  - Help
           → or ^D  - Next char        F2 or ^QF - Find text
Dear Pa    ^← or ^A - Previous word    F3 or ^QU - Find previous
           ^→ or ^F - Next word        F4 or ^L  - Find next
Thanks     ↑ or ^E  - Previous line    F5 or ^KW - Write block
impress    ↓ or ^X  - Next line        F6 or ^KP - Print block
program    ^QS      - Begin of line    F7 or ^KB - Mark begin block
diction    ^QD      - End of line      F8 or ^KK - Mark end block
like th    ^Home    - Begin of file    F9 or ^OK - Open another file
Thanks     ^End     - End of file      F10      - Auto block
           PgUp     - Previous page    ^KH - Hide block
Sincere    PgDn     - Next page        ^QR - Begin of file
           Home     - Begin of screen  ^QC - End of file
Brad Br    End      - End of screen    ^QG - Toggle file format
           Space    - Next char
           Backspace - Previous char   ^W - Scroll down
           Tab or ^I - Tab             ^Z - Scroll up
                     └─ Press any key to continue ─┘

F1Help  F2Locate F3Prev  F4Next  F5Write F6Print F7Begin F8End  F9Open  10Auto B
```

4. Press **F9** and notice the "Open File:" prompt at the lower, left-hand corner of the display screen.

5. Type a valid WordStar filename and press **Return**. Notice that two files are now displayed for viewing.

6. Repeat steps 4 and 5, above, to display a third file.

7. Type a period (.) to close the last file added. This is like "peeling off a file layer."

8. Press **Esc** to close the second file; notice how either Esc or period are used to perform the same operation.
9. Experiment with the following function keys to determine their effect:

F2 Locate	F7 Begin (block)
F4 Next	F8 End (block)
F3 Previous	F10 Auto Block

10. Press **Esc** to close the viewed document.
11. Press **F8** to exit ProFinder.
12. Turn to Module 87 to continue the learning sequence.

Module 69
PROTECT A FILE

> Classic: C
> Pull-Down: F, select "Protect/unprotect a file..."

DESCRIPTION

One of the options available from the OPENING menu is "Protect/unprotect a file" from change. When you type FC, the filename, and press Return to protect a file, the prompt "The file is currently not protected. Protect it? (Y/N)" is displayed.

The prompt reports the protected status of the file. You can reverse the protected status, either on or off, by typing Y. Cancel the operation with N or by pressing Ctrl-U. This procedure applies to both documents and nondocuments. Files with the .BAK extension are automatically protected from change.

When a protected file is displayed, "Prtect" appears on the status line. Your attempts to change the document result in a "beep," which reminds you that you cannot make changes to a protected file.

APPLICATIONS

You may wish to protect an original, master, special form, or final version of a document from accidental or undesired alterations or deletions. This is especially true if other people have access to your files. Use protect to prevent unplanned changes.

TYPICAL OPERATION

In this activity, you follow the procedure for protecting, editing, and unprotecting files using the file named MYLTR. Begin at the OPENING menu.

1. Type **FC MYLTR** and press **Return**. Notice the protect status prompt.

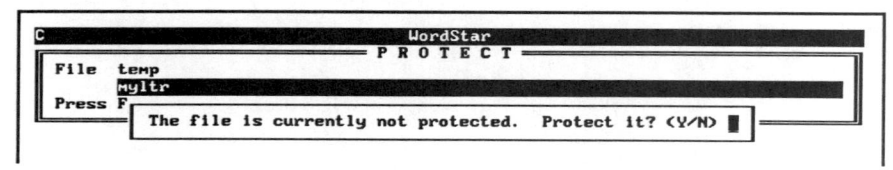

```
C                        WordStar
                    ═══ P R O T E C T ═══
File  temp
      myltr
Press F
         The file is currently not protected.  Protect it? (Y/N) █
```

Protect a File

2. Type **Y** in response to the prompt.
3. Type **FY** to delete a file, specify MYLTR as the file, and press **Return**.
4. Notice the "Can't delete a protected file. Press Esc to continue." prompt. Press **Esc**.
5. Type **FC**, specify MYLTR, press **Return**, and type **Y** to unprotect the file MYLTR.
6. Turn to Module 17 to continue the learning sequence.

Module 70
REFORMAT (REALIGN) TEXT

> Classic: ^B
> Pull-Down: Alt-L, select "Align rest of paragraph"

DESCRIPTION

WordStar's reformat function lets you reformat, or realign, a paragraph to conform to the margin settings, line spacing, right-hand justification, hyphenation, and indent levels in effect at the time. The reformat function is also used when auto-align is turned off with Ctrl-OA.

When reformat is used, the formatting takes place from the current position of the cursor to the next hard return. A hard return is indicated by a less than symbol (<) at the right margin of the display screen. It is produced when the Return key is pressed at the end of a line. A hard return terminates a line and moves the cursor to the beginning of the next line.

Because the reformat operation affects a paragraph at a time, you should place the cursor at the beginning of a paragraph before pressing Ctrl-B. If an entire document is to be reformatted, you can perform the process automatically by positioning the cursor at the beginning of the document and pressing Ctrl-QU. The paragraph at the cursor is aligned, the cursor pauses briefly at the end of the paragraph (hard return), and continues to the end of the document or until interrupted with Ctrl-U.

Any text that you do not want reformatted can be protected by inserting the dot command .AW OFF at the left margin of the line preceding the text to be protected. Entering the dot command .AW ON following the text allows the automatic realignment of the document to resume.

APPLICATIONS

The ability to reformat a paragraph lets you vary spacing, margins, right-hand justification, hyphenation, and indent levels after text has been typed, saved, and even printed. After printing or using page preview to examine the document, you may decide that it would look better with changes in indent levels, margins, and spacing. The reformat function lets you reopen the document and adjust it at will. You may want to use page preview before printing it. See Module 54 for details on the page preview operation.

TYPICAL OPERATION

In this activity, begin with the document MYLTR displayed. Change the right margin and line spacing and use the reformat function to see its effect.

1. Open the document MYLTR and position the cursor at the first line of the letter paragraph.
2. Press **Ctrl-OR**, enter **5.00"** as the right margin value, and press **F10** to set the right margin to five inches.
3. Press **Ctrl-OS**, type **2**, and press **F10** to set double spacing.
4. With the cursor on the first word in the paragraph, press **Ctrl-B** to reformat the paragraph. Move the cursor to the beginning of the document and notice the results.

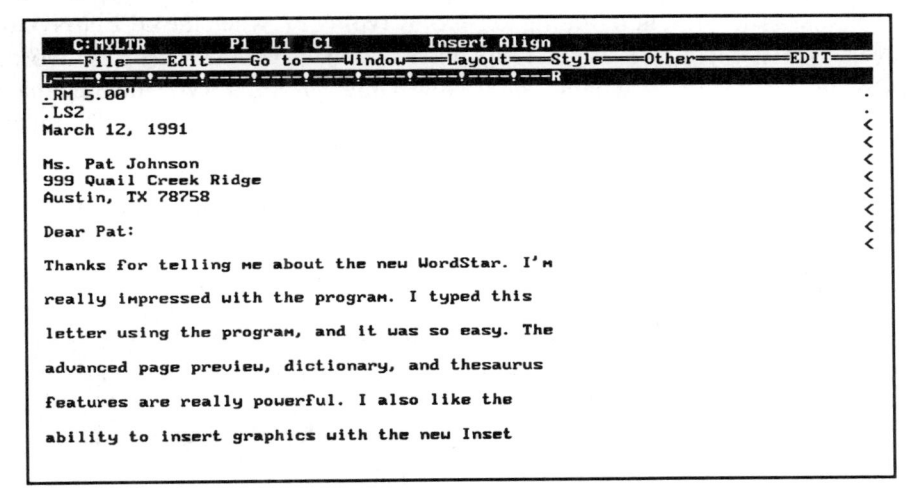

```
  C:MYLTR        P1  L1  C1         Insert Align
====File====Edit====Go to====Window====Layout====Style====Other====EDIT====
L----!----!----!----!----!----!----!----!---R
.RM 5.00"                                                              .
.LS2
March 12, 1991                                                         <
                                                                       <
Ms. Pat Johnson                                                        <
999 Quail Creek Ridge                                                  <
Austin, TX 78758                                                       <
                                                                       <
Dear Pat:                                                              <
                                                                       <
Thanks for telling me about the new WordStar. I'm

really impressed with the program. I typed this

letter using the program, and it was so easy. The

advanced page preview, dictionary, and thesaurus

features are really powerful. I also like the

ability to insert graphics with the new Inset
```

5. Continue to experiment with the reformat function until you are satisfied that you understand its operation. Return line spacing and line length to normal settings.
6. Press **Ctrl-KQ** and type **Y** to abandon the document without saving the changes.
7. Turn to Module 5 to continue the learning sequence.

Module 71
RENAME A FILE

> Classic: E, ^KE
> Pull-Down: F, (or Alt-F), select "Rename a file..."

DESCRIPTION

You may rename a file without returning to DOS by typing FE when the OPENING menu is displayed. When the EDIT menu is displayed, you can press Ctrl-KE. WordStar responds by displaying "Current name" and "New name" prompts. Type the filename you wish to change, press Return, type the new filename, and press Return. The name is changed.

You may abort the process at any point before pressing Return by pressing Ctrl-U.

APPLICATIONS

There are many reasons to change the name of a file. Filenames are assigned to describe the file contents. When several versions of the same file are needed, it is helpful to add a number to the end of the filename or assign a different extension name to reflect the version. You can also combine dates with filenames to reflect the date of origin.

TYPICAL OPERATION

In this activity, you change the name of the file named MYDOC to MYLTR. Begin at the OPENING menu.

NOTE
Always check the directory display of the logged disk to verify the exact spelling of the filename to be changed.

1. Type **FE**; WordStar displays the Current name, New name prompts.

Rename a File

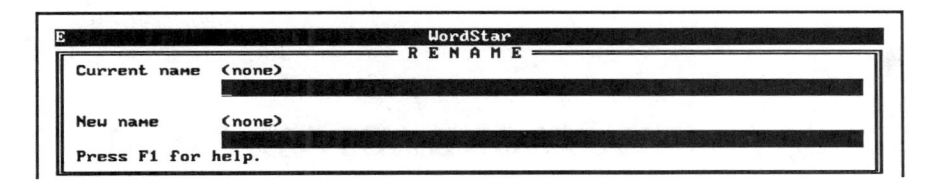

```
┌─────────────────── WordStar ───────────────────┐
│═══════════════════ R E N A M E ═══════════════│
│ Current name    <none>                         │
│                 ▓▓▓▓▓▓▓▓▓▓▓▓▓▓▓▓▓▓▓▓▓▓▓▓▓▓▓▓▓ │
│                                                │
│ New name        <none>                         │
│                 ▓▓▓▓▓▓▓▓▓▓▓▓▓▓▓▓▓▓▓▓▓▓▓▓▓▓▓▓▓ │
│ Press F1 for help.                             │
└────────────────────────────────────────────────┘
```

2. Type **MYDOC** as the Current name and press **Return** (or use the arrow keys to point to MYDOC in the displayed directory and press **Return**).

3. Type **MYLTR** at the New name prompt and press **Return**. Notice that the new filename MYLTR replaces the name MYDOC.

4. Turn to Module 74 to continue the learning sequence.

Module 72
REPEAT A KEYSTROKE AUTOMATICALLY

> ^QQ, type key to repeat

DESCRIPTION

WordStar offers a unique feature that lets you repeat a keystroke or EDIT menu command automatically until you interrupt it by pressing the Spacebar. For example, to repeat a series of Xs automatically, press Ctrl-QQ, then type X. The X is typed from left to right until you interrupt the process by pressing the Spacebar.

You can make the repeat operation run faster or slower by typing a number between 0 and 9 where the higher number is slower.

APPLICATIONS

The automatic repeat operation is sometimes useful for doing things like making dashed lines with the hyphen or drawing an underline without having to type each character.

TYPICAL OPERATION

In this activity, you open a document and use the repeat operation to draw a row of hyphens.

1. Open a new document named TEMP.
2. Press **Ctrl-QQ**; then type **-** (hyphen). Notice that hyphens are typed automatically from left to right.
3. Type **8** to slow the process.
4. Type **1** to speed up the process.
5. Press the **Spacebar** to stop the repeat operation.
6. Experiment with other repeat sequences and speeds to see how they work.
7. Press **Ctrl-KQ** and type **Y** to abandon the document without saving.
8. Turn to Module 85 to continue the learning sequence.

Module 73
RUN A PROGRAM

> Classic: R, ^KF
> Pull-Down: O (or Alt-O), select "Run a DOS command..."

DESCRIPTION

WordStar's OPENING menu contains an option that lets you run a program by typing OR. From the EDIT menu, the same function uses Ctrl-KF. WordStar responds by displaying the RUN menu.

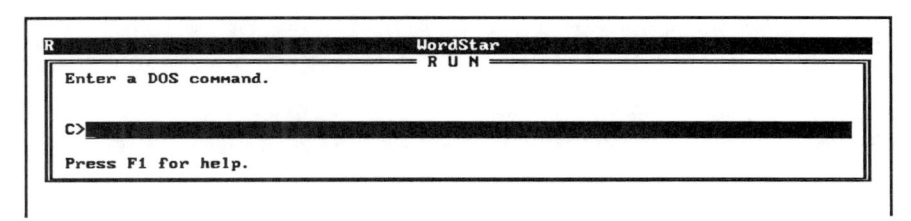

```
R                          WordStar
                           = R U N =
  Enter a DOS command.

  C>

  Press F1 for help.
```

You can type a program name, such as dBASE or BASIC, or a DOS command such as CHKDSK. You can run a program on any disk drive or another file path by prefixing the program name with the drive designator or file path name. When the program is finished, WordStar displays "Press any key to return to WordStar." Typing a key returns you to the previous cursor position.

APPLICATIONS

Running a program from WordStar eliminates the need to exit and return to DOS to run standard programs. This not only saves keystrokes, it also lets you retain established document formats, including margins, tabs, and line spacing. Running programs from an open document means you don't have to leave your word processing and return to the OPENING menu to run a program.

Many programmers use WordStar's nondocument mode to write program source code. You can move in and out of the program with the Run option. For example, if you are preparing a dBASE command file, you can edit the command file, run dBASE to check it out, and return to your data file to make modifications. Make sure your computer has sufficient memory to run both WordStar and dBASE simultaneously.

Module 73

TYPICAL OPERATION

In this example, you display a directory from the RUN menu and then press the Spacebar to return to the OPENING menu. Begin at the OPENING menu.

1. Type **OR** and notice the RUN menu.
2. Respond by typing **DIR** and pressing **Return**.
3. Notice that the directory is displayed followed by the prompt "Press any key to return to WordStar."
4. Press the **Spacebar**; notice that the OPENING menu is redisplayed.
5. Turn to Module 80 to continue the learning sequence.

Module 74
SAVE AND EXIT DOCUMENT

> Classic: ^KD, ^KT
> Pull-Down: Alt-F, select "Save file, go to Opening screen"
> Alt-F, select "Save and name file"

DESCRIPTION

Once a document is created, you can save it and return to WordStar's OPENING menu by pressing Ctrl-KD. Block and file operations are performed with the BLOCK & SAVE menu, which is displayed using Ctrl-K. You can think of the D option as "done."

If you have just created the document, its filename is displayed in the file directory. If the document existed before you opened, edited, and saved it, the filename also appears in the directory with a .BAK file extension. WordStar always keeps the last version of the document in a .BAK file for "backup" purposes. In case you accidentally destroy needed text, you can retrieve the .BAK file by renaming it with WordStar's rename function, described in Module 71.

If you edit an existing document and save it with a new name by pressing Ctrl-KT, typing the new name, and pressing Return, this preserves the existing document in its original form.

APPLICATIONS

Saving a document and returning to the OPENING menu is the most common filing method used. Once you are back at the OPENING menu, you can begin work on another document, print a document, perform file operations, or exit WordStar.

The save and name file operation, achieved by pressing Ctrl-KT, is convenient for using a document that serves as a basis for a new document. Once the original document is modified, Ctrl-KT preserves the original document for future use.

TYPICAL OPERATION

In this activity, you open a document, save the document, and return to the OPENING menu.

1. Open a document named MYLTR by typing **FD MYLTR** and pressing **Return**.

Module 74

2. From the EDIT menu, with the contents of MYLTR displayed, press **Ctrl-KD**.
3. Notice the "Saving... " message as the document is saved to disk.

NOTE
If you kept the MYLTR file from the exercise in Module 71, notice that the file directory displays the file MYLTR.BAK.

4. Turn to Module 77 to continue the learning sequence.

Module 75
SAVE AND EXIT WORDSTAR

> Classic: ^KX
> Pull-Down: Alt-F, select "Save file, exit WordStar"

DESCRIPTION

Module 74 described the procedure for saving a document and returning to the OPENING menu. The procedure for saving a document and exiting WordStar is similar except that it causes you to exit from WordStar to DOS instead of returning to the OPENING menu.

The Ctrl-KX key sequence performs the same job as saving the document with Ctrl-KD and then exiting WordStar by typing X while the OPENING menu is displayed. As the file is being saved, the message

```
Saving...
```

is displayed. Once the file is saved, the DOS prompt is displayed.

APPLICATIONS

Saving a document and exiting WordStar is normally done when you have completed a document and are finished with your word processing work. As mentioned in the description, this operation also prevents the necessity of returning to the OPENING menu and then pressing X to exit WordStar.

TYPICAL OPERATION

In this activity, you open the document MYLTR, then save the document and exit WordStar. Begin at the OPENING menu.

1. Type **FD**, type **MYLTR**, and press **Return** to open the document.
2. Press **Ctrl-KX** to save and exit.
3. Notice that the "Saving... " message is displayed as the document is saved to disk.
4. Notice that when the document is saved, the DOS prompt is displayed.
5. Turn to Module 83 to continue the learning sequence.

Module 76
SAVE AND PRINT DOCUMENT

```
^PrtSc
```

DESCRIPTION

When your document is complete and you are ready to save it, print it, and return to the OPENING menu, press Ctrl-PrtSc. The document is saved and the print options are displayed. The name of the file just saved appears as the File name. When printing is complete, the OPENING menu is redisplayed.

You cannot use this procedure to merge print, so the prompt asking if you wish to merge print does not appear as usual before the print menu options.

APPLICATIONS

Combining the steps that quit and save and then print from the OPENING menu is a convenient way to save keystrokes. The entire process is reduced to one simple key sequence.

TYPICAL OPERATION

In this activity, you open a document, save the document, print it, and return to the OPENING menu. Be sure your printer is ready. Begin at the OPENING menu.

1. Open the document MYLTR.
2. Press **Ctrl-PrtSc** when the document MYLTR is displayed. Notice the prompt "Saving..." followed by the PRINT menu.

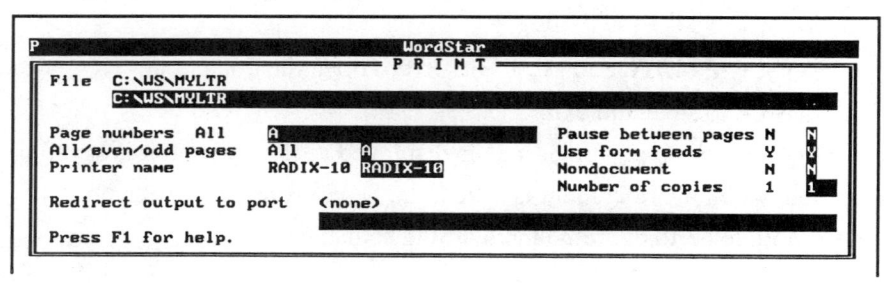

```
P                          WordStar
                         ─ P R I N T ─
    File  C:\WS\MYLTR
          C:\WS\MYLTR

    Page numbers   All      A             Pause between pages  N   N
    All/even/odd pages      All   A       Use form feeds       Y   Y
    Printer name            RADIX-10 RADIX-10  Nondocument     N   N
                                              Number of copies 1   1
    Redirect output to port  (none)

    Press F1 for help.
```

Save and Print Document

3. Press **F10** to accept the print defaults as displayed (or press **Ctrl-U** or **F2** if you do not wish to print).
4. Notice that the OPENING menu is redisplayed when printing stops; the file MYLTR has been saved and printed.
5. Turn to Module 72 to continue the learning sequence.

Module 77
SAVE AND RESUME EDIT

> Classic: ^KS
> Pull-Down: Alt-F, select "Save file, resume editing"

DESCRIPTION

During text editing, you can save a document to disk and resume editing without interruption. This is done by pressing Ctrl-KS, where S stands for "Save." WordStar briefly displays "Saving..." as the document is written to the disk. When the file is saved, the cursor returns to the previous position in the file.

When a document is saved and you resume editing, you will notice that when you finally save the document and return to the OPENING menu by pressing Ctrl-KD, the filename with a .BAK (for "backup") extension is also displayed.

The .BAK extension is an automatic WordStar security feature. WordStar always generates a backup copy of existing saved documents that are displayed for text editing. The same is true of the save and resume edit function. The last version saved prior to final filing appears on the file directory with a .BAK extension.

APPLICATIONS

At any time during the text-editing process, you may wish to save your document on disk. This is often done to prevent potential loss of the document in the event of a power failure or system malfunction. The save and resume edit function writes the file to disk, where it is stored for safekeeping while you continue your word processing tasks. To reduce the potential for loss, you should periodically save your document to disk with Ctrl-KS.

TYPICAL OPERATION

In this activity, you open the MYLTR document, modify it, and use the save and resume function. Begin at the OPENING menu.

1. Open the document MYLTR. Press **Del** to delete the text (your name) and type the following letter. It is used again in other operations.

Save and Resume Edit

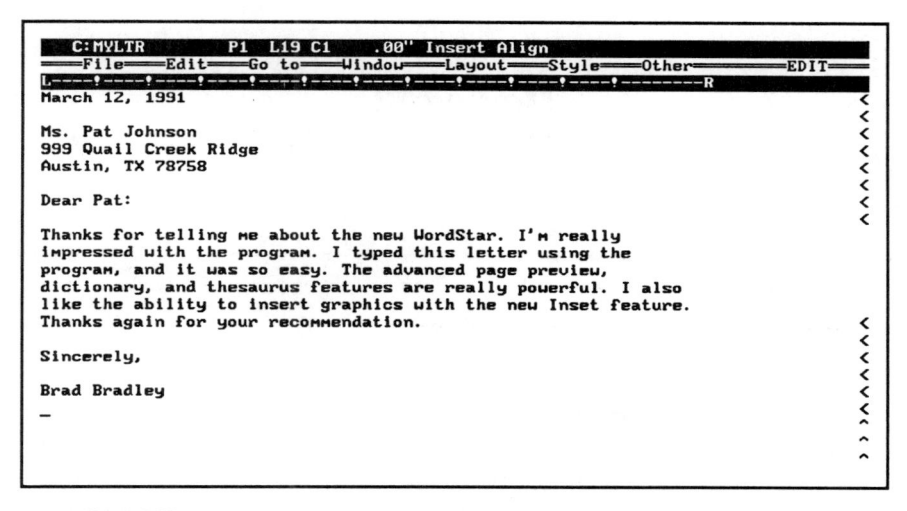

```
╔══════════════════════════════════════════════════════════╗
║ C:MYLTR      P1  L19 C1     .00" Insert Align            ║
║═══File═══Edit═══Go to═══Window═══Layout═══Style═══Other═══════EDIT═══║
║L----!----!----!----!----!----!----!----!----!----!--------R         ║
║March 12, 1991                                          < ║
║                                                        < ║
║Ms. Pat Johnson                                         < ║
║999 Quail Creek Ridge                                   < ║
║Austin, TX 78758                                        < ║
║                                                        < ║
║Dear Pat:                                               < ║
║                                                        < ║
║Thanks for telling me about the new WordStar. I'm really  ║
║impressed with the program. I typed this letter using the ║
║program, and it was so easy. The advanced page preview,   ║
║dictionary, and thesaurus features are really powerful. I also ║
║like the ability to insert graphics with the new Inset feature. ║
║Thanks again for your recommendation.                   < ║
║                                                        < ║
║Sincerely,                                              < ║
║                                                        < ║
║Brad Bradley                                            < ║
║                                                        < ║
║ _                                                      < ║
║                                                        ^ ║
║                                                        ^ ║
╚══════════════════════════════════════════════════════════╝
```

2. Press **Ctrl-KS** to save and resume editing.

3. Notice that the "Saving..." message is displayed as the document is saved to disk and the cursor resumes its previous position.

4. Press **Ctrl-KQ** to abandon the saved document.

5. Turn to Module 4 to continue the learning sequence.

Module 78
SCROLL SCREEN

> ^W, ^Z, ^C or PgDn, ^R or PgUp

DESCRIPTION

Modules 17 and 18 described the use of WordStar's cursor control keys. You can use the cursor keys to move the document up and down a line at a time. Another way to move a document is by scrolling it up or down, either a line at a time or a screen at a time. Scrolling is like looking at a document through a window while the document is moving. Vertical scrolling is when the document moves up or down. Horizontal scrolling is when the document moves left or right.

Horizontal scrolling occurs when the right margin is set beyond column 79 or when the margin release (Ctrl-OX) is active and the cursor moves to column 80 or higher. This causes the cursor to pass the right screen boundary and the entire document moves to the left. Margin settings are described in Module 49.

Here, vertical scrolling is examined. Module 79 describes continuous scrolling using WordStar's classic QUICK menu.

The classic EDIT menu indicates the control characters used for vertical line and screen scrolling. The following list summarizes these.

Vertical Scrolling	Control Key Sequence
Text moves up one line	Ctrl-Z
Text moves down one line	Ctrl-W
Text moves up one screen	Ctrl-C or Pg Up (9)
Text moves down one screen	Ctrl-R or Pg Dn (3)

Note that R and C are the same characters used for jumping the cursor to the top and bottom of the file from the QUICK menu (Module 18). When you scroll the screen up or down (Ctrl-R or Ctrl-C), the screen moves 11 lines. If you suppress the EDIT menu display by using a help level lower than 3, the screen scrolls 17 lines.

APPLICATIONS

The ability to move the screen up and down, either a line or screen at a time, is helpful when reviewing text. Being able to manipulate entire screens of text lets you scan a document for information in an efficient manner.

TYPICAL OPERATION

In this activity, you open a document and note the cursor position. You scroll a few lines up and down, then scroll the screen up and down. Begin at the OPENING menu.

1. Open the MYLTR document.
2. Press **Ctrl-Z** a few times and notice how the lines scroll up.
3. Press **Ctrl-W** a few times and notice how the lines scroll down.
4. Press **Ctrl-C** (or **Pg Dn**) and notice how the screen scrolls up.
5. Press **Ctrl-R** (or **Pg Up**) and notice how the screen scrolls down.
6. Press **Ctrl-KQ** to abandon the document.
7. Turn to Module 79 to continue the learning sequence.

Module 79
SCROLL SCREEN, QUICK

> ^QZ, ^QW

DESCRIPTION

In Module 78 you learned to scroll up and down one line or one screen at a time. In this module, WordStar's classic QUICK menu is used to allow automatic vertical scrolling. Not only can you control the direction of vertical scrolling (up or down), but you can also control the speed of vertical scrolling.

Description	Control Key Sequence	Scrolling Speed	
		Fastest	Slowest
Scroll text up	Ctrl-QZ	0	9
Scroll text down	Ctrl-QW	0	9
Stop scrolling	Spacebar		

To cause the screen to scroll up continuously, press Ctrl-QZ. To change the scrolling speed, type 0 for the fastest speed and 9 for the slowest. You will probably settle on 2 or 3 for comfort. WordStar's default is 3. To stop the scrolling action, press the Spacebar. Press Ctrl-QW to scroll text down.

APPLICATIONS

The ability to scroll the screen up and down at varying speeds lets you read a document without having to use a cursor or manual line scrolling. Just set a comfortable speed and let WordStar do the rest. If you wish to skim a document for format or continuity, you may wish to speed up the scrolling process by typing the 1 or 2 key.

TYPICAL OPERATION

In this activity, you open a document, then scroll the document up and experiment with the speed settings. When you are near the bottom, press the Spacebar to stop the process. Before abandoning the document, you may want to experiment with the scrolling operation. Begin at the OPENING menu.

1. Open the MYLTR document.
2. Press **Ctrl-QZ** and watch the document scroll up a line at a time.
3. Experiment with the speed by typing **1**, then **9**, and finally **3**.
4. Press the **Spacebar** to stop the scrolling action when the last line of the document approaches the top of the screen.
5. Press **Ctrl-QW** to scroll text down.
6. Press the **Spacebar** to stop scrolling when the top line of the document approaches the top of the screen.
7. Press **Ctrl-KQ** to abandon the document.
8. Turn to Module 43 to continue the learning sequence.

Module 80
SHORTHAND (MACRO SUBSTITUTION)

> Classic: Esc
> Pull-Down: Esc

DESCRIPTION

The term *macro substitution* means that you can substitute a few designated keystrokes for many. This is a shorthand technique designed to save time. WordStar's SHORTHAND menu is displayed by pressing Esc. The SHORTHAND menu resembles the following illustration.

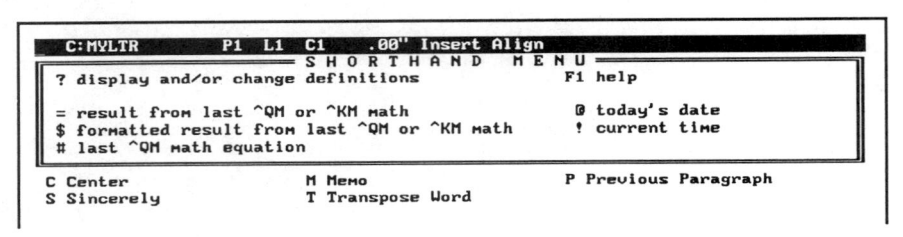

```
  C:MYLTR       P1 L1 C1    .00" Insert Align
══════════════════════ S H O R T H A N D   M E N U ══════════════════════
  ? display and/or change definitions         F1 help

  = result from last ^QM or ^KM math          @ today's date
  $ formatted result from last ^QM or ^KM math ! current time
  # last ^QM math equation

  C Center                    M Memo              P Previous Paragraph
  S Sincerely                 T Transpose Word
```

The macro definitions are stored in the WSSHORT.OVR file supplied with WordStar. When new macro definitions are created and saved, they are stored in this file.

STANDARD MACRO CHARACTERS A number of standard macro keys are supplied with WordStar. Typing one of the indicated characters within the menu box enters the indicated result in an open document at the cursor position. The following list describes the effect of each key listed in the menu.

Esc Key	*Results*
=	Inserts the results of the last math calculation.
#	Inserts the last math equation used.
$	Inserts the results of the last math calculation truncated to two decimal places.
@	Inserts the current system date in the form April 2, 1988.
!	Inserts the current time in the form 5:00 PM.
F1	Displays shorthand help information.
?	Displays current custom macros and definitions; lets you modify macros or create new ones.

The letters and corresponding descriptions below the menu box represent macro substitution keys that can be created and labeled by you, the user. You can use A through Z and 0 through 9 for a total of 36 macro substitution keys. The remainder of this section describes the creation and use of macros.

CREATING AND CHANGING MACROS Pressing Esc and then typing ? displays a screen similar to the following.

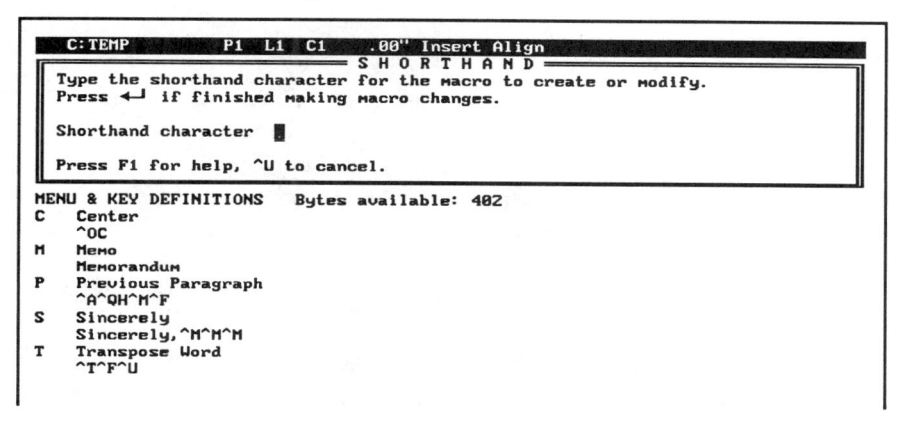

```
C:TEMP           P1  L1  C1    .00" Insert Align
========================= S H O R T H A N D =========================
Type the shorthand character for the macro to create or modify.
Press ← if finished making macro changes.

Shorthand character  █

Press F1 for help, ^U to cancel.

MENU & KEY DEFINITIONS    Bytes available: 402
 C    Center
      ^OC
 M    Memo
      Memorandum
 P    Previous Paragraph
      ^A^QH^M^F
 S    Sincerely
      Sincerely,^M^M^M
 T    Transpose Word
      ^T^F^U
```

You can type the letter of your choice used to call a macro. Then type a description and press Return. Finally, type the definition (or macro string) and press Return. Press Ctrl-U to return to the document. A save prompt is displayed to let you save the macro to disk. Type Y to save, N to retain it temporarily in memory. If N is used, the macro disappears when you exit WordStar.

If you wish to change an existing macro definition, type the letter, and the description and definition automatically appear. Edit the string and save it in the normal fashion.

Notice that the remaining amount of memory is displayed. The available memory for macros can be increased using the WSCHANGE utility.

A clarifying example is provided. Assume that you want to use Esc U for underline, which is usually achieved with Ctrl-PS. Your entry would resemble the following. (Use Ctrl-P Ctrl-P to produce ^P.)

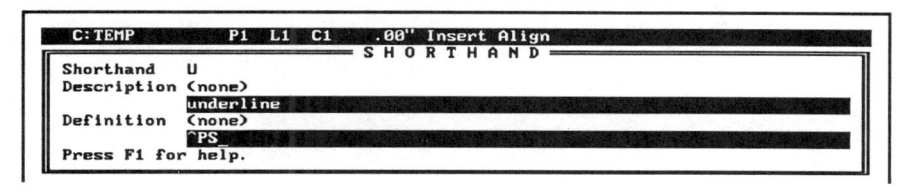

```
C:TEMP           P1  L1  C1    .00" Insert Align
========================= S H O R T H A N D =========================
Shorthand    U
Description  (none)
             underline
Definition   (none)
             ^PS
Press F1 for help.
```

247

Module 80

Always enter control characters with Ctrl-P. Ctrl-P Ctrl-P displays ^P. The Return key is entered with Ctrl-P Ctrl-M, which displays ^M. The Esc key is produced with Ctrl-P Ctrl-Esc and is represented by ^[.

The Typical Operation section of this module guides you through macro creation for a company invoice which enters the company name, the word INVOICE, and the current date, and centers them in the text.

APPLICATIONS

Macro substitution (shorthand) is a productive time saver. You can use it to recall a number of keystrokes automatically, including control characters. You can also prepare multiple macros and call them in sequence. For example, if you must make multiple passes in a global search and replace operation, you can number each pass. To show an example of this, look at the following macro definitions:

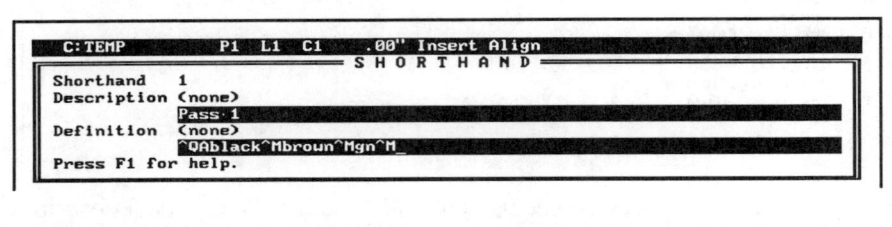

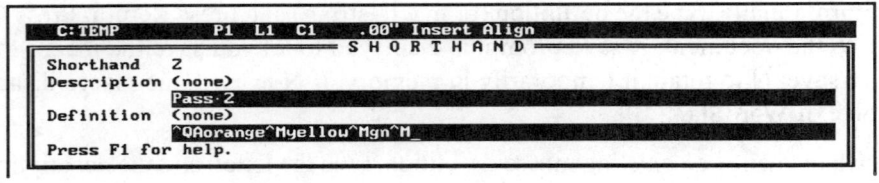

```
C:TEMP           P1  L1  C1    .00" Insert Align
================= S H O R T H A N D =================
Shorthand    1
Description  (none)
             Pass 1
Definition   (none)
             ^QAblack^Mbrown^Mgn^M_
Press F1 for help.
```

```
C:TEMP           P1  L1  C1    .00" Insert Align
================= S H O R T H A N D =================
Shorthand    2
Description  (none)
             Pass 2
Definition   (none)
             ^QAorange^Myellow^Mgn^M_
Press F1 for help.
```

You should recall that the *gn* replace option designates global, replace without asking.

The result of these keystrokes is displayed in the MENU & KEY DEFINITIONS area as

```
MENU & KEY DEFINITIONS    Bytes available: 344
 1   Pass 1
     ^QAblack^Mbrown^Mgn^M
 2   Pass 2
     ^QAorange^Myellow^Mgn^M
```

These two macros globally replace the words black with brown and orange with yellow. Notice that the first macro is called "Pass 1"; the second is called "Pass 2."

Shorthand (Macro Substitution)

You can also combine the two macros into a single two-pass instruction with the definition line:

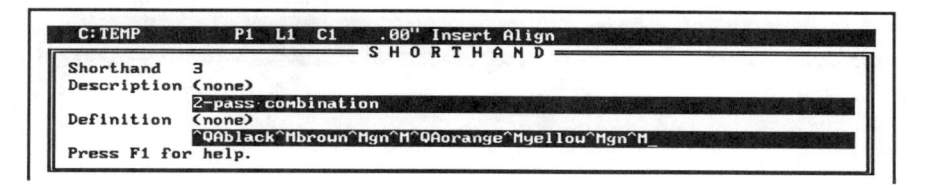

```
  C:TEMP          P1 L1 C1    .00" Insert Align
                        S H O R T H A N D
 Shorthand    3
 Description  (none)
              2-pass combination
 Definition   (none)
              ^QAblack^Mbrown^Mgn^M^QAorange^Myellow^Mgn^M_
 Press F1 for help.
```

TYPICAL OPERATION

In this activity, you create an invoice heading automatically, using WordStar's shorthand. Begin at the OPENING menu. Remember to use Ctrl-P and a letter to convert it to a control character. For instance, Ctrl-P Ctrl-M produces ^M.

1. Open a new document named TEMP.
2. Press **Esc ?** and notice the following display:

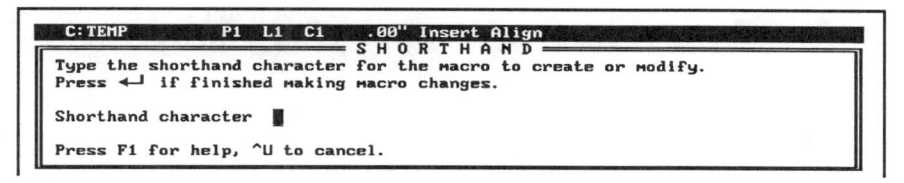

```
  C:TEMP          P1 L1 C1    .00" Insert Align
                        S H O R T H A N D
 Type the shorthand character for the macro to create or modify.
 Press  <-'  if finished making macro changes.

 Shorthand character  ▮

 Press F1 for help, ^U to cancel.
```

3. Type **I** as the defined character.
4. Type **Invoice** as the description and press **Return**.
5. Carefully type the following string on the Definition line and end by pressing **Return**. Remember that ^B is achieved with Ctrl-P Ctrl-B. Similarly, ^O is achieved with Ctrl-P Ctrl-O.

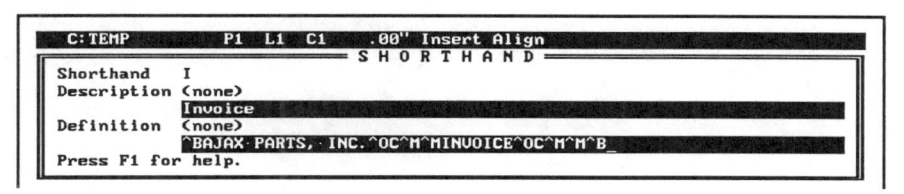

```
  C:TEMP          P1 L1 C1    .00" Insert Align
                        S H O R T H A N D
 Shorthand    I
 Description  (none)
              Invoice
 Definition   (none)
              ^BAJAX PARTS, INC.^OC^M^MINVOICE^OC^M^M^B_
 Press F1 for help.
```

6. Press **Ctrl-U**; then type **N** in response to the save prompt.

249

Module 80

7. Press **Esc I** and notice how the macro produces an invoice heading similar to the following one:

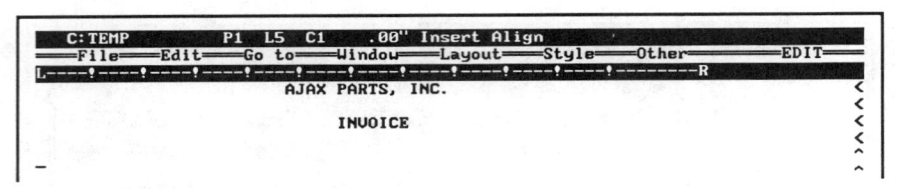

```
 C:TEMP           P1  L5  C1     .00" Insert Align
====File====Edit====Go to====Window====Layout====Style====Other====        ====EDIT====
L----!----!----!----!----!----!----!----!----!----!-------R
                     AJAX PARTS, INC.                          <
                                                               <
                         INVOICE                               <
                                                               <
 -                                                             ^
```

8. Press **Ctrl-KQ** and type **Y** to abandon without saving.
9. Turn to Module 82 to continue the learning sequence.

Module 81
SORT BLOCKS OF TEXT

> ^KZ

DESCRIPTION

WordStar lets you perform an alphanumeric sort on lines within a marked block. To sort the following entries, mark the text as a block.

    Cherries
    Bananas
    Apples

Press Ctrl-KZ to select the sort operation. Then type A to sort in ascending order. The list is sorted accordingly.

    Apples
    Bananas
    Cherries

You can also sort lines based on the entries within a single column. Look at the following example.

Name	Number	Date
Jones	3453	90/12/07
Smith	4544	89/01/15
Johnson	6566	91/02/20

The column mode is turned on by pressing Ctrl-KN.

The name, number, or date column is marked as a column using Ctrl-KB at the upper left-hand corner and Ctrl-KK at the lower right-hand corner. If the names in the column are marked (excluding the column heading "Name"), pressing Ctrl-KZ and typing A sorts the table as shown:

Name	Number	Date
Johnson	6566	91/02/20
Jones	3453	90/12/07
Smith	4544	89/01/15

Module 81

WordStar's sort command is not *case sensitive*. That is, it treats uppercase and lowercase letters as having the same value. In instances where uppercase and lowercase letters are mixed, the first letter encountered is placed first.

The sort precedence, in ascending order, is shown in the following line of characters.

, 0-9 a-z ! " # $ % & ' ( ) * + - . / : ; = ? @ [\ ] ^ ` { | } ~

APPLICATIONS

The sort command is used to rearrange information in alphabetical, numerical, or alphanumerical order. This lets you enter a list of names or numbers in random order and then sort them when you complete your keyboard work.

The sort command is used with personnel rosters, phone directories, indexes, and financial tables, where looking up information alphabetically or by numeric value or date is helpful. The ability to sort in either ascending or descending order is sometimes an important factor, when you want to list the highest values first, as in a wage and salary analysis.

The fact that WordStar's sort is not case sensitive is important in the preparation of alphabetical indexes. This keeps all letters together instead of grouping entries by case, with the uppercase letters ahead of the lowercase letters. This is what happens when using the DOS sort utility.

TYPICAL OPERATIONS

In this activity, you enter the table shown in the Description section of this module and sort the table on the Date column.

1. Open a new document named TEMP.
2. Enter the table of names, numbers, and dates as shown in the following illustration.
3. Turn on the column mode by pressing **Ctrl-KN**.
4. Block mark the Date column by placing the cursor at the upper left-hand corner of the column and pressing **Ctrl-KB**.

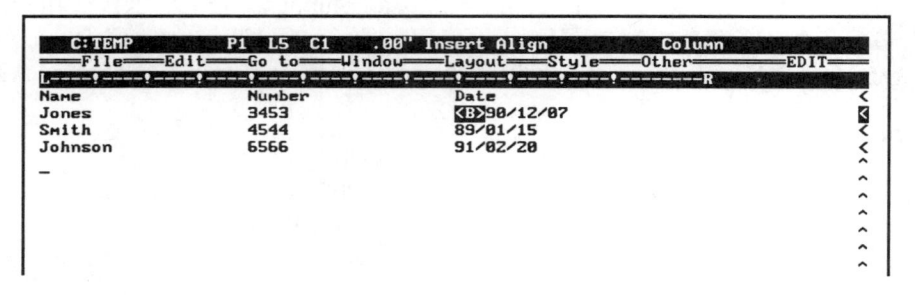

```
      C:TEMP         P1  L5  C1      .00" Insert Align        Column
    ==File====Edit====Go to====Window====Layout====Style====Other====EDIT==
    L----!----!----!----!----!----!----!----!----!----!----!----R
    Name              Number            Date                                <
    Jones             3453              <B>90/12/07                         <
    Smith             4544              89/01/15                            <
    Johnson           6566              91/02/20                            <
    _                                                                       ^
                                                                            ^
                                                                            ^
                                                                            ^
                                                                            ^
```

5. Move the cursor to the lower right-hand corner of the Date column and press **Ctrl-KK**. Your table should resemble the following illustration.

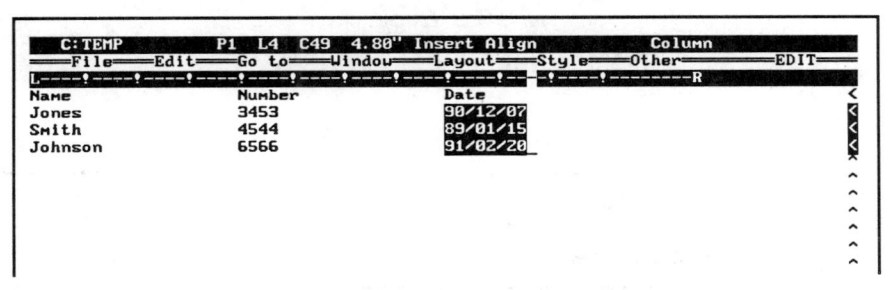

```
    C:TEMP            P1  L4  C49  4.80"  Insert Align        Column
======File======Edit======Go to======Window======Layout======Style======Other======EDIT======
L----!----!----!----!----!----!----!----!--·-!----!---------R
Name              Number            Date
Jones             3453              90/12/07
Smith             4544              89/01/15
Johnson           6566              91/02/20
```

6. Press **Ctrl-KZ** and type **A** for ascending. Notice that the table is rearranged in ascending order according to the date value.

7. Continue to experiment with the sort command until you are comfortable with its operation.

8. Press **Ctrl-KQ** and type **Y** to abandon the document.

9. Turn to Module 13 to continue the learning sequence.

Module 82
SPELLING CHECK

> Classic: ^QL, ^QN, ^QO
> Pull-Down: Alt-O, select "Check document spelling..."
> Alt-O, select "Check word spelling..."

DESCRIPTION

WordStar's spelling check operation uses a large main dictionary, an internal dictionary, and a personal dictionary. The words within the displayed document are compared with those in the main and internal dictionaries, in addition to those words that you add to the personal dictionary. Typically, personal dictionary words are unique to your working vocabulary and sometimes include proper nouns such as the names of cities, companies, and people.

In addition to checking for wrong spellings, double words, like "the the" are found and challenged. Spelling check commands are displayed from the QUICK menu. These include:

Command	Description
Ctrl-QL	Spell checks the rest of the current document
Ctrl-QN	Spell checks the word starting at the cursor
Ctrl-QO	Spell checks a typed word

SPELLING CHECK COMMANDS Pressing Ctrl-QL spell checks the entire document beginning at the cursor position. The SPELLING CHECK menu resembles the following illustration:

```
QL C:TEMP        P1 L1 C8    .70" Insert Align
================ S P E L L I N G  C H E C K  M E N U ================
    I ignore, check next word      E enter correction           ^U quit
    A add to personal dictionary   G global replacement is off  F1 help
    B bypass this time only

        Word:  "trila"
    Suggestions:  1 trial  2 trill  3 trail  4 truly  5 trawl  6 troll
                  M display more suggestions
```

254

Spelling Check

To check an entire document, move the cursor to the top of the file before pressing Ctrl-QL. When an unrecognized word is encountered, as in the previous screen illustration, the word and corresponding suggestions are displayed. In the example, type 1 to replace the unrecognized word with "trial." Type 2 for "trill."

Checking a Single Word Pressing Ctrl-QN checks the word following the cursor. Be sure the cursor is in front of the entire word. This command also checks words to the right of dot commands. The Ctrl-QL function ignores words on dot command lines.

Checking the word "command" with Ctrl-QN displays the following prompt and alternate words:

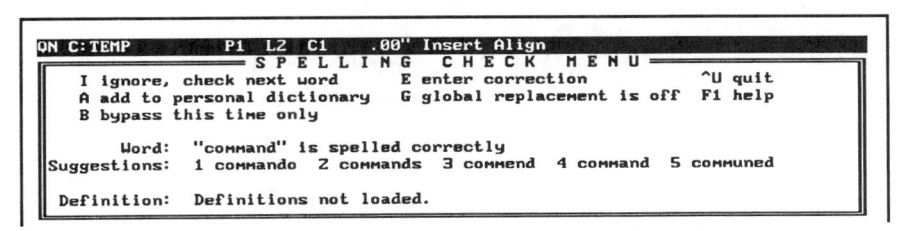

```
QN C:TEMP          P1 L2 C1    .00" Insert Align
================ S P E L L I N G   C H E C K   M E N U ================
     I ignore, check next word       E enter correction         ^U quit
     A add to personal dictionary    G global replacement is off F1 help
     B bypass this time only

         Word:  "command" is spelled correctly
   Suggestions:  1 commando  2 commands  3 commend  4 command  5 communed

   Definition:   Definitions not loaded.
```

When checking a word that is correctly spelled, the Definition line appears at the bottom of the menu. WordStar provides definitions when Definition is turned on with WSCHANGE.

Checking a Guess Pressing Ctrl-QO lets you type a word to verify the correct spelling before you enter the word into your document. Alternate spellings are suggested. Checking the word "word" with Ctrl-QO displays the following prompt and alternate words:

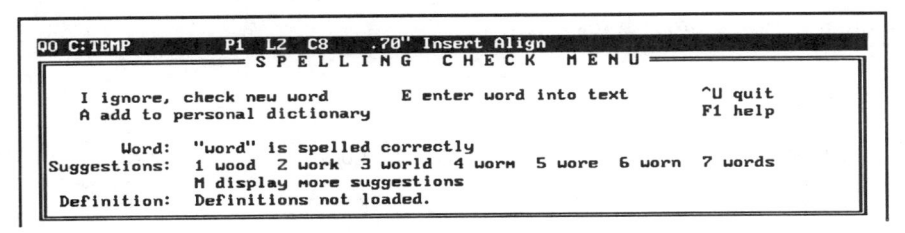

```
QO C:TEMP          P1 L2 C8    .70" Insert Align
================ S P E L L I N G   C H E C K   M E N U ================
     I ignore, check new word        E enter word into text      ^U quit
     A add to personal dictionary                                F1 help

         Word:  "word" is spelled correctly
   Suggestions:  1 wood  2 work  3 world  4 worm  5 wore  6 worn  7 words
                 M display more suggestions
   Definition:   Definitions not loaded.
```

Interrupting the Spelling Check You can press Ctrl-U to discontinue the spelling check. Press Ctrl-QL to resume the spelling check.

SPELLING CHECK OPTIONS The spelling check options listed on the menu are described in the following list:

Module 82

Option	Description
I	Type I to ignore the challenged word. This word is ignored for the balance of the current spelling check. When using Ctrl-QN, I lets you check a continuous series of words, skipping the current word and moving to the next one. When using Ctrl-QO, I lets you type another word to check.
A	Type A to add the challenged word to your personal dictionary. The added word is now accepted during spelling checks.
B	Type B to bypass the challenged word one time. Subsequent occurrences continue to be checked.
E	Type E to display a "Replace with" prompt and enter the correction from the keyboard. The typed word is automatically checked before the spelling check moves to the next word.
G	Type G to turn global replacement on and off. When global replacement is on, all occurrences of the misspelled word are replaced. When off, only the current word is affected.

APPLICATIONS

The spelling check operation is used to find misspelled words and typographical errors and correct them. Of course, it cannot find correctly spelled words used in error. The ability to develop a personal dictionary of your own keeps the spelling checker from challenging words and terms that you use.

Be sure that words are spelled correctly before they are added to your personal dictionary. You can use WordStar's nondocument mode to check the contents of the personal dictionary by opening the file PERSONAL.DCT. Words can be edited, added, or deleted using standard editing procedures.

TYPICAL OPERATION

In this activity, you try the three methods offered to check spelling in the document. Begin at the OPENING menu.

1. Open the document MYLTR.
2. Type **r** before "t" in the word "telling" to create a misspelled word to check.
3. Press **Ctrl-QN** to check the next word with the cursor at the beginning of the word "rtelling." The screen should resemble the following.

Spelling Check

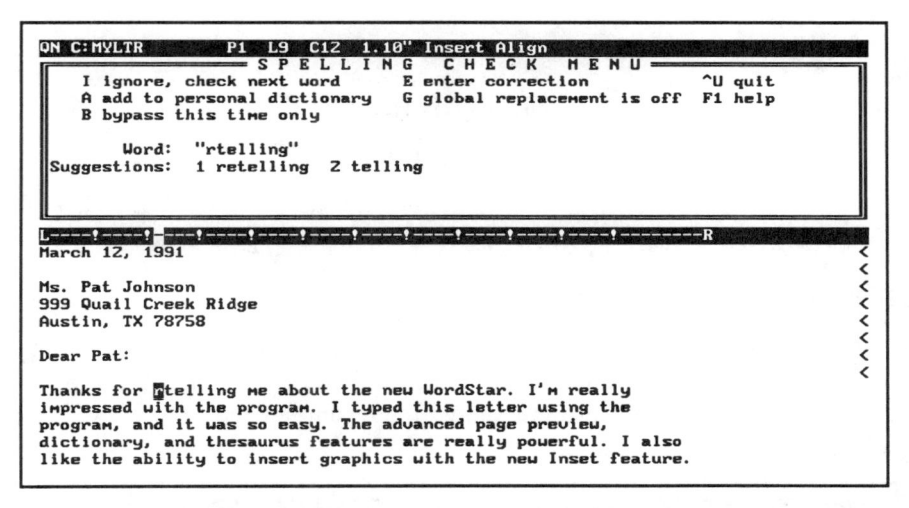

```
ON C:MYLTR        P1  L9  C12  1.10" Insert Align
══════════════════ S P E L L I N G   C H E C K   M E N U ══════════════════
    I ignore, check next word      E enter correction        ^U quit
    A add to personal dictionary   G global replacement is off  F1 help
    B bypass this time only

         Word:  "rtelling"
    Suggestions:  1 retelling  2 telling


L----!----!----!----!----!----!----!----!----!----!--------R
March 12, 1991                                                <
                                                              <
Ms. Pat Johnson                                               <
999 Quail Creek Ridge                                         <
Austin, TX 78758                                              <
                                                              <
Dear Pat:                                                     <
                                                              <
Thanks for [r]telling me about the new WordStar. I'm really
impressed with the program. I typed this letter using the
program, and it was so easy. The advanced page preview,
dictionary, and thesaurus features are really powerful. I also
like the ability to insert graphics with the new Inset feature.
```

4. Type **2** to accept the corrected word suggestion. The misspelled word is corrected and the SPELLING CHECK menu disappears.

5. Position the cursor somewhere in the paragraph and press **Ctrl-QO**. Notice the SPELL CHECK screen and the Word line.

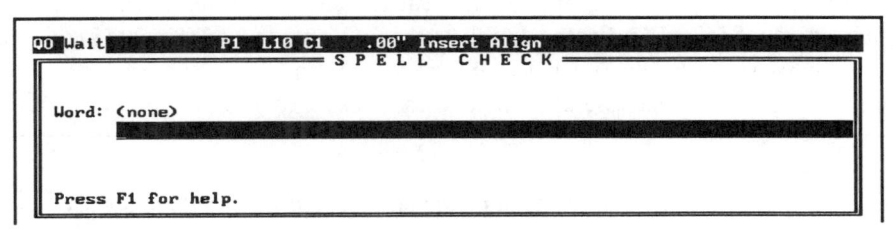

```
QO Wait         P1  L10  C1   .00" Insert Align
═══════════════════════ S P E L L   C H E C K ═══════════════════════

    Word: (none)



    Press F1 for help.
```

6. Type a misspelled word, press **Return**, then type **E** to enter it into the text for the next step.

7. Move the cursor to the beginning of the paragraph and press **Ctrl-QL** to spell check the entire file.

8. Choose your own response to the menu to experiment with the options available and to correct the misspelled word.

9. Press **Ctrl-KQ** and type **Y** to abandon the document.

10. Turn to Module 11 to continue the learning sequence.

Module 83
STATUS LINE

DESCRIPTION

When you open a document, the first line you see is the status line at the top of the page. This line contains valuable information including the file status, filename, cursor location, and line spacing. The classic WordStar status line resembles the following sample line during a find and replace operation:

```
QA C:MYLTR       P1 L12 C8    .70" Insert Align   LinSp-2        Replace Y/N
L----!-!----!----!----!----!----!----!----!----!--------R
```

In this example, QA indicates the search and replace command is in progress; C:MYLTR names the logged drive (C) and filename (MYLTR); P, L, and C indicate the position of the cursor by page, line, and column; .70" indicates inches from the left margin. Insert is on, Align is on, and LinSp-2 indicates double spacing. Replace Y/N appears in the process of selecting which words you wish to replace in the find and replace operation. The following list describes these and other status line messages and information.

Message	*Description*
Command	Appears while menu commands entered with the Ctrl key such as block, print, onscreen, and quick are in progress.
Filename	Including drive, shows which file is being edited.
Wait	Replaces Filename during pauses in disk operations.
Cursor	Shows Page, Line, Column, and inch number locations of cursor.
Insert	Indicates Insert on; display suppressed when insert is turned off with either Ctrl-V or Ins key.
Prtect	Replaces "Insert" when document is protected.
Align	Usually on unless turned off by dot command .AW OFF.
Mar-Rel	Replaces "Align" when margin is released with Ctrl-OX.
Preview	Replaces "Align" when preview is turned on with Ctrl-OP.
LinSp-2	Indicates any line spacing greater than 1.
Column	Indicates column mode.
ColRepl	Replaces "Column" when column replace is added to column mode.
Decimal	Replaces "Column" when tabbing to a decimal tab.
Replace Y/N	Appears during process of find and replace operations.
Large-File	Replaces "Replace Y/N" to warn when file is becoming too large.

Message	Description
Dot-Limit	Replaces "Replace Y/N" to warn when too many dot commands are in use.
Printing	Replaces "Replace Y/N" when background printing is in progress.
Print wait	Replaces "Replace Y/N" when background printing is paused; requires response to menu prompt to continue printing.
RgtJust	Appears over R for right margin to indicate right-justification is on.

APPLICATIONS

The status line is a valuable source of information that is helpful for keeping your place with the cursor indicator. The line number shows you how close you are to filling the page and how many pages are in the file. A glance at Insert informs you whether typing new text will erase existing text or add to it. The Column mode reminds you that text you are marking for copy, move, or delete, is in column form rather than block form.

TYPICAL OPERATION

In this activity, you create a temporary file and experiment with various messages that appear on the status line. Start WordStar and begin at the OPENING menu.

1. Open a new document named TEMP.
2. Type a few lines of text and observe the numbers in the middle of the status line as they change with cursor movement.
3. Press **Ctrl-V** or **Ins** to turn off Insert. Notice the space on the status line where Insert previously appeared.
4. Press **Ctrl-OS**, type **3** for spacing and press **F10**. Notice the status line.

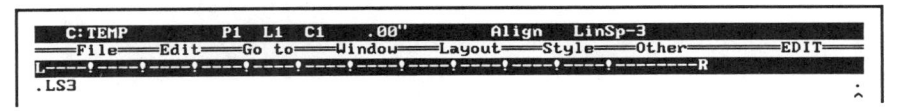

```
  C:TEMP          P1 L1 C1    .00"     Align    LinSp-3
 =File===Edit===Go to===Window===Layout===Style===Other=====EDIT=
 L----!----!----!----!----!----!----!----!----!----!--------R
 .LS3                                                            ^
```

5. Press **Ctrl-K** for BLOCK & SAVE and notice the status line.

```
 K  C:TEMP        P1 L1 C1    .00"     Align    LinSp-3
                  = B L O C K  &  S A V E   M E N U =
         SAVE              BLOCK              FILE              CURSOR
```

6. Type **Q** and then **Y** to finish the abandon without saving command.
7. Turn to Module 69 to continue the learning sequence.

Module 84
TAB SETTINGS (DECIMAL OR ALIGN)

> Classic: ^OI
> Pull-Down: Alt-L, select "Margins and tabs"

DESCRIPTION

Setting, using, and clearing decimal tabs, sometimes called align tabs, is another important formatting tool associated with word processing. The decimal tab automatically aligns decimal points (periods) in a vertical column. When you tab to a decimal tab position, characters move from right to left as they are typed. When a period (or decimal point) is typed, the decimal aligns beneath the decimal tab position on the format ruler. If you type additional characters, they move from left to right in the normal manner.

The number symbol (#) is displayed on the format ruler to designate a decimal tab. A standard tab is designated by an exclamation mark (!).

The procedure for setting the align tab is nearly identical to that of setting a standard tab (Module 85). The main difference is that the number sign (#) is entered in front of the tab setting number. The key sequence for setting a decimal tab 4 inches from the left margin is:

1. Press Ctrl-OI to display the MARGINS & TABS menu.
2. Insert # in front of the 4.00" so it resembles the following:

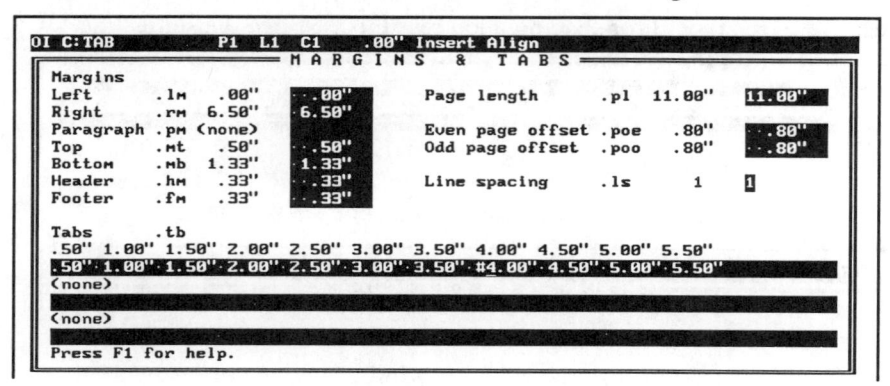

```
OI C:TAB           P1  L1  C1      .00" Insert Align
                          MARGINS  &  TABS
Margins
Left        .lm   .00"      ..00"    Page length      .pl  11.00"    11.00"
Right       .rm  6.50"      6.50"
Paragraph   .pm  <none>              Even page offset .poe  .80"      ..80"
Top         .mt   .50"      ..50"    Odd page offset  .poo  .80"      ..80"
Bottom      .mb  1.33"      1.33"
Header      .hm   .33"      ..33"    Line spacing     .ls    1        1
Footer      .fm   .33"      ..33"

Tabs        .tb
 .50" 1.00" 1.50" 2.00" 2.50" 3.00" 3.50" 4.00" 4.50" 5.00" 5.50"
 .50" 1.00" 1.50" 2.00" 2.50" 3.00" 3.50" #4.00" 4.50" 5.00" 5.50"
<none>

<none>

Press F1 for help.
```

3. Press F10 to return to the editing screen. Check the inserted dot code and resulting format ruler.

Tab Settings (Decimal or Align)

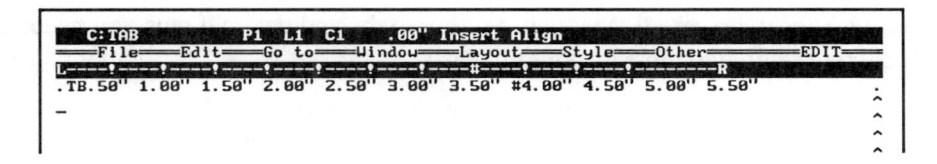

```
  C:TAB          P1  L1  C1    .00" Insert Align
====File====Edit====Go to====Window====Layout====Style====Other====        ====EDIT====
L----!----!----!----!----!----!----#----!----!----!---------R
.TB.50"  1.00"  1.50"  2.00"  2.50"  3.00"  3.50"  #4.00"  4.50"  5.00"  5.50"
-
```

Like the standard tab, you can enter tab settings by typing a dot code directly into the document. This is an alternative to using the MARGINS & TABS menu.

You can create custom sets of tabs for any number of formats by typing new format rulers and activating them with Ctrl-OO and dot command .RR. Whatever format ruler the cursor moves below becomes active. These formats are stored and become a permanent part of your file. The previous two methods are active only while the document is open (See Module 49).

Once a decimal tab is set, it is ready for use. If the string $289.95 is entered under a decimal tab, the following sequence is used:

1. Press Tab until the cursor is aligned with the decimal tab symbol. The status line displays the word "Decimal" when you access a decimal tab.
2. Type $289 (these characters move from right to left as typed).
3. Type . (the period aligns under the decimal tab symbol).
4. Type 95 (these characters move from left to right as typed).

Regardless of the method used, the format ruler displays a number sign (#) at the decimal tab location.

Clearing decimal tabs is accomplished in a manner similar to that of setting them, except that you can clear all tabs simultaneously by pressing Ctrl-Y to delete all tab settings on the Tabs line of the MARGINS & TABS menu.

You can change the decimal tab character using WordStar's installation utility WSCHANGE. If you are working on numeric notation for Europe, commas are used instead of periods to indicate the decimal place. WordStar lets you make the necessary changes.

APPLICATIONS

Decimal tabs are extremely helpful when typing tables and financial documents that have columns of numbers containing decimal fractions. For example, a financial document with columns of dollars and cents is a perfect candidate for WordStar's decimal tab function. By tabbing to the decimal tab location, all that is necessary is to type the number and decimal and then tab to the next column. The alignment of all numbers is done automatically without having to align each entry by hand. Before typing the document,

Module 84

you may wish to first clear all tabs, then set those tabs and decimal tabs you need. This saves the time required to tab past unused tabs.

Another use of the decimal tab is for the creation of flush-right text. Remember, characters move from right to left until a period is typed. If you press Tab or Return before a period is typed, the text stays to the left of the decimal tab position giving it a flush right appearance.

Look at the following example of flush-right text:

>   This
>   is an example
>   of flush right text

As you can see, each line is aligned with the decimal tab, giving a smooth right margin.

TYPICAL OPERATION

In this activity, you open a new document, clear all tabs, and then set a decimal tab at column 3.50". Next, type three rows of financial figures.

1. Open a new document named DECIMAL.
2. Press **Ctrl-OI**, type **Ctrl-Y**, type **#3.5**, and press **F10**.
3. Check for the dot code and a format ruler that resembles the one shown in the following screen illustration.

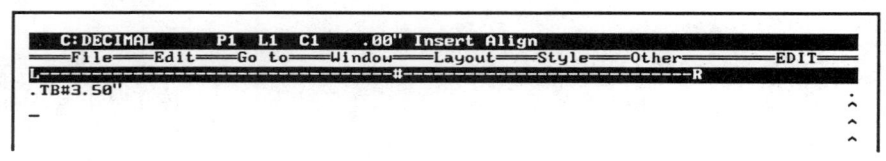

```
  C:DECIMAL       P1  L1  C1    .00" Insert Align
====File====Edit====Go to====Window====Layout====Style====Other====EDIT====
L-----------------------------------#----------------------------R
.TB#3.50"
 _
```

4. Using the Tab key to advance the cursor to the tab setting, type the following column of numbers. At the end of each number entry, press **Return** and **Tab** to advance the cursor to the next entry point.

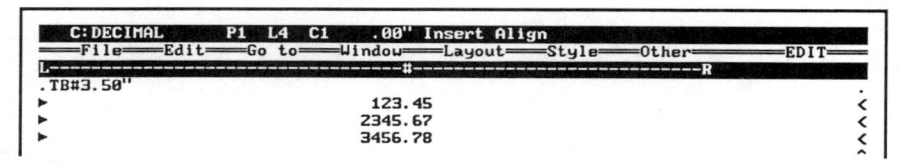

```
  C:DECIMAL       P1  L4  C1    .00" Insert Align
====File====Edit====Go to====Window====Layout====Style====Other====EDIT====
L-----------------------------------#----------------------------R
.TB#3.50"
 ▶                         123.45                                <
 ▶                        2345.67                                <
 ▶                        3456.78                                <
```

5. Continue experimenting with the decimal tab function until you are comfortable with its use.
6. Press **Ctrl-KQ** and type **Y** to abandon the document without saving.
7. Turn to Module 53 to continue the learning sequence.

Module 85
TAB SETTINGS (TYPEWRITER)

> Classic: ^OI
> Pull-Down: Alt-L, select "Margins and tabs..."

DESCRIPTION

Setting, using, and clearing standard typewriter-like tab stops is an important formatting tool associated with word processing. Notice the following format ruler.

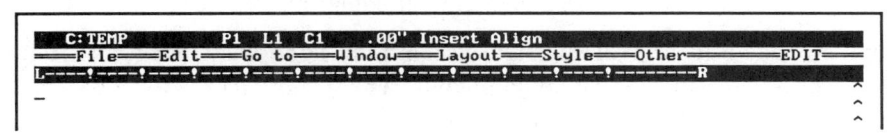

```
C:TEMP          P1  L1  C1    .00" Insert Align
===File===Edit===Go to===Window===Layout===Style===Other===EDIT===
L----!----!----!----!----!----!----!----!----!----!----!--------R
```

The positions of tabs are indicated by the exclamation marks (!). You can set or clear a tab using the MARGINS & TABS menu. Tabs are set, deleted, or moved by pressing Ctrl-OI. WordStar displays the tab settings within the MARGINS & TABS menu as shown in the following example.

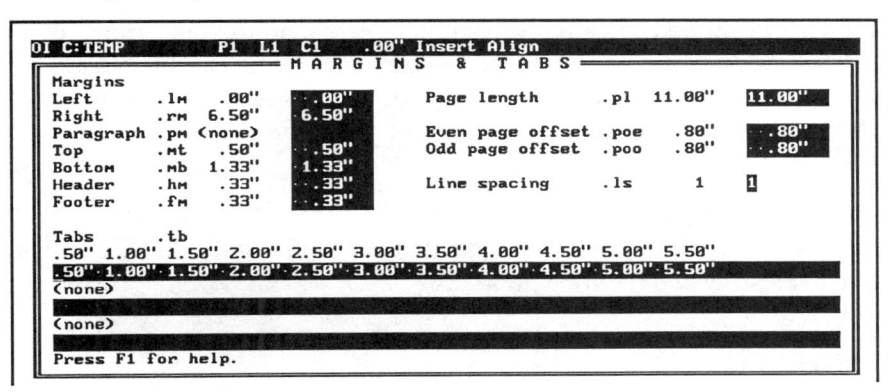

```
OI C:TEMP        P1  L1  C1    .00" Insert Align
===================== M A R G I N S  &  T A B S ===================
Margins
Left        .lm    .00"     .00"   Page length      .pl  11.00"    11.00"
Right       .rm   6.50"    6.50"
Paragraph   .pm  (none)            Even page offset .poe   .80"      .80"
Top         .mt    .50"     .50"   Odd page offset  .poo   .80"      .80"
Bottom      .mb   1.33"    1.33"
Header      .hm    .33"     .33"   Line spacing     .ls    1         1
Footer      .fm    .33"     .33"

Tabs        .tb
 .50"  1.00"  1.50"  2.00"  2.50"  3.00"  3.50"  4.00"  4.50"  5.00"  5.50"
 .50"  1.00"  1.50"  2.00"  2.50"  3.00"  3.50"  4.00"  4.50"  5.00"  5.50"
(none)
(none)
Press F1 for help.
```

Respond by typing the tab positions you want, like 1.25" and 1.75" for tabs at 1.25 and 1.75 inches from the left margin. Then press F10 to record the setting and resume editing.

You can clear all tabs by pressing Ctrl-OI and Ctrl-Y. You can restore the previous tabs by pressing Ctrl-R.

An alternate method of setting tabs is with the tab dot code, .TB, followed by either a number or the inch expression. The following two dot code expressions are examples of how to set tabs on either column positions or as inches from the left margin.

.TB 5,10,15
.TB .5",1",1.5"

You can create custom tabs for any number of formats by typing new format rulers and activating them with Ctrl-OO and dot command .RR. Whatever format ruler the cursor moves below becomes active. These formats are embedded and stored with your file. The previous two methods are temporary tab setting changes (See Module 49).

Decimal (or align) tabs are preceded with a number sign (#). These are discussed in detail in Module 84.

If you check your format ruler, you can see that WordStar's default tab settings are every five spaces beginning at column 6 and ending at column 65.

Tab stops are fixed at intervals of eight columns in nondocument mode. This can be changed by pressing Ctrl-O and responding with a new interval (2, 4, 8, and so on). These are temporary changes and are not saved with the nondocument file.

APPLICATIONS

WordStar's tabs are used in the same way as standard typewriter tabs. Tabs are normally used to indent paragraphs or to align columns of text while typing tables.

You may wish to set your own tab spacing to correspond to your printed output. The 5-space setting corresponds to 1/2-inch spacing for 10-pitch (10-character-per-inch) printing. If you are using 12-pitch type (12 characters per inch), set your tabs every 6 spaces instead of every 5. The 6-space setting corresponds to 1/2-inch tab spacing for 12-pitch printing.

WordStar makes setting and clearing tabs easy. The ability to use dot codes and enter the precise tab locations in either inches or with a column number is also a convenient alternative to clearing and resetting new tabs.

TYPICAL OPERATION

In this activity, you open a new document and practice setting and clearing tabs.

1. Open a new document named TAB. Notice WordStar's default tab settings.
2. Press **Ctrl-OI**. Notice that WordStar displays the MARGINS & TABS menu.

Tab Settings (Typewriter)

3. Press **Ctrl-Y** and press **F10**. Notice that the tab positions disappear from the format ruler and the dot code .TB is embedded in your document.

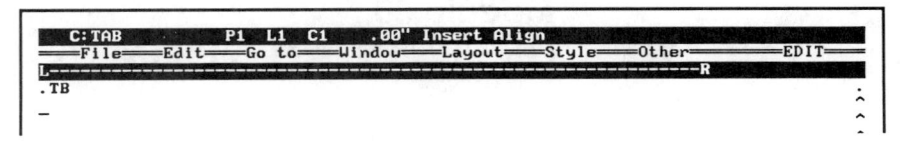

```
 C:TAB            P1  L1  C1      .00"  Insert Align
===File====Edit====Go to====Window====Layout====Style====Other====      ====EDIT===
L------------------------------------------------------------R
.TB
```

4. Press **Ctrl-OI**. Notice that the tab position line is clear.
5. Type **.5,1,1.5** and press **F10**. Notice that tabs are displayed at .50", 1.00", and 1.50" on the format ruler and check the corresponding dot code line.

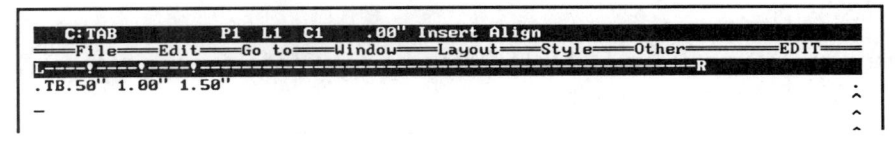

```
 C:TAB            P1  L1  C1      .00"  Insert Align
===File====Edit====Go to====Window====Layout====Style====Other====      ====EDIT===
L----!----!----!---------------------------------------------R
.TB.50"  1.00"  1.50"
```

6. Continue experimenting with setting and clearing tabs until you are comfortable with tab operations. Be sure to enter tabs using the .TB and .RR dot codes. Also experiment with Ctrl-OO.
7. Press **Ctrl-KQ** and type **Y** to abandon the document without saving.
8. Turn to Module 84 to continue the learning sequence.

Module 86
TABLE OF CONTENTS CREATION

> Classic: .TC
> Pull-Down: Alt-O, select "Table of contents entry..."

DESCRIPTION

WordStar provides an automatic table of contents generation feature that uses the .TC dot command. The form of the entry is

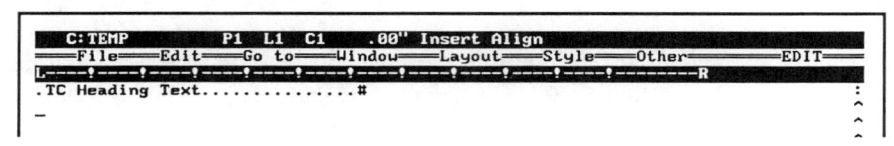

```
C:TEMP            P1  L1  C1      .00" Insert Align
====File====Edit====Go to====Window====Layout====Style====Other====    ====EDIT====
L----!----!----!----!----!----!----!----!----!----R
.TC Heading Text..............#
```

where the .TC is an extra line located at the left margin of the document. It is usually placed immediately above or below the actual printable heading.

The number sign is replaced by the current page number. Once the document is saved, you can create a table of contents file which is a derivative of the embedded .TC lines. Just type OT from the OPENING menu. The TABLE OF CONTENTS menu is displayed.

```
                        WordStar
================ TABLE  OF  CONTENTS ================
File    C:\WS\TEMP
        C:\WS\TEMP

Page numbers        All A
All/even/odd        All A

Press F1 for help.
```

Enter the File name, and press Return. Enter the Page numbers with either a series of pages (such as 2-11), or press Return to accept A for All. Respond to the "All/even/odd" prompt for all, even, or odd-numbered pages. Pressing Return or F10 prepares the table of contents document. If you wish to prepare a complete table of contents and bypass the prompts, just type the File name and press F10.

The table of contents file uses the filename of the original document with the extension .TOC. You can have ten .TOC files per document. Subsequent files are tagged with extensions .TO1 through .TO9.

When the original document is printed, the .TOC dot command lines are ignored.

By block marking and copying existing .TC lines each time a new entry is required, you can save the time required to enter a dot leader and number sign. In addition, the lines are more apt to retain a uniform format. WordStar's dot leader feature (entered with Ctrl-P.) saves the time normally used to enter periods individually. Refer to Module 25 for more information about dot leaders.

APPLICATIONS

Tables of content are used in large, segmented documents such as books, reports, and proposals. The ability to have multiple tables of content is useful in cases where each chapter within a document requires an individual table of contents in addition to the master table of contents located at the front of a book.

The ability to insert the .TC dot command as you create a document saves the time required to compile tables of content manually by going back through the screens or printed output of the document.

TYPICAL OPERATION

In this activity, you create and save a document named TEMP that includes .TC dot commands. Then you use the table of contents utility, which creates the file TEMP.TOC. Finally, you open the table of contents document and examine its contents.

1. Create the following document named TEMP. (See Module 25 for help with dot leaders.)

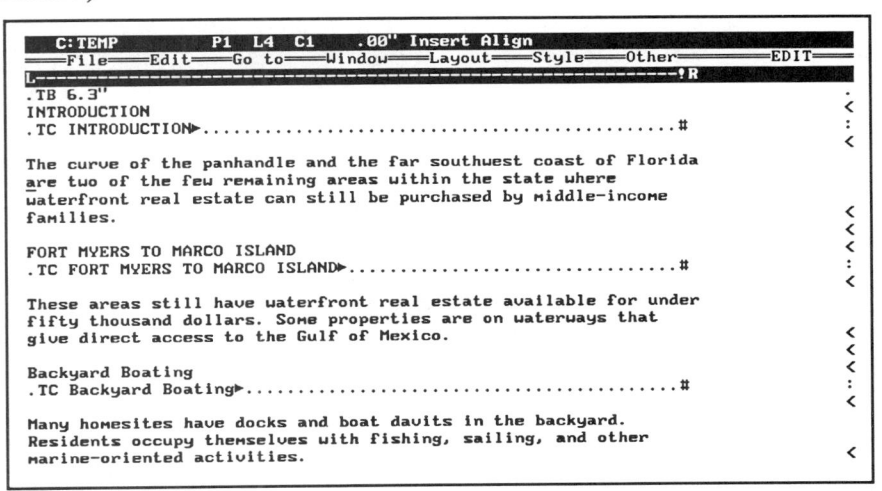

```
  C:TEMP          P1  L4  C1    .00" Insert Align
  ====File====Edit====Go to====Window====Layout====Style====Other====    =EDIT=
  L--------------------------------------------------!R
  .TB 6.3"
  INTRODUCTION                                                              <
  .TC INTRODUCTION►.........................................#              :
                                                                            <
  The curve of the panhandle and the far southwest coast of Florida
  are two of the few remaining areas within the state where
  waterfront real estate can still be purchased by middle-income
  families.                                                                 <
                                                                            <
  FORT MYERS TO MARCO ISLAND                                                <
  .TC FORT MYERS TO MARCO ISLAND►..............................#           :
                                                                            <
  These areas still have waterfront real estate available for under
  fifty thousand dollars. Some properties are on waterways that
  give direct access to the Gulf of Mexico.                                 <
                                                                            <
  Backyard Boating                                                          <
  .TC Backyard Boating►........................................#           :
                                                                            <
  Many homesites have docks and boat davits in the backyard.
  Residents occupy themselves with fishing, sailing, and other
  marine-oriented activities.                                               <
```

Module 86

2. Save the document and return to the OPENING menu.
3. Type **OT**, type **TEMP**, and press **F10** to accept the default values.
4. Open the TEMP.TOC file after the table of contents preparation activity ceases and examine its contents.

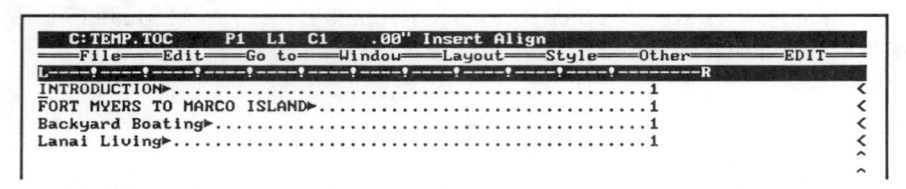

```
  C:TEMP.TOC      P1  L1  C1     .00" Insert Align
=====File=====Edit=====Go to=====Window=====Layout=====Style=====Other=====         =EDIT=
L----!----!----!----!----!----!----!----!----!----!---------R
INTRODUCTION►.......................................1              <
FORT MYERS TO MARCO ISLAND►.........................1              <
Backyard Boating►...................................1              <
Lanai Living►.......................................1              <
                                                                   ^
                                                                   ^
```

5. Press **Ctrl-KQ** to abandon the document.
6. Erase the files TEMP and TEMP.TOC to recover disk space.
7. Turn to Module 42 to continue the learning sequence.

Module 87
TELMERGE

> Classic: AT
> Pull-Down: A, select "TelMerge..."

DESCRIPTION

TelMerge is a feature-packed computer telecommunications package that is included with WordStar. This module summarizes its setup, commands, use, and applications and provides a brief hands-on experience with the program.

SETTING UP TELMERGE   Before attempting to use TelMerge, you must have:

- An internal Hayes-compatible modem card or an asynchronous communications card and an external Hayes-compatible modem
- A private telephone line with a standard RJ11C telephone wall jack
- A computer with at least 128K of memory and 100K of available disk space.

You should avoid running RAM-resident programs with TelMerge until you check their compatibility through testing. Also, if you have "call waiting" on your phone system, the call click will disrupt your communications session resulting in garbled data or possibly a disconnect.

The switch settings for an external Hayes modem are:

1	Down	Data Terminal Ready (not used)
2	Up	Result codes printed (CONNECT, DISCONNECT, RING, etc.)
3	Down	Sends result codes to your computer
4	Up	Modem commands displayed during dialing sequence
5	Down	Turns auto-answer off
6	Down	Carrier detect ignored by TelMerge
7	Up	Configures modem for single-line phone
8	Down	Modem commands recognized

The switch settings for a Hayes 1200B (internal) modem are:

1	On for COM1, Off for COM2
2	Off for single-line phone
3	Off to ignore carrier detect

Module 87

STARTING TELMERGE To start TelMerge from WordStar, check that the TELMERGE.EXE and TELMERGE.SYS files are on the same disk and directory as your WordStar program files, then type A and select TelMerge from the OPENING menu. You can also start TelMerge from the DOS prompt by typing TELMERGE and pressing Return. The following screen is displayed.

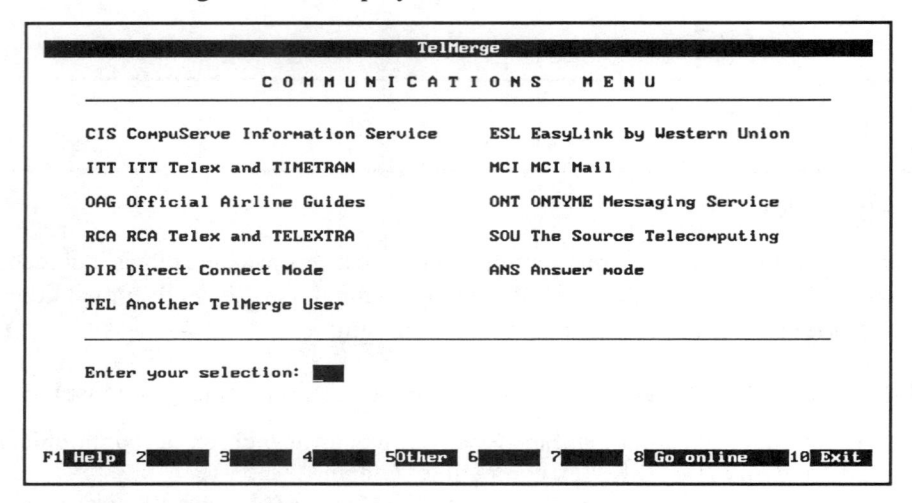

```
                              TelMerge
                    C O M M U N I C A T I O N S    M E N U

         CIS  CompuServe Information Service    ESL  EasyLink by Western Union
         ITT  ITT Telex and TIMETRAN            MCI  MCI Mail
         OAG  Official Airline Guides           ONT  ONTYME Messaging Service
         RCA  RCA Telex and TELEXTRA            SOU  The Source Telecomputing
         DIR  Direct Connect Mode               ANS  Answer Mode
         TEL  Another TelMerge User


         Enter your selection: 



    F1 Help  2        3        4        5 Other  6        7        8 Go online    10 Exit
```

CREATING A SERVICE FILE You can create a custom service file of your own for a communications service that you use by pressing F5 (for Other). The following prompts are displayed.

```
                    ─Choose/Create Control File─
         Type the name of a control file to use for dialing, or press
         ↵ to create a new one.
         You don't need to include an extension. TelMerge adds the ".tel"
         extension for you:
```

Assuming you want to create a control file for the Computer User's Group (or CUG) system, type CUG and press Return. A series of prompts is displayed. Type your response and press Return.

```
              Creating a file to save dialing information
         Phone number to dial:                              Escape
```

For the following prompts, type your answer, press Return to skip the question, or press Esc to accept all default values.

270

```
      Service name: cug
        User ID: myid
        Password: mypw
      Baud rate (300 1200 2400 4800 9600): 1200
      Serial Port (Com1, Com2): com2
      Network (Tymnet, Telenet, Uninet, Enter=none):
      HostID (tells network who to call):
```

You can view or edit the resulting file, CUG.TEL, using WordStar's nondocument mode. The file's contents are contained in the following listing.

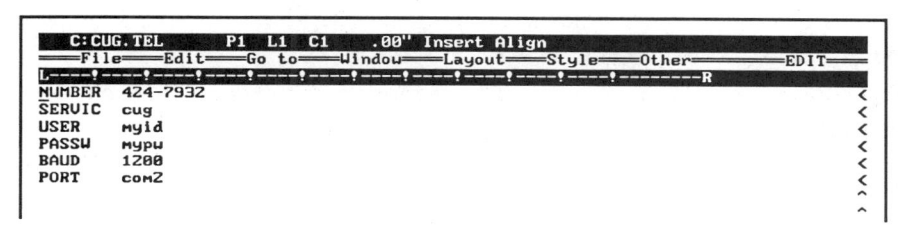

```
    C:CUG.TEL        P1  L1  C1      .00" Insert Align
  ====File====Edit====Go to====Window====Layout====Style====Other====EDIT====
  L----!----!----!----!----!----!----!----!----!----!----R
  NUMBER   424-7932                                                          <
  SERVIC   cug                                                               <
  USER     myid                                                              <
  PASSW    mypw                                                              <
  BAUD     1200                                                              <
  PORT     com2                                                              <
                                                                             ^
                                                                             ^
```

Notice that in this example, Com2 was used assuming that Com1 is used with a serial mouse or other serial device. Com1 is the TelMerge default port, but you can modify the default by editing the TELMERGE.SYS file, discussed later in this module.

USING THE CONTROL FILE After connecting your equipment and setting the modem switches as suggested, you can use the control file by pressing F5, typing the name of the control file (such as CUG), and pressing Return. Your computer dials the number and uses the information found in the CUG.TEL file. The screen dialogue resembles the following.

```
      Dialing CUG  Logfile TELMERGE.LOG  Printer PRN  9

      Commands to modem
        and responses:
      ATQ0V1
      OK
      ATE1
      OK
      ATDT642-7165
```

The "CONNECT" message is also displayed if a satisfactory connection is made. A "NO CARRIER" message is usually followed by a redial in about 45 seconds. Notice the Logfile TELMERGE.LOG — this file collects the communications dialogue for later review. The commands for turning the Logfile on and off and creating logfiles for specific services are discussed in the following paragraphs.

Module 87

ADDING A SERVICE TO THE TELMERGE.SYS FILE If you want to select a file directly from the first menu rather than having to use F5, you can modify the TELMERGE.SYS file using WordStar's nondocument mode. Use the following steps to add CUG to the file.

1. Open the TELMERGE.SYS file as a nondocument.
2. Press PgDn twice to move to the System Section and edit default values to suit your system.
3. Press PgDn a few more times until you reach the Menu Section. You can replace NEW with CUG to add your new CUG service.
4. Page down to the Service Section. This section contains scripts for each service. You can read the CUG.TEL file (using Ctrl-KR) into this section and modify it as necessary or type the script file. A series of optional commands is presented for your use in the script if required.

Command	Description
ANSWERBACK *string*	Sends your personal ID code in response to a telex WHO ARE YOU request.
APPEND	Adds dialogue to the end of an existing LOG file.
ATDELAY *n*	Pauses n tenths of a second before sending to service.
ATTENTION *c*	Sends special character such as ^C or ^M.
AUTOLOG *yes* or *no*	Sets automatic log-on to on or off.
BAUD *rate*	Use 110, 300, 1200 (default), 2400, 4800, or 9600.
BITS *n*	Use 7 or 8 (default).
CALL	Calls service; begin immediate dialing.
CLS	Clears the screen.
DUPLEX *half* or *full*	Full (default) echoes typed characters; some services require half.
ELSE	See IF.
EMULATE *type*	Use VT100 (default), VIDTEX, or NONE.
END	Ends script.
ENDIF	See IF.
EXIT	Ends TelMerge session and exits to WordStar.
FILESEND *filename*	Sends specified file.
FIRST *c*	Waits for character c from service before displaying text on screen.
FK *text*	Programs function keys F7 or F8 to issue special commands; to program F7 to send a Return, CUG, and the command CREATE, use FK1R,CUG CREATE.
FULLSCREEN *yes* or *no*	Used with EMULATE for full screen display; yes is default.
GOTO *name*	Transfers command file execution to label.
GRAPHIC *yes* or *no*	Yes (default) displays extended character set.
HANGCOM *string*	Use with a hangup string if ATH (default) is not used by your modem.
HANGUP	Hangs up phone in preparation for another call.
HARDCOPY	See PRINT.

TelMerge

Command	Description
HOSTID *string*	Issues up to 30 characters as a network's internal "phone number" for the called service such as HOST CUG.
IF, IFNOT *string*	Tests for condition; used with ELSE and ENDIF.
INCLUDE *filename*	Branches from current script to INCLUDE file.
INIT, INIT2 *string*	Initializes modem prior to dialing; INIT2 lets you add more information.
INTERACTIVE *number*	Specifies phone number of a telex real-time system.
LABEL *name*	Marks position within a control file for a GOTO.
LINEDELAY *n*	Pauses at end of each line (in tenths of a second) when sent with F4.
LOGFILE *filename*	Filename that records a communication session such as CUG.LOG.
LOGGING ON or OFF	Turns communications session logging ON or OFF.
LOGON *string1*|*string2*|...	Used to automate logon session with a service (up to 80 characters).
MODEM *acoustic*	Used for an acoustic coupled modem.
MODEM *answer*	Used for computer-to-computer file transfer.
MODEM *automatic*	Default setting for automatic dialing and answering.
MODEM *direct*	Used for direct cable connection to another computer.
MODEM *hayes*	Automatically dials and answers.
MODEM *hayes 2400*	Used for Hayes Smartmodem 2400.
NETWORK *name*	Telephone network used to contact the service such as TYMNET, Telenet, or UNINET.
NUMBER *number*	The telephone number to dial.
PARITY *setting*	Use none (default), odd, even, zero, or one.
PASSWORD *string*	Your password for the service (up to 30 characters).
PAUSE *secs*	Waits a specified number of seconds.
PORT *Com1* or *Com2*	Selects communications port.
POSTMODEM *string*	Sends characters to an electronic switch after calling.
PREFIX *string*	Lets you change from ATDT (default) to another dialing prefix.
PREMODEM *string*	Sends string to communications port before modem is initialized.
PRINT *string*	*Yes* prints a communications session; *No* (default) suppresses printing; *filename* saves session to file; *LPT2* prints to LPT2.
PROMPT *string*	Adds up to 14 characters, nine deep to prompts received from a service by TelMerge; legal characters are: @ : = ! ? > ^ Q
PROTOCOL *type*	Lets you change from XMCHK (default) to XMCRC protocol.
QUIET *secs*	Waits a specified number of seconds after remote has finished sending.
SAY *text*	Displays text on screen (up to 80 characters).
SEND *word*	Sends word (or words) to the service.
SERVICE *string*	Name of the service; displayed in status line during connection (up to 32 characters).
STOPS *1* or *2*	Number of stop bits; 1 is the default value.

Command	Description
SUFFIX *string*	Sends up to 30 characters following the dialed number.
TERMINAL *string*	Up to a 6-character string specifies your terminal type.
TRY *1 to 99*	Number of dial retries when number is busy; waits approximately 45 second between retries; default is 2.
USEDTR *yes* or *no*	Change to *yes* for modems that use DTR signal for hangup.
USERID *string*	User identification code used by the service (up to 30 characters).
WAIT *string*	Waits for specified string from the service after logging on.

The script file for CUG should resemble the following one within the TELMERGE.SYS file.

```
Label     CUG
Service   CUG
Logfile   CUG.LOG
Number    642-7165
Userid    MYID
Password  MYPW
Baud      1200
Port      Com2
End
```

NOTE

If you are using a telex service, two additional lines are inserted above the Number line. These are:

Interactive	interactive phone number	(used for real-time session)
Answerback	your answerback number	(used to verify receipt)

5. Once the script file is completed, save the TELMERGE.SYS file and try it out.

If you discover a need to intercept and respond to additional prompts from your service, or if you wish to issue service commands automatically, such as going directly to MCI Mail's Dow Jones Service, you can embed these in your script file.

SENDING A DOCUMENT   TelMerge is designed to send WordStar documents. Once a script is prepared, such as CUG, start TelMerge and perform the following steps.

1. Type CUG and press Return; TelMerge dials CUG.
2. When CUG answers, TelMerge issues your user identification number and password.
3. Press F4 to send a file. Type the full name of the file including the directory name.
4. When prompted for an end-of-text marker, type / and press Return.
5. Use required service commands necessary to complete sending your document.
6. Use service commands to exit the service; then press F10 to hang up and press F10 again to exit TelMerge.

Sending ASCII Files   To send an ASCII file, specify any service other than SERVICE or SERVICE CIS and press F4. An ASCII file transfer is made.

Sending Program Files with the XMODEM Protocol   Use F6 (XM SND) instead of F4 to send a *protocol* file. The XM stands for XMODEM protocol, which lets you transfer files containing characters above 128 decimal.

RECEIVING A DOCUMENT   To receive a document from a selected service, ensure the logging feature is on. This makes a copy of the session, including received documents. There should be sufficient space on your disk to receive and store incoming documents.

You may want to add RECEIVE and ORIGINATE services to your TELMERGE.SYS file. The RECEIVE service script should include the following lines:

```
Label       RECEIVE
Say         Receiving Computer
Modem       ANSWER
End
```

The ORIGINATE service script should include these lines:

```
Label       Originate
Say         Calling Computer
Number      phone number
End
```

You may need to set your modem's auto-answer switch ON and restart your modem to reinitialize it for auto-answer.

APPLICATIONS

The TelMerge communications package serves as a general purpose telecommunications package that you can use to send and receive any kind of computer-based information. You can use its automatic dialing and logon features to initiate communications with any service with a few simple keystrokes. Setting up and using script files helps office workers who are unfamiliar with communications jargon. Just show them how to start the TelMerge program and select a service. Your script file does the rest.

As a WordStar user, you should be pleased that TelMerge sends your document files to other WordStar users without a hitch. If the recipient is using another word processing package, such as WordPerfect or Microsoft Word, you can print your document to an ASCII file and send the ASCII image. The ASCII format is selected because almost all word processing programs can read and write ASCII files.

You can also do direct file transfers from one computer to another by telephone or through a cable (called a *null modem*). This is handy for transferring files from a laptop computer to a desktop computer when they use different size disk media. For example, if you have a laptop computer that uses 3 1/2-inch diskettes and a desktop computer that uses 5

1/4-inch media, interconnect them and use TelMerge to transfer files in either direction. When you use a direct cable connection, experiment with faster baud rates up to 9600 to speed the file transfer process.

TYPICAL OPERATION

In this activity, you add a local access (telephone) number to the TELMERGE.SYS file for an available service in your area. You should be a subscriber having an access code. If you are new to telecommunications, you may want to subscribe to a service. For example, you can subscribe to MCI Mail by dialing 1-800-MCI-MAIL and requesting a subscriber package. Once you establish a personal or company ID and password, you can dial the service and check your mailbox for information. As a minimum, you can view the day's news highlights before you exit.

Before beginning, you must have the equipment called for in the Setting Up TelMerge paragraph. Otherwise, skip this activity and turn to Module 93 to continue the learning sequence.

1. From the OPENING menu, type **FN** and open TELMERGE.SYS as a nondocument file.
2. Page down until you find the MCI script file.
3. Add the local access telephone number to the Number line. Your script file should now resemble the following one.

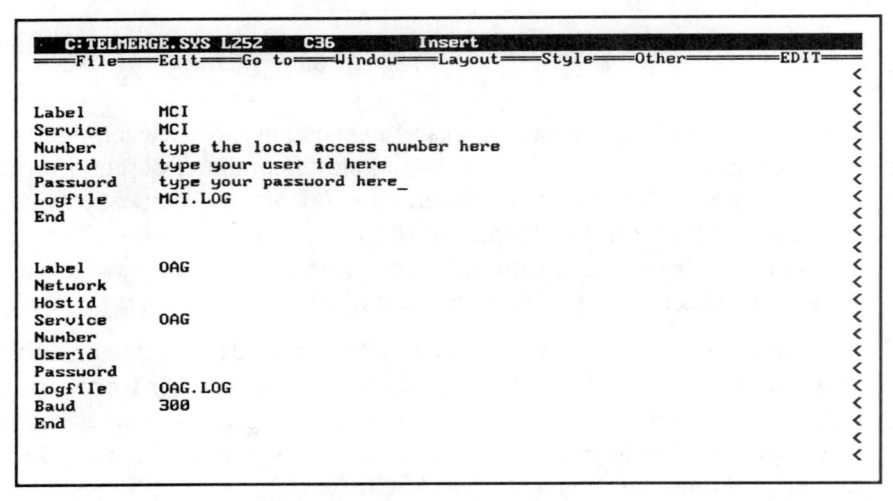

```
 C:TELMERGE.SYS L252    C36          Insert
====File====Edit====Go to====Window====Layout====Style====Other====EDIT====
                                                                          <
                                                                          <
  Label        MCI                                                        <
  Service      MCI                                                        <
  Number       type the local access number here                          <
  Userid       type your user id here                                     <
  Password     type your password here_                                   <
  Logfile      MCI.LOG                                                    <
  End                                                                     <
                                                                          <
                                                                          <
  Label        OAG                                                        <
  Network                                                                 <
  Hostid                                                                  <
  Service      OAG                                                        <
  Number                                                                  <
  Userid                                                                  <
  Password                                                                <
  Logfile      OAG.LOG                                                    <
  Baud         300                                                        <
  End                                                                     <
                                                                          <
                                                                          <
```

4. Press **Ctrl-KD** to save the TELMERGE.SYS file.

5. Start the TelMerge program from either the OPENING menu or DOS prompt. The TelMerge COMMUNICATIONS menu is displayed.

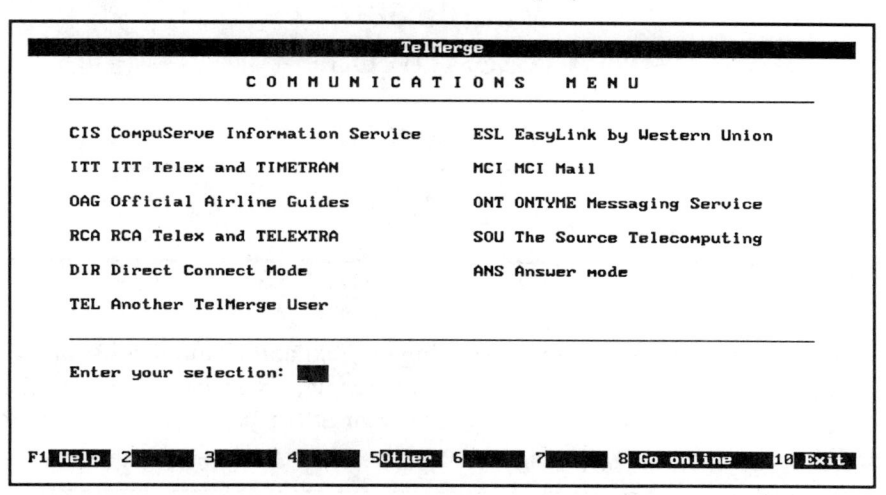

```
                         TelMerge
                  COMMUNICATIONS    MENU

     CIS CompuServe Information Service    ESL EasyLink by Western Union
     ITT ITT Telex and TIMETRAN             MCI MCI Mail
     OAG Official Airline Guides            ONT ONTYME Messaging Service
     RCA RCA Telex and TELEXTRA             SOU The Source Telecomputing
     DIR Direct Connect Mode                ANS Answer mode
     TEL Another TelMerge User


     Enter your selection: ▪


 F1 Help  2      3      4      5 Other  6      7      8 Go online  10 Exit
```

6. Type **MCI** and press **Return** to dial MCI Mail. Watch the communications dialogue on your screen.
7. Use service-specific commands to view help and other information.
8. Type **exit** (or the appropriate service command) to exit.
9. Press **F10** to exit TelMerge.
10. Turn to Module 93 to continue the learning sequence.

Module 88
THESAURUS

> Classic: ^QJ
> Pull-Down: Alt-O, select "Thesaurus..."

DESCRIPTION

The Thesaurus feature lets you select a word in your text and examine a list of alternate words having the same or a similar meaning. For example, if you want to find a substitute for the word "determine," you can place your cursor at the beginning of the word and press Ctrl-QJ. The following screen is displayed.

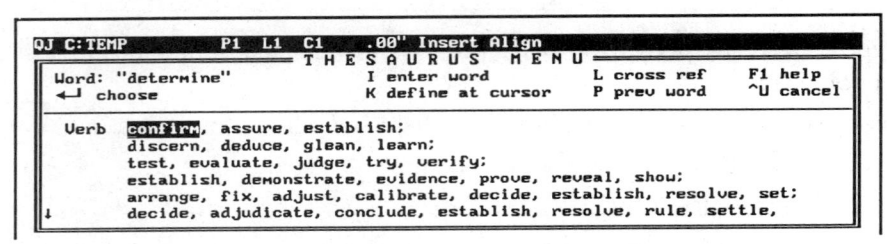

```
QJ C:TEMP           P1  L1  C1      .00" Insert Align
                      THESAURUS  MENU
 Word: "determine"            I enter word        L cross ref    F1 help
 ↵  choose                    K define at cursor  P prev word    ^U cancel

   Verb  confirm, assure, establish;
         discern, deduce, glean, learn;
         test, evaluate, judge, try, verify;
         establish, demonstrate, evidence, prove, reveal, show;
         arrange, fix, adjust, calibrate, decide, establish, resolve, set;
 ↓       decide, adjudicate, conclude, establish, resolve, rule, settle,
```

You can select a word by pointing to it using the arrow keys. Once selected, press Return to make the replacement. If you decide to keep the original word, press Ctrl-U to return to your text.

There are several options available with the Thesaurus. These are called by typing the letters I, K, L, or P. Each is described in the following list.

Option	Description
I	Type another word and find its synonym.
K	Display a definition for the selected word.
L	Display a synonym list for a word selected in the THESAURUS menu.
P	Redisplay the previous list of words after using the L option.

APPLICATIONS

A thesaurus is a standard tool of the word processing, writing, and editing trades. Having a thesaurus on line saves the time required to look up a word for substitutions. Most WordStar users who experience the power and speed of the Thesaurus utility, in comparison to a paper-based thesaurus, generally agree that it is a valuable addition to the program.

TYPICAL OPERATION

In this activity, the Thesaurus is used to find a substitute for the word "bad." Begin by opening a new document named TEMP.

1. Type the word **bad** and reposition the cursor to the "b" in "bad."
2. Press **Ctrl-QJ** and notice the following screen.

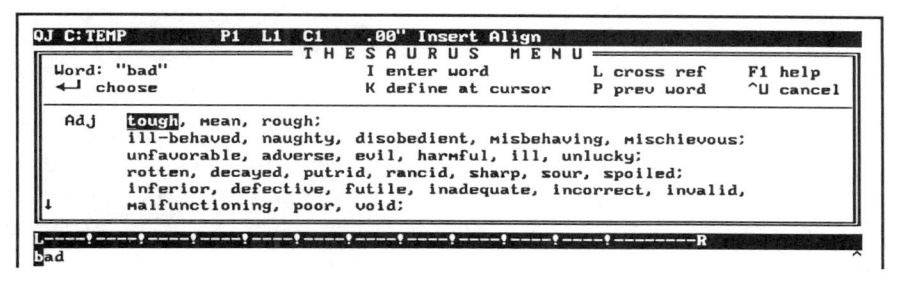

```
QJ C:TEMP          P1 L1 C1    .00" Insert Align
                  = T H E S A U R U S   M E N U =
  Word: "bad"                  I enter word        L cross ref     F1 help
  ↵ choose                     K define at cursor  P prev word     ^U cancel

  Adj    tough, mean, rough;
         ill-behaved, naughty, disobedient, misbehaving, mischievous;
         unfavorable, adverse, evil, harmful, ill, unlucky;
         rotten, decayed, putrid, rancid, sharp, sour, spoiled;
         inferior, defective, futile, inadequate, incorrect, invalid,
  ↓      malfunctioning, poor, void;
 L----!----!----!----!----!----!----!----!----!----!--------R
 bad                                                         ^
```

3. Press **Down Arrow** or **PgDn** to see additional words.

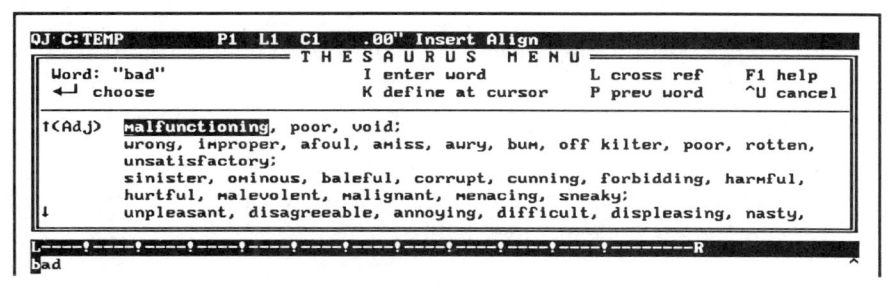

```
QJ C:TEMP          P1 L1 C1    .00" Insert Align
                  = T H E S A U R U S   M E N U =
  Word: "bad"                  I enter word        L cross ref     F1 help
  ↵ choose                     K define at cursor  P prev word     ^U cancel

  ↑(Adj) malfunctioning, poor, void;
         wrong, improper, afoul, amiss, awry, bum, off kilter, poor, rotten,
         unsatisfactory;
         sinister, ominous, baleful, corrupt, cunning, forbidding, harmful,
         hurtful, malevolent, malignant, menacing, sneaky;
  ↓      unpleasant, disagreeable, annoying, difficult, displeasing, nasty,
 L----!----!----!----!----!----!----!----!----!--------R
 bad                                                     ^
```

4. Point to "corrupt" and press **Return**. Notice that the word "bad" is replaced with the word "corrupt."
5. Experiment with other words until you are familiar with the use of Thesaurus.
6. Press **Ctrl-KQ** and type **Y** to abandon the document.
7. Turn to Module 50 to continue the learning sequence.

Module 89
UNDO, UNERASE

> Classic: Ctrl-U
> Pull Down: Alt-E, select "Undo"

DESCRIPTION

WordStar's undo function is used to interrupt an operation before it is completed. For example, you can type a command sequence from either the OPENING menu or the EDIT menu, and then undo (or abort) the sequence with Ctrl-U (or F2) before it takes effect. The F2 key is WordStar's default function key setting. It is possible that the function of your F2 is different, depending on whether or not WordStar's WSCHANGE utility was used to redesignate the function key values.

WordStar also allows you to undo an erasure or "unerase" some characters under some conditions. Ctrl-U unerases the last characters you erased if more than 1 and less than 500 characters were erased using one key sequence (such as Ctrl-Y). The deleted text is restored at the cursor position.

APPLICATIONS

Undo is often used to abort printing, deleting, renaming, copying, diskette logging, and other file operations before they are completed. You can also use undo to abort operations like spelling check or find and find-replace during text editing functions.

Unerase is used to restore the most recent word, line, or block of text that was deleted. Being able to restore text that was erased accidentally is a convenience that anyone who has ever pressed the wrong key can appreciate.

TYPICAL OPERATION

In this activity, you use the undo or unerase command to abort a print command; then you restore a line of deleted text. Type WS from the DOS prompt to start WordStar.

1. Type **FP** from the OPENING menu to display the PRINT menu.
2. Press **Ctrl-U** to undo the printing operation. The OPENING menu is redisplayed.

3. Press **FD** to open a file. Type **TEMP** as the filename and press **Return**. Type **Y** to respond to the prompt "Create a new one (Y/N)?"
4. Type **This is a test to see how unerase works.**
5. Press **Ctrl-Y** with the cursor positioned on the typed sentence. The line of text is deleted.
6. Press **Ctrl-U** to restore the deleted text. Notice that the line returns beginning at the cursor position.
7. Press **Ctrl-KQ** and type **Y** at the prompt to abandon the document without saving.
8. Turn to Module 39 to continue the learning sequence.

Module 90
UPPER/LOWER CASE CONVERSION

> Mark block, then press ^K', ^K", or ^K.

DESCRIPTION

WordStar lets you convert a marked block of text from uppercase to lowercase, or from lowercase to uppercase. Pressing Ctrl-K', where ' is an apostrophe, converts all characters within a marked block to lowercase. Ctrl-K", where " is a double quote, converts all characters within a marked block to uppercase. Use ^K. to convert to sentence case where the first letter following a period, question mark, or exclamation point and a space is capitalized. The rest of the block (except for the letter I used alone) converts to lowercase.

APPLICATIONS

There are times when you may type a passage of text using all capital letters. You can convert the text to lowercase by marking it as a block and pressing Ctrl-K'. The reverse is accomplished with Ctrl-K". If you are editing paragraph headings, which should be in the opposite case, it is much faster to mark and convert the case compared to retyping long titles. Of course, you may have to retype the first letter of words within a paragraph title or proper nouns within a block of text.

TYPICAL OPERATION

In this activity, you create a document and enter a small column of text. Then you convert it to uppercase. Next you type a sentence in all caps and convert it to sentence case. Begin at the OPENING menu.

1. Open a document named TEMP.
2. Type the following list using uppercase and lowercase as shown.

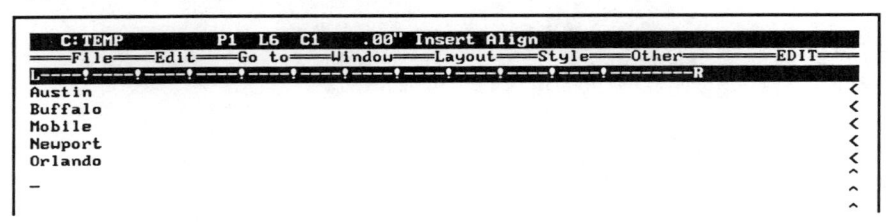

```
  C:TEMP           P1  L6  C1     .00" Insert Align
 ==File====Edit====Go to====Window====Layout====Style====Other====         =EDIT==
 L----!----!----!----!----!----!----!----!----!----R
 Austin                                                                      <
 Buffalo                                                                     <
 Mobile                                                                      <
 Newport                                                                     <
 Orlando                                                                     <
 -                                                                           ^
                                                                             ^
```

Upper/Lower Case Conversion

3. Mark the entire list as a block and press **Ctrl-K"**. Notice the result.

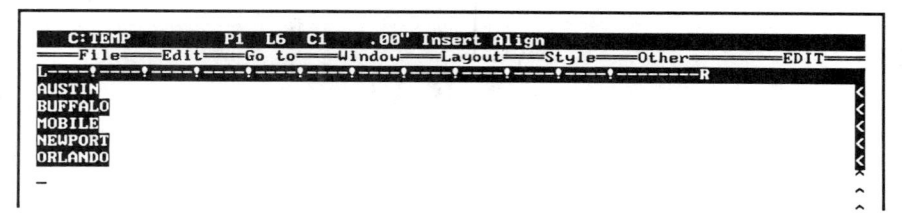

```
C:TEMP        P1  L6  C1    .00"  Insert Align
=File====Edit====Go to====Window====Layout====Style====Other====EDIT==
L----!----!----!----!----!----!----!----!----!----!--------R
AUSTIN
BUFFALO
MOBILE
NEWPORT
ORLANDO
-
```

4. Delete the block by pressing **Crtl-KY**. Press **Caps Lock** and type the following sentence.

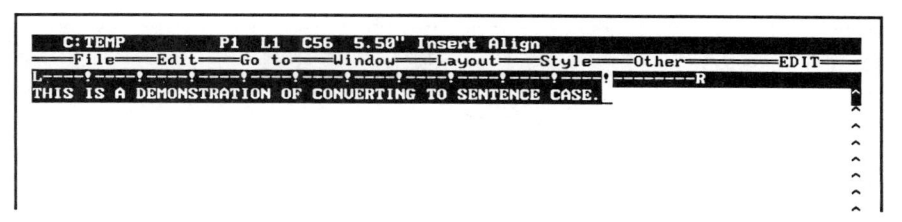

```
C:TEMP        P1  L1  C56  5.50"  Insert Align
=File====Edit====Go to====Window====Layout====Style====Other====EDIT==
L----!----!----!----!----!----!----!----!----!----!--------R
THIS IS A DEMONSTRATION OF CONVERTING TO SENTENCE CASE.
```

5. Press **Ctrl-K.** (period) and notice the result.

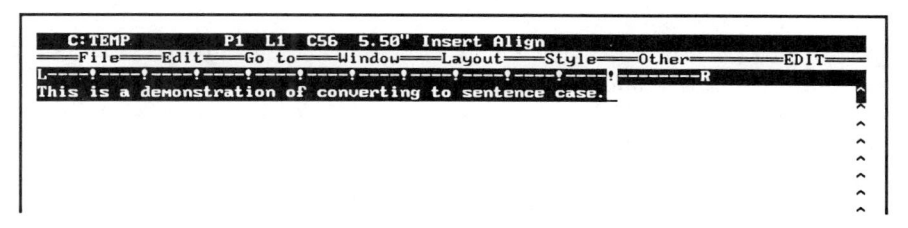

```
C:TEMP        P1  L1  C56  5.50"  Insert Align
=File====Edit====Go to====Window====Layout====Style====Other====EDIT==
L----!----!----!----!----!----!----!----!----!----!--------R
This is a demonstration of converting to sentence case.
```

6. Press **Ctrl-KQ** and type **Y** to abandon the document.
7. Turn to Module 91 to continue the learning sequence.

Module 91
WINDOW
(WORKING WITH TWO DOCUMENTS)

> Classic: ^OK
> Pull-Down: Alt-W, select "Open/switch between windows"

DESCRIPTION

WordStar's window function lets you open and work with two documents at the same time. To use the window function, open one document in the normal manner. Then press Ctrl-OK, enter the name of a second document, and press Return. The second document is displayed at the bottom half of the screen. The second document may already exist, or you can create it when you open the window.

Once a window is open, you can move between windows by pressing Ctrl-OK. You can also mark and copy or move blocks between windows. The pull-down menu (Alt-W) for window displays window-related commands.

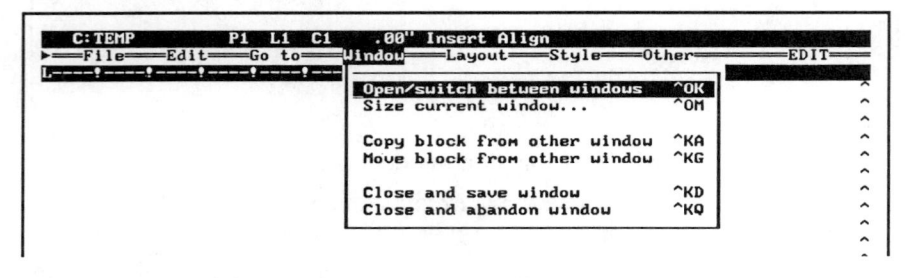

```
C:TEMP           P1  L1  C1    .00" Insert Align
═══File═══Edit═══Go to═══Window═══Layout═══Style═══Other═══════EDIT═══
L────!────!────!────!────!─┌──────────────────────────────┐
                           │ Open/switch between windows ^OK │
                           │ Size current window...       ^OM │
                           │                                  │
                           │ Copy block from other window ^KA │
                           │ Move block from other window ^KG │
                           │                                  │
                           │ Close and save window        ^KD │
                           │ Close and abandon window     ^KQ │
                           └──────────────────────────────┘
```

MARKING AND MOVING OR COPYING BLOCKS You can mark a block in the active window using the block mark command (Ctrl-KB/KK). Once a block is marked, move to the other window with Ctrl-OK. Then use Ctrl-KA to copy the marked block. Use Ctrl-KG to move the block from one window to the other.

SAVING OR ABANDONING A WINDOW The document in the current window is saved in the normal way (with Ctrl-KD). Similarly, it is abandoned using Ctrl-KQ. Once saved or abandoned, the cursor moves to the remaining document. It is saved or abandoned in the same way.

SIZING WINDOWS The number of lines used by the active window is easily changed by pressing **Ctrl-OM**. The SIZE WINDOW screen is displayed.

Change the size of the window by entering a number that corresponds to the lines you want to display in the active window. When you close a window, the screen size of the remaining window returns to normal.

APPLICATIONS

WordStar's window feature is an excellent way to move passages of text, tables, boxes, or formats from one document to another. It is also useful for examining one document while editing another. For example, you may need to refer to certain information during the creation of a new, related document. You can use the window function to open and browse a second document. Once the information is found, it can either be copied or paraphrased.

TYPICAL OPERATION

In this activity, you open the document named MYLTR. Next you open a document named TEMP. The first paragraph in MYLTR is marked and moved to TEMP.

1. Open the document MYLTR.
2. Press **Ctrl-OK**, type **TEMP**, press **Return**, and then type **Y**. Notice that the blank TEMP document is at the bottom half of the screen.

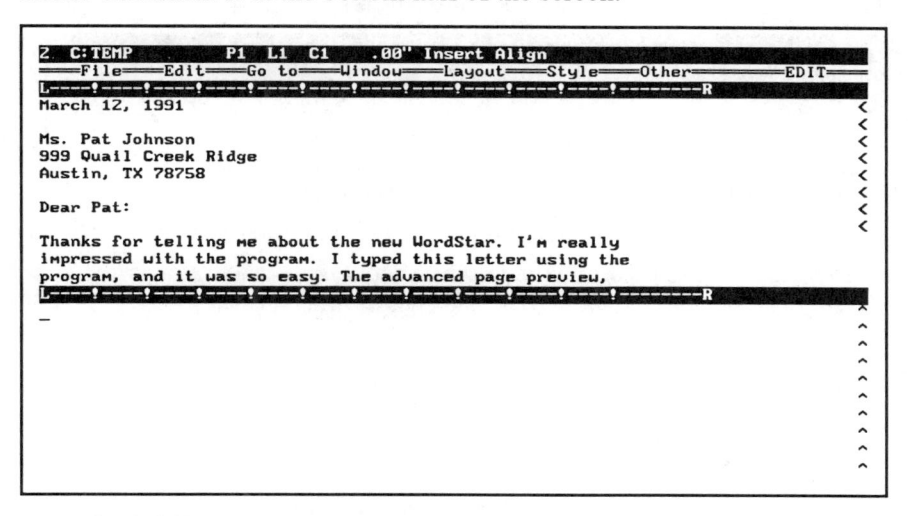

```
2  C:TEMP           P1  L1  C1    .00" Insert Align
====File====Edit====Go to====Window====Layout====Style====Other====    ====EDIT====
L----!----!----!----!----!----!----!----!----!----!--------R
March 12, 1991                                                          <
                                                                        <
Ms. Pat Johnson                                                         <
999 Quail Creek Ridge                                                   <
Austin, TX 78758                                                        <
                                                                        <
Dear Pat:                                                               <
                                                                        <
Thanks for telling me about the new WordStar. I'm really
impressed with the program. I typed this letter using the
program, and it was so easy. The advanced page preview,
L----!----!----!----!----!----!----!----!----!----!--------R
-                                                                       ^
                                                                        ^
                                                                        ^
                                                                        ^
                                                                        ^
                                                                        ^
                                                                        ^
                                                                        ^
                                                                        ^
```

3. Press **Ctrl-OK** to move the cursor to the top window.
4. Mark the address of MYLTR as a block (Ctrl-KB, Ctrl-KK).
5. Press **Ctrl-OK** to move to the bottom window.

Module 91

6. Press **Ctrl-KA** to copy the marked block from MYLTR to TEMP.

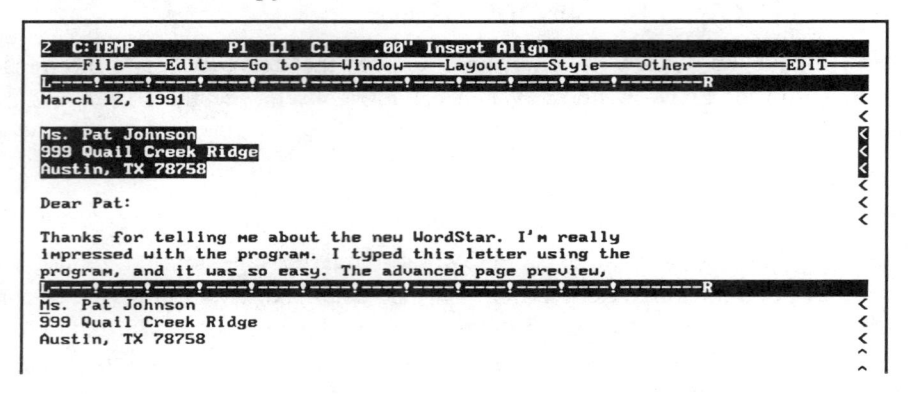

```
2 C:TEMP         P1  L1  C1     .00" Insert Align
====File====Edit====Go to====Window====Layout====Style====Other====EDIT===
L----!----!----!----!----!----!----!----!----!----!----!----!--------R
March 12, 1991                                                          <
                                                                        <
Ms. Pat Johnson                                                         <
999 Quail Creek Ridge                                                   <
Austin, TX 78758                                                        <
                                                                        <
Dear Pat:                                                               <
                                                                        <
Thanks for telling me about the new WordStar. I'm really
impressed with the program. I typed this letter using the
program, and it was so easy. The advanced page preview,
L----!----!----!----!----!----!----!----!----!----!----!----!--------R
Ms. Pat Johnson                                                         <
999 Quail Creek Ridge                                                   <
Austin, TX 78758                                                        <
                                                                        ^
                                                                        ^
```

7. Experiment with marking, moving, and copying text.
8. Press **Ctrl-OM** to change the size of the windows.

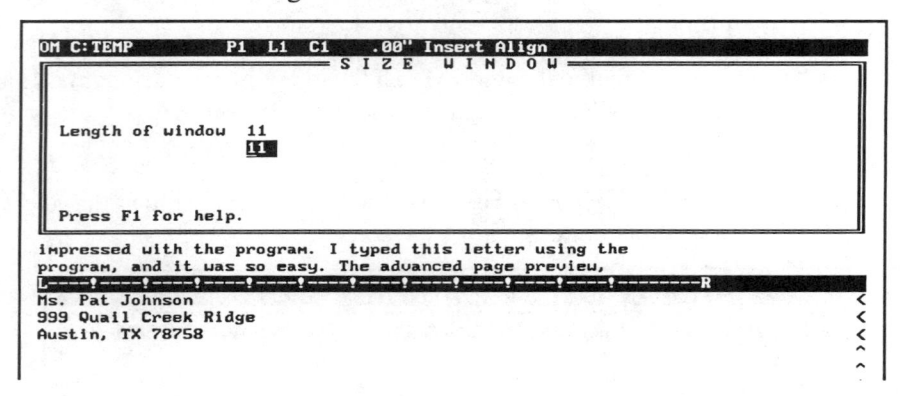

```
OM C:TEMP         P1  L1  C1     .00" Insert Align
                         ═══ S I Z E   W I N D O W ═══


   Length of window  11
                     11


   Press F1 for help.

impressed with the program. I typed this letter using the
program, and it was so easy. The advanced page preview,
L----!----!----!----!----!----!----!----!----!----!----!----!--------R
Ms. Pat Johnson                                                         <
999 Quail Creek Ridge                                                   <
Austin, TX 78758                                                        <
                                                                        ^
                                                                        ^
```

9. Press **Ctrl-KQ** and type **Y** to abandon the current window.
10. Press **Ctrl-KQ** and type **Y** to abandon the remaining document.
11. Turn to Module 55 to continue the learning sequence.

Module 92
WORD WRAP OFF/ON

> ^OW

DESCRIPTION

The automatic word wrap function lets you type text without worrying about line endings. Automatic word wrap moves those words that are too long to fit at the end of the current line to the beginning of the next line. When a word wraps, WordStar places what is known as a *soft return* at the end of the line. A hard return can be replaced with a soft return by pressing Ctrl-6 at the end of a line and then pressing Ctrl-B to reformat the current paragraph.

You can turn off automatic word wrap by pressing Ctrl-OW. Turn it on again by repeating Ctrl-OW. You can check the status of automatic word wrap by looking at the ONSCREEN menu. The status of format functions that are toggled on or off can be viewed there.

When automatic word wrap is off, it is necessary to end each line by pressing Return. Otherwise, displayed text scrolls to the left as you type text at the right side of the screen. A beep is sounded as you enter the region beyond the right margin. To wrap a long line of text, even when word wrap is off, put the cursor at the beginning of the line and press Ctrl-B to reformat the line. WordStar's reformat function is described in Module 70.

APPLICATIONS

Automatic word wrap is a productive word processing function that allows "free-form" typing. It lets you keep your eyes on your reference text, eliminates the need to press Return at the end of each line, and increases typing speed.

TYPICAL OPERATION

In this activity, begin by opening a new document. Type about 90 characters of text and watch the automatic word wrap work. Then turn off word wrap and type the same line to see how the text scrolls horizontally.

Module 92

1. Open a new document named TEMP.
2. Type the following passage of text; then press **Return** twice.

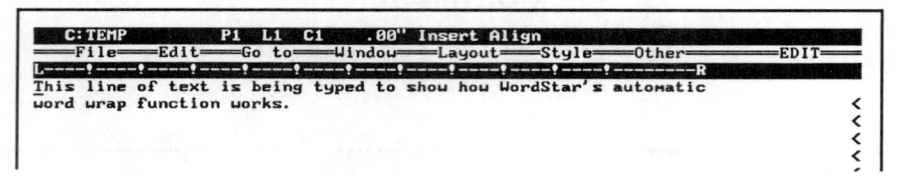

```
 C:TEMP         P1 L1 C1    .00" Insert Align
====File====Edit====Go to====Window====Layout====Style====Other====EDIT====
L----!----!----!----!----!----!----!----!----!--------R
This line of text is being typed to show how WordStar's automatic
word wrap function works.                                              <
                                                                       <
                                                                       <
                                                                       <
```

3. Press **Ctrl-OW** and type the same line of text followed by a **Return**.

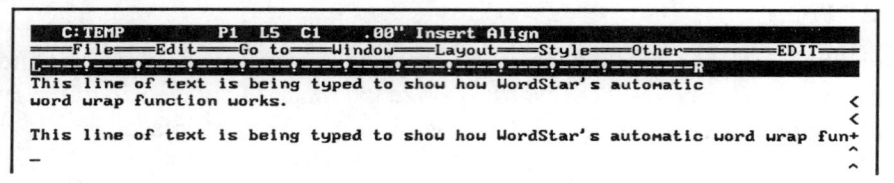

```
 C:TEMP         P1 L5 C1    .00" Insert Align
====File====Edit====Go to====Window====Layout====Style====Other====EDIT====
L----!----!----!----!----!----!----!----!----!--------R
This line of text is being typed to show how WordStar's automatic
word wrap function works.                                              <
                                                                       <
This line of text is being typed to show how WordStar's automatic word wrap fun+
 _                                                                      ^
                                                                        ^
```

4. Move the cursor to the beginning of the line and press **Ctrl-B** to reformat the line.
5. Press **Ctrl-O** and check the status of word wrap.

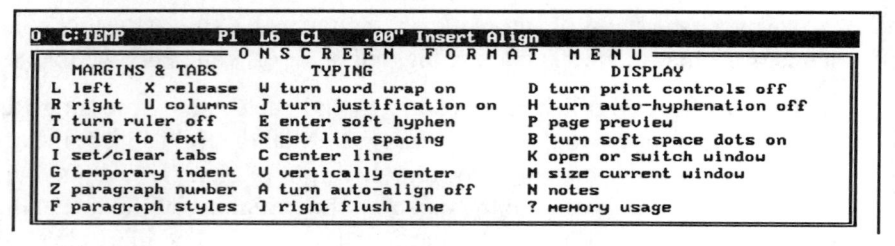

```
O  C:TEMP         P1 L6 C1    .00" Insert Align
============== O N S C R E E N   F O R M A T   M E N U ==============
      MARGINS & TABS            TYPING                  DISPLAY
   L left    X release    W turn word wrap on     D turn print controls off
   R right   U columns    J turn justification on H turn auto-hyphenation off
   T turn ruler off       E enter soft hyphen     P page preview
   O ruler to text        S set line spacing      B turn soft space dots on
   I set/clear tabs       C center line           K open or switch window
   G temporary indent     V vertically center     M size current window
   Z paragraph number     A turn auto-align off   N notes
   F paragraph styles     ] right flush line      ? memory usage
```

6. Type **W** (completes the Ctrl-O in step 5) to toggle word wrap back on.
7. Press **Ctrl-KQ** and type **Y** to abandon the document without saving.
8. Turn to Module 10 to continue the learning sequence.

Module 93
WSCHANGE AND PRCHANGE
(CUSTOMIZING WORDSTAR)

DESCRIPTION

The WordStar program is delivered with utility programs used for installing and changing the way WordStar works. The WINSTALL.EXE program is used as an initial installation utility. Here, you can establish a number of system settings including the default disk drive, printer and monitor types, dictionary files, and so on. You can also access WSCHANGE and PRCHANGE from the WINSTALL program.

The WSCHANGE.EXE program lets you customize your WordStar program. The WSCHANGE program also makes use of the PRCHANGE program, which can be run separately if you intend to add or modify a printer driver file, which controls the way WordStar interacts with a specified printer.

A few of the special PRCHANGE screens are shown at the end of this module.

Because WSCHANGE has a complete setup repertoire with only a few PRCHANGE exceptions, it is recommended as the primary setup and change utility.

STARTING WSCHANGE WSCHANGE is started by typing WSCHANGE WS at the DOS prompt and pressing Return. This displays the Main Menu. You can press Ctrl-X and type Y at any time to exit the WSCHANGE program.

WSCHANGE MENUS The following menus and submenus, in A to E order, are displayed when working your way through the WSCHANGE utility.

```
                         WSCHANGE Main Menu
    A  Console......Monitor              Function keys         Video attributes
                    Monitor patches      Keyboard patches

    B  Printer......Choose a default printer
                    Change printer name  Printer defaults      Printer interface

    C  Computer.....Disk drives          Operating system      Memory usage
                    WordStar files       Directory display     Patches

    D  WordStar.....Page layout          Editing settings      Help level
                    Spelling checks      Nondocument mode      Indexing
                    Shorthand            Merge print           Miscellaneous

    E  Patching.....General patches      Reset all settings    Auto-patcher

    X  Finished with installation

    Enter your menu selection..._        F1 = Help
                                         ^C = Quit and cancel changes
```

Module 93

Each of the menus and most submenus are shown in the following screen illustrations. Preceding each menu is a path to the menu. This path shows each menu option letter and name in the order of selection.

A Console:

```
                        Console Menu

       A   Monitor............Monitor selection    Monitor name
                              Screen sizing

       B   Function keys......Define keys          Onscreen Labels

       C   Video attributes   Screen display
                              (colors, bold...)

       D   Monitor patches....Special characters   Cursor control
                              Video attributes     Save colors and attributes
                              Cursor sizing

       E   Keyboard patches...Function keys        Save function keys

       X   Finished with this menu
```

A Console—>A Monitor:

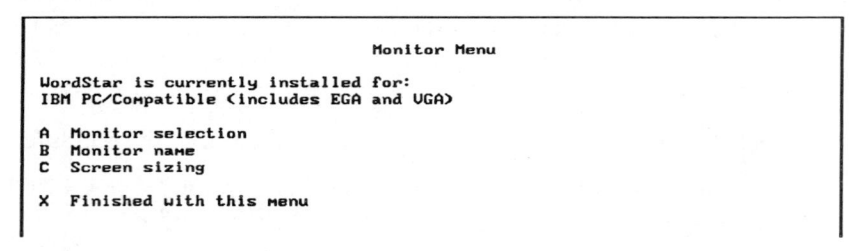

```
                        Monitor Menu

       WordStar is currently installed for:
       IBM PC/Compatible (includes EGA and VGA)

       A   Monitor selection
       B   Monitor name
       C   Screen sizing

       X   Finished with this menu
```

A Console—>B Function keys:

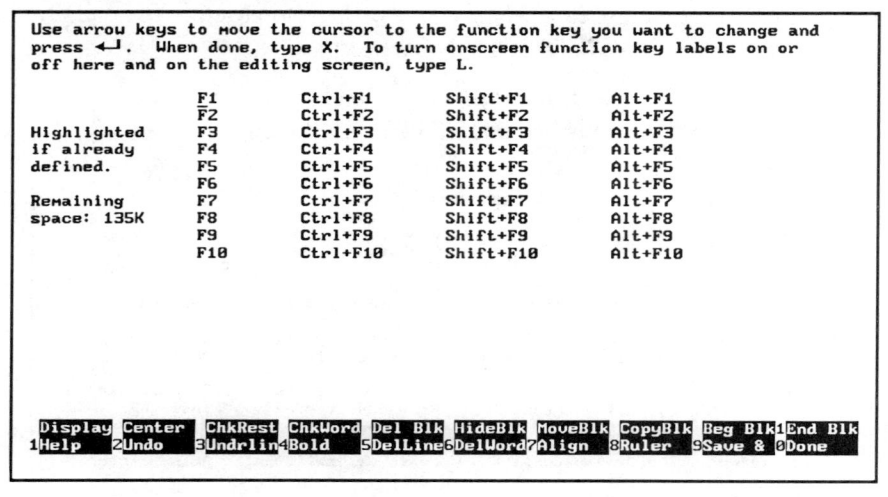

```
       Use arrow keys to move the cursor to the function key you want to change and
       press ↵. When done, type X. To turn onscreen function key labels on or
       off here and on the editing screen, type L.

                    F1       Ctrl+F1    Shift+F1    Alt+F1
                    F2       Ctrl+F2    Shift+F2    Alt+F2
       Highlighted  F3       Ctrl+F3    Shift+F3    Alt+F3
       if already   F4       Ctrl+F4    Shift+F4    Alt+F4
       defined.     F5       Ctrl+F5    Shift+F5    Alt+F5
                    F6       Ctrl+F6    Shift+F6    Alt+F6
       Remaining    F7       Ctrl+F7    Shift+F7    Alt+F7
       space: 135K  F8       Ctrl+F8    Shift+F8    Alt+F8
                    F9       Ctrl+F9    Shift+F9    Alt+F9
                    F10      Ctrl+F10   Shift+F10   Alt+F10




        Display Center  ChkRest ChkWord Del Blk HideBlk MoveBlk CopyBlk Beg Blk End Blk
       1Help   2Undo   3Undrlin4Bold   5DelLine6DelWord7Align  8Ruler  9Save & 0Done
```

A Console—>C Video attributes:

```
                    Video Attributes Menu
         A  Select colors individually
         B  Color display default
         C  Monochrome display default
         D  Shipped default

         X  Finished with this menu
```

A Console—>D Monitor patches:

```
                    Monitor Patches Menu
         A  Special characters
         B  Cursor control
         C  Video attributes
         D  Save colors
         E  Cursor size for monochrome monitors
         F  Cursor size for all other monitors

         =  Enter User Area address
         X  Finished with this menu
```

A Console—>E Keyboard patches:

```
                    Keyboard Patches Menu
         A  Function Keys
         B  Keyboard repeat rates
         C  Save Function Keys

         =  Enter User Area address
         X  Finished with this menu
```

B Printer:

```
                         Printer Menu
         A  Choose a default printer

         B  Change printer name on sign-on screen

         C  Printing defaults

         D  Printer interface...Printer busy handshaking    Printer subroutines
                                Background printing

         X  Finished with this menu
```

B Printer—>A Choose a default printer:

```
                    Default Printer Selection Menu
         Choose the printer (and printer description file) to use if no other printer
         is specified at print time.  Current PDF: RADIX-10

         Menu 1  of 1

         Printer Name                                        PDF Name
         A   ASCII    -Diskfile: 128 Char. Set               ASCII.PDF
         B   Draft    -Generic: Non-backspacing              DRAFT.PDF
         C   Apple Laserwriter Postscript                    LASERPS.PDF
         D   Star Radix-10/15                                RADIX-10.PDF
         E   WS4                                             WS4.PDF
```

Module 93

B Printer—>B Change printer name on sign-on screen:

```
                       Default Printer Name Menu
    The name of your default printer appears on the WordStar sign-on screen.
    If you want to change the current name, press Y, type a new name (up to
    37 characters), and press ↵.

    The current printer name is:  Star Radix-10/15
```

B Printer—>C Printing defaults:

```
                       Printing Defaults Menu #1
    A   Print nondocument as default.................OFF       PNODOC
    B   Bidirectional printing........................ON       .bp
    C   Letter quality printing (NLQ)................DIS       .lq
    D   Microjustification...........................DIS       .uj
    E   Underline blanks.............................OFF       .ul
    F   Proportional spacing.........................DIS       .ps
    G   Normal character font.......................No font name
    H   Alternate character font....................No font name
    I   Strikeout character..........................."-"      STKCHR
    J   Line height (1440ths/inch)...................240       INIEDT+40
    K   Sub/superscript roll (1440ths/inch)..........90        .sr

    Z   Printing Defaults Menu #2
    X   Finished with this menu
```

C Computer:

```
                             Computer Menu
    A   Disk drives........Valid disk drives    Delay disk access if typing

    B   Operating system....Single-user system  Multi-user or network system
                            IBM compatibility

    C   Memory usage........System allocations  WordStar allocations

    D   WordStar files......File names          Search path

    E   Directory display...Defaults

    F   Computer patches

    X   Finished with this menu
```

C Computer—>A Disk drives:

```
                            Disk Drives Menu
    A   Valid disk drives............................0A58      LGLDRV
    B   Delay disk access if typing..................0         DDISK

    X   Finished with this menu
```

WSCHANGE and PRCHANGE (Customizing WordStar)

C Computer—>B Operating System:

```
                     Operating System Menu
        A   Single-user system
        B   Multi-user or network system
        C   IBM compatibility

        X   Finished with this menu
```

C Computer—>C Memory usage:

```
                     Memory Usage Menu #1
        A   WordStar RAM resident (turns help off).......OFF       NWFLG
        B   Entire main dict. to RAM if room.............OFF       SPFLAG
        C   Speller, thesaurus, hyphenator memory usage..023D      MEMFLG
        D   Main spelling buffer (kbytes)..................71      SPLMEM
        E   Personal dictionary memory (kbytes)............2       UDMEM
        F   Messages and menus buffer (records)............4       VMSIZE
        G   Text spillover, 0=auto (records)...............0       TVSIZE
        H   Shorthand buffer size (records)................4       HANMAX
        I   Dot command buffer, RR, etc. (bytes).........4000      DSTKSZ

        2   Memory Usage Menu #2
        X   Finished with this menu
```

```
                     Memory Usage Menu #2
        A   Memory allocated for unerase buffer (bytes)..500       UNSIZE
        B   Memory allocated for editor (kbytes).........64        EDTMEM
        C   Header and footer size (bytes).............2048        HFSIZE
        D   Memory for merge print (kbytes)..............4         MRGMEM
        E   Number of menu font definitions............100         MFDSIZ
        F   Number of font family member definitions....20         FAMSIZ
        G   Number of proportional space data tables.....4         PSTSIZ
        H   PDF buffer size (records)...................16         LRUSIZ
        I   Footnote buffer size (records)...............8         FNSIZE
        J   Endnote buffer size (records)................2         ENSIZE

        1   Memory Usage Menu #1
        X   Finished with this menu
```

C Computer—>D WordStar files:

```
                     WordStar Files Menu #1
        A   Define default search path...................0BB9      DEFPTH
        B   Reassign drive and path for all WordStar files
        C   Messages and menus file.....................C:WSMSGS.OVR(1)
        D   Indexer exclusion list file.................C:WSINDEX.XCL(1)
        E   Shorthand storage file......................C:WSSHORT.OVR(1)
        F   Help overlay................................C:WSHELP.OVR(1)
        G   Paragraph styles library file...............C:WSSTYLE.OVR(1)
        H   TelMerge from Additional Menu...............C:TELMERGE.EXE(5)
        I   MailList from Additional Menu...............C:WSLIST.COM(6)

        2   WordStar files menu #2
        3   WordStar files menu #3
        4   WordStar files menu #4
        X   Finished with this menu
```

Module 93

```
                    WordStar Files Menu #2

        A   Spelling checker overlay....................C:WSSPL000.OVR(2)
        B   Main spelling dictionary file...............C:SPLMN000.DCT(2)
        C   Personal spelling dictionary file...........C:PERSONAL.DCT(2)
        D   Foreign language dictionary (if required)...C:SPLIN000.DCT(2)
        E   Thesaurus overlay file......................C:WSTHS000.OVR(2)
        F   Thesaurus dictionary........................C:THESR000.DCT(2)
        G   Thesaurus definitions overlay...............C:DEFIN000.DCT(2)
        H   Advanced Page Preview work files............C:????????.CRT(3)
        I   Advanced Page Preview file..................C:PREVIEW.OVR(3)
        J   Location of FONTID.CTL for Page Preview.....C:FONTID.CTL(3)

        1   WordStar files menu #1
        3   WordStar files menu #3
        4   WordStar files menu #4
        X   Finished with this menu
```

```
                    WordStar Files Menu #3

        A   Hyphenation overlay.........................C:WSHYP000.OVR(1)
        B   Main data file for hyphenation..............C:HYPMN000.DCT(1)
        C   Index file for hyphenation..................C:HYPIN000.DCT(1)
        D   Printer description files...................C:????????.PDF(1)
        E   Printer overlay files.......................C:????????.OVR(1)
        F   Print from keyboard template file...........C:KEYBOARD.MRG(1)
        G   Inset program for print-time loading........C:INSET.EXE(4)
        H   Graphics files directory display............12A1        GRPHMK
        I   Graphics files file extension...............129C        GRPHFT

        1   WordStar files menu #1
        2   WordStar files menu #2
        4   WordStar files menu #4
        X   Finished with this menu
```

```
                    WordStar Files Menu #4

        A   Backup file type............................BAK         BAKTYP
        B   Temporary text file type....................$A$         AFTYPE
        C   Temporary text file type....................$B$         BFTYPE
        D   Temporary block file type...................$C$         BLKTYP
        E   Newspaper column file type..................$D$         NCLTYP
        F   Endnote file type...........................$E$         ENOTYP
        G   Footnote file type..........................$F$         FNOTYP
        H   Workfile for paragraph styles...............$G$         WRKTYP
        I   Messages buffer size (records)..............4           WMSIZE
        J   Make backup files when saving...............ON          INIBAK

        1   WordStar files menu #1
        2   WordStar files menu #2
        3   WordStar files menu #3
        X   Finished with this menu
```

C Computer—>E Directory display:

```
                    Directory Display Menu

        A   Display file directory......................ON          INIDIR
        B   Directory in alphabetical order.............ON          DIRSRT
        C   File types excluded from directory..........0D1C        NOTYPE
        D   Filenames that are shown....................0E84        DIRFIL
        E   Initial directory log-on....................0CE2        INILOG
        F   Show space remaining on disk................ON          DSPACE
        G   Show size of each file......................ON          SHOSIZ
        H   Show files with changing drive/dir..........OFF         SDIRFL
        I   Display file directory at filename prompts..ON          DIRSIZ

        X   Finished with this menu
```

C Computer—>F Computer patches:

```
                    Computer Patches Menu
    A  Initialization string......................0569      TRMINI
    B  Un-initialization string...................056E      TRMUNI
    C  Initialization subroutine..................0573      INISUB
    D  Un-initialization subroutine...............0576      UNISUB
    E  General patch area.........................06EB      MORPAT
    F  Printer patch area.........................09B0      PRNPAT
    G  Extra patch area...........................1321      EXTRA
    H  Multi-user control.........................023C      MPMFLG
    I  WordStar control...........................023B      NWFLG

    =  Enter User Area address
    X  Finished with this menu
```

D WordStar:

```
                         WordStar Menu
    A  Page layout........Page size and margins   Headers and footers
                          Tabs                    Footnotes and endnotes
                          Stored ruler lines      Paragraph styles

    B  Editing settings....Edit screen, help level  Typing
                           Paragraph alignment      Blocks
                           Erase and unerase        Lines and characters
                           Find and replace         WordStar compatibility
                           Paragraph numbering      Line numbering

    C  Other features......Spelling check          Nondocument mode
                           Indexing                Shorthand (key macros)
                           Merge printing          Miscellaneous
                           Char conversion patches

    X  Finished with this menu
```

D WordStar—>A Page layout:

```
                        Page Layout Menu
    A  Page size and margins
    B  Headers and footers (page numbers)
    C  Tabs
    D  Footnotes and endnotes
    E  Stored ruler lines
    F  Paragraph styles
    G  Units of measurement

    X  Finished with this menu
```

D WordStar—>A Page layout—>A Page size and margins:

```
                    Page Sizing and Margins Menu
    A  Page length......................11.00"    INIEDT+18    .pl
    B  Top margin........................0.50"    INIEDT+14    .mt
    C  Bottom margin.....................1.33"    INIEDT+16    .mb
    D  Header margin.....................0.33"    INIEDT+1F    .hm
    E  Footer margin.....................0.33"    INIEDT+21    .fm
    F  Page offset on even page..........0.80"    INIEDT+24    .poe
    G  Page offset on odd page...........0.80"    INIEDT+26    .poo
    H  Left margin.......................0.00"    RLRINI       .lm
    I  Right margin......................6.50"    RLRINI+2     .rm
    J  Paragraph margin (-1 for none)....(none)   RLRINI+4     .pm

    X  Finished with this menu
```

D WordStar—>A Page layout—>B Headers and footers (page numbers):

```
            Headers and Footers Menu (Includes Page Numbering)

    A  Print page numbers..........................ON      INIEDT+1C  .op
    B  Position of page number (-1 = center).......(center) INIEDT+1D  .pc
    C  Initial page number.........................1        INIEDT+1A  .pn

    X  Finished with this menu
```

D WordStar—>A Page layout—>C Tabs:

```
                              Tabs Menu

    A  Regular tab stops
    B  Decimal tab stops

    X  Finished with this menu
```

D WordStar—>A Page layout—>D Footnotes and endnotes:

```
                      Footnotes and Endnotes Menu #1

    A  Footnote font and style.....................187F    FNFONT
    B  Footnote repeating character table..........1891    FNRCH
    C  Footnote reference mark in text.............18A4    FNTXT
    D  Footnote reference mark in note.............18AE    FNTXT+0A
    E  Footnote tag type...........................188F    FNTYP
    F  Footnote separator..........................18B4    FNSEP
    G  Footnote continuation text..................197D    FNCNTU
    H  Footnote position...........................0       FNPOSN
    I  Running footnote format.....................8       FNRUN
    J  Footnote UMI lines..........................1A43    FNUMI
    K  Footnote file type..........................$F$     FNOTYP
    L  Footnote buffer size (records)..............8       FNSIZE

    Z  Footnote and Endnote Menu #2
    X  Finished with this menu
```

```
                      Footnotes and Endnotes Menu #2

    A  Endnote font and style......................1887    ENFONT
    B  Endnote repeating character table...........189B    ENRCH
    C  Endnote reference mark in text..............18B8    FNTXT+14
    D  Endnote reference mark in note..............18C2    FNTXT+1E
    E  Endnote tag type............................3       ENTYP
    F  Endnote UMI text lines separation...........1A4B    ENUMI
    G  Endnote file type...........................$E$     ENOTYP
    H  Endnote buffer size (records)...............2       ENSIZE

    1  Footnote and Endnote Menu #1
    X  Finished with this menu
```

D WordStar—>A Page layout—>E Stored ruler lines:

```
                    Stored Ruler Lines Menu

       A   Default ruler line
       B   1st stored ruler line
       C   2nd stored ruler line
       D   3rd stored ruler line
       E   4th stored ruler line
       F   5th stored ruler line
       G   6th stored ruler line
       H   7th stored ruler line
       I   8th stored ruler line
       J   9th stored ruler line

       X   Finished with this menu
```

D WordStar—>A Page layout—>F Paragraph styles:

```
                      Paragraph Styles

   A   Library of paragraph styles................C:WSSTYLE.OUR(1)
   B   Default paragraph style....................185F        PARSTY
   C   Temporary file extension...................$G$         WRKTYP
   D   Storage buffer size........................8           STYSIZ

   X   Finished with this menu
```

D WordStar—>A Page layout—>G Units of measure:

```
                   Units of Measurement Menu

   A   Horizontal unit...............................Inches      DBUNITH
   B   Vertical unit.................................Inches      DBUNITV
   C   Line height unit..............................Inches      DBUNITL
   D   Font size unit................................Points      DBUNITP
   E   Unit for all measurements.....................(mixed)

   X   Finished with this menu
```

D WordStar—>B Editing settings:

```
                      Editing Settings Menu

       A   Edit screen, help level
       B   Typing
       C   Paragraph alignment
       D   Blocks
       E   Erase and unerase
       F   Lines and characters
       G   Find and replace
       H   WordStar compatibility
       I   Paragraph numbering
       J   Line numbering

       X   Finished with this menu
```

Module 93

D WordStar—>B Editing settings—>A Edit screen, help level:

```
                    Edit Screen, Help Level Menu #1
       A  Help level............................4         INIHLP    ^JJ
       B  Display function keys at help level 4........OFF   LABHP4
       C  Status line..............................ON        INISTA
       D  Status line filler character.................." "  STFILL
       E  Soft space display.......................OFF       INIEDT+0D
       F  Soft space character................... · FA       SOFTSP
       G  Page break character........................- C4   SOFTSP+1
       H  Binding space character.................... ■ FE   SOFTSP+2
       I  Snaking column character...................≡ F0    SOFTSP+3
       J  Column break character......................= CD   SOFTSP+4
       K  Dot leader character........................"."    SOFTSP+5
       L  Print control display........................ON    INIEDT+3  ^od

       Z  Edit Screen Menu #2
       3  Edit Screen Menu #3
       X  Finished with this menu
```

```
                    Edit Screen, Help Level Menu #2
       A  Ruler line..............................ON        INIEDT+5  ^ot
       B  Default onscreen function key labels.........ON    FUNLAB
       C  HMI (1800ths) units for ruler line..........180    RLUNIT
       D  VMI (1440ths) units for line height.........240    INIEDT+40
       E  Hard return ending character................"<"    SCMARK
       F  Soft return ending character................" "    SCMARK+1
       G  Long line character.........................."+"   SCMARK+2
       H  End of file character......................."^"    SCMARK+3
       I  Overprint line character...................."-"    SCMARK+4

       1  Edit Screen Menu #1
       3  Edit Screen Menu #3
       X  Finished with this menu
```

```
                    Edit Screen, Help Level Menu #3
       A  Line feed character........................."J"    SCMARK+5
       B  Form feed character........................."F"    SCMARK+6
       C  Page break character........................"P"    SCMARK+7
       D  Column break character......................"C"    SCMARK+8
       E  Window separator character.................."W"    SCMARK+9
       F  Dot command character......................."."    SCMARK+0A
       G  Dot command at start of page................"1"    SCMARK+0B
       H  Merge print dot command character..........":"     SCMARK+0C
       I  Unknown dot command character..............."?"    SCMARK+0D

       1  Edit Screen Menu #1
       2  Edit Screen Menu #2
       X  Finished with this menu
```

D WordStar—>B Editing settings—>B Typing:

```
                              Typing Menu
       A  Word wrap at right margin....................ON    INIEDT+1  ^ow
       B  Insert characters............................ON    INIEDT+2  ^v
       C  Fast typing display pause....................50    DFAST
       D  Fast typing page/line/column delay...........75    UPDLY
       E  Disk access pause.............................0    DDISK
       F  Automatic backspace characters..............0F0A   AUTOBS
       G  Scroll speed..................................3    INIEDT+9

       X  Finished with this menu
```

WSCHANGE and PRCHANGE (Customizing WordStar)

D WordStar—>B Editing settings—>C Paragraph alignment:

```
                  Paragraph Alignment Menu
     A  Right-justification.........................OFF     INIEDT  ^oj
     B  Line spacing................................1       INIEDT+8 ^os
     C  Auto-hyphenation............................OFF     INIEDT+4 ^oh
     D  Characters before auto-hyphenation..........5       HYMAX
     E  Auto-align..................................ON      INIEDT+0E
     F  Delay value for auto-alignment..............500     DALIGN
     G  Watch progress of ^QU alignment.............OFF     RFINTR

     X  Finished with this menu
```

D WordStar—>B Editing settings—>D Blocks:

```
                        Blocks Menu
     A  Column mode.................................OFF     INIEDT+6 ^kn
     B  Column replace mode.........................OFF     INIEDT+7 ^ki
     C  Beginning block marker......................04B7    BBLOCK
     D  Ending block marker.........................04BC    KBLOCK

     X  Finished with this menu
```

D WordStar—>B Editing settings—>E Erase and unerase:

```
                   Erase and Unerase Menu
     A  Maximum characters that can be unerased.....500     UNSIZE
     B  Unerase single character erasures...........OFF     UNONE
     C  Del erases to left (not at cursor)..........OFF     DELFLG
     D  Erasing and cursor type-ahead...............OFF     AHEAD

     X  Finished with this menu
```

D WordStar—>B Editing settings—>F Lines and characters:

```
                 Lines and Characters Menu #1
     A  Characters that are part of a word..........0EC2    LGLCHR
     B  Characters for moving across words..........0EE6    MOVCHR
     C  Soft space display..........................OFF     INIEDT+0D
     D  Soft space character........................· FA    SOFTSP
     E  Page break character........................- C4    SOFTSP+1
     F  Binding space character.....................■ FE    SOFTSP+2
     G  Snaking column character....................≡ F8    SOFTSP+3
     H  Column break line character.................= CD    SOFTSP+4
     I  Dot leader character........................"."     SOFTSP+5
     J  Thousands number separator..................","     SPLCHR
     K  Decimal point...............................". "    SPLCHR+1

     Z  Lines and Characters Menu #2
     3  Lines and Characters Menu #3
     X  Finished with this menu
```

Module 93

```
                    Lines and Characters Menu #2
        A  Hard return character........................"<"     SCMARK
        B  Soft return character........................" "     SCMARK+1
        C  Long line character.........................."+"     SCMARK+2
        D  End of file character........................"^"     SCMARK+3
        E  Overprint line character....................."-"     SCMARK+4
        F  Line feed character.........................."J"     SCMARK+5
        G  Form feed character.........................."F"     SCMARK+6
        H  Page break character........................."P"     SCMARK+7
        I  Column break character......................."C"     SCMARK+8
        J  Window separator character..................."W"     SCMARK+9

        1  Lines and Characters Menu #1
        3  Lines and Characters Menu #3
        X  Finished with this menu
```

```
                    Lines and Characters Menu #3
        A  Dot command character........................"."     SCMARK+0A
        B  Dot command at start of page................."1"     SCMARK+0B
        C  Merge print dot command character............":"     SCMARK+0C
        D  Unknown dot command character................"?"     SCMARK+0D

        1  Lines and Characters Menu #1
        2  Lines and Characters Menu #2
        X  Finished with this menu
```

D WordStar—>B Editing settings—>G Find and replace:

```
                       Find and Replace Menu
        A  Default find and replace options............1271     INIFIN
        X  Finished with this menu
```

```
                    Find and Replace Options Menu
        When you find or find and replace text, you can choose from a number of
        options.  Choose which option you want for the default.

                W  whole words only            R  rest of file
                U  ignore case                 N  replace without asking
                M  maintain case               A  align paragraph after replace
                B  backwards search            ?  wild cards
                G  whole file


        Current default options:  None


        Do you want to change this? (Y/N) _
```

300

D WordStar—>B Editing settings—>H WordStar compatibility:

```
                    WordStar Compatibility Menu
      A   ^H moves left (not erase left)...............OFF       CTLHFL
      B   ^6 hard to soft carriage return/auto-align...OFF       CASEFL
      C   Del erases left (not at cursor)..............OFF       DELFLG
      D   Cursor stays in column 1 at marker............ON       BLKFLG
      E   No extra soft lines at paragraph end.........OFF       LSPFLG
      F   Esc acts like ^R and ⏎ .....................OFF       ESCFLG
      G   Automatically fill out last record............ON       SETEOF
      H   ^QX goes to right side of screen..............ON       QUXFLG
      I   Classic commands at Opening pull-down menu...OFF       PULFLG
      J   Dot commands automatically put into file.....ON        USEDOT

      X   Finished with this menu
```

D WordStar—>B Editing settings—>I Paragraph numbering:

```
                    Paragraph Numbering Menu
      A   Paragraph numbering style....................1836      IPFRMT
      B   Paragraph numbering separator at end.........OFF       PPRSEP
      C   Outline style numbering......................OFF       PROUTL

      X   Finished with this menu
```

D WordStar—>B Editing settings—>J Line numbering:

```
                    Line Numbering Menu
      A   Line numbering font...........................No font name
      B   Continuous line numbering....................OFF       INIEDT+42
      C   Line spacing between line numbers.............0        INIEDT+42
      D   Left margin for line number..................0.70"     LNMCH
      E   Left margin character for line number........‖ BA      LNMCH+2
      F   Right margin for line number.................7.40"     LNMCH+3
      G   Right margin character for line number....... | B3     LNMCH+5
      H   Space between number and left margin character....0.30"  LNMCH+6

      X   Finished with this menu
```

D WordStar—>C Other features:

```
                    Other Features Menu
      A   Spelling check
      B   Nondocument mode
      C   Indexing
      D   Shorthand (macros)
      E   Merge printing
      F   Character conversion patches
      G   Miscellaneous

      X   Finished with this menu
```

Module 93

D WordStar—>C Other features—>A Spelling check:

```
                    Spelling Check Menu
   A  Spelling check overlay......................C:WSSPL000.OUR(2)
   B  Main spelling dictionary file...............C:SPLMN000.DCT(2)
   C  Thesaurus overlay file......................C:WSTHS000.OUR(2)
   D  Personal spelling dictionary file...........C:PERSONAL.DCT(2)
   E  Dictionary usage............................1293         SPFLAG
   F  Main spelling buffer (kbytes)...............71           SPLMEM
   G  Personal dictionary memory (kbytes).........2            UDMEM
   H  Smallest word checked.......................2            SPMIN
   I  Turn spelling check on or off...............ON           SPLMEM/UDMEM
   J  Check for double word.......................ON           CKDBL
   K  Watch progress of spelling check............OFF          SPINTR

   X  Finished with this menu
```

D WordStar—>C Other features—>B Nondocument mode:

```
                    Nondocument Mode Menu
   A  Nondoc. file when in command line...........OFF          ININON
   B  Print nondocument as default................OFF          PNODOC
   C  ^B and ^QU strip MSB of characters..........ON           STRPFL
   D  Tabs and auto-indent by file type...........0E95         EDCOND

   X  Finished with this menu
```

D WordStar—>C Other features—>C Indexing:

```
                    Indexing Menu
   A  General exclusion list file.................C:WSINDEX.XCL(1)
   B  Normally index every word...................OFF          IDXALL

   X  Finished with this menu
```

D WordStar—>C Other features—>D Shorthand (macros):

```
                    Shorthand (Key Macros) Menu
   A  Shorthand storage file......................C:WSSHORT.OUR(1)
   B  Storage buffer size (records)...............4            HANMAX
   C  Format for today's date.....................12AC         FDATE
   D  Format for current time.....................12B4         FTIME
   E  Dollar format for numbers...................12BC         DOLLAR

   X  Finished with this menu
```

D WordStar—>C Other features—>E Merge printing:

```
                    Merge Printing Menu
   A  Separator between data items................","          DATSEP
   B  Variable name indicator.....................'&'          DATSEP+1
   C  Date format for &@& variable................12AC         FDATE
   D  Time format for &!& variable................12B4         FTIME

   X  Finished with this menu
```

WSCHANGE and PRCHANGE (Customizing WordStar)

D WordStar—>C Other features—>F Character conversion patches:

```
                    Character Conversion Patches Menu
  A  Uppercase table...........................1521      UPCASE
  B  Lowercase table...........................1621      LOCASE
  C  Collating sequence table..................1721      COLATE
  D  Keystroke code translation................1821      KBXLAT

  =  Enter User Area address
  X  Finished with this menu
```

D WordStar—>C Other features—>G Miscellaneous:

```
                          Miscellaneous Menu
  A  Sign-on message..........................0A30       INITID
  B  Longest delay (sign-on)..................2000       DLONG
  C  Medium delay (menus).....................1000       DMED
  D  Short delay (doc align)..................200        DSHORT
  E  Erasing and cursor type ahead............OFF        AHEAD
  F  ^N split line (or hard RET to soft)......ON         CTLNFL
  G  Window prompt for document/nondoc........OFF        WPRMPT
  H  Size of other window.....................128        WRATIO
  I  Auto-backup..............................0          AUTSAV
  J  Go to top of page........................OFF        GPGFLG
  K  Language default.........................1          LNGCOD
  L  Current code page support................437        CODEPG

  X  Finished with this menu
```

E Patching:

```
                            Patching Menu
  A  Auto-patcher.............................Patch from file
  B  Save settings............................Make file for auto-patcher
  C  Reset all settings.......................Original settings

  =  Enter User Area address
  X  Finished with this menu
```

E Patching—>A Auto-patcher:

```
                          Auto-Patcher Menu
  The auto-patcher reads the patches that you have stored in a nondocument
  file.  The format of each line in the file is:

                            USERADDR=PATCHES

  USERADDR is an address containing either a label name or hex number.  You
  may use add (+), subtract (-), multiply (*), or divide (/) to calculate an
  address.  Use hex numbers for calculating addresses.

  PATCHES can be one or more bytes, strings (enclosed within either single or
  double quotes) or equations.

            For example:  CRTID="XYZ Console",CR,LF,0

  Enter file name (or Press ↵ to quit)..._
```

E Patching—>B Save settings:

```
                      Save Settings Menu
You can save some of the current WordStar settings in a nondocument
file that can later be used by the auto-patcher. You can either save
all settings at once, or enter one User Area label at a time. A patch
will be stored that encompasses all bytes between that label and the
next one in the User Area.

Warning: Data lengths may change from one version of WordStar to
         another. Check your patch file against the user area.

Enter file name to hold settings (or Press ↵ to quit)..._
```

E Patching—>C Reset all settings:

```
                     Reset All Settings Menu
This selection will erase any modifications already made to your
WordStar and will restore the default values as supplied on the
distribution disk for each and every item that can be installed.

Are you sure you want to reset everything? (Y/N) _
```

As you can see, WSCHANGE does many things. Most are easily used by the average user. There are a few changes and special patches that may require additional documentation. For example, you must consult your printer manual to determine which control codes are appropriate for your printer.

A good way to learn the effect of the WSCHANGE program is to install WordStar in a temporary subdirectory. Then you can experiment with the WSCHANGE menus to see what effect they have on the temporary version of WordStar.

PRCHANGE

The PRCHANGE program is run from WINSTALL or by typing PRCHANGE WS and pressing Return. The opening screen and some of the option screens are shown in the following illustrations.

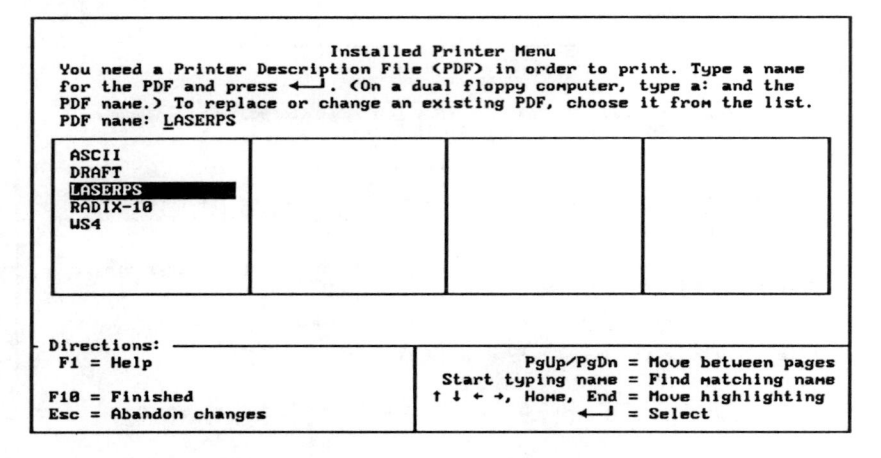

```
                        Installed Printer Menu
 You need a Printer Description File (PDF) in order to print. Type a name
 for the PDF and press ↵. (On a dual floppy computer, type a: and the
 PDF name.) To replace or change an existing PDF, choose it from the list.
 PDF name: LASERPS
 ┌─────────────┬─────────────┬─────────────┬─────────────┐
 │ ASCII       │             │             │             │
 │ DRAFT       │             │             │             │
 │ LASERPS     │             │             │             │
 │ RADIX-10    │             │             │             │
 │ WS4         │             │             │             │
 │             │             │             │             │
 └─────────────┴─────────────┴─────────────┴─────────────┘
 ┌ Directions: ─────────────────────────────────────────────
 │ F1 = Help                    PgUp/PgDn = Move between pages
 │                        Start typing name = Find matching name
 │ F10 = Finished         ↑ ↓ ← →, Home, End = Move highlighting
 │ Esc = Abandon changes             ↵ = Select
```

```
                        Printer Type Menu
         HP LJ & compat (GS, CO# cart)
         HP LJ & compat (A-Z, Pro cart)
         HP LaserJet compat--no HP cart
         Canon lasers and HP DeskJets
         Other lasers
         Others A-N (incl. generic)
         Others O-Z




 Use arrow keys to move the highlighting to the description that
 best fits your type of printer and press ←┘.
─Directions:──────────────────────────────────────────────────────
 F1 = Help
                              Start typing name = Find matching name
                              ↑ ↓ ← →, Home, End = Move highlighting
 Esc = Installed Printer Menu       ←┘ = Select
```

```
        Put the disk containing Printer Data 1 in drive A. Type A:
        and press F10. (If you copied printer data to your hard
        disk, type the location, for example C:\WS.)



          Press Esc to cancel.        Press F10 when finished.
```

```
                        Printer Selection Menu
        Highlight the name of the printer to install and press ←┘.

         AST TurboLaser                  HP LaserJet IID PostScript 2 up
         Apple Laserwriter Postscript    HP LaserJet IID PostScript cart
         Apple Laserwriter Postscript 2-up IBM 4019 (IBM ASCII mode)
         Cordata LP-300                  IBM 4216 Postscript
         Cordata LP-300X                 IBM 4216 Postscript 2-up
         Dataproducts Postscript         NEC LC850 (IBM mode)
         Dataproducts Postscript 2-up    NEC LC890 Postscript
         Destiny PageStyler Postscript   NEC LC890 Postscript 2-up
         Destiny PageStyler Postscript 2-up NewGen TurboPS PostScript
         Epson GQ3500 Laser              NewGen TurboPS PostScript 2 up

         Printers are listed in alphabetical order by manufacturer.
```

```
                      Additional Installation Menu

              Select printer adapter port
              Install sheet feeder
              Go to Printer Information Menu
              Add or delete font groups
              Return to Installed Printer Menu
```

Module 93

```
                    Change Printer Adapter Port
         AUX
         PRN
         LPT1
         LPT2
         LPT3
         COM1
         COM2
         Printer protocol selection
         User-defined disk
         User-defined device
         Save and return to previous menu

Your printer is currently connected to:
```

```
                    Sheet Feeder Selection Menu
Select a sheet feeder for your printer.
         Manual/Cassette feed
```

```
                    Printer Information Menu
         View printer information
         Print printer information
         Save printer information to a disk file
         Return to Additional Installation Menu
```

These are just a few of the available PRCHANGE screens. To see all of the PRCHANGE features, you may wish to look at the screens by starting PRCHANGE and reviewing them.

If you are using a serial printer, you should run the DOS MODE command to ensure that the data exchange parameters are properly configured. For example, if you are using a PostScript laser printer attached to COM1, you can type MODE COM1:1200,n,8,1,p and press Return from the DOS prompt before starting WordStar.

If you have difficulty making your printer work, you may wish to use the DOS COPY command to send the SETDTR.PS file to your printer using COPY SETDTR.PS COM1. This assumes that your printer is attached to your COM1 serial port.

You can also see errors by using COPY EHANDLER.PS COM1, which provides error messages for a PostScript printer interface.

Check for the README.COM and README.TXT files on your WordStar disk and type README and press Return to review Sections 10 and 11, which describe printer installation and use.

Appendix A
TERMS AND DEFINITIONS

Some computer and word processing terms used in this book are defined in this appendix. The word processing functions that are the subjects of entire modules are defined in the first paragraph of their respective modules. Therefore, those terms are not repeated in this appendix.

Term	Definition
ASCII	Acronym for *A*merican *S*tandard *C*ode for *I*nformation *I*nterchange. Used as a standard for configuring characters, punctuation, and data control codes used by computers.
AUTOEXEC.BAT	A file that automatically executes when a computer is turned on or rebooted. Commonly used to set file paths, the DOS prompt style, and to load and run one or more specified programs. Each line in a .BAT file is executed as encountered.
Backup file	The previous version of a file that is automatically produced by WordStar each time a file is opened and saved. The backup file has the extension .BAK. Backup files serve as insurance in the event that information in an updated file is lost.
Batch file	A file that automatically performs a series (or *batch*) of operations. WordStar batch files are often used to print multiple documents using a series of file insert (.FI) dot codes.
Bidirectional printing	Printing forward and backwards, or from left to right and right to left.
Boilerplate	A frequently used, standard passage of text that is available for use to create derivative documents. A standard term or condition paragraph is a typical example of this.
Boot	Starting or turning on a computer; derived from the term *bootstrapping*, an early term applied to the computer startup procedure, which involved the use of an electrical jumper, or "bootstrap."
Case sensitive	A command or computer operation that requires the use of or differentiates between uppercase or lowercase characters.
Character	A letter, number, punctuation mark, space, or symbol displayed on a screen or printed on paper.
Character position	A specified position on the display screen, such as the intersection of display screen line 3, character position 45.
Character string	Any unique sequence of characters.

Appendix A

Term	Definition
Character width	The space occupied by a printed character. Printers that use a fixed space for each character are called *monospace printers* and are measured in characters per inch, or *pitch*. For example, ten pitch is ten characters per inch. Typeset material and proportional-space printers assign unit widths to each character in proportion to its size. For example, an "i" is narrower than a "w."
Classic menus	Menus that resemble those used with WordStar Professional Release 4.
Close document	The act of filing a displayed document to the system storage medium.
Columns	Aligned, vertical strips of text. A column of text aligned five spaces from the left margin is said to be in "column 5." WordStar's status line displays the column number occupied by the cursor.
Continuous-form paper	Paper that is fan-folded, each sheet being separated by perforations. Used to eliminate the need to feed individual cut sheets of paper.
Control key	A key used in combination with other standard keys, such as Ctrl-I for Tab or Ctrl-H for Backspace. The control key must be pressed and held before the corresponding character key is pressed, like holding the Shift key down to type a capital letter.
Cursor	A flashing square or underscore that shows the display screen position at which a typed character will appear.
Cut-sheet paper feeder	A device used on printers to feed cut sheets of paper automatically to the printer on demand. Eliminates the need to feed cut-sheet paper manually.
Data file	A data file contains information, such as customer or student records, arranged in a predetermined uniform order.
Default settings	A group of predetermined settings that are the normal mode when the system is turned on. WordStar's default right margin is often 65; the default insert setting is ON. These settings are selected with WSCHANGE.
Directory	A list of files stored on the disk.
DOS	An acronym for Disk Operating System.
Dot command	An embedded code used by WordStar and merge print to control document formatting.
Drive	An electromechanical device used to read and write information to and from a magnetic disk. A disk may be removable or fixed.
Embedded code	A special key sequence typed within text which performs some special function, such as stopping the printer (stop code).
Error messages	A message that is displayed on a computer screen to indicate an entry or operational error.
Escape	A key sequence used to complete or cancel a system operation. The Esc key is used.

Term	Definition
Execute	The key sequence, which involves pressing one or more special keys, to complete an operation.
Exit	To quit a program or operation.
Extension	An optional 1- to 3-character filename suffix. Often used to designate the file type.
Filename	The name given to a document by the system user. Filenames are limited to eight characters with a three-character extension. The extension is separated from the filename by a period in the form FILENAME.EXT.
Flag column	The right column of the WordStar screen displays symbols (or flags) that correspond to dot commands, hard returns, continuing text, etc.
Format ruler	A display at the top of the screen showing the left and right margin and tab settings.
Formatting	The structure of a document is called the format. This includes such elements as margin, tab, and line spacing settings. WordStar lets you change margin and indent settings and realign text. This is called reformatting.
Function keys	The keys F1 through F10 (or F12) located on your computer's keyboard. These keys are often assigned special functions, or key sequences.
Graphics	When applied to computers, graphics includes special symbols and colors or shades of gray used to prepare illustrations, charts, and graphs.
Hardware	The equipment components that make up a computer system.
Key sequence	Any keystroke or combination of keystrokes.
Logged drive	The active disk drive and filepath (or file or directory).
Macro substitution	The substitution of one or two keystrokes to produce a larger, more involved series of keystrokes or operations.
Memory	A computer's temporary storage area. Most computers use semiconductor memory, referred to as random access memory, or RAM. A computer loses information stored in memory when power is turned off. Computer programs are usually loaded and reside in a computer's memory during program execution.
Menu	A list of available options for user selection.
Nondocument	An ASCII file that is created using WordStar's nondocument mode. Nondocuments are void of contaminating format control characters that can interfere with the operation of merge print data files and program source files.
Numeric Keypad	A calculator-like section of the keyboard that is often used for numerical entry. The keypad may be switched from numeric keys to function keys, such as Home, End, PgUp, and PgDn by using a "NumLock" key.

Appendix A

Term	Definition
Open document	The act of retrieving and displaying a stored document for editing or creating a new document. The file that is currently active on the screen.
Operating system	A computer program designed to interface a computer and applications software designed to operate on that computer.
Page format	A predefined page organization. Format considerations include such items as heading and body text styles and margin widths.
Path	Often used in place of the term filepath or file directory.
Pitch	A horizontal unit of measure for type size expressed in characters per inch. For example, twelve pitch is 12 characters per inch.
Printer driver	The control file used by a program to interface with a specific type or model of printer. WordStar has a number of selectable printer drivers. Each printer driver converts format control codes to operate properly with the printer for which it was designed.
Printer port	The parallel or serial connector to which printers are connected. The number of printer ports varies with the computer. Parallel printer ports are usually designated LPT1 and LPT2; serial printer ports are designated COM1 through COM3.
Program disk	The disk containing the operating program. Usually found on the disk in drive A on a two-floppy disk system and on drive C on a fixed disk system.
Prompt	A screen display to indicate that the system is ready for operator action or to provide information to the operator.
RAM	Random-access memory. See Memory.
Reading a file	Importing a file stored on disk into an open document.
Return (Enter)	The key used to terminate a line of text or enter a computer command. Also called the Enter key.
Root directory	The initial, or top, directory found on a disk. Usually found on hard disks.
Ruler	See Format ruler.
Scrolling	Horizontal or vertical movement of text on the display screen.
Software	The programs (computer instructions) and data files that reside on magnetic media, paper, or in the computer hardware.
Status line	A line of information at the top of the screen showing the filename and the page, line, and column position of the cursor. Other information, such as line spacing, insert on/off status, margin release, and column editing mode, is also displayed.
Storage medium	A magnetic storage device, such as a disk, tape, or card, used to save documents.
Subdirectory	A directory, or filepath, that is subordinate to a higher level directory.

Term	Definition
Supershift	An extra keyboard shift, activated by a special key sequence, that allows standard character keys to type a third character set, where lowercase and uppercase are the first two character sets.
Text	Words, sentences, paragraphs, or financial information used to make up the body of a document.
Toggles	Functions, such as ruler display or word wrap, that can be turned (or "toggled") on and off by the same key sequence.
Type face	The specific type style, such as Gothic or italic.
Type font	The mechanical device, such as a daisy wheel or Selectric ball, containing the type characters. Sometimes used to refer to a type face.
Variable	A changeable value. Merge print data values are referred to as variables.
Wild card	A character that is used to represent any legitimate value. The asterisk symbol (*) is used to represent any legitimate filename in DOS commands.
Writing a file	The act of storing, printing, or outputting a data or program file.

Appendix B
CONVERTING FILES FROM OTHER WORD PROCESSORS

DESCRIPTION

The Star Exchange program supplied with WordStar 6.0 is a separate utility used to convert a file created by another word processing program to WordStar. It can also be used to convert a WordStar file for use with another word processor. Word processor files that can be converted to or from WordStar 6.0-compatible files include:

- WordStar 2000
- WordStar 3.31
- WordStar 3.4
- WordStar 4.0
- WordPerfect®
- WordPerfect® 5
- Microsoft Word 4
- Microsoft Word 5
- MultiMate 3.6
- MultiMate Advantage 2
- DisplayWrite™ (uses DCA/RFT)
- ASCII (accepted by WordStar 6.0 without conversion)

The ASCII file conversion is helpful when sharing documents with other word processors that feature an ASCII file import/export capability. For example, you may wish to convert a WordStar 6.0 document to ASCII to give another user, not equipped with WordStar 6.0, access to your document using his or her ASCII import feature. You can also use ASCII conversion to prepare a document for electronic mail transfer.

The Star Exchange program is ideal for use in environments where a variety of word processing software is used. A file conversion utility is also invaluable if you are a user who receives disk-based documents from various contributing authors. Star Exchange lets you assemble and produce a final WordStar 6.0 document made up of files that were originally produced by users of such word processors as WordStar 2000, WordPerfect, Microsoft Word, MultiMate, and DisplayWrite.

INSTALLING STAR EXCHANGE

Star Exchange is distributed on three 360K floppy diskettes or two 720K diskettes. A subdirectory, such as C:\WS\CONVERT, should be prepared for the Star Exchange files. Once the subdirectory is prepared using the DOS MD command, and assuming your Star Exchange diskettes are inserted into drive A, you can copy the files to your hard disk using the DOS COPY command:

Converting Files form Other Word Processors

```
COPY A:*.* C:\WS\CONVERT
```

Repeat this command for each of the Star Exchange diskettes. Once the program files are copied, Star Exchange is ready for use.

RUNNING STAR EXCHANGE

The Star Exchange program is run by typing CONVERT and pressing Return from the DOS prompt. The first screen, called OPTIONS, resembles the following illustration.

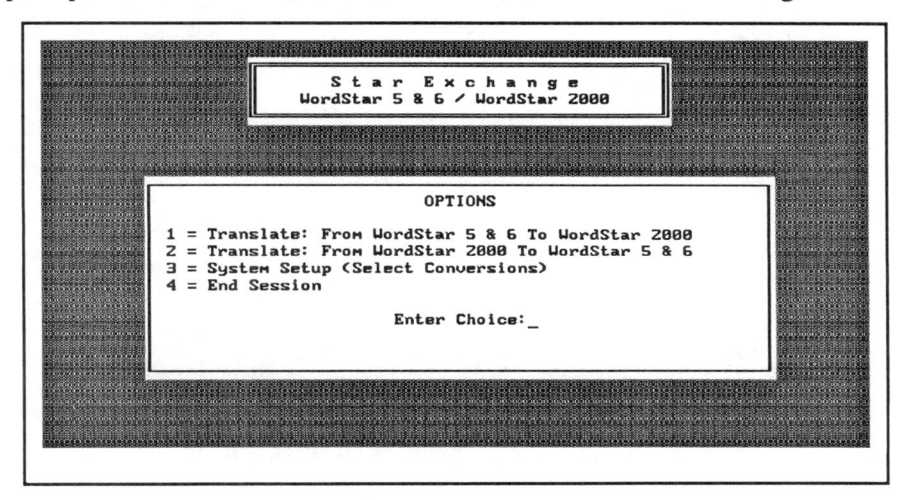

```
          Star Exchange
      WordStar 5 & 6 / WordStar 2000


              OPTIONS

  1 = Translate: From WordStar 5 & 6 To WordStar 2000
  2 = Translate: From WordStar 2000 To WordStar 5 & 6
  3 = System Setup (Select Conversions)
  4 = End Session

              Enter Choice: _
```

Use selection 3, System Setup, to select the type of conversion you want. The System Setup menu resembles the following illustration:

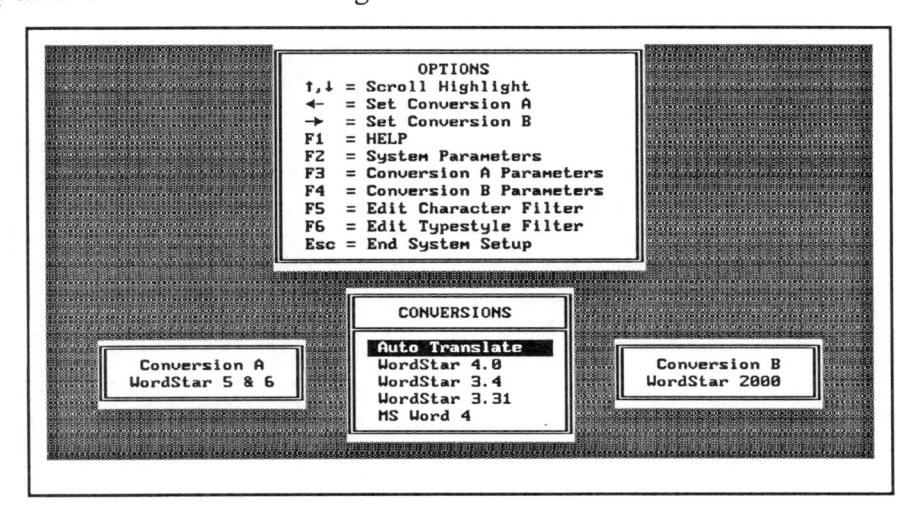

```
                    OPTIONS
       ↑,↓ = Scroll Highlight
       ←   = Set Conversion A
       →   = Set Conversion B
       F1  = HELP
       F2  = System Parameters
       F3  = Conversion A Parameters
       F4  = Conversion B Parameters
       F5  = Edit Character Filter
       F6  = Edit Typestyle Filter
       Esc = End System Setup


                   CONVERSIONS
                   Auto Translate
    Conversion A   WordStar 4.0      Conversion B
    WordStar 5 & 6 WordStar 3.4      WordStar 2000
                   WordStar 3.31
                   MS Word 4
```

Appendix B

Use the Down and Up Arrow keys to select one of the involved word processors. Use the Right Arrow to display the names of Conversion B word processors; the Left Arrow to display names of Conversion A word processors. The Auto Translate selection causes Star Exchange to analyze the input file and then the input file is converted automatically to WordStar 6.0 file format. When Auto Translate is active, only "Translate from Auto Translate to WordStar" is displayed as a conversion choice on the OPTIONS menu.

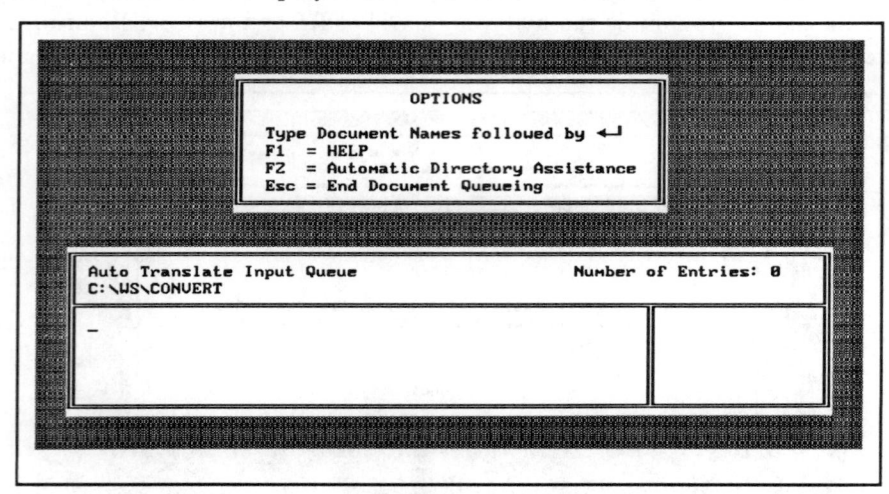

```
                    OPTIONS
    Type Document Names followed by ↵
    F1  = HELP
    F2  = Automatic Directory Assistance
    Esc = End Document Queueing

    Auto Translate Input Queue          Number of Entries: 0
    C:\WS\CONVERT
```

Help information and a number of setup parameters are available using the function keys F1 through F6. These are described in the following list.

Function Key	Description
F1	Displays help information about Star Exchange. Pressing F1 from the System Setup menu describes other function keys that are available.
F2	System Parameters. You can view or change system parameters such as the working directory, the keyboard type, and the active character filter file (see F5). The system work area is a directory where temporary conversion files are processed and then erased. A work file is approximately 1.5 times the size of the file being converted. The keyboard type is changed by highlighting Keyboard Type and pressing the Return key. Finally, the Character Filter File is typed. The filename must match one that was created, named, and saved using selection F5.
F3	Conversion A Parameters. This selection lets you change or view certain conversion parameters. You can designate an output directory for your converted files. You can also establish file naming conventions. For example, you can supply a unique filename and file extension or use the original filename with your own extension. You can also replace an unreadable character with one that is readable when the source word processor produces a character that is not compatible with the target word processor.

Converting Files form Other Word Processors

Function Key	Description
F4	Conversion B Parameters. This selection is identical to F3 except that it is for Conversion B.
F5	Edit Character Filter. This selection lets you adjust a conversion table that translates input characters to a different character value in the output file. A table is displayed with the hex values and generated character. You can modify the input and output characters as necessary for accurate conversion. Once you have modified the default table values, you can save the file with a meaningful name. Then use F2, System Parameters, and enter the filename as the Character Filter File.
F6	Edit Typestyle Filter. This selection lets you convert a typestyle in the input file to a similar typestyle in the output file. A table is displayed and used to choose typestyles. Only the output typestyles may be adjusted. Use the Up or Down Arrow to highlight a typestyle conversion. Then press F2 and highlight a typestyle from the window listing available typestyles. Once highlighted, press F3 to accept the selected typestyle. Press F10 to save changes, Esc to exit without storing changes.

You can use F1 for help during the setup process. Context-sensitive help is available from within Star Exchange submenus.

When you are finished with system setup and the desired word processor names, directories, file naming conventions, and translation filters are prepared, press Esc to End Setup and redisplay the OPTIONS menu.

To make a conversion, press either 1 or 2 and a series of menus are displayed to help you select files. Automatic directory assistance lets you display a desired directory and point to the input file. Once highlighted, press Return to queue it for conversion. You can queue a number of documents and then convert them in a single operation. Press F10 to begin the translation process. If you have not assigned a filename, the output filename will assume the extension WS.

Appendix C
WORD PROCESSING EXERCISES

1. About This Book
    a. List any three of five word processing features included with WordStar.
    b. How much computer memory is required for WordStar operation?
    c. What must be contained in the CONFIG. SYS file?
    d. How can you find information about a word processing function in this book?

2. Program Overview
    a. What are some file handling advantages offered by WordStar?
    b. What can you do with WordStar's menus as you become an advanced WordStar user?
    c. What should you do with the DOS PATH command and why?
    d. What system does the WordStar classic menus resemble?
    e. What is the purpose of the WSCHANGE program?
    f. What is the first menu displayed when starting WordStar?

3. A Sample Session with WordStar
    a. What line should be contained in the CONFIG. SYS file for WordStar to operate properly?
    b. Describe the use of control key sequences.
    c. How do you log disk drive B from WordStar's OPENING menu?
    d. What does the format ruler show you?
    e. How does automatic word wrap help you?
    f. How do you save a document?
    g. What does the < symbol designate at the right edge of the screen?
    h. What is a merge print data file?
    i. What is a delimiter?
    j. How do you quit WordStar?

4. Abandon Document without Changes
    a. What are some reasons for abandoning a document?
    b. What is the difference between WordStar's screen messages when abandoning an edited document compared to abandoning an unedited document?
    c. What key sequence is used to abandon an edited document?

5. Aligning Text (Auto-Align)
    a. What effect does Auto-Align have when it is on?
    b. How do you turn Auto-Align off?

Word Processing Exercises

6. Block Hide/Display
    a. What is meant by hiding a marked block of text?
    b. What key sequence is used to hide and redisplay a marked block?
7. Block Math
    a. What does the block math function do?
    b. How is a group of numbers identified for a block math calculation?
    c. How are negative values identified and treated?
    d. Where is the result of a block math calculation displayed?
    e. How is a block math result entered into an open document as dollars and cents?
8. Block Selection
    a. Describe a block of text.
    b. How do you mark the beginning of a block of text?
    c. How do you mark the end of a block of text?
    d. Name four things you can do with a marked block of text.
9. Calculator (Quick Math)
    a. Describe two practical uses for the Calculator.
    b. How do you access the Calculator screen?
    c. What keystrokes are used to multiply 25 times 321?
    d. What keystrokes are used to divide the result by 4?
    e. How do you exit the Calculator?
    f. Give two keystroke series used to insert the previous Calculator result on the screen.
10. Centering Text on a Line or Page
    a. Describe the purpose of the line-centering function.
    b. Describe the method used to center a short line of text.
    c. How can you reverse the text centering process?
11. Character Count
    a. Describe two uses for the Character Count feature.
    b. What key sequences are used to obtain a word count for:
        (1) A paragraph?
        (2) The entire document?
12. Columnar Editing
    a. Describe the difference between a marked block and a marked column.
    b. What key sequence is used to turn the column-editing function on and off?
    c. Once the column-editing function is active, describe the steps required to mark a column of text.
    d. Once a column is marked, what key sequence is used to delete it?

Appendix C

      e. How is the column replace function turned on?
      f. What is the difference between column replace and column insert?
      g. What is a typical use for column editing?

13. Copy Block to File (Write Block)
      a. Give a reason for writing a block of text to a file.
      b. What happens if you specify a filename that already exists?
      c. What key sequence is used to write a block to a file named TEMP. 001?
      d. What key sequence is used to append a block to an existing file named TEMP.001?

14. Copy Blocks of Text
      a. How do you designate the location of a copied block?
      b. What happens to the text at the original block location?
      c. What happens to the text following the copied block?
      d. Once a block of text is marked, what key sequence is used to copy the marked block?

15. Copy File
      a. Which filename (source or destination) is typed first?
      b. What happens if you specify a destination filename that already exists?
      c. What keystrokes are used to copy a file named CONTENTS from disk A to disk B when A is the logged disk drive?

16. Copy File into Document (Read File)
      a. How can reading a file and writing a block be used together?
      b. How do you designate the point within a document at which a read file is copied?
      c. What happens to the text following the inserted (read) file?
      d. What key sequence is used to read the file CHAP4. TXT into an open document?

17. Cursor Control
      a. Describe the purpose of the cursor.
      b. What key sequence is used to move the cursor one character to the right?
      c. What key sequence is used to move the cursor one word to the right?
      d. What key sequence is used to move the cursor up one line?
      e. Where can you see the exact line and column position of the cursor?

18. Cursor Movement, Quick
      a. What key sequence is used to display the QUICK menu?
      b. What is meant by "jumping" the cursor?
      c. What key sequence is used to jump the cursor to the bottom of a file?
      d. What key sequence is used to jump the cursor to the right edge of a line?

19. Custom Print Codes
    a. What program(s) is used to install custom print codes?
    b. What key sequence is used to select a custom print code?
    c. How can you assign a value to the Ctrl-PQ, W, E or R keys?
    d. What effect does the dot command .xq 0F have on an Epson dot matrix printer?
    e. How is a custom print code canceled?

20. Delete Blocks of Text
    a. What key sequence is used to delete a marked block of text?
    b. What happens to the following text when a block is deleted?
    c. How might you delete a paragraph if you choose not to use the block delete function?
    d. How can a block of text be unerased?
    e. Does the unerase command have a size limitation? Explain.

21. Delete Characters, Words, and Lines
    a. What key sequence is used to delete one character to the right of the cursor?
    b. What key sequence is used to delete one word to the right of the cursor?
    c. What key sequence is used to delete an entire line of text?
    d. What key sequence is used to delete all text to the right of the cursor?

22. Delete File
    a. What keystrokes are required to delete a file named LIST.DAT from the disk in drive A when A is the logged disk drive?
    b. How can you verify that a file has been deleted?
    c. What key sequence is used to delete a file from the EDIT menu?
    d. Give two reasons for deleting a file.

23. Disk Drive and Directory Selection
    a. How can you tell what disk drive or directory is logged when the OPENING menu is displayed?
    b. Describe the procedure for logging disk drive B when disk drive A is the logged disk drive.
    c. If the WordStar program is on disk drive A, where can document files be accessed, edited, and saved if you have a two-drive computer?

24. Dot Commands (Print and Format Control Codes)
    a. Where are text-embedded dot commands placed?
    b. How many lines do dot commands occupy?
    c. What effect does the .PO code have?
    d. What effect does the .PA code have?
    e. How can you suppress the effect of dot commands during printing?

Appendix C

25. Dot Leader
    a. What is a dot leader?
    b. How is a dot leader inserted in text?
    c. How do you control the length of a dot leader?

26. Drawing Lines and Boxes
    a. What ten key combinations are used to draw box elements?
    b. How can you change box elements?
    c. Give three reasons to use lines and boxes.

27. Exit WordStar
    a. What key is used to exit WordStar from the OPENING menu?
    b. What key sequence is used to exit directly to DOS from the EDIT menu?
    c. What is displayed on the screen when you've exited WordStar?

28. File Directory Display
    a. How can you turn off the file directory of the logged disk when the OPENING menu is displayed?
    b. When the EDIT menu is in use, how is the file directory displayed?
    c. Why might you wish to view the file directory during editing operations?

29. File Operations During Word Processing
    a. What is meant by "file operations"?
    b. Name four file operations that can be performed during word processing.
    c. What key sequence is used to rename a document when the EDIT menu is displayed?

30. Find and Find-Replace Again
    a. Describe a use for the find/replace again key sequence.
    b. What happens when Ctrl-L is pressed after a find or find-replace operation has been used?
    c. What key sequence is used to recall the last find or replace string used?

31. Find Block Marker
    a. Describe how block markers are used to find text.
    b. Can a block marker be found when a block has been hidden? Explain.
    c. After hiding a marked block, what is displayed on the screen when you jump to a beginning block marker?
    d. What key sequence is used to jump the cursor to the location within a document from which a block has been moved?

32. Find Place Marker
    a. What is the purpose of place markers?
    b. How many place markers are available?
    c. What key sequence is used to set place marker number 1?

d. What key sequence is used to jump to place marker number 1?
e. What key sequence is used to hide place marker number 1?

33. Find-Replace
    a. Describe a typical use for the find-replace function.
    b. How many "find" characters can you use?
    c. How can you include a hard Return in your find string?
    d. Describe the procedure for converting a WordStar file into a clean ASCII file.

34. Find-Replace, Global
    a. Define global find and replace.
    b. What option characters are used to perform a global, no ask, ignore case find-replace operation?
    c. How can you speed up the global find and replace function when the no query option is used?
    d. What effect does the option string RNW have on the find-replace operation?

35. Find Specified Page, Character
    a. What key sequence is used to find page 3?
    b. What effect does this key sequence have in the nondocument mode?
    c. If you started at the beginning of the document, where does the cursor go after jumping to page 3?
    d. How can you jump the cursor to the end of a sentence?
    e. How can you jump the cursor to the beginning of a sentence?

36. Find Text String
    a. What is a unique text string?
    b. Describe the use of the W option.
    c. Describe the use of the U option.
    d. What is meant by wild card?
    e. How can you find the third occurrence of a text string?

37. Footnotes, Endnotes, Annotations, and Comments
    a. What is a footnote?
    b. Give the procedure for entering footnote text?
    c. How is the display of embedded footnote markers changed?
    d. What is the difference between a footnote and an endnote?
    e. What is an annotation?

38. Format Ruler
    a. What is the purpose of the format ruler?
    b. What key sequence is used to turn the format ruler off?
    c. Why might you wish to turn the format ruler off?
    d. If the format ruler is off, how do you turn it back on?
    e. What is accomplished with the key sequence Ctrl-OO?
    f. What dot command is used to store a format ruler within a document?

Appendix C

39. Help and Help Levels
    a. What is the purpose of HELP menus?
    b. Describe why you might change from pull-down help to level 3 or 2.
    c. How do you change the help level from the OPENING pull-down menu?
    d. What keystrokes are required to change the help level from 4 to 3 when the pull-down EDIT menu is displayed?

40. Hyphenation
    a. Describe the operation of auto-hyphenation.
    b. What key sequence is used to turn auto-hyphenation on and off?
    c. When auto-hyphenation is on, how are hyphens inserted within existing paragraphs of text?
    d. What is a soft hyphen?
    e. How is a soft hyphen entered into a document?

41. Indent (Paragraph Tabs)
    a. Describe two uses for the paragraph (or indent) tab.
    b. What key sequence is used to indent a paragraph to the second tab?
    c. What key is pressed to cancel an indent?

42. Indexing
    a. What indexing options are available from the OPENING menu?
    b. What is the name of an index file that corresponds to a document file named CHAP2?
    c. How are words marked for inclusion in an index?
    d. How is a line of text marked for inclusion in an index?

43. Insert On/Off
    a. Describe what happens to text to the right of the cursor when typing with Insert on.
    b. What happens to text at the cursor when in the strikeover mode?
    c. How do you turn the insert mode off and on?

44. Inset (Merging Graphics)
    a. What is the purpose of WordStar's Inset program?
    b. What program is used to install Inset?
    c. What "hot key" is used to start the Inset program?
    d. Describe a *graphic tag*.
    e. Can graphics and text be placed on the same line? Explain.
    f. What are some ideal uses for merging graphics and text?

45. Justification Off/On
    a. How does WordStar justify the right-hand margin?
    b. What is meant by the term ragged-right?
    c. What key sequence is used to turn off right-hand justification?
    d. What dot codes are used to turn justification on and off?

46. Line Numbering
    a. What elements are specified within the line number dot command?
    b. Where are the line numbers displayed?
    c. What happens when you place the line number dot command in the middle of a page?

47. Line Spacing
    a. How can you determine the current line spacing setting?
    b. What key sequence is used to set your document to double line spacing?
    c. When in double line spacing, what happens when you press Return?
    d. What dot code is used to embed double spacing?

48. MailList
    a. Describe uses for the MailList program.
    b. What are the names of the two prepared forms supplied with WordStar?
    c. How is the MailList program started?
    d. What is a data file as used with the MailList program?

49. Margin Settings
    a. Which menu is used to control margins, tabs, and line spacing?
    b. Describe two ways to set the right margin.
    c. What key sequence is used to release the right margin?
    d. When released, how is the right margin reinstated?
    e. Describe the difference between .RM 65 and .RM 6.5".

50. Merge Print
    a. Define the term *list merge*.
    b. Define the term *document assembly*.
    c. What is a base document?
    d. What is a data file?
    e. List eight uses for merge print dot commands.
    f. Define the term *delimiter*.
    g. List four predefined variables used with merge print.
    h. What is a format variable?

51. Move Blocks of Text
    a. How do you designate the location of a moved block?
    b. What happens to text following a moved block of text?
    c. What happens to text following the spot to which a block is moved?
    d. Once marked, what key sequence is used to move a block?

52. Open a Document or Nondocument File
    a. What are some differences between a document and a nondocument file?
    b. What keystrokes are required to open a document file named PRACTICE.TXT?
    c. Which type of WordStar file is often used by programmers?

Appendix C

53. Page Breaks, Page Length
    a. What is a page break?
    b. What happens to the status line when you move through a page break?
    c. How can you change the default page length value?
    d. What dot command is used to enter a page break?
    e. What is a conditional page break?

54. Page Preview
    a. Give two uses for the page preview function.
    b. What key sequence is used to access the page preview function?
    c. Describe the purpose of each of the page preview submenus:
       (1) Go to
       (2) Options
       (3) View
       (4) Return to Editing

55. Paragraph Numbering
    a. What key sequence is used to display the PARAGRAPH NUMBER menu?
    b. How do you insert paragraph number 1 at the cursor position?
    c. What are the Left and Right Arrow keys used for?
    d. If you delete or insert a paragraph number, what happens to following numbers?
    e. How can you adjust the starting paragraph number?

56. Paragraph Styles
    a. Why would you wish to change a paragraph style?
    b. What is a library-resident style sheet?
    c. Where is a local style sheet stored?
    d. Describe how paragraph styles are useful.

57. PC-Outline
    a. How is the PC-Outline utiltiy started?
    b. What keystrokes are used to remove PC-Outline from memory?
    c. How do you display a PC-Outline Help screen from the outline screen?
    d. What function key is used to access the menu bar?
    e. How is a specific menu option selected, once the cursor is on the menu bar?
    f. Give some typical uses for PC-Outline, and describe advantages offered over a standard text editor.

58. Print Alternate Pitch
    a. What are the most common pitch settings used in word processing?
    b. How many characters are printed in an inch when 10 pitch is used?
    c. What key sequence is used to change to the alternate pitch setting?
    d. What key sequence is used to change back to the normal pitch setting?

Word Processing Exercises

59. Print Binding (Non-Break) Space
    a. Define a non-break space.
    b. When might you require the use of a non-break space?
    c. What key sequence is used to place a non-break space between SAN and FRANCISCO?

60. Print Color
    a. What key sequence is used to display the COLORS menu?
    b. How can you pick a color?
    c. How is a color tag removed from your document?

61. Print Document
    a. What is done to a document before it is printed?
    b. What key sequence is used to print from the EDIT menu?
    c. How can you suppress page formatting (dot commands) during printing?
    d. When a document is printed, what is displayed on the screen?
    e. Define the term simultaneous printing.

62. Print Extended Character Set (Special Symbols)
    a. What key sequence is used to access the EXTENDED CHARACTER menu?
    b. How are vertical arrows entered into a document?
    c. How can you use the Alt key to enter extended characters into a document?

63. Print from Keyboard
    a. What is meant by *typewriter mode*?
    b. Describe the purpose of a template file.
    c. When would you want to use WordStar's typewriter mode?

64. Print Pause (Stop) Code
    a. Describe some uses for the printer pause.
    b. What key sequence is used to embed a printer pause?
    c. How is printing resumed from the OPENING menu after pausing?
    d. How is printing resumed from the EDIT menu after pausing?

65. Print Phantom Space and Rubout (Special Characters)
    a. What are phantom spaces and rubouts?
    b. How can you check to see what your system produces when a phantom space or rubout is used?
    c. What is an alternate use for phantom space and rubout?

66. Print Special Effects
    a. How is a passage of text underlined?
    b. How is a passage of text bold-faced?
    c. How is a passage of text italicized?
    d. What is a use for the strikeout character?
    e. How are superscripts and subscripts typically used?

Appendix C

67. Printer Select
    a. What is the purpose of the printer select function?
    b. How is the CHANGE PRINTER menu displayed?
    c. How can you select an alternate printer?

68. ProFinder
    a. Describe some uses for ProFinder.
    b. What key is pressed to change directories?
    c. Name three parameters used to arrange filenames within ProFinder's file display?
    d. What can you do with the gray plus key?

69. Protect a File
    a. What is the procedure for protecting a file?
    b. How can you determine whether or not a file is protected when it is displayed?
    c. What kind of documents are candidates for protection.

70. Reformat (Realign) Text
    a. What key sequence is used to reformat a paragraph?
    b. How can you reformat an entire document?
    c. What key sequence is used to suppress reformatting of a specified passage of text?
    d. Why might you want to suppress reformatting of a passage of text?

71. Rename a File
    a. What filename conventions are followed when renaming a document?
    b. What keystrokes are used to rename B:CHAPTER. 5 to B:CH5?
    c. What key sequence is used to rename a file from the EDIT menu?
    d. Give two reasons for changing a filename.

72. Repeat a Keystroke Automatically
    a. Why would you use the repeat keystroke function?
    b. Describe the key sequence used to repeat a series of underlines.
    c. How do you speed up and slow down the repeat function?
    d. How do you stop the repeat function?

73. Run a Program
    a. Why would you want to run a program from within WordStar?
    b. When you run a program from WordStar's OPENING menu, what prompt is displayed?
    c. How can you run a program when a document is displayed?
    d. Once you've run a program, what is done to return to WordStar?

74. Save and Exit Document
    a. What key sequence is used to save a document and return to the OPENING menu?
    b. Explain the purpose of a file that has a . BAK extension.
    c. When is a . BAK file created?
    d. What must be done to a . BAK file before it can be edited?
75. Save and Exit WordStar
    a. What key sequence is used to save a document and exit WordStar?
    b. When is this function normally used?
76. Save and Print Document
    a. What key sequence is used to save and print a document without redisplaying the OPENING menu?
    b. Can you perform merge print with save and print?
    c. What is displayed during printing?
77. Save and Resume Edit
    a. Describe the purpose of the save and resume edit function.
    b. What key sequence is used to save a document and resume editing?
    c. Where does the cursor go when editing is resumed after saving?
78. Scroll Screen
    a. Describe the difference between vertical and horizontal scrolling.
    b. Describe the difference between cursor movement and screen scrolling.
    c. What key sequences are used to scroll an entire screen up or down?
79. Scroll Screen, Quick
    a. What key sequence is used to cause a continuous scroll up?
    b. How do you slow down the speed of automatic scrolling?
    c. How do you stop automatic scrolling?
    d. Give a reason for using automatic scrolling.
80. Shorthand (Macro Substitution)
    a. Define macro substitution.
    b. What key sequence is used to enter the system date into a document?
    c. How many macro substitution keys are available for use?
    d. How can you display shorthand help information?
    e. What key sequence is used to enter a Return code within a key definition?
    f. If key definitions are not saved to disk, what happens to them when you quit WordStar?
81. Sort Blocks of Text
    a. Why might you wish to sort a block of text?
    b. What must be done prior to a sort?
    c. Describe the process used to sort on the middle column of a three-column list.

Appendix C

82. Spelling Check
    a. What key sequence is used to start a spelling check?
    b. Where does a spelling check begin?
    c. What key sequence is used to check a single word?
    d. How can you check a spelling guess?
    e. Define the I, A, B, E, and T spell check options.

83. Status Line
    a. Where is the status line located?
    b. What kind of information is displayed on the status line?
    c. How can you determine when the margin release is active?
    d. How can you determine if the Insert function is active?
    e. What meaning does the status line display L12 C25 have?

84. Tab Settings (Decimal or Align)
    a. Describe a common use for a decimal tab.
    b. How do you move the cursor to a decimal tab?
    c. How does text entry differ before and after typing a decimal point?
    d. What key sequence is used to set a decimal tab at column 42?

85. Tab Settings (Typewriter)
    a. What are "typewriter" tabs?
    b. How can you clear all tab settings?
    c. What symbol is used on the format ruler to designate the position of a tab?
    d. Describe two ways to set a tab.
    e. How can you store a format ruler in your document?

86. Table of Contents Creation
    a. How is a table of contents entry identified?
    b. Write a dot code line that enters "Introduction," a series of periods (or a dot leader), and the current page number.
    c. How can block copy be used to save time?

87. TelMerge
    a. What might memory resident programs do to TelMerge operation?
    b. What effect can call waiting have on telecommunications?
    c. How is TelMerge started?
    d. What is a Service File?
    e. What is the TELMERGE. LOG file used for?
    f. What is a *null modem*?

88. Thesaurus
    a. Why would you want to use the Thesaurus?
    b. How are words selected?
    c. What keys are pressed to start the Thesaurus?
    d. How can you display a brief definition of a Thesaurus word?

89. Undo, Unerase
    a. What is the purpose of the undo command?
    b. Name three operations that are commonly undone.
    c. You are in the middle of the printing prompts and decide not to print. What can you do?
    d. Describe a use and limitation of the unerase function.

90. Upper/Lower Case Conversion
    a. What must first be done to a passage of text before it is converted?
    b. What key sequence is used to convert to uppercase?
    c. What key sequence is used to convert to lowercase?
    d. What key sequence is used to retain capitals on the first word of each sentence within a marked passage?

91. Window (Working with Two Documents)
    a. What is a *window*?
    b. How do you open a window?
    c. How can you copy information between documents within displayed windows?
    d. How do you close a window?

92. Word Wrap Off/On
    a. What benefit is offered by the automatic word wrap function?
    b. What is a soft return?
    c. What sequence is used to turn automatic word wrap off and on?

93. WSCHANGE and PRCHANGE (Customizing WordStar)
    a. What two setup utilities are available with WordStar?
    b. What is the purpose of WSCHANGE?
    c. How do you start the WSCHANGE utility?
    d. After you have worked your way to the proper menu and made your changes, how do you work your way back to the WSCHANGE Main Menu and the DOS prompt?
    e. What key sequence is used to exit WSCHANGE without saving any changes?
    f. What is the purpose of PRCHANGE?
    g. Name three modifications that can be made with PRCHANGE.
    h. Which program is used to install a laser printer?

Index

abandon, 21, 29
Advanced Page Preview, 128
align tab, 260
alternate font, 56
alternate pitch, 188
annotations, 103, 106
append, 42
ASCII, 4, 161, 165, 195, 198, 275, 307, 312
AUTOEXEC.BAT, 5, 15, 307
automatic repeat, 232
automatic word wrap, 17, 190, 287
auto-align, 23-25, 150
auto-hyphenation, 117

BAK extension, 235, 240, 307
base document, 157, 161
binding space, 190
block, 26, 163
block, copy, 44
block, delete, 62
block, hide, 23,
block, move, 163
block, show, 23
block markers, 26, 30, 87
block math, 27-29
block operations, 30
boilerplate files, 42, 46
bold, 209, 211
boxes, 78

Calculator, 32-34
case conversion, 282
center text, 35
Change drive/directory, 68
change fonts, 210
change printer, 213
changing format ruler, 109
changing macros, 247
character count, 37
classic menus, ix, 1, 6, 11-14, 308
color, 191
column, 38-41
column block, 38
column dot commands, 39

column editing, 38-40
column replace, 38
columns, 251, 308
comma delimited, 157, 161
comments, 103
compressed print, 188
conditional page breaks, 169
CONFIG.SYS, 3, 5, 15
control codes, 193
control file, 270-271
control keys, 142, 308
convert block of text to lowercase, 282
convert block of text to sentence case, 282
convert block of text to uppercase, 282
convert file, 195, 312
copy a file, 46, 48
creating macros, 247
cursor, 50, 53, 242, 308
cursor control keys, 50, 242, 244
cursor movement, quick, 53
custom print codes, 56-61
custom print fonts, 58
custom tabs, 264

data file, 157, 161, 308
database files, 48
decimal tabs, 260
default margins, 195
delete file, 66
delete operations, 64
directory, 68
document, 165, 193, 235
DOS, 3, 5, 68, 80, 233
dot codes, 18
dot commands, 35, 39, 58, 70-75, 104-105, 136, 148, 153-156, 168, 173, 201, 266,
dot leader, 76, 267
double strike, 209, 211
endnotes, 103

exit WordStar, 80
extended characters, print, 198

331

Index

file conversion, 312
file directory, 81
file operations, 83-84
find and replace, 91,
find and replace, global, 95
find and replace options, 91-92, 95-96
find and replace strings, special, 93
find character, 98
find page, 98
find text, 100
find text options, 101
fonts, 56, 210
footnotes, 103
format ruler, 109-111, 261, 264, 309
function key tags, 215

Go To, 98, 170
go to commands, 50
graphic tags, 128
graphics, 127, 131, 309

hard returns, 93, 139, 228
Hayes modem, 269
help, 113-114
help levels, 113
highlighting, 23, 30
hyphenation, 17, 23, 117

Illustrated books, ix, 161
indent, 119
indent tabs, 119
index, 106, 121-123
index file, 121
insert, 125
Insert a file, 48
insert function, 125
Inset program, 127
INSTALL, 127
INVENTORY, 141

justification, 17, 23, 134

library paragraph style, 176
line editors, 51
line numbers, print, 136
line spacing, 138
local paragraph style, 176,
logged drive, 68

macro definitions, 246
macro substitution, 246, 248, 309
MailList, 140-147
margin release, 150
margins and tabs, 148-152, 260, 263
marked block, 44, 62, 163
marking words for index, 122
menus, 113
merge print, 18-20, 153, 161
move block, 163
move blocks between windows, 284

newspaper-style columns, 39
nondocument files, 165, 233, 309
non-break space, 190
notes, 103-105

open a document, 165, 310
overprint lines, 209
overstrike, 209

page break, 74, 168
page length, 168
page number, 74
page offset, 73, 149
page preview, 39, 170
paragraph margins, 150
paragraph numbers, 173
paragraph styles, 176
paragraph tabs, 119
PC-Outline, 180-187
phantom rubout code, 206
phantom space code, 206
pitch, 149-151, 188, 310
place marker, 89
PRCHANGE, 289, 304-306
print a file, 193
print color, 191
print from keyboard, 201
print legal size page length, 73
print line numbers, 136
print prompts, 194
print styles, 208
print to file, 195-196
printer pause, 204
printing, 18, 194
printing, stop, 195

ProFinder, 215-223
protect a file, 226
pull-down menus, ix, 1, 6-11, 165

quick math, 32-34

read file, 48
reformat, 228
rename a file, 230
repeat a keystroke, 232
run a program, 233

save and name file, 235
save and print document, 238
save file, exit WordStar, 237
save file, go to Opening screen, 235
save file, resume editing, 240
saving a window, 285
scalable fonts, 210
script, 272-275
scroll text, 244
scrolling, 242, 244
scrolling speed, 244
service file, 270
shorthand, 246, 248
sizing windows, 285
soft hyphen, 117
soft return, 93, 287
sort, 251
sort columns, 251
sort lines, 251
speed write, 166
spelling check, 254
spelling check options, 256
spreadsheets, 48
standard macro keys, 246
standard tabs, 263

Star Exchange, ix, 2, 312-315
status line, 258, 310
stored format rulers, 110
strikeout, 209, 211
strikeover, 125
subscripts and superscripts, 209, 212
suppress page numbering, 73
SWITCH.COM, 15

tab setting, 260, 263
table of contents, 266
TelMerge, 269
text string, 100
Thesaurus, 278
type fonts, 56
typewriter mode, 201
typing machines, 14

underline, 208, 211
undo, 280
unerase, 62, 280
unprotecting files, 226
user print control, 59

variables, 157-160, 311

window operation, 42
windows, 284
WINSTALL, 3, 5, 289
word wrap, 287
write block, 42
WSCHANGE, 3, 5-6, 12, 18, 23, 30, 104, 110, 188, 193, 289-304
WSCHANGE menus, 289-304
WSLIST, 140
WSSETUP, 5

Other Books from Wordware Publishing, Inc.

Business-Professional Books
Business Emotions
The Business Side of Writing
Consulting Handbook for the High-Tech Professional
Hawks Do, Buzzards Don't
How to Win Pageants
Innovation, Inc.
Investor Beware
MegaTraits
Occupying the Summit
Steps to Strategic Management

Computer Aided Drafting
Illustrated AutoCAD (Release 9)
Illustrated AutoCAD (Release 10)
Illustrated AutoCAD on the Mac II
Illustrated AutoLISP
Illustrated AutoSketch 1.04
Illustrated AutoSketch 2.0
Illustrated GenericCADD Level 3

Database Management
The DataFlex Developer's Handbook
Illustrated dBASE II (2nd Ed.)
Illustrated dBASE III Plus
Illustrated dBASE IV
Illustrated Force 2.0
Illustrated FoxPro
Illustrated Paradox 3.0 Volume II (2nd Ed.)

Desktop Publishing
Achieving Graphic Impact with Ventura 2.0
Desktop Publisher's Dictionary
Handbook of Desktop Publishing
Illustrated PFS:First Publisher 2.0
Illustrated PageMaker 3.0
Illustrated Ready, Set, Go! 4.5 (Macintosh)
Illustrated Ventura 2.0
Ventura Troubleshooting Guide

General Advanced Topics
Illustrated Dac Easy Accounting 3.0
Illustrated Dac Easy Accounting 4.1
Illustrated Harvard Graphics 2.3
Illustrated Novell NetWare 2.15
Novell NetWare: Adv. Tech. and Applications

Integrated
Illustrated Enable/OA
Illustrated Framework III
Illustrated Microsoft Works 2.00
Illustrated Q & A 3.0 (2nd Ed.)

Programming Languages
Illustrated C Programming (ANSI) (2nd Ed.)
Illustrated Clipper 5.0

Programming Languages (cont.)
The DataFlex Developer's Handbook
The FOCUS Developer's Handbook
Graphic Programming with Turbo Pascal 5.5
Illustrated Turbo C++
Illustrated Turbo Pascal 4.0
Illustrated Turbo Pascal 5.5

Spreadsheet
Illustrated Lotus 1-2-3 2.01
Illustrated Lotus 1-2-3 Rel. 3.0
Illustrated Lotus 1-2-3 Rel. 2.2
Illustrated Microsoft Excel 2.10 (IBM)
Illustrated Microsoft Excel 1.5 (Macintosh)
Illustrated Quattro
Illustrated SuperCalc 5

Systems and Operating Guides
Illustrated Microsoft Windows 2.0
Illustrated MS/PC DOS 3.3
Illustrated MS/PC DOS 4.0 (6th Ed.)
Illustrated UNIX

Word Processing
Illustrated DisplayWrite 4
Illustrated Microsoft Word 5.0
Illustrated Microsoft Word for the Mac
Illustrated WordPerfect 1.0 (Macintosh)
Illustrated WordPerfect 5.0
Illustrated WordPerfect 5.1
Illustrated WordStar 3.3
Illustrated WordStar 6.0
Illustrated WordStar Professional (Rel. 5)
WordPerfect: Advanced Applications Handbook
WordPerfect Wizardry

Popular Applications Series
Presentations with Harvard Graphics
Learn WordPerfect in a Day
Mailing Lists using dBASE
WordPerfect Macros

Regional
Exploring the Alamo Legends
Forget the Alamo
The Great Texas Airship Mystery
100 Days in Texas: The Alamo Letters
Rainy Days in Texas Funbook
Texas Highway Humor
Texas Wit and Wisdom
That Cat Won't Flush
They Don't Have to Die
This Dog'll Hunt
Unsolved Texas Mysteries

Call Wordware Publishing, Inc. for names of the bookstores in your area
(214) 423-0090